유희태
일반영어 ① 기본

LSI 영어연구소 유희태 박사 저

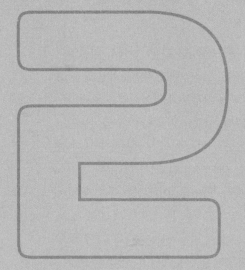

《2S2R》시리즈를 <워드북> 출판사에서 출간했었지만, 출판사의 사정으로 더이상 교재를 낼 수 없는 상황이 되었다. 자본이 충분치 않은 소규모 출판사의 한계를 결국 넘지 못하고, 주저 앉게 된 점 무척 안타깝게 생각한다. 출판사 대표와의 인연으로 인해 더 나은 조건을 제시했 던 다른 회사들의 제안을 모두 거절했었다. 《2S2R》시리즈의 판매로 그나마 출판사가 유지되 었기 때문이었다. 하지만 이제 그 출판사가 세상에 없는 상황이 되었는지라, 2021년도부터는 《2S2R》시리즈를 <박문각> 출판사에서 출간하게 되었다. 한국의 전통 있는 출판사 중 하나인 <박문각>은 이전의 작은 출판사와는 비교할 수 없을 정도로 시스템이 잘 되어있는 장점이 있 다. 이전 출판사 교재들의 고질적 문제였던 편집상 실수에서 비롯되던 오류 등을 박문각의 편 집자는 모든 글을 하나하나 다 읽고 걸러낼 뿐만 아니라 저자가 미처 생각지 못했던 문제점까 지 찾아내서 교정해주었다. 아무쪼록 <박문각> 출판사가 《2S2R》시리즈의 좋은 안식처가 되 길 바라본다.

시간은 흘러 《2S2R 기본》이 세상에 나온 지 12년이 되었다. 처음 나올 때의 제목은 《2S2R 최고 의 독해 비결》이었는데, 많은 수험생이 '최독비'라는 애칭으로 불렀었다. 지금은 사라진 <비욘 드> 출판사에서 2009년에 첫 출간 되었다. 아직도 마감을 맞추느라 당시 LSI 영어연구소의 연 구원들과 출판사 직원들이 몇 날 밤을 새웠던 기억이 또렷하다. 그만큼 애정도 많았고 연구에 시간도 많이 들였던 책이었다. 비록 완벽하진 않지만, 한국의 Reading Comprehension 분야에 일조한다는 마음으로 준비한 책이었다. 처음 이 교재를 출간했을 때 가졌던 생각과 다짐 그리 고 방법은 여전히 유효하리라 생각하여 여기에 다시 옮겨본다.

노량진에 있는 국공립학교 영어 교사 양성시험을 대비하는 교원임용고시학원에서 일반영어 를 강의하며 많은 수험생으로부터 받아왔던 공통적인 질문이 하나 있다. "어떻게 하면 글을 정 확히, 그리고 빨리 읽을 수 있나요?" 아마 한국에서 시행되는 대부분의 영어시험을 준비하는 다른 수험생들도 마찬가지의 고민을 지니고 있을 줄로 안다. 이것은 우리나라 수험생들뿐만 아니라 미국의 수험생 또는 대학생들(매주 상당한 양의 논문과 책을 읽고 보고서를 써내야 하 는)에게도 유사하게 해당하는 질문이기도 하다. 미국의 한 대학에서 학부생들에게 읽기 지도 를 하면서 그 학생들도 마찬가지의 고민을 하고 있음을 보며, '영어'를 '이해'하는 문제가 얼마 나 보편적인지를 깨닫게 된다. 영어 독해를 할 때, 지문이 말하고자 하는 내용도 다 알겠고, 독 해도 다 된 것 같은데, 문제를 풀면 항상 한두 문제는 틀리는 일이 발생하는 것은 왜일까? '나의 이해'와 '정답' 사이의 거리는 왜 항상 발생하는 것일까? 도대체 뭐가 문제일까? 저자는 그것이

근본적으로 영어를 넘어선 '언어'에 대한 논리적 이해의 결핍에서 오는 것이라 본다. 그렇다면, 어떻게 하면 영어 더 넓게는 '언어'를 잘 이해할 수 있을까? 저자는 그 하나의 가설적 대안으로 "대화적 읽기"를 제시하고자 한다. 대화적 읽기는 처음엔 시간이 오래 걸리겠지만 결국 실전 문제 풀이에서 분석적(구조적)으로 지문을 읽을 때 큰 도움이 될 것이다.

'대화적 읽기'란

우리는 매일 일상에서 수많은 읽을거리를 접하게 된다. 잡지의 기사, 신문의 사설 또는 한 조각의 광고 문구를 읽으며 스스로 "이것의 메시지는 뭐지?" "이것이 함축하는 것은 또 뭘까?" 등의 질문을 던지게 된다. 액면 그대로(at face value)를 받아들이기보다 그것의 표면 아래(beneath the surface)를 보려는 노력이 필요함은 물론이다. 우리는 어렴풋이 다음과 같은 질문을 글쓴이에게 하게 된다.

1) 이 글은 도대체 무엇에 관한 것인가요?
2) 그것을 통해 당신이 말하고자 하는 바는 무엇인가요?
3) 당신의 그 진술을 뒷받침할 수 있는 것인가요?
4) 근거가 너무 주관적인 것 아닌가요?
5) 사실관계가 명확한 것인가요?
6) 그 용어를 어떻게 정의하는 것인가요?
7) 어떻게 그런 결론을 내렸죠?
8) 그래서 어떻다는 거죠? 왜 그것이 중요한 것인가요?
9) 당신 도대체 어떤 태도로 대상을 바라보는 것이죠? 비꼬는 것인가요?
10) 왜 이런 패턴으로 글을 쓴 것이죠? 너무 나열식 아닌가요?
11) 당신 글엔 모순이 있군요.
12) 당신 주장은 알겠는데, 동의할 순 없군요.
13) 좋은 주장이군요. 미처 생각하지 못했는데.

의식적이든 무의식적이든 위와 같은 반응은 이미 여러분이 읽은 것에 대해 '대화적으로(dialogically)' 사고한다는 것을 나타낸다. 개념에 대해 질문을 하고, 정보를 평가하고, 증거를 찾고, 가설을 하며, 그리고 판단한다. 한마디로 여러분은 다른 사람의 말(주장)을 그대로 흡수

(take in)하는 수동적 관찰자로서가 아니라 그 주장을 가공(process)하고 있는 능동적 대화자의 자질이 있는 것이다. 글을 읽을 때, 읽는 '나'와 읽히는 '너'가 만나 새로운 하나의 '나와 너'가 만들어져 '지문(텍스트)에 나타나 있는 의미'를 넘어서는 새로운(창조적) 의미를 발견하는 것이 대화적 읽기이다.

왜 대화적 읽기인가?

하나, 대화적 읽기는 발견의 역동적 과정이기 때문이다. 여러분은 어느 한 주제에 관한 글쓴이의 관점을 발견하게 된다. 그런 다음, 그가 말하는 내용 또는 주장의 강함과 약함을 발견한다. 그리고 그 주장을 동의할지 동의하지 않을지를 결정하게 된다. 저자에게 질문을 하고, 그 저자가 서 있는 지점과 여러분이 서 있는 지점이 대비 또는 충돌이 됨으로써 평면적이 아닌 입체적인 이해를 하도록 해준다. 마지막 귀결점으로 글을 쓴 저자와 그 이슈에 대해 더 잘 이해하게 된다.

둘, 대화적 읽기는 다른 이의 글을 목수가 집을 바라보듯이 읽도록 해준다. 그는 세부 사항을 꼼꼼히 보며, 그런 다음 어떻게 그 세부 사항이 전체와 연결되고 동시에 전체를 만들어 내는지를 본다. 또한 대화적 읽기는 자신이 읽은 글에 대해 스스로 평가하도록 해준다. 남의 글에 대해 충실히 분석하고 반응할수록 그 글에 대한 이해에서도 더욱 그렇게 하게 된다.

셋, 대화적 읽기는 교원임용고시, 수능, 공무원, 편입, 토익, 토플, 심지어 GRE 등 한국에서 시행되는 대부분의 시험에서 단골로 출제되는 유형인 요지찾기, 제목(주제)찾기, 순서맞추기, 글의 흐름파악하기, 요약하기 문제 등 '논리'를 물어보는 문제에 적극적으로 대처할 수 있도록 만들어 준다.

어떻게 대화적으로 읽을 것인가? 독해전략 4단계 2S2R

글을 '대화적'으로 읽기 위해 구체적 방법론으로 저자는 2S2R 독해전략을 제시하고자 한다. 2S2R 독해전략은 '빠르고 정확한 읽기'를 위한 훈련의 과정이다.

1단계 Survey 개관하기

2S2R 독해전략의 1단계로 텍스트(읽을거리)를 미리 훑어보는 것을 말한다. 개관하기는 각 문단의 첫 문장과 끝 문장을 유심히 읽은 다음 나머지를 훑어본다. 이것은 주어진 지문의 주요 화

제(topic), 구조, 부분 그리고 특색 등에 대한 전체적인 생각을 하도록 해준다. 이 1단계에서 여러분이 구체적으로 해야 할 것은 1) key words 찾기 2) signal words 찾기이다. 이 단계를 마치면, 여러분은 각각의 구체적인 문단들과 부분들이 얼마나 잘 짜여 있는지 이해하게 만들어 주는 '지적 얼개(a mental framework)'를 형성하게 된다.

2단계 Reading 읽기

2S2R 독해전략의 2단계는 읽기 단계로 여러분이 해야 할 것은 다음과 같다.

하나, 글의 목적(purpose) 파악하기

둘, 글의 어조(tone) 파악하기

셋, 글의 구조(pattern) 파악하기: 2S2R 독해전략에서 가장 강조하는 부분이다.

넷, 글의 요지(main idea) 파악하기

3단계 Summary 읽은 것 요약하기

2S2R 독해전략의 3단계는 2단계 Reading에서 했던 내용을 요약하는 것이다.

요약하기는 글의 중요한 부분을 훨씬 짧은 길이로 다시 서술하는 것으로, 요약을 잘하기 위해서는 다음의 조건을 지켜야 한다.

하나, 좋은 요약은 요지와 주된 논거(major supporting points)를 포함한다. 요지는 가능하면 첫 문장에 제시한다.

둘, 좋은 요약은 단서가 되는 단어들(signal words)을 포함한 각 단락의 핵심어를 포함한다.

셋, 좋은 요약은 작은 세부 사항, 반복되는 세부 사항, 읽는 이의 의견을 포함하지 않는다.

넷, 좋은 요약은 본문에 있는 단어나 어구를 그대로 사용하지 않고 가능하면 다른 말로 바꿔 쓰기(paraphrase) 한다.

다섯, 일반적으로 원 본문의 길이를 25%로 줄이는 것을 원칙으로 한다.

4단계 Recite 요약한 것 소리 내어 말하기

2S2R 독해전략의 4단계는 3단계에서 했던 것을 입으로 정리하는 것을 말한다. 3단계가 철저히 훈련되었다면 자연스럽게 진행될 수 있는 단계이다. 지문을 읽은 후 멈춰 서서 읽은 것에 대해 정리를 한다. 이때 반드시 입 밖으로 정리한 것을 소리를 내야 한다는 점에 유념하자. 머릿속에만 가지고 있는 것, 즉 언어로 표현되지 않은 것은 내 것이 아니다.

우리는 유전자가 모든 것을 결정한다는 이야기를 요즘 들어 더욱 자주 듣게 된다. 타고난, 즉, 부모로부터 물려받은 좋은 머리(높은 IQ로 상징되는)야말로 우리의 성공의 근원이라는 것이다. 그러나, 과연 그럴까? 최근의 연구들에 따르면, 유전자가 우리의 성공을 결정지을 확률은 '집적된 시간'이 끼치는 영향보다 훨씬 적다는 것이다. 우리가 꾸준히 노력해서 1만 시간에 가까운 시간을 자신의 전공 분야에 기울인다면, 누구나 성공에 이를 수 있다는 것이다. 비틀즈 (The Beatles)의 성공에는 바로 1만 시간에 가까운 그들의 반복된 노력에 있었지, 그들의 유전자에 있었던 것이 아니었다고 한다. 애플 컴퓨터의 창립자인 스티브 잡스(Steve Jobs)가 성공한 것도 그의 유전자가 좋아서라기보다는 오히려 자신이 살던 곳인 마운틴뷰—지금은 너무나 유명해진 실리콘밸리 지역—가 그에게 많은 기회를 주었기 때문이라고 전문가들은 지적한다. 그의 이웃에는 휴렛패커드의 엔지니어들로 가득해서 그는 그들로부터 어린시절 컴퓨터에 관한 수많은 이야기를 들을 수 있었고, 심지어 휴렛패커드의 창립자인 빌 휴렛(Bill Hewlett)과 개인적으로 접촉하여 직접 영향을 받을 수 있었다. 그것을 통해 그는 어린 시절부터 자신이 좋아하는 것을 정확히 알 수 있었고, 그 좋아하는 것을 꾸준히 노력 및 반복함으로써 성공을 할 수 있었다. 이때 그가 들인 시간이 약 1만 시간 정도라고 한다.

필자는 이 1만 시간이란 말을 은유로 받아들인다. 곧이곧대로 1만 시간이 중요하다는 것이 아니라, 그만큼 자신이 하고자 하는 것을 성취하기 위해서는 그에 요구되는 꾸준한 노력과 반복 학습이 필요하다는 것이다. 이것보다 더 확실한 것은 없다. 단, 그 노력과 반복 학습을 좀 더 나은 방식으로 한다면 더할 나위 없이 좋을 것이다. A라는 사람이 하루에 단어를 10개 외우고, B라는 사람이 20개를 외운다고 하자. 그렇다면, 이 둘의 집적된 시간은 어떻게 될까? A에게 하루가 24시간이라면 B에게는 하루가 48시간이 된다. 시간은 절대적이지만 동시에 상대적이기도 하다. 그렇다면, A가 아니라 B가 되도록 하는 것이다. 이 교재가 여러분을 A가 아닌 B가 되도록 하는 데 조금이라도 이끈다면 더 바랄 나위가 없겠다. 이제 '난 머리가 나빠서 안 되나 봐!'라는 좌절감에 빠질 필요는 전혀 없다. 스스로 부족하다 싶은 것은 더 많은 시간과 그 시간을 좀 더 효율적으로 만들 수 있는 좋은 방법론으로 만회하면 된다. 그 하나의 방법론으로 2S2R 독해전략을 권하고 싶다.

임용고시영어를 준비하는 대다수의 수험생이 일반영어의 시작을 《2S2R 기본》으로 공부한다고 한다. 저자로서는 기쁘면서도 무거운 책임감을 동시에 느낀다. 그래서 현재에 안주하지 않고 최선을 다해 좀 더 나은 지문과 분석력으로 한 걸음 더 진보된 교재를 만들어야겠다는 다짐을 항상 하곤 한다.

《유희태 일반영어》시리즈를 효과적으로 활용하는 방법은, 대학 1학년 때《2S2R 기본》을 최소 3회독, 평균 5회독하여 일반영어 기본이론을 확실하게 다진 뒤, 2학년 때《2S2R 유형》을 최소 3회독하여 임용 유형에 기본이론을 확장 적용하는 훈련을 하고, 3학년 때《2S2R 기출》을 2회독한 다음, 처음으로 임용시험을 치르는 4학년 때《2S2R 문제은행》을 가지고 공부하는 것이다. 이 과정에서《기출 VOCA 30days》는 1학년 때부터 주 6회 매일 20분씩 꾸준히 공부하기를 추천한다.

이 7판 작업을 하면서 많은 분들의 도움을 받았다. 원고를 보기 좋은 최종 결과물로 만들어준 박문각의 변수경 편집자와 박용 회장님께 고마움을 전한다. 또한 영어지문의 함축의미, 문화적 맥락, 그리고 답안 등을 두고 토론하고 때로는 격렬한 논쟁을 했던 LSI 영어연구소의 Sean Maylone 수석연구원에게도 인사를 전한다. 아무쪼록 이 7판 교재가 수험생 여러분의 합격에 일조하기를 깊은 마음으로 바란다.

2022년 새해를 앞두고 LSI영어연구소에서

유희태

CONTENTS

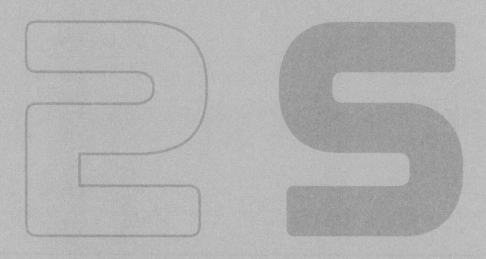

유희태 일반영어 ①

2S2R

기본

_Part

01

2S2R 원리

General & Specific

2S2R 독해전략을 이해하기 위해 우리가 가장 먼저 해야 할 것은 general일반적과 specific세부적을 구별하는 것이다. **모든 영어 논리의 기본은 바로 일반적인 것과 세부적인 것을 구분하는 것에서부터 시작한다는 점을 명심하자.** General이란 말은 'broad'하면서 'not limited'란 뜻이다. 누군가가 어떤 단어나 생각을 'general하다'라고 말하면, 그것은 **하나의 큰 것 속에 많은 다양한 작은 것들(세부사항들)**이 들어 있음을 의미한다.

예를 들어 sports라는 하나의 범주 안에는 football, baseball, and basketball 등의 다양한 종류의 세부사항들이 들어 있다. 여기서 sports는 general이고 football, baseball, and basketball은 specific한 것이 된다. 이렇듯 specific은 하나의 큰 그룹 안에 속해 있는 세부적인 것을 말한다.

> **영어의 거의 대다수의 글은 'general한 것에서 specific한 것'으로 진행된다!**

모든 영어 독해의 가장 기본이 되는 것이 general과 specific을 정확하게 구별하는 능력이라 할 수 있다. 지금까지 영어 독해 학습에서 이것이 간과되었다는 것은, 기존의 학습이 토대가 튼튼하지 못한 부실공사와 같은 것이었음을 말해주는 것이다. 2S2R 독해전략에서는 이 둘을 구별하는 능력이 모든 것의 근본이 됨을 강조한다. 따라서 이 책에 실린 연습문제들을 푸는 과정에서 영어 논리력의 기본이 쌓일 것이라 생각한다.

General과 specific의 관계를 정확히 아는 것이 중요한 이유는 여러 가지겠지만, 특히 순서 맞추기 문제나 글의 흐름상 어색한 것 고르기 문제 등에선 이것을 모르고는 좋은 점수를 얻을 수 없다. 아래에 제시되어 있는 예제를 풀다보면, 여러분은 general과 specific의 개념이 무엇인지 자연스럽게 체득할 것이라 본다.

📝 예제

[1-2] 다음을 general에서 specific한 순서로 배열하시오.

01
  ① dentist   ② man   ③ Dr. Sam

02
  ① animal   ② mammal   ③ dog
  ④ Jack terrier   ⑤ Eddie, the dog on the Fraiser television show

[3-5] Read each pair of sentences. Then label the general sentence G and the specific one S.

03
  ① After years of suffering and pain, South African leader Nelson Mandela experienced the sweet taste of triumph. _____
  ② After spending almost thirty years in South African prisons, Nelson Mandela became that country's president. _____

04
  ① Early on in the history of the United States, newspapers didn't even pretend to be without political bias. _____
  ② In the eighteenth century, American politicians created and controlled newspapers to further their interests. _____

05
  ① In the past twenty years, health care around the world has markedly improved; this is especially true where infants are concerned. _____
  ② Thanks to improved health care, the number of babies who die in the first year of life has decreased markedly over the last twenty years. _____

정답 | **01** ② – ① – ③
    02 ① – ② – ③ – ④ – ⑤
    03 G / S
    04 G / S
    05 G / S

[6-7] 다음의 문장을 가장 general한 것으로부터 가장 specific한 것으로 재배열하시오.

06

① In particular, his studies of Jupiter's moons and the planet Venus proved the heliocentric, or sun-centered, theory of the solar system.

② Galileo Galilei(1564-1642), Italian astronomer, mathematician, and physicist, was one of the greatest scientists of all time.

③ His concepts of motion and the forces that produce motion opened up an entirely new approach to astronomy.

_____ → _____ → _____

07

① For example, in my small town, we have a very fancy coffee shop called the SAM, which serves different types of coffees and sells T-shirts, coffee mugs, and croissants.

② Upscale coffee shops that serve special coffees and offer other merchandise have become very popular in the last few years.

③ One of the most popular coffees at the SAM is the "Sam Whip," which is a large $6.00 cup of coffee with chocolate syrup and whipped cream all whipped together.

_____ → _____ → _____

[8-9] 먼저 general sentence를 읽고, 그런 다음 그 general sentence를 뒷받침 또는 설명해주는 specific sentences의 기호를 써넣으시오.

08

General sentence: It's easy to understand why the threat of rabies inspires great fear.

Specific sentences:

① In its final stages, rabies produces hallucinations.

② Few people recover from rabies once symptoms appear.

③ Rabies has been around a long time; there are references to it as early as 700BC.

④ Once the disease takes hold, the victim can neither stand nor lie down comfortably.

⑤ Recently, scientists have improved the treatment for rabies; the new treatment is much less painful than the old.

⑥ In the early stages of rabies, a dog is likely to appear tired and nervous; it will try to hide, even from its master.

_____

09 General sentence: In the last decade, Americans have displayed a growing interest in haiku, a type of Japanese poetry that must be composed using only three lines and seventeen syllables.

01

Specific sentences:

① From 1990 to 1997, the Haiku Society of America grew from a small club to a national group with ten regional leaders.

② In Japan, haikus are printed on tea cans that are sold in public vending machines.

③ Ancient haikus often celebrated the beauties of nature, but today's haikus might focus on movies, cartoon characters, junk food, or rock bands.

④ When a U.S. newspaper, the *Christian Science Monitor*, sponsored a haiku contest in 1996, editors received 30,000 entries — three times as many as they got in 1986.

⑤ The World Wide Web hosts hundreds of haiku sites designed by residents of all fifty states, and the number of haikus on Internet bulletin boards increases every year.

⑥ Haiku fans in Europe throw parties where guests read their poems aloud and compete to write the best haiku in five or ten minutes.

정답 | **06** ② — ③ — ①
07 ② — ① — ③
08 ①, ②, ④
09 ①, ④, ⑤

예제 03 ① 수년간의 고통과 아픔 뒤에 남아프리카 공화국의 지도자 넬슨 만델라는 달콤한 승리를 맛보았다.
② 남아공 감옥에서 거의 삼십 년을 보낸 후 넬슨 만델라는 그 나라의 대통령이 되었다.

04 ① 미국 역사의 전반부에 신문은 정치적으로 편향되어 있지 않은 척 하지도 않았다.
② 18세기, 미국 정치인들은 자신들의 이익을 더 창출하기 위해 신문을 만들고 관리했다.

05 ① 지난 20년 동안 세계 보건은 눈에 띄게 개선되었다; 유아들의 문제에서 특히 그렇다.
② 나아진 보건 덕분에 생애 첫해에 죽던 수많은 아기들이 지난 20년간 현저히 줄어들었다.

06 ① 특히 목성의 달과 금성에 대한 그의 연구는 태양 중심의 태양계 이론을 증명하였다.
② 이탈리아의 천문학자이며 수학자이고 물리학자인 갈릴레오 갈릴레이는 역사상 가장 위대한 과학자 중 한 사람이다.
③ 움직임과 움직임을 생성하는 힘에 대한 그의 개념은 천문학에 있어서 완전히 새로운 접근 방식을 열었다.

07 ① 예를 들어 우리 작은 동네에 샘이라는 아주 멋진 커피숍이 있는데, 이곳은 여러 가지 종류의 커피와 티셔츠, 커피 머그 그리고 크로아상 등을 판다.
② 지난 몇 년간 특별한 커피와 다른 상품들을 파는 고급 커피숍들이 아주 인기를 얻게 되었다.
③ 샘의 가장 인기 있는 커피 중 하나는 '샘 휩'으로, 초콜릿 시럽과 휩크림이 같이 섞인 큰 컵의 6불짜리 커피이다.

08 General sentence: 광견병의 위협이 왜 큰 공포를 불러오는지를 알기는 쉽다.
Specific sentences:
① 최종 단계에서 광견병은 환각을 부른다.
② 한번 증상이 나타나면 낫는 사람이 많지 않다.
③ 광견병은 오랫동안 존재해 왔다; 빠르게는 기원전 700년에도 언급이 있다.
④ 병이 지속되면 병자는 편히 서지도 눕지도 못한다.
⑤ 최근 과학자들은 광견병의 치료를 증진하였다; 새로운 치료법은 기존의 것보다 훨씬 고통이 적다.
⑥ 광견병의 초기 단계에 개는 지치고 불안해 보인다; 개는 심지어 주인에게서도 숨으려고 한다.

09 General sentence: 지난 10년 미국인들은 오직 삼 행과 열일곱 음절만을 사용하는 일본 시인 하이쿠에 더 많은 관심을 보여 왔다.
Specific sentences:
① 1990년에서 1997년 사이 작은 모임에서 시작한 미국 하이쿠 학회는 열 개의 지역 지도자가 있는 전국적인 모임이 되었다.
② 일본에서 하이쿠는 자판기에서 판매되는 차 캔에 쓰여 있다.
③ 고대의 하이쿠는 자연의 아름다움을 많이 노래했지만, 오늘날의 하이쿠는 영화와 만화 주인공, 패스트푸드나 록 밴드에 집중하는 것 같다.
④ 1996년 미국 신문인 "크리스천 과학 모니터"가 하이쿠 대회를 개최했을 때, 편집자들은 1986년의 세 배인 삼만 편을 접수받았다.
⑤ 월드와이드 웹은 50개의 모든 주 거주자들이 만든 수백 개의 하이쿠 사이트를 갖고 있으며 인터넷 불레틴 보드에 있는 하이쿠 수는 매년 늘어나고 있다.
⑥ 유럽의 하이쿠 팬들은 손님들이 자신의 시를 낭송하고 5분에서 10분 사이에 최고의 하이쿠를 짓는 시합을 하는 파티를 연다.

CHAPTER 02 Fact & Opinion

2S2R 독해전략을 이해하기 위해 우리가 가장 먼저 해야 할 것은 general과 specific을 구별하는 것이었다. 이제 그 다음으로 파악할 것은 사실과 의견을 구별하는 일이다. 우리는 영어 독해를 배우면서도 실제 이것의 중요성은 많이 간과하는 오류를 범하기 쉽다. 하지만, 글에서 저자의 주장이 설득력이 있는지 아니면 억측에 기반한 비논리적인 것인지를 판단할 때 가장 기본이 되는 것은 사실과 의견을 구별하는 능력에 있다.

Fact사실란 조사나 증명이 가능한 정보나 진술a piece of information or a statement that can be checked or proven 을 말한다. 가장 알기 쉬운 fact는 통계, 사건, 날짜 등과 같은 데이터를 포함한다. 예를 들어, '60살 넘는 사람들은 20대보다 투표율이 2배가 높다.'는 fact이다. 여러분이 이 진술을 읽는다면, 여러분은 그것이 옳은 것이라 가정한다. 왜냐하면, 이 진술의 사실성은 투표 조사를 통해 사실인지 아닌지 조사와 검증이 가능하기 때문이다.

Opinion의견이란 사실에 대한 해석an interpretation of facts으로, 믿음, 감정, 판단, 태도, 선호를 나타내는 것이다. 이것들은 세계에 대한 자기 자신의 인식에 기반하고 있기에 확증하기가 쉽지 않다. 따라서 끊임없이 논쟁이 되고 다른 의견이 제기될 수 있다.

하나의 예를 들어보자. '60살 넘는 사람들이 20대보다 투표율이 2배가 높은 이유는 투표하는 방식이 젊은 사람들에겐 공정하지 못하기 때문이다.' 여기선 '60살 넘는 사람들이 20대보다 투표율이 2배가 높다.'는 fact에 대해 글쓴이가 자신의 해석, 즉 '투표하는 방식이 젊은 사람들에겐 공정하지 못하기 때문이다.'라는 해석을 가미하고 있다. 따라서 이 문장은 opinion이다. 이렇게, opinion엔 facts를 포함시킬 수도 있다. 하지만, 그렇지 않고 자신의 의견만을 진술하는 경우가 일반적으로 더욱 많다.

위에서 말했듯이, 2S2R 독해전략에선 이 둘을 구별하는 능력이 영어 논리를 이해하는 데 있어서 중요함을 강조한다. 사실에 기반한 근거를 대는가, 아니면 자신의 의견만을 강요하는 글인가를 정확하게 이해함으로써 글을 비판적, 논리적으로 읽는 데 도움이 되기 때문이다. 다음에 제시되어 있는 예제를 풀다보면, 여러분은 영어 논리력의 기본 중 하나인 사실과 의견을 구별하는 안목이 자연스럽게 쌓일 것이라 생각한다.

다음의 어구들이 나오면 fact보다는 opinion일 확률이 높다.

1. I think; I believe
2. good; bad; awful; ridiculous; (un)fair; wonderful; interesting; boring; disgusting; beautiful; difficult; terrific; fantastic; discouraging
3. bigger; most important; strangest; silliest
4. some; several; many; quite a few; most; large numbers; often; usually
5. sometimes; frequently; seldom; rarely
6. all; every; never; each; always; none; no
7. may be; could be; seems; appears; probably; apparently; seemingly

다음의 것들이 의견을 표현하는 대표적인 예들이다.

BELIEF 믿음 : If you want to live an ethical life, you must follow the Ten Commandments.
FEELING 감정 : We should be ashamed of our failure to get homeless people the help they need.
JUDGMENT 판단 : People who don't keep their lawns neatly trimmed are lazy and inconsiderate toward their neighbors.
ATTITUDE 태도 : A mother with a preschooler should not work outside the home full time.
PREFERENCE 선호 : Singers should not try to improve upon "The Star-Spangled Banner" because the melody is fine the way it was written.

번역 BELIEF : 윤리적인 삶을 살고 싶으면 십계명을 따라야 한다.
FEELING : 우리는 노숙자들이 필요한 도움을 받지 못하게 된 것을 부끄럽게 느껴야 한다.
JUDGMENT : 자기 집 잔디밭을 깨끗이 깎지 않는 사람들은 게으르고 이웃에 대한 배려를 하지 않는 것이다.
ATTITUDE : 유아원 다니는 아이가 있는 엄마는 집 밖에서 풀타임으로 직장을 가져서는 안 된다.
PREFERENCE : 멜로디가 쓰여진 그대로 좋기 때문에, 가수들은 미국 국가인 "The Star-Spangled Banner"에 뭔가를 가미해 더 잘하려고 해서는 안 된다.

예제

[1-10] 다음 문장을 읽고 사실에 대한 진술이면 F, 의견에 대한 진술이면 O를 쓰시오.

01 Rosa Parks was arrested on December 1, 1955, in Montgomery, Alabama, for refusing to give up her seat on a bus to a white passenger. _____

02 Everybody living in Montgomery, Alabama, at the time should have agreed with what many activists did. _____

03 The majority of handgun owners in America are Republicans who are out of touch with the violence problem. _____

out of touch with : ~와 멀리 떨어져서 (잘 모르는)

해설 The majority(대다수)란 글쓴이의 의견일 뿐 객관적 사실은 아니다.

04 A panel of federal judges struck down Montgomery's bus segregation laws as unconstitutional. _____

segregation : 분리, 차별
unconstitutional : 위헌적인

05 Without Rosa Parks's brave act and the boycott that followed, African-Americans would never have been able to change the laws. _____

06 The 2000 presidential election was so close that we had to have the Supreme Court decide who won. _____

해설 The 2000 presidential election was close는 사실에 대한 진술이지만 we had to have the Supreme Court decide who won은 의견을 말하는 것이다. 따라서, O

정답 **01** F **02** O **03** O **04** F **05** O **06** O

07 The 2000 presidential election was so close that all of the ballots should have been recounted in the state of Florida to decide who won. _____

*ballots : 투표

해설 The 2000 presidential election was close는 사실에 대한 진술이지만 all of the ballots should have been recounted in the state of Florida to decide who won은 의견을 말하는 것이다. 따라서, O

08 President Bush said that there were weapons of mass destruction in Iraq, so we needed to invade that country to keep the world safe. _____

해설 이 문장은 비록 옳지 않은 정보이지만, 부시 대통령이 이라크에 대량 무기가 있어 침공을 해야 한다고 말한 것은 사실이다. 따라서, F

09 *The New York Times* is a very informative newspaper. _____

10 Jjang-gu is my son's favorite show. _____

11 다음 글을 읽고 각각의 문장들이 사실을 제공하면 (F), 의견을 제공하면 (O)를 쓰시오.

(1) Your child may be at risk of being swept up in one of the fastest growing health epidemics to hit kids in recent years. (2) That's the bad news. (3) The good news is that protecting your kid may be as simple as turning off the tube, hoofing it around the block, or stocking the fridge with fruits and veggies instead of cakes and cookies. (4) One out of every four children in this country is dangerously overweight. (5) And with increasing obesity rates, there has been an explosion in Type 2 diabetes, a disease once so rarely seen in children it was called "adult-onset diabetes." (6) Ten years ago, it accounted for just 4 percent of diabetes cases in children. (7) But today, that figure has jumped to as high as 45 percent in some parts of the country. (8) Of the children diagnosed with Type 2 diabetes, 85 percent are obese. (9) "It's a very serious problem" says Janet H. Silverstein, M.D., the American Academy of Pediatrics' representative on the U.S. Health Care Financing Administration's Diabetes Quality Improvement Project Leadership Council. (10) "It is really an epidemic."

* sweep up : 휩쓸다 * epidemic : 유행병
* tube : TV를 일컬음 * fridge : 냉장고 * obesity : 비만

Sentence 1 _____	Sentence 6 _____
Sentence 2 _____	Sentence 7 _____
Sentence 3 _____	Sentence 8 _____
Sentence 4 _____	Sentence 9 _____
Sentence 5 _____	Sentence 10 _____

[12-13] 다음 글을 읽고 근거가 충분한 글(informed)인지 아니면 근거가 충분하지 않은(uninformed) 글인지 찾으시오.

12

Public schools are better than private schools. In my opinion, public schools are more diverse in their student population. You never see a diverse student population in a private school class, yet public school classes often have students from all over the globe. Public schools also offer more programs, and have better teachers. People think private school teachers are better educated than public school teachers, but they're not. Public school teachers are very knowledgeable and caring. Public school buildings are more modern because many were built in the 1990s, like the ones in my town. The buildings in my town are clean, fairly new, and updated often. Private school buildings are often from the early 1920s and look it. For this reason, and the others mentioned above, I think public schools are better.

diverse : 다양한

informed _____   uninformed _____

13

America cannot solve its energy problems by finding more oil in our own lands. Proponents of Arctic drilling say that the Arctic National Wildlife Refuge alone could provide us with enough oil to significantly reduce Americans' dependence on foreign oil. They claim the Arctic could yield 1.5 million barrels a day at peak production in, say, 2020. That is a significant amount of oil. However, it also assumes the discovery of 15 billion barrels under the refuge's coastal plain, which the United States Geological Survey regards as an extremely remote possibility. Official estimates of "economically recoverable" oil are in fact much lower than 15 billion barrels. Yet even if the most optimistic estimates prove to be right, the Arctic reserves — or any other major domestic discoveries, for that matter — would not guarantee anything approaching energy independence. The reason is simple: according to the U.S. Department of Energy, this country accounts for about 25 percent of global oil consumption but only has about 3 percent of proven global oil reserves. Even if we can generate 1.5 million barrels a day, we still need 2.5 million to meet demand.

proponents : 지지자(supporters)
*yield : 생산하다, 내놓다   *reserve : 보유량*

informed _____   uninformed _____

해설 제시된 근거들이 주로 opinion보다는 fact로 되어 있고, 권위를 인정받는 자료를 사용하고 있으며, 검증 가능한 정보들로 이루어져 있다. 따라서 의심스러운 사실관계(개인의 편견에 기반한)나 불충분한 양의 증거에 기반하고 있지 않다. 따라서, informed가 맞다.

정답 07 O 08 F 09 O 10 F 11 F, O, O, F, F, F, F, F, O, O 12 uninformed 13 informed

한글 번역

예제 | **01** 1955년 12월 1일 로사 파크스는 백인 승객에게 자리를 양보하길 거부했기 때문에 앨라바마주 몽고메리에서 체포되었다.

02 앨라바마주 몽고메리에 사는 모든 이들은 그 당시 많은 활동가들이 한 일에 동의했어야 했다.

03 미국의 대다수의 소지 총을 소유한 사람들은 폭력 문제에 눈을 감는 공화주의자들이다.

04 판사단은 몽고메리의 버스 차별법이 반헌법적이라며 그것이 더 이상 효력이 없다고 선고했다.

05 로자 파크스의 용감한 행동과 그에 따른 보이콧이 없었다면 흑인들은 법을 바꿀 수 없었을 것이다.

06 2000년 미 대선은 너무나 박빙이었기에 대법원에서 누가 승자인지를 가려야 했다.

07 2000년 미 대선은 너무나 박빙이었기에 플로리다주의 모든 투표는 누가 승자인지를 가려내기 위해 다시 세어졌어야 했다.

08 부시 대통령은 이라크에 대량 살상무기가 있어서, 세계를 안전하게 지키기 위해 이라크를 침공해야 한다고 말했다.

09 *New York Times*는 아주 정보력이 있는 신문이다.

10 짱구는 내 아들이 가장 좋아하는 프로그램이다.

11 ⑴ 당신의 아이는 어쩌면 최근 가장 빠른 속도로 아이들을 공격하고 있는 질병에 휩쓸릴 위험에 놓여 있는지도 모른다. ⑵ 이것은 나쁜 소식이다. ⑶ 좋은 소식은 텔레비전을 끄고, 집 주변을 돌며 냉장고를 케익과 쿠키 대신 야채와 과일로 채우는 것 같은 간단한 방법으로 당신의 아이들 보호할 수 있다는 것이다. ⑷ 우리나라의 4명 중 한 아이가 심각한 비만이다. ⑸ 그리고 비만율의 증가에 따라 2군 당뇨병, 즉 한때는 어린이에게서는 거의 보이지 않았기 때문에 성인 당뇨병으로 불렸던 질병이 폭발적으로 증가하고 있다. ⑹ 10년 전에는 4% 정도의 당뇨병이 어린이에게서 나타났다. ⑺ 그러나 오늘날 우리나라의 어느 지역에서는 이 숫자가 45%로 급증했다. ⑻ 2군 당뇨병으로 진단받은 아이들 중 85%가 비만이다. ⑼ 미국 건강자금 위원회의 당뇨 질 개선 프로젝트 리더십 위원회의 미국 소아과 대표인 재닛 실버스타인 박사는 "정말 심각한 문제입니다." ⑽ "이건 정말 유행병이에요."라고 말한다.

12 공립학교들은 사립학교들보다 더 낫다. 내 생각에 공립학교들은 학생 구성이 더 다양하다. 사립학교 교실에서는 다양한 학생군을 거의 볼 수 없지만 공립학교 교실에는 세계 여러 곳에서 온 학생들이 있다. 공립학교는 또한 더 많은 프로그램을 제공하고 더 나은 선생님들을 갖고 있다. 사람들은 사립학교 선생이 공립학교 선생보다 더 좋은 교육을 받았다고 생각하지만, 그렇지 않다. 공립학교 선생들은 대단히 지식이 많고 아이들을 사랑한다. 공립학교 건물들은 시내의 건물들과 마찬가지로 대부분 1990년대에 지어졌기 때문에 더 현대적이다. 우리 마을 건물들은 깨끗하고 상당히 새것이며 자주 보수된다. 사립학교 건물들은 1920년대 것들이 많으며 오래 되어 보인다. 이런 이유와 위에 언급한 이유로 나는 공립학교가 좋다고 생각한다.

13 미국은 우리 자신의 땅에서 더 많은 석유를 찾으려 해서는 에너지 문제를 해결할 수 없을 것이다. 북극을 시추하자는 의견의 동조자들은 ANWR에서만도 미국의 외국 석유 의존도를 상당히 줄일 수 있을 만한 충분한 석유를 얻을 것이라고 말한다. 그들은 가령 2020년도에 북극에서 하루 최고 150만 배럴의 석유를 생산할 수 있다고 주장한다. 그것은 상당한 양이다. 그러나 이는 또한 이곳 해안가의 150억 배럴의 발견을 가정하고 말하는 것인데, 미 지질조사단은 이것이 대단히 희박한 가능성인 것으로 보고 있다. 실질적으로 '경제적으로 회수 가능한' 양은 150억 배럴보다 훨씬 적은 것으로 추정된다. 그러나 설령 가장 낙관적인 추정이 맞다 하더라도 이 문제에 있어서 북극의 저장분, 아니면 국내에서의 어떤 발견도 에너지 독립에 근접시킬 수 있다는 보장을 할 수 없다. 이유는 간단하다. 미 에너지국에 의하면 우리나라는 전 세계의 35%의 석유를 사용하지만 3%의 입증된 석유 보유를 하고 있는 것이다. 우리가 하루에 150만 배럴을 생산한다 해도 우리는 여전히 수요에 맞추기 위해 250만 배럴이 필요한 것이다.

Signal Words

2S2R 독해전략의 1단계인 Survey에서 연결어와 패턴을 나타내주는 단어나 구와 같은 signal words를 찾는 것은 매우 중요하다. 그것을 미리 파악함으로써 2S2R 독해전략의 2단계인 Reading의 단계에서 할 것을 미리 예측하여 전체 독해의 큰 그림을 그릴 수 있기 때문이다.

　예를 들어 글의 중간에 '그러나'라는 연결사가 나오고 그 다음에 어떠한 signal words가 나온 것이 없다면, 그 글은 '그러나' 다음에 나오는 내용이 저자가 말하고자 하는 주장이 될 확률이 높다. 따라서 시험 시간이 부족할 경우 여러분은 '그러나' 이하의 문장만 꼼꼼히 읽어도 전체 내용을 파악할 수 있고, 저자의 요지도 파악할 수 있다. 1단계에서 signal words를 빨리 체크함으로써 글 전체에 대한 지도를 그릴 수가 있는 것이다.

01　다양한 패턴의 Signal Words

1. Series(열거)를 나타내는 Signal Words

also	in addition	too	another
one	furthermore	first, second, third	first of all
and	for one thing	finally	lastly
most importantly	moreover	next	several
many	two, three, four, etc.	number of	numerous
examples	reasons	points	classes
types	categories	groups	goals
kinds	characteristics	methods	advantages
ways	forms	tips	

예제

다음 글을 읽고 series pattern의 signal words에 밑줄을 치시오. 그런 다음 topic을 쓰시오.

These days, it is important to know something about computers. There are a number of ways to learn. Some companies have computer classes at work. Also, most universities offer day and night courses in computer science. Another way to learn is from a book. There are many books about computers in bookstores and libraries. Or, you can learn from a friend. After a few hours of practice, you too can work with computers. You may not be an expert, but you can have fun!

Topic : _____

번역 오늘날 컴퓨터에 대해 아는 것은 중요하다. 배우는 방법은 여러 가지가 있다. 일부 회사들은 회사에 컴퓨터 강좌가 있다. 또한 대부분의 대학들은 컴퓨터공학과에서 밤낮으로 강의를 제공한다. 또 다른 방법은 책이다. 서점과 도서관에는 컴퓨터에 관련된 서적들이 많다. 아니면 친구에게 배울 수도 있다. 몇 시간만 연습하면 여러분도 컴퓨터로 작업할 수가 있다. 전문가는 아니겠지만 재미있을 것이다!

정답 These days, it is important to know something about computers. There are a number of ways to learn. **Some** companies have computer classes at work. **Also**, most universities offer day and night courses in computer science. **Another** way to learn is from a book. There are many books about computers in bookstores and libraries. **Or**, you can learn from a friend. After a few hours of practice, you too can work with computers. You may not be an expert, but you can have fun!
Topic : ways to learn about computers

2. Comparison and Contrast(비교와 대조)를 나타내는 Signal Words

■ Comparison Pattern의 Signal Words

alike	similar	same	(and) also	both

■ Contrast Pattern의 Signal Words

different	unlike	비교급(more… than/less… than)	
however	but	yet	although
instead (of)	in opposition	in spite of	just the opposite
though	nevertheless	on the one hand/on the other hand	
rather (than)	on the contrary	actually	despite
while	unfortunately	in contrast	conversely
even though	still	nonetheless	whereas
in reality	as opposed to		

예제

다음 글을 읽고 comparison or contrast의 signal words에 밑줄을 치시오. 그런 다음 topic을 쓰시오.

If you travel around Europe, you will find many differences in how doctors work. For example, English doctors are quick to give strong antibiotics for colds, but German doctors usually are not. The Germans, on the other hand, give medicine for low blood pressure, but the English do not think low blood pressure is a problem. German doctors seem very concerned about heart problems. They give six times as many heart drugs as English doctors do. Patients in the two countries are different, too. The English are more likely to accept their doctors' orders without question. The Germans, however, are likely to ask their doctors to explain their treatment.

Topic : _____

번역 유럽을 여행하면 의사들이 일하는 것에서 많은 차이점을 발견하게 될 것이다. 예를 들어 영국의 의사들은 감기에 금방 항생제를 처방하지만 독일의 의사들은 보통 그렇지 않다. 반면 독일인들은 저혈압에 약을 주지만 영국인들은 저혈압이 문제가 된다고 생각하지 않는다. 독일 의사들은 심장 질환에 아주 염려하는 것처럼 보인다. 그들은 영국 의사들이 심장약을 주는 것의 6배를 준다. 두 나라의 환자들도 다르다. 영국인들은 의사의 말에 질문 없이 잘 따르는 편이다. 그러나 독일인들은 치료에 대해 설명해 달라고 의사에게 요구하는 편이다.

정답 If you travel around Europe, you will find many **differences** in how doctors work. **For example**, English doctors are quick to give strong antibiotics for colds, **but** German doctors usually are not. The Germans, **on the other hand**, give medicine for low blood pressure, **but** the English do not think low blood pressure is a problem. German doctors seem very concerned about heart problems. They give **six times as** many heart drugs **as** English doctors do. Patients in the two countries are **different**, too. The English are more likely to accept their doctors' orders without question. The Germans, **however**, are likely to ask their doctors to explain their treatment.
Topic : how doctors work in England and Germany

3. Time Order(시간순서)를 나타내는 Signal Words

■ Time-Order Signal Words

first, second, third	before	now	ago
nowadays	then	after	while
next	soon	in the beginning	once
today	previously	often	as
when	until	later	since
eventually	last	meanwhile	finally
over time	in the end	during, in, on, or by *(followed by a date)*	
originally	in just one year	from~to~	events
steps	stages	developments	procedure
process	history		

📝 **예제**

[1-2] 다음 글을 읽고 signal words에 밑줄을 치시오. 그런 다음 topic을 쓰시오.

01

> Albert Einstein was born in 1879 in Ulm, Germany. He graduated from the University of Zurich in Switzerland in 1905. In 1905 he also did some of his most famous work in physics. In 1921 he won the Nobel Prize for Physics. Between 1919 and 1933 he lived in Germany and traveled a lot to talk to other scientists. Then in 1933 he had to leave Germany because of Hitler and the Nazi party. He moved to the United States. From 1933 until his death he lived in Princeton, New Jersey. He died on April 18, 1955.

Topic : _____

번역 알버트 아인슈타인은 1879년 독일 울름에서 태어났다. 그는 1905년에 취리히 대학을 졸업했다. 1905년에 그는 또한 물리학에서 그의 가장 유명한 업적들을 달성했다. 1921년에 그는 노벨 물리학상을 받았다. 1919년에서 1933년 사이에 독일에 살면서 다른 과학자들과 교류하기 위해 많은 여행을 했다. 그리고 1933년 히틀러와 나치 당을 연유로 독일을 떠나야 했다. 그는 미국으로 갔다. 1933년부터 죽을 때까지 그는 뉴저지 프린스턴에 살았다. 그는 1955년 4월 18일 사망했다.

02

In the United States, some people did not want the war. In the early 1960s only a few people felt this way. But by the late 1960s many people believed Americans should not be fighting in Vietnam. Finally, the U.S. government had to listen to these people. In May 1968, the Americans began to talk to North Vietnam about stopping the war. For the next few months, fewer bombs were used against the North. By the end of the year, the bombing stopped. It still took a long time to end the war. American soldiers started to go home in 1970. The last Americans left three years later.

Topic : _____

번역 미국에서 일부 사람들은 전쟁을 원치 않았다. 1960년대 초반에는 이렇게 생각하는 사람이 많지 않았다. 그러나 1960년대 후반에는 많은 사람들이 미국이 베트남에서 싸워서는 안 된다고 믿었다. 마침내 미국 정부는 이들의 말을 들어야 했다. 1968년 5월 미국인들은 월맹(북 베트남)과 정전을 논하기 시작했다. 이후 몇 달 동안 전보다 적은 양의 폭탄이 월맹에 사용되었다. 그 해 말, 폭격은 멈추었다. 그러나 여전히 전쟁이 끝나는 데는 오랜 시간이 걸렸다. 1970년 미국 군인들은 귀환하기 시작했다. 3년 후 마지막 미국인들이 떠났다.

정답 01 Albert Einstein was born in **1879** in Ulm, Germany. He graduated from the University of Zurich in Switzerland in **1905**. In **1905** he also did some of his most famous work in physics. In **1921** he won the Nobel Prize for Physics. Between **1919 and 1933** he lived in Germany and traveled a lot to talk to other scientists. Then in **1933** he had to leave Germany because of Hitler and the Nazi party. He moved to the United States. From **1933 until his death** he lived in Princeton, New Jersey. He died on **April 18, 1955**.
Topic : The Life of Albert Einstein

02 In the United States, some people did not want the war. In **the early 1960s** only a few people felt this way. But **by the late 1960s** many people believed Americans should not be fighting in Vietnam. Finally, the U.S. government had to listen to these people. In **May 1968**, the Americans began to talk to North Vietnam about stopping the war. **For the next few months**, fewer bombs were used against the North. **By the end of the year**, the bombing stopped. It still took a long time to end the war. American soldiers started to go home in **1970**. The last Americans left **three years later**.
Topic : how the Americans stopped fighting in Vietnam or the process of ending the Vietnam War in the US

4. Cause and Effect(인과관계)를 나타내는 Signal Words

If the arrow goes **C(cause)** ──────▶ **E(effect)**, use these signal words:

so	can make	is a cause of	lead to
stops	result in	cause	have an effect on
(can) help	effect	is the reason for	produce
want			

If the arrow goes **E(effect)** ◀────── **C(cause)**, use these signal words:

is the effect of	the effect of	are caused by	because (of)
is caused by	is due to	results from	

기타 **signal words** :

consequences	outcomes	chain reaction	factors
impact			

예제

[1-2] 다음 글을 읽고 signal words에 밑줄을 치시오. 그런 다음 topic을 쓰시오.

01

Aspirin is a simple drug. It has many useful effects. It can stop a headache or an earache. It helps take away pain in the fingers or knees. Aspirin can stop a fever if you have the flu, and it can make you feel better if you have a cold. Some doctors believe that aspirin also can result in a healthy heart. They say that some people should take an aspirin every day. For those people, aspirin may stop heart disease.

Topic : _____

> 번역 아스피린은 단순한 약품이다. 이것은 많은 유용한 효과들이 있다. 두통이나 귀의 통증을 멈춰주기도 한다. 손가락이나 무릎의 통증도 없애준다. 독감에 걸렸다면 열을 멈춰 줄 수도 있고 감기라면 좀 덜 아프게 해주기도 한다. 일부 의사들은 아스피린이 심장 건강에 좋다고 믿는다. 그들은 어떤 사람들은 아스피린을 매일 먹어야 한다고 말한다. 이 사람들에게 아스피린은 심장질환을 멈춰줄 수도 있다.

02

In the United States, many of the poor city children have health problems. Some of the children are ill because of their diet. They do not get enough food, or they do not get healthy food. Their poor health is also caused by bad housing. Many children live in poor apartments which have no heat in the winter and little fresh air in the summer. Some of the children have poor health because they do not receive good medical care. Many poor children do not see a doctor for checkups or for shots to keep them healthy.

Topic : _____

번역 미국에서 가난한 도시의 많은 아이들이 건강에 문제가 있다. 일부 어린이들은 식생활 때문에 몸이 아프다. 그들은 충분한 음식을 얻지 못하거나, 건강한 음식을 얻지 못한다. 그들의 열악한 건강의 원인은 주거에 있기도 하다. 많은 아이들이 겨울에는 난방이 잘 안 되고 여름에는 환기가 잘 안 되는 열악한 아파트에 산다. 또 일부 아이들은 양질의 의료 혜택을 받지 못해 건강이 나쁘다. 많은 아이들이 건강을 지키기 위한 정기검진이나 예방접종을 받기 위해 의사를 찾지 못한다.

정답 **01** Aspirin is a simple drug. It has many useful **effects**. It **can stop** a headache or an earache. It **helps** take away pain in the fingers or knees. Aspirin **can stop** a fever if you have the flu, and it **can make** you feel better if you have a cold. Some doctors believe that aspirin also **can result in** a healthy heart. They say that some people should take an aspirin every day. For those people, aspirin **may stop** heart disease.
Topic : Aspirin, a useful drug

02 In the United States, many of the poor city children have health problems. Some of the children are ill **because of** their diet. They do not get enough food, or they do not get healthy food. Their poor health is **also** **caused by** bad housing. Many children live in poor apartments which have no heat in the winter and little fresh air in the summer. Some of the children have poor health **because** they do not receive good medical care. Many poor children do not see a doctor for checkups or for shots to keep them healthy.
Topic : the poor city children's health in the United States

5. Definition(정의)을 나타내는 Signal Words

정의 패턴은 종종 하나 또는 그 이상의 보기examples를 포함하는데, 따라서 다음과 같은 signal words들이 주로 나타난다.

means	—(dash)	definition	define
meaning	is/are	is/are called	for example
for instance	to illustrate	as an illustration	in one instance
such as	in one case	describe	more precisely
specifically	what one calls		

예제

다음 글을 읽고 signal word를 제시하고, 글의 패턴은 무엇인지 밝히시오.

The World Health Organization defines obesity as a condition in which a person's body-mass index, or MBI, is greater than 30.

번역 세계보건기구는 비만을 체질량지수 혹은 MBI가 30보다 높은 상태로 정의한다.

Signal words의 중요성은, 일반적인 영어시험에서는 빈칸 채우기 형식으로 출제가 되는 문제에서 두드러진다. 이런 유형에선 signal words를 아는 것이 문제를 푸는 핵심이 되며, 답을 정확히 동시에 빨리 풀 수 있도록 해준다. 다음의 문제를 보자.

정답 이 글의 signal word는 "defines"이다. 따라서, 글의 패턴은 'definition'이 된다.

실전문제

Read the following and answer the question.

2010학년도 임용고시 9번

There are two words whose meanings reflect our somewhat warped attitudes toward levels of commitment to physical and mental activities. These are the terms *amateur* and *dilettante*. Nowadays, these labels are slightly _____(1)_____. An amateur or a dilettante is someone not quite up to par, a person not to be taken very seriously, one whose performance falls short of professional standards. But originally, "amateur," from the Latin verb *amare*, "to love," referred to a person who loved what he was doing. Similarly, a "dilettante," from the Latin *delectare*, "to find delight in," was someone who enjoyed a given activity. The earliest meanings of these words therefore drew attention to experiences rather than _____(2)_____. They described the subjective rewards individuals gained from doing things, instead of focusing on how well they were achieving. Nothing illustrates as clearly our changing attitudes toward the value of experience as the fate of these two words. There was a time when it was admirable to be an amateur poet or a dilettante scientist, because it meant that the quality of life could be improved by engaging in such activities. But increasingly the emphasis has been to value behavior over _____(3)_____ states; what is admired is success, achievement, the quality of performance rather than the quality of experience.

Which of the following best fits in the blanks above?

	(1)	(2)	(3)
①	derogatory	accomplishments	subjective
②	condescending	failures	ideal
③	cryptic	enjoyment	disorderly
④	conciliatory	accomplishments	emotional
⑤	pejorative	failures	natural

정답 ┃ ①

🔊 친절한 해설

자 우리 기억합시다. **"좋은 빈칸 문제는 항상 논리성을 띄고 있다"**는 것을. (물론 때때로 출제위원이 개념 없이 출제를 하는 경우도 있긴 하지만, 그렇지 않을 거라 우리 그냥 믿어버리자구요.) 빈칸 채우기 문제가 나오면, ① 글 전체의 Topic sentence를 찾을 수 있으면 찾아보고(일반적으로 첫째나 둘째 문장에 있음), ② 빈칸의 앞뒤 문장을 꼼꼼히, 특히 signal words에 주목해서 두 번 이상 읽기 바랍니다.

우선 첫 번째 빈칸에 들어갈 단어를 찾을 때 역시나 논리적으로 중요한 키워드가 있네요. 우선 "Nowadays," "But" "originally" "similarly"에 밑줄을 쫙 그으세요. 단어나 숙어는 정확히 몰라도 문맥 안에서 파악을 할 수 있어요. 예를 들어 "up to par"는 어떤 것이 기준에 부합하는 것으로 어려운 의미의 숙어예요(참고로, 단어 공부하실 때 그 단어가 긍정이냐(+), 부정이냐(−), 중립이냐(○)를 우선 결정하는 것이 중요해요). 하지만 이 숙어를 몰라도 논리구조 속에서 의미 파악을 해야죠. 첫 번째 빈칸의 논리구조는 다음과 같아요.

> Nowadays _____(1)_____. + "심각하게 고려되지 않고 있는 사람".
> But originally ………. Similarly ………

여기서 But은 역접인데다가 바로 뒤에 originally라는 시간의 구조가 있네요. 즉, "현재는 ……(A)……한데, 과거엔(원래는) ……(B)……했다"의 구조잖아요. 그럼 이 문제의 핵심은 (B)의 내용이죠. 그런데 (B)의 내용을 보니 긍정적인 것들이네요. 따라서 (A)엔 부정의 의미의 단어가 들어가야 돼요. 따라서 derogatory(경멸스러운)나 그것의 유사한 의미를 지닌 pejorative가 올 수 있지요. Similarly 다음은 읽을 필요가 없어요. 부연일 따름이니까요. 시간 절약해야죠.

그런 다음, 빈칸 (2)를 푸는 데에도 중요한 구조적 힌트가 있어요. 즉 rather than과 instead of이란 (유사)비교급 구조가 있잖아요. 그렇다면,

> (1) 첫 번째 CLUE는 다음의 구조죠.
> ……(A)…… rather than ……(B)………

> (2) 두 번째 CLUE는 다음의 구조죠.
> ……(A)…… instead of ……(B)………

이 두 개의 구조를 보면, (A)에 들어갈 것과 (B)에 들어갈 것이 같음을 알 수 있어요. 따라서, (A)에 experience가 왔으니, 그것과 대비되는 단어가 (B)에 와야 되겠지요. 특히 두 번째 CLUE의 (B)엔 "how well they were achieving"이란 문장이 있지요. 즉, achievement와 연관이 있네요. 그러면 당연히 빈칸 (2)에는 achievement의 비슷한 의미인 accomplishments가 와야 하지요. 그런 다음은? 읽지 마세요. 시험에선 시간을 절약하는 것이 가장 아름다운 미덕중 하나니까요. 답은 ①번이죠.

**실전
문제** 육체적이고 정신적인 활동에 관련하는 정도에 대한 우리의 다소 왜곡된 사고를 반영하는 의미를 가진 두 단어가 있다. 이것들은 아마추어와 애호가라는 용어들이다. 오늘날, 이 명칭들은 다소 경멸적이다. 아마추어나 애호가는 평균에 이르지 못하는 사람, 심각하게 여겨지지 않는 사람, 그의 솜씨가 전문적 기준에 이르지 못하는 사람이다. 그러나 원래 *amare* 라는 라틴어 동사에서 나온 아마추어라는 말은 자신이 하는 일을 사랑하는 사람을 일컬었다. 유사하게, '그 안에서 즐거움을 찾다.'를 의미하는 *delectare*라는 라틴어에서 나온 애호가라는 말은 주어진 활동을 즐기는 사람을 말한다. 따라서, 이 단어들의 원래의 의미는 성취보다는 오히려 경험에 대해 관심을 기울였다. 그들은 그들이 얼마나 그 일을 잘 성취했는지에 초점을 맞추는 대신, 그 일을 함으로써 개인들이 얻게 되는 개인적인 보상들을 묘사했다. 이 두 단어의 운명만큼 경험의 가치에 대한 우리의 변화하는 생각을 분명히 보여주는 것은 없다. 아마추어 시인이거나 애호가 수준의 과학자임이 존경 받던 때가 있었다. 그러한 활동들에 참여함으로써 삶의 질이 향상될 수 있음을 의미했기 때문이다. 그러나, 점차적으로 주관적인 수준을 넘어서는 행동에 가치를 두는 것이 강조되어 가고 있는 데 존중받는 것은 성공, 성취, 그리고 경험의 질보다는 성취의 질이 되고 있다.

Topic

일반적인 글 읽기의 과정을 포함해서 대화적 읽기에서 가장 기본이 되고 가장 먼저 확인해야 할 것은 이 글이 '무엇'에 관한 글인지를 파악하는 것이다. 해당 글이 '무엇에 관한 글인가about what?' 라는 질문을 던지고 그에 대한 답을 찾았다면 글의 주제topic를 파악했다고 할 수 있다. 문단 혹은 전체 글이 말하고자 하는 바가 요지main idea인데 그 요지의 근본이 되는 것이 주제이므로, 2S2R 독해전략의 모든 과정에서 일관되게 고려되어야 할 것도 '주제'라고 할 수 있다.

2S2R 독해전략의 1단계 개관하기Survey에서 지문의 주요 화제를 찾는 것이 곧 주제를 파악하는 것이다. 그리고 각각의 구체적인 문단들이 얼마나 잘 짜여 있는지를 평가하는 것도 주제를 중심으로 평가되어야 한다. 2단계 읽기Reading에서 주석을 달거나 주장과 근거들을 도식화하는 과정에서도 주제를 중심으로 작업이 진행되어야 한다. 3단계 요약하기Summarizing에서 좋은 요약이 각 문단의 주제어를 포함해야 함은 당연한 것이다.

01 주제와 요지의 구별

주제와 요지는 구별되어야 한다. 다음의 예문을 보자.

① 서울은 외국 관광객에게 인기가 없다.
② 서울은 500년 동안 조선의 수도였다.
③ 서울은 자동차가 아주 많아 대기가 깨끗하지 않다.

위의 세 문장은 모두 서울을 주어로 하여 주장이나 설명을 하고 있다. 이때 서울이 topic이며 세 문장은 모두 요지에 해당한다. 즉 요지는 topic을 통해서 글쓴이가 독자에게 말하고자 하는 요점이다. 따라서 topic을 이해한다는 것은 그 주제에 대해서 글쓴이가 어떤 주장 혹은 설명을 하고자 하는지를 이해하기 위한 관문에 해당한다. 요지가 드러나는 문장을 주제문이라고 할 때, 주제와 주제문의 관계는 아래와 같은 구조로 나타낼 수 있다. 따라서 '무엇'에 대한 글인지를 잘못 이해한다면 글의 핵심 주장을 파악할 수 없음은 자명한 이치이다.

주제문(topic sentence) = 주제(topic) + 서술어(controlling idea)

예 서울은 외국 관광객에게 인기가 없다(topic sentence) = 서울(topic) + 외국 관광객에게 인기가 없다 (controlling idea)

02 주제 찾기 방법

일반적으로 주제를 파악하는 방법은 2가지로 제시할 수 있다. **먼저 문단에서 가장 많이 언급되는 대상을 찾는 방법**이다. 일반적으로 주제는 ① 반복되어 나오는 ② 개념어가 될 가능성이 가장 높다. 따라서 지문에서 언급되는 대상 혹은 개념들의 빈도를 파악하는 것은 주제를 찾는 한 방법이 된다.

■ Key Point

> Topic은 다음의 3가지 원칙을 지켜야 한다.
> 1. Topic은 too general해서는 안 된다.
> 2. Topic은 too specific해서는 안 된다.
> 3. Topic엔 읽는 사람 개인의 생각이 들어가선 안 된다.

다음의 예를 들어보자.

예 다음 중 어느 것이 topic이 될 수 있나?
① Korea ② Japan ③ China ④ Country ⑤ East Asian countries

여기서, ①, ②, ③번은 너무 세부적(too specific)이다. 왜? 만약 ①이 답이 된다면 ②, ③도 답이 되어야 하니까 말이 안 된다. 서로 등가의 것이니까. 그러면, ④번에 있는 Country는? 이것은 또 너무 포괄적(too general)이다. 동아시아에 있는 나라를 다루는 데 국가라는 큰 개념을 쓸 필요는 없기 때문이다. 그래서 답은 ⑤ East Asian countries가 된다. 만일 ⑤가 선택지에 없다면? 물론 ④가 답이 된다.

우리는 1장에서 general과 specific에 대해서 공부를 하였다. 그것을 기반으로 하여 지금부터 topic을 알아보도록 하자.

예제

[1-6] What is the topic? Write it.

01 yellow / purple / white / color / green

Topic : _____

> 해설 yellow, purple, white, green은 서로 등가의 것들이므로 나머지를 포괄할 수 없다. 따라서 topic이 될 수 없다. color만이 전체를 포괄한다.

02 nose / ears / eyes / head / mouth

Topic : _____

03 table / chair / chest / bed / furniture

Topic : _____

04 doctor / X-rays / medicine / hospital / patients

Topic : _____

05 physics / chemistry / astronomy / geology / biology

Topic : _____

> 해설 주어진 단어들 중에서는 나머지를 포괄할 수 있는 것이 없다. 모두가 서로 등가의 것이기 때문이다. 이런 경우 이것들의 공통 속성을 추론해서 답을 찾아야 한다. 물리학, 화학, 천문학, 지질학, 생물학 ⇨ 이것들은 모두 과학이라는 공통의 속성을 지니고 있다. 따라서 답은 sciences가 되는 것이다.

06 Colorado / California / Florida / Arizona / Texas

Topic : _____

[7-8] One word does not belong with the others. Cross out the word. Then write the topic.

07 roof / tree / window / door / floor / wall

Topic : _____

> 해설 roof, window, door, floor, wall 등은 모두 어떤 건물을 구성하는 부분들이다. 하지만 나무는 그것과 직접적인 관련이 없다. 따라서 제외시켜야 한다.

08 ice cream / candy / cake / carrots / pie / cookies

Topic : _____

[9-11] What is the topic of the paragraph? Write it.

09

All clouds are made of many little drops of water. But not all clouds are alike. There are three kinds of clouds. Cirrus clouds are one kind. These are made of ice drops. They look soft and light. Cumulus clouds are another kind of cloud. They are large and deep and flat on the bottom. We usually see cumulus clouds on warm summer days. Finally, there are stratus clouds, which cover the whole sky. These clouds make the sky gray and the sun does not shine at all.

Topic : _____

> 해설 clouds라 답을 하신 분들도 있으리라 본다. 하지만 그것은 too general하다. 또한 cirrus clouds도 topic이 될 수 없다. 앞서 봤지만 topic은 전체를 포괄할 수 있어야 하는데 이것은 그렇지 못하기 때문이다. 이것은 too specific하다. 만약 cirrus clouds이 topic이 된다면, cumulus clouds와 stratus clouds도 topic이 될 수 있다. 그렇게 되면 **하나의 문단에는 단 하나의 topic만이 있어야 한다**는 대원칙을 어기게 되어 오류가 된다.

정답 | **01** color   **02** head   **03** furniture   **04** hospital   **05** sciences   **06** states in the United States
07 parts of a building   **08** sweets or desserts   **09** three kinds of clouds

10

Many American scientists are worried about the drinking water in the United States. They think that soon there may be no more clean drinking water. Dirt, salt, and chemicals from factories can get into the water, making it unsafe to drink. This is already true in some places. One example is a small town in Massachusetts. Many children in this town became sick because of chemicals in the water. Another place with water problems is California. The water near old Air Force airports is not safe to drink. Many other cities and towns have water problems, too.

Topic : _____

해설 9번 문제보다는 약간 난이도가 높은 문제이다. 따라서 원리를 적용하여 푸는 것이 도움이 되겠다. 우선 가장 많이 반복되는 단어나 구를 찾아보자. drinking water란 어구가 첫째, 둘째 그리고 셋째 문장에 모두 반복되어 나온다. 그렇다면 이것은 틀림없이 중요한 key words에 해당한다. 그런 다음 그것에 대해 어떠한 말들이 언급되는지 보자.

문장 1 : Many American scientists are **worried about** the drinking water in the United States.

문장 2 : They think that soon there may be **no more clean** drinking water.

문장 3 : **Dirt, salt, and chemicals from factories** can get into the water, making it **unsafe** to drink.

위에서 밑줄 친 것들을 다시 한번 읽어보자. '걱정하다' '더 이상 깨끗하지 않은' '공장에서 나오는 쓰레기, 염분, 화학약품들' '안전하지 않은' 따위의 부정적인(negative) 의미를 지닌 것들 뿐이다. 이제 이것들을 한마디로 요약하는 것이 필요하다. 무엇이라고 할까? 답을 내기 전에 다시 원리로 돌아가 보자. 앞에서 우리는 다음과 같은 것을 배웠다.

physics / chemistry / astronomy / geology / biology ⇨ 이 5개를 한 단어로 정리하면, 답은 sciences이다.

그렇다면, 이 원리를 여기에 적용해보자. 'worried about' 'no more clean' 'Dirt, salt, and chemicals from factories' 'unsafe' 이것들의 의미의 공통 속성을 끄집어내보자. 그렇다면, problems란 단어가 가장 적합할 것이다. 여기까지 정리 해보면, problems with safe drinking water가 topic이 된다. 하지만, 이것은 topic이 되기엔 too general하다. 왜냐하면, 위의 글은 한국의 문제도 중국의 문제도 우간다의 문제도 아닌, 바로 미국의 문제이기 때문이다. 따라서 다시 정리를 해보면, American problems with safe drinking water 또는 problems with safe drinking water in the United States가 topic이 된다.

11

The tendency to help others begins early, although at first it is not spontaneous; children have to learn to be helpful. In most cultures, very young children usually help others only when they are asked to do so or are offered a reward. Still, Carolyn Zahn-Waxler and her associates found that almost half of the two-year-olds they observed acted helpfully toward a friend or a family member. Even before their second birthday, some children offer help to those who are hurt or crying by snuggling, patting, or offering food or even their own teddy bears. As they grow older, children use helping behavior to gain social approval, and their efforts at helping become more elaborate. The role of social influence in the development of helping is seen as children follow examples set by people around them. Their helping behaviors are shaped by the norms established by their families and the broader culture. In addition, children are usually praised and given other rewards for helpfulness, but scolded for selfishness. Eventually most children come to believe that being helpful is good and that they are good when they are helpful. By the late teens, people often help others even when no one is watching and no one will know that they did so.

Topic : _____

해설 앞의 10번 문제보다도 난이도가 높은 문제이다. 따라서 10번과 같이 원리를 적용하여 푸는 것이 도움이 되겠다. 우선 가장 많이 반복되는 단어나 구를 찾아보자. 다시 문장을 읽어 보자.

문장 1 : The tendency to **help others** begins early, although at first it is not spontaneous; children have to learn to be helpful.

문장 2 : In most cultures, very young children usually **help others** only when they are asked to do so or are offered a reward.

문장 3 : **Still**, Carolyn Zahn-Waxler and her associates found that almost half of the two-year-olds they observed acted **helpfully toward a friend or a family member**. (a friend or a family member는 others로 바뀔 수 있다)

문장 4 : Even before their second birthday, some children offer **help to those who** are hurt or crying by snuggling, patting, or offering food or even their own teddy bears.

문장 5 : As they grow older, children use **helping behavior** to gain social approval, and their efforts at **helping** become more elaborate.

문장 6 : By the late teens, people often **help others** even when no one is watching and no one will know that they did so.

helping others; helping behavior; helping이란 어구가 첫 문장에서부터 마지막 문장에까지 반복되어 나온다. 그렇다면 이것을 모두 포괄할 수 있는 것은 helping others이다. 따라서 그것이 topic이 될 수 있다. helping은 too general하고, helping behavior는 남을 돕는다는 의미를 지니고 있긴 하지만 직접적으로 남을 돕는다는 의미를 지닌 helping others가 더욱 좋다.

정답 | **10** American problems with safe drinking water　**11** helping others

실전문제

01 **What is the title of the passage?**　　　　　　　　　　　　　　7급 공무원

> Whatever their position, partisans often invoke examples from other cultures to support their ideas about the proper role of each sex. Because women are clearly subservient to man in many societies, some experts conclude that the natural pattern is for men to dominate. But among the Semai tribe no one has the right to command others, and in West Africa women are often chiefs. The place of women in these societies supports the argument of those who believe that sex roles are not fixed, that if there is a natural order, it allows for many different arrangements. The argument will never be settled as long as the opposing sides toss examples from the world's cultures at each other like intellectual stones. But the effect of biological differences on male and female behavior can be clarified by looking at known examples of the earliest forms of human society and examining the relationship between technology, social organization, and sex roles. The problem is to determine the conditions in which different degrees of male dominance are found.
>
> **toss : 던지다(throw)*

① Argument and Sex Roles
② Sex Roles in Different Societies
③ Women in West Africa
④ Understanding Different Cultures
⑤ Gender Problems

02 What is the best title of the passage?

Noah Webster's goal in life was to promote the adoption of an American language. He wanted to free Americans from British English as they had freed themselves from the British crown. To this end he published a series of three textbooks : a speller in 1783, a grammar in 1784, and a reader in 1785. Webster objected to the way certain words had been borrowed from other languages but had not been repelled. The result, he claimed, was a confusing mixture of letters, many of which were not pronounced the way they looked, and others of which were not pronounced at all. Webster urged Americans to simplify their spelling. For example, he argued that "head" should he spelled "had" and "bread" should be spelled "bred". Most of Webster's suggestions did not catch on, but his textbooks sold millions of copies.

* *promote* : 진행시키다, 촉진하다, 진척시키다
* *adoption* : 채택, 채용
* *crown* : 국왕의 지배, 통치
* *repel* : 저항하다, 쫓아버리다
* *catch on* : 인기를 얻다
* *urge* : 설득하다, 주장하다

① The Three Books of Noah Webster
② Noah Webster and the Adoption of an American Language
③ Simplification of Spelling
④ American English and British English
⑤ Noah Webster and His Greatness

정답 | 01 ② 02 ②

03   What is the best title of the passage?

Work is desirable, first and foremost, as a preventive of boredom, for the boredom that a man feels when he is doing necessary though uninteresting work is regarded as nothing in comparison with the boredom that he feels when he has nothing to do with his days. With this advantage of work another is associated, namely that it makes holidays more delicious when they come. Provided a man does not have to work so hard as to impair his vigor, he is likely to find more zest in his free time than an idle man could possibly find.

desirable : 바람직한
first and foremost : 맨 앞의, 선두의
preventive : 예방책
boredom : 지루함
provided : 만일 ~라면
impair : 해치다, 손상시키다
vigor : 활기, 힘
zest : 열정

① Work and Boredom
② Danger of Boredom
③ Merit of Work
④ Value of Free Time
⑤ Merit of Boredom

04 What is the best title and main idea of the passage? 교원임용고시

First is the concern that only the rich will have access to such life-saving technologies as genetic screening and cloned organs. Such fears are justified, considering that companies have been patenting human life. The obesity gene, the premature aging gene, and the breast cancer gene, for example, have already been patented. These patents result in gene monopolies, which could lead to astronomical patient costs for genetic screening and treatment. A biotechnology industry argues that such patents are the only way to recoup research costs that, in turn, lead to further innovations. The commercialization of technology causes several other concerns, including issues of quality control and the tendency for discoveries to remain closely guarded secrets rather than collaborative efforts. In addition, industry involvement has made government control more difficult because researchers depend less and less on federal funding. Finally, although there is little doubt that profit acts as a catalyst for some scientific discoveries, other less commercially profitable but equally important projects may be ignored.

Title : _____

Main idea : _____

_____

정답 | 03 ③

04 Title : Commercialization of biotechnology

Main idea : Commercialization of biotechnology causes several concerns.

🔊 친절한 해설

우선 중요한 key words나 signal words에 밑줄을 그어보세요. 그런 다음 topic도 찾아보지요. 그런 다음 글의 pattern of organization과 main idea도 찾아보고요. 그리고 맨 마지막에 summary도 해보지요. 자, 준비됐나요?

> <u>First</u> is the <u>**concern**</u> that only the rich will have access to such <u>life-saving technologies</u> as genetic screening and cloned organs. Such <u>fears</u> are justified, considering that companies have been patenting human life. The obesity gene, the premature aging gene, and the breast cancer gene, <u>**for example**</u>, have already been patented. These patents <u>result in</u> gene monopolies, which could <u>lead to</u> astronomical patient costs for genetic screening and treatment. A biotechnology industry argues that such patents are the only way to recoup research costs that, in turn, lead to further innovations. The <u>**commercialization of technology**</u> <u>**causes**</u> several <u>**other concerns**</u>, including issues of quality control and the tendency for discoveries to remain closely guarded secrets rather than collaborative efforts. <u>In addition</u>, industry involvement <u>**has made**</u> government control more difficult <u>because</u> researchers depend less and less on federal funding. <u>Finally</u>, although there is little doubt that profit acts as a catalyst for some scientific discoveries, other less commercially profitable but equally important projects may be ignored.

우선 signal words나 key words에 밑줄을 치니 위와 같이 되네요. 이미 앞에서 설명했듯이, topic은 너무 구체적(too specific)이거나 너무 일반적(too general)이지 않은 "반복되는 단어나 어구"(특히 개념어)라고 말했던 것 기억나시죠? 그러면, topic이 될 만한 것을 찾아보죠.

우선 ① concern(s) — 그것의 유사어인 fear(s) — ② patent 등이 나오다가 조금 있으니, ③ commercialization of technology라는 단어가 반복해서 나오는군요. 여기서 저자는 paraphrase를 계속 사용하고 있는데, industry, companies 등을 commercialization과 같은 개념으로 서로 번갈아 가면서 쓰고 있네요. ① concern은 too general하고 ② patent는 too specific하네요. 따라서 가장 타당한 것은 ③ commercialization of technology이네요. 그런데 좀 더 정확히는 단순한 technology가 아니라 life-saving technologies라는 구체적인 것을 언급하므로 biotechnology가 되어야 해요. 이 글의 topic은 고로, commercialization of biotechnology가 되네요.

그러면 다음으로 요지를 찾아보죠. 다음 5장에서 배우겠지만, 이 글은 series의 패턴으로 쓰여졌어요. 이 패턴의 signal words가 First; other; In addition; Finally이고요. 이 유형에서 가장 중요한 것은 **일반화**(generalization)의 기술이에요. 즉, 다른 말로 하면, 각각의 supporting details의 **공통 속성**을 찾아내는 것이 중요하다는 말이죠. (이 방법에 대해 우리는 본문 3장과 5장 Signal words와 Patterns of Organization에 대한 이론에서 좀 더 자세히 살펴볼 것이기에 여기선 간략히 다루겠음).

이 지문에서 First; other; In addition; Finally 사이엔 사소하고 지엽적인 내용상 차이가 있을 뿐, 그 어떠한 외적·범주적인 큰 차이도 없어요. 다시 말하면, First 다음에 나오는 것도 concern에 관한 것이고 other; In addition; Finally 다음에 나오는 것도 모두 concern에 관한 것일 따름이지요. 좀 더 부연하면, 첫 번째 우려처럼 오직 부자들만이 생명을 살리는 기술에 접근하고 가난한 사람들은 접근 못할 것이란 점이든; 두 번째 우려처럼 품질 관리를 어떻게 할 것인가와 협동 노력보다는 자기들끼리 몰래 함으로써 낮게 되는 문제점 등을 지적하든; 세 번째 우려처럼 정부의 통제를 더욱 어렵게 만든다는 등 총 4가지의 이유를 제시하고 있지만, 이것들 각각에서 하나의 **공통 속성**을 뽑아내면, 그것은 바로 concern(fear)이라는 점이네요.

01

그러면, 도대체 뭐 때문에 concern이 쭉 열거가 될까요? 이 질문을 품고 글의 구조를 좀 더 꼼꼼히 보니 또 하나의 pattern이 사용되었네요. 바로 인과관계(cause and effect) 패턴이네요. 인과관계 패턴에 많이 사용되는 signal words는 다음과 같지요.

so	can make	is a cause of	leads to
stops	results in	causes	makes
had an effect on	can help	creates	effects
is the reason for	is the effect of	the effect of	are caused by
because of	is caused by	is the reason for	is due to
results from	because		

이런 경우 대다수의 글의 요지는 "A가 B에게 (이러저러)한 영향을 주었다"라든가 "A는 B라는 결과를 야기시켰다" 따위와 유사한 것이 되지요. 이 지문엔 result in; lead to; causes; has made; because 등의 signal words들이 있어요. 따라서 이 글의 main idea를 써보면, commercialization of biotechnology causes several concerns가 되지요. 다음의 공식을 명심하세요.

주제문(topic sentence or main idea) = 주제(topic) + 서술어(controlling idea)

⇨ commercialization of biotechnology causes several concerns = commercialization of biotechnology (topic) + causes several concerns (controlling idea)

자, 그럼 이 지문을 summary한다면, 어떻게 해야 할까요? 마지막 장에서 나오겠지만, 미리 한 번 보죠. 다음에 나오는 summary의 원리를 적용하면 쉽게 풀 수가 있어요.

1. 좋은 요약은 요지와 주된 논거(major supporting points)를 포함한다. 요지는 가능하면 첫 문장에 제시한다.
2. 좋은 요약은 단서가 되는 언어들(signal words)을 포함한 각 문단의 핵심어를 포함한다.
3. 좋은 요약은 작은 세부사항, 반복되는 세부사항, 읽는 이의 의견을 포함하지 않는다.
4. 좋은 요약은 본문에 있는 단어나 어구를 그대로 사용하지 않고 다른 말로 바꿔쓰기(paraphrase)한다.
5. 일반적으로 원 본문의 길이를 25%(4분의 1)로 줄이는 것을 원칙으로 한다.

이 원칙을 따르면, 본문을 다음과 같이 요약할 수가 있겠네요.

Biotechnology for profit has several problems. These include the rising cost of genetic treatment and the possibility of companies withholding discoveries. Since governments no longer provide the major research funding, their control has slackened. Research becomes guided by profit than by true benefit.

예제 09 모든 구름은 많은 작은 물방울로 만들어져 있다. 그러나 모든 구름이 같은 것은 아니다. 세 가지 종류의 구름이 있다. 덩굴 구름이 한 종류이다. 이것들은 얼음 방울로 되어 있다. 이들은 부드럽고 가벼워 보인다. 적운은 또 다른 종류의 구름이다. 이것들은 크기가 크고 깊으며 바닥이 널찍하다. 우리는 보통 따뜻한 여름날 적운을 본다. 마지막으로 층운이 있는데 이는 전체 하늘을 다 덮는다. 이것들은 하늘을 회색으로 만들고 태양도 전혀 빛나지 못한다.

10 많은 미국 과학자들은 미국의 식수에 대해 우려를 한다. 그들은 곧 깨끗한 식수가 없어질 거라고 생각한다. 공장에서 나오는 오염물, 염분, 화학물질이 물로 들어갈 수 있고 먹기에 안전하지 않게 만들 것이다. 일부 지역에서는 이것이 이미 사실이다. 하나의 예는 메사추세츠의 작은 마을이다. 이 마을의 많은 아이들은 물에 든 화학물질 때문에 병이 났다. 물 문제가 있는 또 다른 지역은 캘리포니아이다. 오래된 공군 비행장 주변의 물은 먹기에 안전하지 않다. 다른 많은 도시들과 마을들 역시 물 문제가 있다.

11 비록 처음에는 즉각적이지는 않더라도 다른 이들을 돕는 성향은 일찍 시작된다. 아이들은 도움이 되는 사람이 되도록 배워야 한다. 대부분의 문화에서 아주 어린 아이들은 요청을 받았을 때에만 다른 사람을 돕거나, 도우면 보상을 제공받는다. 그러나 캐롤라인 잔 웩슬러와 그녀의 동료들은 거의 절반의 2살배기들이 자신의 친구나 가족에게 도움이 되는 행동을 하는 것을 발견했다. 심지어 두 돌이 되기도 전에 일부 어린이들은 다치거나 우는 아이들을 안거나 토닥이거나 음식을 주거나 심지어 자신의 테디베어를 주면서 도움을 주려고 한다. 나이가 들면서 아이들은 사회적인 인정을 얻기 위해 도움 행위를 이용하고 그들의 도움의 노력은 좀 더 발달된다. 도움 행동의 발달에 있어서 사회적인 영향의 역할은 아이들이 자기 주변 사람들이 설정한 예들을 따르면서 나타난다. 그들의 도움 행동은 그들의 가족과 그 외부의 문화에 의해 설정된 기준에 의해 형성된다. 더불어 어린이들은 도움을 주려 하는 태도에 대해 칭찬과 보상을 받고 이기적일 때 혼이 난다. 결국 대부분의 아이들은 도움이 되는 것이 좋은 것이며 자신이 도움이 될 때 착한 것이라고 믿게 된다. 10대 후반에 사람들은 남들이 보지 않고 아무도 그들이 그렇게 한 것을 모를때조차 남을 종종 돕게 된다.

실전 문제 01 그들의 입장이 무엇이든 간에, 당파주의자들은 종종 다른 문화의 예에 호소해서 남녀 각각의 적절한 성 역할에 대한 그들 생각을 방어한다. 여성들은 분명히 많은 사회에서 남성들에게 복종하는 경향이 있기 때문에 어떤 전문가들은 자연의 패턴은 남성이 지배하는 것이라고 결론을 내린다. 그러나 Semai 종족 사이에서는 어떤 누구도 사람에게 명령을 할 권리가 없다. 그리고 서아프리카에서는 여자가 종종 족장이다. 이런 사회에서 여성의 위치는 성의 역할이 고정되어 있지 않고, 만일 타고난 질서가 있다면 서로 다른 많은 배열을 허용한 것이라 믿는 사람들의 주장을 뒷받침해준다. 서로 세상에 있는 문화로부터 자신들의 지적 초석으로 여러 예들을 사용하는 한 논쟁은 결코 해결되지 않을 것이다. 그러나 생물학적 차이가 남녀 행동에 영향을 준다는 것은 인간 사회의 초창기 형태의 알려진 예를 통해, 그리고 기술, 사회조직, 성 역할 사이의 관계를 살펴보면 분명해진다. 문제는 조건들—그 안에서 서로 다른 정도의 남성 지배가 발견되는—이 도대체 무엇인지를 결정하는 것이다. (즉, 어떤 사회에서 남성 지배가 더 강하고 다른 사회에서는 남성 지배가 덜 강하다면, 그런 상황을 만들어내는 '조건들'이 도대체 무엇인가를 결정하는 것이 중요하다는 점을 저자는 말하고 있다.)

02 노아 웹스터의 인생 목표는 미국식 영어의 채택을 증진시키는 것이었다. 그는 미국인들이 영국 국왕의 지배로부터 자신들을 해방시킨 것처럼 미국인들을 영국식 영어로부터 해방시키기를 원했다. 이런 목적으로 그는 3권의 교본을 시리즈로 출판했다. 1783년에 철자 교본, 1784년에 문법 교본, 그리고 1785년에 독해 교본이었다. 웹스터는 특정한 어휘들을 다른 언어로부터 빌려오기만 하고 저항하지 않았던 방식에 반대했다. 그가 주장하건대, 그 결과는 문자의 혼란스러운 혼합이었다. 문자 중 많은 것들은 그것이 생긴 모양처럼(철자처럼) 발음되지 않았고, 다른 것들은 전혀 발음되지 않았다. 웹스터는 미국인들이 철자를 단순화할 것을 촉구했다. 예를 들어서, 그는 "head"는 "had"로, "bread"는 "bred"로 쓰여야 한다고 주장했다. 웹스터의 제안 대부분은 인기를 얻지는 못했지만 그의 교본들은 수백만 부가 팔렸다.

03 일은 무엇보다도 지루함에 대한 예방책으로 바람직하다. 왜냐하면 사람이 재미는 없지만 필요한 일을 하고 있을 때 느끼는 지루함은 사람이 할 일이 없을 때 느끼는 따분함과 비교하면 아무것도 아닌 것으로 간주되기 때문이다. 이러한 일의 장점과 연결되어 있는 또 다른 것이 있다. 즉, 휴일이 올 때 일은 휴일을 더 달콤하게 만든다. 만일 어떤 사람이 자신의 활기를 해칠 만큼 열심히 일할 필요가 없다면, 그는 아마 할 일 없는 사람(즉, 일하지 않는 사람)이 찾을 수 있는 것보다 더 많은 열정을 자신의 자유 시간 중에 발견할 것이다.

04 첫 번째 우려는 오직 부자들만이 (개인의 유전적 질병의 발견과 예방을 위한 조사인) 유전자 검사나 복제된 기관들과 같은 생명을 살리는 기술에 접근할 것이란 점이다. 그와 같은 걱정은, 기업체들이 인간 생명을 특허를 내는 것을 고려할 때, 정당한 근거가 있다. 예를 들어, 비만 유전자, 정상보다 빨리 노화되는 유전자, 그리고 유방암 유전자 등은 벌써 특허를 내고 있다. 이런 특허는 유전자 독점이란 결과를 낳게 되는데, 이 독점은 유전자 검사와 (그런 다음) 치료를 해야 하는 부모들에게 천문학적인 비용을 들게 할 수 있다. 생명공학 산업계는 그와 같은 특허는 연구 비용을 벌충하는 유일한 방법이고, 이걸 통해 앞으로 더 나은 혁신을 가져올 수 있다는 주장을 한다. 기술을 상업화 하는 것은 여러 우려를 낳게 하는데, 품질 관리의 문제와 협동 노력보다는 연구 성과나 발견이 다른 사람들 모르게 보호되는 경향성 등이 거기에 포함된다. 게다가, 산업의 개입은 정부의 통제를 더욱 어렵게 만드는데, 왜냐하면 연 구자들이 연방정부의 기금에 덜 의존하게 되기 때문이다. 끝으로, 이윤이란 것이 어떤 과학적 발견을 촉진시키는 촉매제라는 것은 거의 의심의 여지가 없음에도, 상업적으론 덜 이익이 나는 것이긴 하지만 마찬가지로 앞의 것 만큼 이나 중요한 다른 계획들이 무시될 수도 있다는 점이다.

CHAPTER 05 Patterns of Organization

01 글의 패턴의 파악과 2S2R

문단의 구성 유형pattern of organization을 파악하는 것이 '빠르고 정확한' 읽기에 어떤 도움이 되는지는 아래와 같은 간단한 실험을 통해 쉽게 이해할 수 있다.

> 다음의 숫자들을 한 번 읽고서 암기해보자.
>
> a. 1, 4, 7, 10, 13, 16, 19
> b. 1, 4, 6, 9, 16, 17, 25
> c. 2, 4, 6, 8, 10, 12, 14
> d. a, b, c, d, e, f, g, h

먼저 a의 경우는 맨 처음의 숫자 1에서부터 차례로 3씩 더해지고 있음을 알 수 있다. c의 경우는 짝수로 구성되어 있다. 그리고 d는 알파벳의 순서로 되어 있다. 따라서 a와 c, 그리고 d는 굳이 암기하지 않고도 정보를 이해하고 기억하는 것이 더 용이하다. 즉 유형pattern화된 정보는 '빠르고 정확한' 이해와 암기에 큰 도움을 준다. 결국 글의 **구성 유형**을 파악하는 것은 글 전체의 정보를 구조화시켜서 정확하게 이해할 뿐만 아니라, 읽은 정보를 빠르게 기억해내는데 기여함을 알 수 있다.

　2S2R 독해전략에서 문단 유형의 파악이 이루어져야 할 부분은 **Reading 단계**이다. 각 문단의 주제topic를 잠정적으로 이해한 뒤에 그 topic sentence를 뒷받침하는 세부사항(논거)들인 supporting details들을 통해서 전체적인 글의 구성유형을 떠올려본다. 이때 글이 어떻게 조직화(패턴화)되어 있는지를 알면 다음 단계에 나올, 저자가 글에서 말하려 하는 요점, 즉 요지를 정확하게 이해하는 데 큰 도움을 준다. 특히, 2S2R 독해전략에서는 글의 구성 유형을 철저하게 이해하는 것을 매우 중시한다. 왜냐면, 다시 강조하지만 글의 요지를 파악하는 데 있어서 supporting details가 어떻게 구성되어 있는 지를 파악하는 것이 가장 급선무이기 때문이다. 다음의 글을 한 번 보자.

> The name *Arkansas* comes from the Sioux word *quapaw,* which means "downstream people." The word *Illinois* comes from the Algonquin word *illini,* "warrior men." *Kentucky* comes from the Iroquois word *kentake,* which means "meadow" or "plains." The name *Michigan* comes from the Chippewa *mica gama,* meaning "grand waters." *Oklahoma* is named after the Choctaw term for "red people," *okla humma.*

번역 알칸사스라는 이름은 '하류쪽의 사람들'을 뜻하는 수족의 단어 *quapaw*에서 온 것이다. 일리노이는 '전사'를 뜻하는 알곤퀸족의 단어 *illini*에서 온 말이다. 켄터키는 '초원'이나 '평야'를 뜻하는 이로쿠아 족의 말 *kentake*에서 온 것이다. 미시간은 '거대한 물'을 뜻하는 취페와족의 용어 *mica gama*에서 온 것이다. 오클라호마는 '붉은 사람들'을 뜻하는 촉타우족의 *okla humma*에서 유래했다.

이 글의 topic과 main idea는 무엇인가? 그냥 무작정 추측할 수는 없는 노릇이다. 그렇다면, 위에서 말했지만 글의 구성 유형을 파악하는 것이 급선무이다. 그런 다음 각각 문장 하나하나를 꼼꼼히 읽고 각 문장의 주제subject를 찾아 리스트화하는 것이다. 자, 우선 이 글을 보니 미국의 5개 주의 이름이 나열되어 있다. 따라서 Series열거패턴으로 구조화되어 있음을 알 수 있다. 구체적으로 각 문장의 주제를 써보면 다음과 같다.

- Sentence 1 subject : the name Arkansas
- Sentence 2 subject : the word Illinois
- Sentence 3 subject : Kentucky
- Sentence 4 subject : the name Michigan
- Sentence 5 subject : Oklahoma

그러면, 이 다섯 문장에서 언급된 것의 **공통 속성**을 끄집어내보자. Arkansas, Illinois, Kentucky, Michigan, Oklahoma 등의 공통 속성은 미국의 '주'라는 것이다. (예를 들어 대전, 부산, 인천, 광주 등 4개가 있다고 할 때 이것들의 공통 속성은 한국의 광역시라는 것이듯.) 그런데 각 문장에서 또 하나의 공통적 요소가 있는데, 그것은 그 주의 이름들의 기원에 대한 것이다. 그런데 그 이름들의 기원이 모두 인디언에게서 왔음을 알 수 있다. 따라서 이 series로 나열되어 있는 다섯 문장을 종합해 보면, '(미국의) 주의 이름 + 이름의 기원 + 인디언 언어'라는 도식이 성립된다. 그러므로 이 글의 topic은 "origins of names of several states"이 되며, main idea는 "Names of several states of the United States originated from Indian languages"가 될 수 있다.

만일 이 글의 구성이 contrast나 definition, 또는 cause&effect 등으로 되어 있었다면, 이 글은 전혀 다른 글이 되었을 것이며, 요지를 찾는 방법도 달랐을 것이다. 하지만, 이 글은 Series로 되어 있기 때문에 그것들의 **공통 속성**을 찾아내서 **일반화**하면 요지를 찾을 수가 있는 것이다.

02 문단의 구성 유형

1. Series 열거에 따른 구성

이 유형에서 저자의 요지main idea는 **일반화**generalization의 형태로 제시된다. 따라서 바로 앞의 예문에서 봤듯이, 각각의 supporting details의 **공통 속성**을 찾아내는 것이 중요하다. 보통 문단의 맨 앞에 일반화되어 제시된 단어를 'key words'라고 한다. key words가 앞에 제시된 열거 방식의 글의 경우 key words와 관련된 항목을 **순차적으로 나열하는 것**이 일반적이다. 이렇게 제시된 항목들은 대등하게 제시된 경우도 있고 점층적으로 제시된 경우도 있다. 따라서 항목들 간의 관계가 어떠한지 살피는 것이 필요하다. 보통 열거의 구성은 ① 예시examples ② 이유reasons ③ 분류classification ④ 다양한 항목들의 특질 설명하기kind of point 등 4가지가 있다. 먼저 이해를 돕기 위해 우리말로 된 열거의 예를 보자.

읽기 연구자들에 의하면 글을 읽고 독자가 구성하게 되는 표상(representation)에는 세 단계가 있다. 첫째는 글의 표층 기억(text surface trace) 표상이다. 이는 실제 쓰인 단어와 구, 글의 직접적 표상의 사실적 입력이다. 표층 기억은 글 기억 표상의 토대를 제공한다. 사람들이 글의 표면적 특징 중 일부를 보유한다고 하더라도, 글 형태에 대한 기억은 글이 처리된 직후에 급속히 사라진다. 둘째는 글 기저(text base) 표상이다. 이는 담화의 의미적, 명제적 표상으로서 글 명제의 의미를 포함한다. 글 기저란 글 자체의 기억을 표상, 그것을 재인, 회상, 요약 등의 형태로 재생하는 독자 능력과 관계가 있다. 마지막으로 상황 모델(situation model) 표상이다. 이 단계에서 결정적인 것은 어떻게 글 정보가 독자의 배경지식 구조에 관련되느냐이다. 그러므로 상황 모델 구성은 글 기저 더하기 지식이라고 할 수 있다. 어떻게 글 정보가 추론을 통해 다른 지식과 결합되며 어떻게 기존 지식 구조를 수정하는가와 관련되어 있는 것이 상황 모델이다.

이 글은 문단의 첫 문장에 key word인 '표상'이 제시되어 있고, 이를 뒷받침하는 항목들이 차례로 설명되어 있는 series 가운데서도 classification에 해당된다. 따라서 이 글의 요지는 '글을 읽고 독자가 구성하게 되는 표상에는 세 단계가 있다'는 것이며, 각 단계인 표층 기억 표상, 글 기저 표상, 상황 모델 표상은 서로 **대등한 지위**를 가지고 있다. 이런 글의 경우 실제 시험에선 나열되어 제시되는 세부 항목에 대한 정보를 묻곤 하므로 처음 읽을 때 정보를 구조화하고 키워드에 표시를 함으로써 이후 필요한 정보를 빠르고 정확하게 찾을 수 있도록 하는 것이 중요하다. 이제 영어 문장을 통해서 파악해 보자.

> The Spanish kings and queens sent **many people** to find out about America. Christopher Columbus was one of these people. Ponce de Leon was **another**. Vasco da Gama was **a third**.

위의 예문은 **열거의 구성**으로 되어 있다. 첫째 문장이 topic sentence이고 나머지 세 문장은 그것을 뒷받침하는 supporting details에 해당하며, one, another, a third는 signal words에 해당한다. 만일 위의 문장이 다음과 같다면?

> Christopher Columbus was **one** of many people who went to find out America. Ponce de Leon was **another**. Vasco da Gama was **a third**.

이 예문은 주어진 topic sentence가 없다. 그러면 어떻게 글의 요지를 파악할 것인가? 이럴 경우 어쩔 수 없이 여러분은 이 글의 요지를 **추론**해야만 한다. 이럴 때 유용한 방법은 다음과 같다. (나중에 Main Idea를 다루는 장에서 더 구체적으로 언급이 될 것이다.)

> Step 1. topic과 관련이 있는 supporting details를 목록화하고,
> Step 2. 글이 어떤 구성으로 되어 있는지를 파악한 다음,
> Step 3. 그 supporting details의 공통점을 찾아내서 그것을 일반화한다.

이 예문은 크게 3개의 문장으로 되어 있는데, 각각의 문장에서 세 사람이 등장한다. 이들을 나열해보면, Christopher Columbus와 Ponce de Leon, Vasco da Gama다. 그런 다음 이 글엔 중요한 signal words가 있다. 그것을 나열해 보자. one, another, a third가 그것이다. 이것은 전형적인 **열거의 패턴**으로 되어 있는 글이다. 즉, key words와 관련된 항목을 순차적으로 대등하게 나열하고 있다.

그렇다면, 각각의 내용은 유사한 것들을 담고 있을 것이다. 즉, Christopher Columbus가 미국을 발견하기 위해 갔던 것처럼, 다른 두 사람도 마찬가지인 것이다. 따라서 이 세 사람의 **공통 속성**을 찾아낼 수가 있다. 그것은 그들이 스페인 사람이란 점도, 그들이 축구를 좋아한다는 점도, 그들이 왕의 총애를 받았다는 점도 아닌, 바로 미국을 발견하기 위해 갔던 사람들이란 점이다. 그것을 찾을 수 있는 중요한 힌트가 one; another; a third 등의 signal words가 있는 **열거의 구성**으로 되어 있다는 것이다.

따라서, 지금까지 언급한 것을 정리해보면, 이 글의 요지는 "There were many people who went to find out America미국을 발견하기 위해 많은 사람들이 갔다."가 되며, "Christopher Columbus was **one** of many people who went to find out America. Ponce de Leon was **another**. Vasco da Gama was **a third**."는 논거(supporting details)가 된다.

2. Comparison and Contrast 비교와 대조에 따른 구성

Comparison은 **similarity**에 기반하고 있고, **Contrast**는 **difference**에 기반하고 있음을 명심하자. 먼저 이해를 돕기 위해 우리말로 된 예문을 보자.

> 고대 중국의 농민들은 관개농사를 했기 때문에 물을 나눠 쓰되 누군가 속이지 않는다는 것을 확실히 할 필요가 있었던 반면 서양의 기원인 고대 그리스에는 개별적으로 포도와 올리브를 키우는 농민이 많았고 그들은 오늘날의 개인 사업가처럼 행동했다. 이런 삶의 방식이 지각 구조에도 영향을 미쳐, 철학자 아리스토텔레스는 바위가 물에 가라앉는 것은 중력 때문이고 나무가 물에 뜨는 것은 부력 때문이라고 분석하면서도 정작 물에 대해서는 아무런 언급을 하지 않았지만, 중국인들은 모든 움직임을 주변 환경과 연관시켜 생각했고 서양인보다 훨씬 전에 조류(潮流)와 자기(磁氣)를 이해했다는 것이다.

이 글은 고대 중국과 고대 그리스의 농업 구조의 차이를 설명하면서 이러한 삶의 방식의 차이가 지각 구조에도 영향을 미쳤음을 이야기하고 있다. 고대 중국과 그리스의 농업 구조에 따른 삶의 방식의 차이와 지각 구조의 차이를 **대조**의 방식으로 기술하고 있는데, 이런 대조의 방식은 일반적으로 평행 구조로 이루어진다. 평행 구조란 농사 방식에 따른 농민들의 주된 관심사와 성향, 지각 구조의 특성 등이 중국과 그리스를 중심으로 대등하게 배치되어 있는 것을 의미한다. 이러한 **대조적 평행 구조**의 글에서 주제 문장은 양 항을 모두 포괄할 수 있는 내용으로 구성되어야 한다. 따라서 '지각 구조의 차이는 경제적·문화적 배경의 차이에서 비롯될 수 있다.'는 문장이 주제문이 될 수 있다. 이제 다음의 영어로 된 예문을 보자.

> A Buick and a Cadillac, both built by General Motors, are alike in many ways. A Buick, which measures over 200 inches in length and weighs over 3,000 pounds, is large and holds the road well. A Cadillac is similar in length and weight. Like a Buick, a Cadillac gets relatively low gas mileage compared with smaller economy cars made by the same manufacturer. The Buick provides an unusually comfortable ride, especially on cross-country trips on the highway, as does a Cadillac. And both cars enjoy a certain status as a luxury automobile.

번역 제너럴 모터스에서 만드는 뷰익과 캐딜락은 여러가지 면에서 닮아 있다. 길이는 200인치가 넘고 무게는 3000파운드가 넘는 뷰익은 크기가 크고 도로에서 잘 달린다. 캐딜락은 그 길이와 무게에서 비슷하다. 뷰익처럼 캐딜락도 같은 회사의 좀 더 작은 경제적인 차들에 비해 상대적으로 연비가 나쁘다. 뷰익은 캐딜락과 마찬가지로 승차감이 매우 좋고 특히 고속도로 대륙 횡단 여행에 아주 좋다. 두 차 모두 고급 차로서의 지위를 누리고 있다.

이 글은 comparison pattern으로 구성되어 있다. 따라서 유사성similarity에 기반하고 있다. 만일이 지문의 첫 번째 문장이 없을 경우 main idea는 어떻게 찾을 수 있을까? 먼저 이 글의 topic부터 찾아보자. topic은 a Buick과 a Cadillac이다. 그런 다음 글의 pattern이 무엇인지

보자. 이 글의 pattern은 alike; like; the same; as does; both 등의 signal words가 나와 있는 것을 보니, comparison이다. 이것들을 종합해보면, a Buick과 a Cadillac의 유사성에 관해서 저자는 말하고 있는 것이다. 따라서, main idea는 "a Buick and a Cadillac have many similarities(또는 a Buick and a Cadillac are similar in many ways)"가 된다.

> The twins are as different as two people can be. Sally, who is always hoping someone will have a party, has black hair, brown eyes, and an outgoing personality. She wants to be an actress or a popular singer. Susan, more serious and studious, has blonde hair, blue eyes, and a somewhat shy manner. Since she has done well in all her classes in graphic arts and math, she plans to become an architect or an engineer.

번역 쌍둥이는 서로 다른 두 사람만큼 다르다. 누군가가 파티를 열기를 항상 바라는 샐리는 검은 머리에 갈색 눈, 그리고 외향적인 성품을 갖고 있다. 그녀는 배우나 유명한 가수가 되기를 바란다. 좀 더 심각하고 공부벌레인 수잔은 금발에 푸른 눈 그리고 좀 수줍은 편이다. 미술과 수학을 반에서 잘하기 때문에 수잔은 건축가나 엔지니어가 되기를 바란다.

이 글은 contrast 패턴으로 구성되어 있다. 따라서 차이성difference에 기반하고 있다. 첫 번째 문장에 main idea가 들어 있다.

> Most Americans would say it is not really possible to establish an ideal society. But time after time, a small dedicated group of people will drop out of the mainstream of American society to try, once more, to live according to the group's concept of an ideal society. Most of these groups have believed in holding their property in common. Most have used the word *family* to refer to all members of the group. Many of these groups, however, have differed widely in their attitudes toward sex and marriage.

번역 대부분의 미국인들은 이상적인 사회를 만드는 것은 진정 불가능하다고 말할 것이다. 하지만 계속해서 소수의 헌신적인 사람들은 미국 주류 사회에서 벗어나 한 번 더 단체의 이상 사회의 개념에 의거해 살아보려고 노력할 것이다. 대부분의 이들 단체들은 재산을 공유하는 신념을 갖고 있다. 대부분은 가족이라는 단어를 단체 전체의 구성원들을 부를 때 쓴다. 그러나 많은 단체들이 성과 결혼의 문제에 있어서 대단히 다른 입장을 취한다.

이 글은 Mixed Comparison and Contrast 패턴으로 구성되어 있다. 따라서 유사성과 차이성 둘 다에 기반하고 있다. 이 글의 첫 번째 문장은 단순한 도입부로서 핵심 key words인 'an ideal society'를 소개하고 있다. 즉, 실제로 저자가 말하고자 하는 부분은 두 번째 문장부터 시작된다. 중요한 signal words는 Most of; in common; however; differed 등이다. 즉 이 signal words를 보면 이 글의 구조는 유사성과 차이성을 다 지니고 있다. 따라서 comparison and contrast 패턴으로 글이 구성되어 있음을 알 수 있다. 이런 경우 main idea는 유사성과 차이성에 대한 언급이 모두 들어가 있어야 한다. 즉, '이상사회를 추구하는 집단들은 그들이 추구하는 공통의 가치도 있지만 그 안에서 다양한 차이점도 또한 존재한다.' 라는 주장이 들어가야 한다.

> Leif Ericson probably had a more difficult trip across the Atlantic Ocean than Christopher Columbus did. Ericson sailed across the cold northern part of the Atlantic, but Columbus sailed across the southern part, where it was warmer.

번역 리프 에릭슨은 대서양을 건널 때 콜럼버스보다 더욱 어려운 여행을 했을 것이다. 에릭슨은 추운 북대서양을 가로질러 항해했지만, 에릭슨은 좀 더 따뜻한 남대성양을 가로질러 항해했다.

이 글은 contrast 패턴으로 구성되어 있다. 따라서 차이성에 기반하고 있다. more; than; but이 signal words이다.

3. Time Order 시간관계에 따른 구성

(1) Narrative(서사적 구성)

Narrative란 이야기를 함축하고 있는 글의 구성을 말한다. 서사를 위해서는 수행자인 '인물'과 수행되는 '사건', 그리고 이 둘을 매개하는 시간의 흐름이 필요하다. 이러한 구성의 글은 글 전체를 하나의 이야기화(누가 무엇을 수행하는가)하여 맥락을 파악하는 것이 필요하며, 이를 통해 주제를 도출할 수 있어야 한다. 다음의 예문들을 보자.

> Gold was first found in California in about 1840. The next ten years in American history are called the California Gold Rush. Many people moved to the West during those years to look for gold. By 1850, there were many new Gold Rush towns in California.

번역 금은 캘리포니아에서 1840년 처음 채취되었다. 미국 역사의 다음 10년 동안은 캘리포니아 골드러시의 시대라고 일컬어진다. 많은 사람들이 금을 찾으려고 이 시기에 서부로 이주했다. 1850년이 되어서는 캘리포니아에 여러 새로운 골드러시 마을이 생겼다.

이 글은 time order 중에서도 narrative로 구성되어 있다. **about 1840; The next ten years; during those years; By 1850** 등이 signal words에 해당한다. 이렇게 시간 순서로 진행되어 있는 것에서 다음과 같은 요지를 도출할 수 있다. '1840년에서 1850년까지 캘리포니아엔 많은 골드러시 마을이 생겼다.'

> Franklin D. Roosevelt was the only president to be elected four times. He was born in Hyde Park, New York, on January 30, 1882, and he began his studies at Harvard in 1903. In 1905, he married Eleanor Roosevelt, a distant cousin, and they had six children. After serving in the New York State Senate, Roosevelt worked in Washington as Secretary of the Navy until 1921. At that time, he became very ill with polio and lost the use of his legs. In 1928, Roosevelt ran for governor of New York. After serving two terms as governor, he was elected to the presidency in 1933. Roosevelt died in office on April 12, 1945.

번역 프랭클린 D. 루스벨트는 유일하게 4번이나 선출된 대통령이었다. 그는 1882년 1월 30일, 뉴욕의 하이드파크에서 태어났으며, 1903년 하버드에서 공부를 시작했다. 1905년, 그는 먼 사촌인 엘리너 루스벨트와 결혼해서 6명의 자녀를 두었다. 뉴욕주 상원의원으로 일한 뒤, 루스벨트는 1921년까지 워싱턴에서 해군 차관으로 일했다. 당시 그는 소아마비로 매우 아팠으며 그로 인해 걸을 수가 없었다. 1928년, 루스벨트는 뉴욕의 주지사로 출마했다. 그는 주지사로 두 번 재임한 뒤, 1933년 대통령으로 선출되었다. 루스벨트는 1945년 4월 12일 직무실에서 사망했다.

이 글은 time order 중에서도 narrative로 구성되어 있다. January 30; 1882; 1903; 1905; After; 1921; At that time; In 1928; After 1933; 1945 등이 signal words에 해당한다. 이렇게 시간 순서로 진행되어 있는 것에서 다음과 같은 요지를 도출할 수 있다. 이 글의 main idea는 "Franklin D. Roosevelt served his county for most of his life"이다.

(2) Process(단계적 구성)

Process란 각 단계별로 어떤 것이 행해지는 방식을 설명하는 구성이다. 따라서 세부사항details 들은 단계들steps or stages로 조직화되어 있다.

> Making orange juice concentrate from fresh oranges is done entirely by machines. First, oranges are dumped onto a moving belt. They travel into a machine which washes them with detergent. Next they are rolled into juicing machines, where seven hundred oranges per minute are split and squeezed. Then the rinds (the skin of the oranges) are thrown out the end of a long tube. At the same time, the juice goes through small holes in the bottom of the tube. Next, the juice goes into another machines called the finisher. There, the seeds and other tiny objects are removed. Last, the juice goes into large tanks, where most of the water is removed.

번역 신선한 오렌지를 응축하여 오렌지 주스를 만드는 것은 전부 기계를 통해 이루어진다. 첫 번째로 오렌지는 움직이는 벨트 위해 올려진다. 그것들은 세척기 안으로 이동한다. 그 다음, 분당 700개의 오렌지를 쪼개서 즙을 내는 기계 안으로 들어가게 된다. 그리고 나서 오렌지의 껍질은 기다란 용기의 끝부분에 던져진다. 동시에 즙은 용기의 바닥에 있는 작은 구멍을 통과한다. 다음, 즙은 마무리 기계 안으로 들어간다. 그 기계에서 씨와 다른 작은 물질들이 제거된다. 마지막으로, 즙은 수분의 대부분을 제거하는 커다란 탱크로 들어가게 된다.

이 글은 time order 중에서도 process로 구성되어 있다. First; Next; Then; At the same time; Next; Last 등이 signal words에 해당한다. 이것을 도식화해보면 다음과 같다.

- Step 1 : Oranges are dumped onto a moving belt. They travel into a machine which washes them with detergent.
- Step 2 : they are rolled into juicing machines, where seven hundred oranges per minute are split and squeezed.
- Step 3 : the rinds (the skin of the oranges) are thrown out the end of a long tube. The juice goes through small holes in the bottom of the tube.
- Step 4 : the juice goes into another machines called the finisher.
- Step 5 : the juice goes into large tanks, where most of the water is removed.

이렇게 시간 순서로 진행되어 있는 것에서 다음과 같은 요지를 도출할 수 있다. "Making orange juice concentrate from fresh oranges is done entirely by machines"이다.

Photocopying machines use a process known as xerography. In transfer xerography, a photoconductive plate, cylinder, or belt is electrostatically charged. A photoconductor, such as selenium, allows charge to leak away when exposed to light. Then the material to be copied is placed face down on the photocopying machine, and a projected image of the page falls on the charged plate. Next, the illuminated portions become conducting and discharge, leaving a charged electrostatic image of the dark regions or print of the page. The photoconductor copy then comes into contact with toner. Finally the toner is attracted to the paper, and heating causes it to be permanently fused to the paper. All this takes place very quickly ─ and outcomes your copy.

번역 복사기는 제로그래피라고 알려진 과정을 이용한다. 광전도의 판금, 실린더 또는 벨트가 정전기적으로 충전된다. 셀레늄과 같은 광전도체가 빛에 노출될 때 방전이 새나가도록 한다. 그리고는 복사될 물체는 뒤집어서 복사기에 놓이고 투사된 이미지는 충전된 판에 떨어진다. 다음으로 빛을 받은 부분은 광전도되고 발사되어 검은 부분 또는 페이지의 프린트 부분의 정전기적 이미지를 남긴다. 그러면 광전도체 사본은 토너와 접촉하게 된다. 마지막으로 토너는 종이에 붙게 되고 열이 종이 위에 이것이 영구적으로 남게 한다. 이 모든 것이 아주 빨리 진행되고 당신의 복사본이 나오게 된다.

이 글은 time order 중에서도 process로 구성되어 있다. process; Then; Next; then; Finally 등이 signal words에 해당한다. 이것을 도식화해보면 다음과 같다.

- Step 1 : Photoconductive plate, cylinder, or belt is electrostatically charged.
- Step 2 : Image of original document is projected onto charged plate.
- Step 3 : Illuminated portions leave a charged image of the dark print on the page.
- Step 4 : Photoconductor copy comes into contact with toner.
- Step 5 : Heat fuses toner to paper.

4. Cause and Effect 인과관계에 따른 구성

Cause and Effect pattern은 원인과 결과에 따라 글을 구성하는 것이다. 일반적으로 원인은 결과보다 먼저 존재하므로 인과관계의 글에서는 시간적인 순서에 따라 글을 이해하는 것이 한 요령이 된다. 또한 인과관계에서 원인은 구체적이고 결과는 일반적인 경우가 많은데, 이러한 글의 경우 귀납적인 논리 전개법을 따르고 있을 가능성이 크므로 글의 요지를 파악하는데 참고할 필요가 있다. 먼저 이해를 쉽게 하기 위해 우리말로 된 글들을 읽어보자.

아래의 글을 인과관계에 따라 정리해 보자.

> 1997년 외환 금융 위기 이후, 자본 시장 개방으로 대규모 외국 자본이 유입되면서 주주의 이익을 극대화하는 경영에 부합하는 가치관과 제도들이 확산되었다. 주주 대표 소송 등 소액 주주의 권한 행사 요건과 절차가 개선되었으며, 사외 이사가 확대되고 사외 이사 중심의 독립적인 감사 위원회가 설치됨으로써 내부 감시 기능도 강화되었다. 소유 구조 및 회계의 투명성도 높아졌다. 이 '주주 가치 경영'은 시장 질서의 확산과 함께 우리나라 기업들의 기업 지배 구조를 개선하고, 기업 경영을 감시하여 기업 가치를 높이는 긍정적인 효과를 낳은 것으로 평가된다.

먼저 지문에서 언급하고 있는 사건이나 변화된 상황을 시간 순으로 정리해보자.

> 1997년 외환 금융 위기 ⇨ 자본 시장 개방 ⇨ 외국 자본의 유입 ⇨ 주주의 이익을 극대화하는 경영 가치관과 제도들의 확산(주주대표 소송, 사외 이사의 확대, 독립적인 감사 위원회의 설치) ⇨ 시장 질서의 확산, 소유 구조 및 회계의 투명성 개선, 기업 가치의 상승

가만히 살펴보면 끝부분의 시장 질서의 확산이나 소유 구조 및 회계의 투명성 개선 등은 주주 대표 소송, 사외 이사의 확대, 독립적인 감사 위원회의 설치 등과 같은 주주 이익 극대화 경영의 가치관과 제도의 확산에 따른 결과물이다. 마찬가지로 그러한 가치관과 제도의 도입은 외국 자본의 유입에 따른 결과물인 것이며, 외국 자본의 유입은 자본 시장 개장을 통해서 가능했던 것이다. 자본 시장 개방은 외환 금융 위기에 대처하기 위해 이루어졌다. 따라서 위의 글은 원인과 결과의 관계를 시간적인 순서에 따라 진술하고 있음을 알 수 있다. 이제 영어로 된 예문들을 살펴보자.

> A whale eats a lot of ocean food every day. That is because it is a very large animal.

- **원인** : A whale is a very large animal.
- **결과** : It eats a lot of food every day.

이 글의 signal word는 That is because이다. 따라서, 글의 패턴은 'cause and effect'가 된다.

> To save money in the early 1980s, Illinois released 21,000 prisoners an average of three months early. The early releases produced 23 homicides, 32 rapes, 262 arsons, 681 robberies, 2,472 burglaries, 2,571 assaults and more than 8,000 other crimes. According to Harvard researchers, the $60 million the state saved cost Illinois crime victims $304 million, directly or indirectly.

번역 1980년대 초반 비용을 절감하기 위하여, 일리노이주는 2만 천 명의 죄수들을 평균 석 달 일찍 출감시켰다. 이 감형은 23건의 살인, 32건의 강간, 262건의 방화, 681건의 강도, 2472건의 도둑질, 2571건의 폭력, 그리고 8000건 이상의 다른 범죄들을 유발시켰다. 하버드 연구진에 의하면, 주 정부가 절감한 6천만 달러는 일리노이의 범죄 피해자들에게 직간접적으로 3억 4백만 달러의 비용을 들게 한 것이다.

- **원인** : the early release of prisoners
- **결과** : an increase in crimes
- **Main idea** : the early release of prisoners caused an increase in crimes in Illinois.

5. Definition 정의에 따른 구성

Definition은 어떤 특정한 단어나 용어 또는 개념의 의미를 진술하고 그런 다음 그것을 설명해주기 위해 하나 또는 그 이상의 예를 드는 것이 일반적이다. 앞 3장에서 봤듯이, 주로 means; definition; define; meaning; is/are; is/are called; is described as 같은 signal words들이 사용된다. 다음과 같은 것이 그 예들이다.

> 1. A triathalon **is** a long-distance race that usually includes phases of running, swimming, and bicycling.
> 2. One **meaning** of Zen is the process of identifying and reducing attachments to beliefs, attitudes, and ideas that cause human suffering.
> 3. Harmful substances that invade the womb and result in birth defects **are called** teratogens.

번역 1. 철인 3종 경기는 일반적으로 달리기, 수영, 자전거 타기 등을 포함하는 장거리 경주이다.
2. 선이라고 하는 것은 인간이 괴로움을 겪도록 만드는 어떤 믿음, 태도, 그리고 견해에 대한 집착이 무엇인지를 밝히고 그것을 줄이려는 과정이다.
3. 자궁을 공격해 선천적 기형을 야기시키는 해로운 물질은 기형발생인자라 불린다.

1. 철인 3종 경기가 무엇인지에 대한 정의를 내리고 있다.
2. 선이 어떠한 의미를 지니는지에 대한 정의를 내리고 있다.
3. 기형발생인자(teratogen)가 어떠한 것인지에 대한 정의를 내리고 있다.

6. Description 묘사에 의한 구성

Description이란 어떤 특정한 사람이나, 장소에 대한 기호, 또는 어느 특정한 대상의 외양 등을 마치 '그림을 보는 듯이 생생하게' 묘사해 강한 인상을 남기는 것을 말한다. 소위 우리가 중·고등학교 시절 배웠던 '붓 가는 대로' 쓰여지는 글에 해당하는 것들이 주로 이 패턴에 속한다고 보면 된다. 수필이라든가 문학작품이 여기에 많이 속한다. narrative와 유사한 면이 있긴 하지만, narrative가 주로 시간 속에서 일어나는 일을 서술한다면, description은 구체적인 대상에 대한 세부적인detail 묘사가 중심이 되며 살아 뛰는 언어를 많이 쓴다. 다음의 예를 보자.

The chair was the one piece of furniture I wanted to take with me when I closed up my parents' house for the final time. To look at it, sitting in the same kitchen corner where it had been for fifty years, you'd wonder how it could be my favorite chair. It was nothing but a straight-backed wooden chair, its seat scratched here and there from the soles of a small boy's shoes. The only thing unusual about it was the intricate design carved into its back. But the carving was what made the chair meaningful to me. I had sat in that chair many times as punishment for errors in my ways. I suppose my mother thought it was defiance that led me to sit cross-legged on the seat with my back to her in the kitchen. But it was not defiance. Rather, in that position my eyes and then my fingers could trace the intertwining leaves and flowers of the design carved in the back of the chair. Each time I sat there I seemed to see lines and shapes I hadn't seen before : a heart-shaped leaf, a budding rose, a blade of grass. Perhaps that chair had something to do with my lasting interest in well-made antique furniture. Who knows? I do know that when I drove away on that last day, the chair, carefully wrapped in several old quilts, lay tenderly cradled on the back seat of my car.

번역 내가 마지막으로 부모님을 집을 정리하며 가져오고 싶었던 단 하나의 가구는 그 의자였다. 같은 부엌 구석에 50년 동안 있어온 이 의자를 보면 왜 이 의자가 내가 가장 아끼는 것인지 의아해 할 것이다. 이것은 그냥 등받이가 반듯한 나무 의자이며, 앉는 자리가 어린 소년의 구두창으로 여기저기 긁힌 의자이다. 유일하게 특이한 점이 있다면 뒷면에 조각된 섬세한 디자인이다. 하지만 바로 이 조각이 이 의자를 내게 특별한 것으로 만드는 그것이다. 난 잘못을 했을 때 그 의자에 많이 앉았다. 내 생각엔 우리 어머니가 내가 어머니로부터 등을 돌리고 다리를 꼬고 그 의사에 앉아 있는 이유가 반항이라고 생각하셨을 것 같다. 하지만 그건 반항이 아니었다. 오히려 그 자세로 내 눈과 그리고 손가락이 의자 뒤에 새겨진 서로 엮인 나뭇잎과 꽃들을 따라갈 수 있었다. 거기에 앉을 때마다 난 이전에 볼 수 없었던 선과 모양을 보는 것 같았다. 심장 모양으로 생긴 나뭇잎, 막 피어나는 장미 봉우리, 잎새. 아마도 이 의자가 잘 만든 고가구에 대한 나의 꾸준한 관심과 연관이 있지 싶다. 누가 알겠는가? 그 마지막 날 떠나오면서, 이 의자가 여러 장의 오래된 퀼트로 조심스레 싸여 내 차의 뒷자리에 놓여 있었다는 것을 나만은 아는 것이다.

이 글에서 의자는 단지 등받이가 반듯한 나무 의자이며, 앉는 자리가 어린 소년의 구두창으로 여기저기 긁힌 의자라고 묘사되어 있다. 하지만 글쓴이는 이 단순한 사물을 살아 뛰는 언어로 생생하게 묘사하고 있다.

7. Combination of Patterns

종종, 지문들은 하나가 아니라 두 개 이상의 패턴으로 되어 있는 경우가 있다. 주로 major supporting details가 어느 한 패턴으로, 하지만 minor supporting details는 다른 패턴으로 되어 있는 경우가 많다.

Time-starved Americans now spend as much time eating out as they do eating at home. How often do you pick up a quick lunch at a Burger King or Taco Bell? In **the 1950s and 1960s**, this trend was just beginning. Consumers **wanted** more restaurants and fast-food outlets. **As a result**, McDonald's, Wendy's, Big Boy, White Castle, Pizza Hut, Godfather's Pizza, and other fast-food outlets flourished. The trend toward eating away from home reached a fevered pitch in **the late 1970s**, when the average number of meals per person eaten out (excluding brown-bag lunches and other meals prepared at home but eaten elsewhere) exceeded one per day. In **the 1980s**, people **wanted** the fast food but didn't want to go get it. By emphasizing delivery, Domino's Pizza and a few other fast-food outlets became very successful. In **the 1990s**, the "takeout taxi" business—where restaurant food is delivered to homes—grew 10 percent per year.

번역 시간에 굶주린 미국인들은 이제 집에서 먹는 시간만큼 외식을 하고 있다. 당신은 얼마나 자주 버거킹이나 타코벨에서 점심을 가져오는가? 1950년대와 1960년대에는 이런 유행이 그저 시작되는 단계였다. 소비자들은 더 많은 식당과 패스트푸드 아울렛을 원했다. 결과적으로 맥도날드, 웬디즈, 빅보이, 화이트 캐슬, 피자헛, 갓 파더스 피자, 그리고 다른 패스트푸드 아울렛들은 번성했다. 외식이 늘어나는 경향은 1970년대 후반, (도시락과 집에서 만들었지만 밖에서 먹게 된 음식들을 빼고) 한 사람당 평균 외식 수가 하루 한 끼 이상이었던 때에 그 열풍의 정점에 달했다. 1980년대에 사람들은 패스트푸드를 먹고 싶었지만 나가서 먹고 싶지는 않았다. 배달에 방점을 둠으로써 도미노 피자와 다른 패스트푸드 아울렛들은 대단한 성공을 거뒀다. 1990년대에는 식당 음식이 집으로 배달되는 '테이크아웃 택시'가 해마다 10%씩 증가했다.

이 글에서 대다수의 details는 time order, 그 중에서도 narrative로 되어 있다. 이 글은 지난 50여 년 동안의 패스트푸드의 발전을 지적하고 있다. 그 와중에 소비자의 욕구가 낳는 **결과**에 대해서도 동시에 언급이 되어 있다. 따라서 이 글은 time order와 cause/effect의 패턴이 혼합되어 있다. 진하게 표시한 것들은 signal words인데, wanted; As a result는 cause/effect를 나타내는 signal words이고, 나머지는 time order이다.

01

An overwhelming **amount of evidence** shows that social support has therapeutic **effects** on both our psychological and physical health. **David Spiegel**, of Stanford University's School of Medicine, came to appreciate the value of social connections many years ago when he organized support groups for women with advanced breast cancer. Spiegel had fully expected the women to benefit, emotionally, from the experience. But he found something else he did not expect : These women lived an average of eighteen months longer than did similar others who did not attend the groups. In **another study**, Lisa Berkman and Leonard Syme surveyed seven thousand residents of Alameda County, California; conducted a nine-year follow-up of mortality rates; and found that the more social contacts people had, the longer they lived. This was true of men and women, young and old, rich and poor, and people from all racial and ethnic backgrounds. **James House and others** studied 2,754 adults interviewed during visits to their doctors. He found that the most socially active men were two to three times less likely to die within nine to twelve years than others of similar age who were more isolated.

번역 엄청난 양의 증거는 사회적 지원이 우리의 몸과 마음의 건강에 치료적인 효과가 있다는 것을 보여준다. 스탠포드 대학 약학과의 데이비드 스피겔은 여러 해 전 유방암 말기의 여성들의 상호 지원 모임을 만들면서 이를 알게 되었다. 스피겔은 이 여성들이 모임을 통해서 감정적으로 도움을 받을 것을 충분히 예측하고 있었다. 그러나 그는 예상치 못한 것을 발견하게 되었다. 이 여성들은 모임에 참여하지 않은 유사그룹보다 평균 18개월을 더 생존했다. 또 다른 연구에서 리사 버크만과 리오나드 심은 캘리포니아 알라메다 카운티의 7천명의 주민들을 조사했다. 그들은 이후 9년 동안의 생존율을 조사했고 사람들이 더 많은 사회적인 접촉을 할수록 더 오래 산 다는 것을 발견했다. 이것은 남녀노소, 빈부, 그리고 인종과 민족적 배경을 불문하고 사실이었다. 제임스 하우스와 다른 이들은 2754명의 성인들이 병원에 왔을 때 인터뷰를 했다. 그는 비슷한 연령대의 고립된 남성들보다 사회적으로 적극적인 사람들이 9년에서 12년 안에 죽을 확률이 두세 배나 낮다는 것을 밝혀냈다.

이 지문은 series와 cause/effect의 패턴이 혼합되어 사용되고 있다. series를 나타내는 signal words는 David Spiegal(여기선, for example 또는 first 등이 생략되어 있다); another study; James House and others(여기서도 signal words인 third나 also 등이 생략되어 있다)이고; cause/effect를 나타내는 signal words는 effects이다.

예제

[1-12] What is the main pattern of organization for this writing?

01 When you study for an exam, you should follow three steps. First, you should make sure you have all the information you need. Next, you should put that information in order. Finally, you should make a list of the most important things.

① Series   ② Time order   ③ Cause/effect

④ Comparison   ⑤ Definition

02 A parakeet is a small bird that lives in tropical forests. The parrot is similar to a parakeet, but it is larger. Both birds sometimes can learn how to say words.

① Series   ② Time order   ③ Cause/effect
④ Comparison/contrast   ⑤ Definition

03 Some kinds of birds cannot fly. The penguin is one of these birds. It lives mostly in the very cold Antarctic climate. Another kind of bird that cannot fly is the ostrich. It lives in Africa.

① Series   ② Time order   ③ Cause/effect
④ Comparison   ⑤ Definition

04 Some people do not like to use computers for writing. They prefer to use typewriters. They know computers are faster and more accurate, but they feel more comfortable with typewriters.

① Series   ② Time order   ③ Cause/effect
④ Comparison/contrast   ⑤ Definition

05 Leif Ericson was probably the first European to see America. He visited some of the northern areas in about 1000. The next European visitor to America was Christopher Columbus in 1492.

① Series   ② Time order   ③ Cause/effect
④ Comparison   ⑤ Definition

06 Cola and ginger ale are both kinds of soft drinks. Both these drinks have a lot of sugar in them, but cola has caffeine in it and ginger ale does not.

① Series   ② Time order   ③ Cause/effect
④ Comparison/contrast   ⑤ Definition

07 Some of the early Americans did not want to come to this country. For example, many Africans had to come as slaves. Some Europeans had to come for religious freedom.

① Series ② Time order ③ Cause/effect
④ Comparison/contrast ⑤ Definition

08 Lisa plans to travel in Europe this summer. In June, she will visit Sicily. In July, she will bicycle in northern Italy. In August, she will travel through France. By September, she hopes to be in Paris.

① Series ② Time order ③ Cause/effect
④ Comparison/contrast ⑤ Definition

09 The clambake is a popular New England dinner. It usually includes many different kinds of seafood. Clams are the most common kind of seafood at a clambake. There may also be lobster and mussels.

① Series ② Time order ③ Cause/effect
④ Comparison/contrast ⑤ Definition

10 Many American Indians died soon after the Europeans arrived. There was one important reason for this. The Europeans brought new kinds of diseases with them. These diseases caused thousands of deaths in a short time.

① Series ② Time order ③ Cause/effect
④ Comparison/contrast ⑤ Definition

정답 | 01 ② 02 ④ 03 ① 04 ④ 05 ②
06 ④ 07 ① 08 ② 09 ① 10 ③

11 During the war in the Vietnam in 1970s, many villages were destroyed. People were left homeless, so they moved to the city. The cities were often overcrowded, with little hope for a good life. This led many people to leave their homeland and move to the United States. Now, many schools and colleges in the United States are expanding their English language programs.

① Series   ② Time order   ③ Cause/effect
④ Comparison/contrast   ⑤ Definition

12

Maya Angelou, an African-American author, had many difficult experiences while she was growing up. Born in 1929 in Long Beach, California, her original name was Marguerite Johnson. Her parents separated when she was three. Then she and her brother went to live with their grandmother in Stamps, Arkansas. Later on, she lived for a while with her mother and grandmother in St. Louis, Missouri. When she was only eight years old, Maya experienced abuse from her mother's boyfriend. Wherever she lived, she was often badly treated because of racial prejudice. But her life was also shaped by the strong influence of love. In her childhood, she learned of love from her grandmother and her brother. As she grew older, she also began to love literature. After junior high school, Maya went to live with her mother in San Francisco. There, in 1945, she graduated from high school. A few months later, she had a baby son, who became the center of her life. In later years, Maya included all of these experiences in her novels, plays, and poems. She has received many honors as a writer and spokes-woman for Afro-Americans. But perhaps her greatest honor came in 1993. President Bill Clinton asked her to write the official poem for his inauguration. Then she read the poem aloud at the ceremony in front of the American public.

① Series   ② Time order   ③ Cause/effect
④ Comparison   ⑤ Definition

정답 | 11 ③   12 ②

📑 **실전문제**

Read the following and answer the question.

교원임용고시

01

> Society regards as true the systems of classification that produce the desired results. The scientific test of "truth," like the social test, is strictly practical, except for the fact that the desired results are more severely limited. The results desired by society may be irrational, superstitious, selfish, or humane, but the results desired by scientists are only that our systems of classification produce predictable results. Classifications determine our attitudes and behavior toward the object or event classified. When lightning was classified as "evidence of divine wrath," no courses of action other than prayer were suggested to prevent one's being struck by lightning. But after Benjamin Franklin classified it as "electricity," a measure of control over it was achieved by the invention of the lightning rod. Certain physical disorders were formerly classified as "demonic possession," and this suggested that we "drive the demons out" by whatever spells and incantations we could think of. The results were uncertain. But when those disorders were classified as "bacillus infections," courses of action were suggested that led to more predictable results. Science seeks only *the most generally useful* systems of classification; these it regards for the time being, until more useful classifications are invented, as "true."

Which of the following would be the best title of this passage?

① The Importance of Societal Classification

② The Eternity of Scientific Classification

③ The Methodology of Effective Classification

④ The Implications of Different Classification Systems

⑤ Societal Classification as a Measure of Predictability

🔊 **친절한 해설**

제목을 찾는 문제인데 논리를 요하는 문제지요. 제목 문제가 나오면 여러분이 가장 먼저 해야 될 것은 '이 글은 무엇에 관한 것일까'를 생각하는 것이죠(즉 topic 찾기, 짧은 글에선 topic은 필연적으로 제목과 연결되어 있거든 요). 그것은 너무 구체적이어서도, 또 너무 일반적이어서도 안 돼요. 두 번째는 '반복되는 단어나 어구'(특히 개념 어)에 밑줄을 긋는 것이에요(즉 key words or phrases 찾기). 작가는 반복을 함부로 하지 않아요. 중요하다 생각 되니까 반복하는 것이죠. 자, 그럼 이 문제로 가볼까요.

우선 이 글은 무엇에 관한 것인가요? 그리고 계속 반복되는 중요한 key words는?

a. systems of classification인 것도 같고, b. scientific classification인 것도 같고 c. societal classification인 것도 같지요. 그럼 여기서 우리 원칙을 되뇌어보죠. 아까 topic은 뭐라 했죠? 그것은 너무 구체적이서도, 또 너무 일반적이어서도 안 된다고 했지요.

예를 들어, 다음 다섯 가지 중에선 어느 것이 topic이 될 수 있을까요?

① Korea ② Japan ③ Thailand ④ Nation ⑤ Asian nation

여기서, ①, ②, ③번은 너무 구체적이죠? 왜? 만약 ①이 답이 된다면 ②, ③도 답이 되어야 하니까 말이 안 되죠. 서로 등가의 것이니까요. 그러면, ④는? ④는 또 너무 일반적이에요. 동아시아에 있는 나라를 다루는 데 국가라는 큰 개념을 쓸 필요는 없어요. 그래서 답은 ⑤가 되는 것이에요. 만일 ⑤가 선택지에 없다면? 물론 ④가 답이 되죠.

이 원리를 적용해 보면 이 글에서 topic은 b. scientific classification와 c. societal classification은 될 수가 없어요. 이것은 조금 전 살펴보았던 'Korea, Japan, Thailand'에 해당되는 것들이죠. 즉 너무 구체적이에요. 따라서 선택지에서 이것들을 제외하고 문제를 풀어보세요. 그러면 아리송한 것들이 명쾌하게 보일 거예요. 게다가 이 글은 contrast의 구조로 쓰여 있네요. 즉 과학과 사회(공동체)라는 서로 다른 영역에서의 분류체계를 다루고 있어요. 여기서 또 다른 하나의 용어 'difference'가 유추가 되네요. 알다시피 contrast와 comparison의 차이는 전자는 'difference'에 후자는 'similarity'에 기반하고 있다는 것이죠. 그러므로 종합해보면, 'different systems of classification'이란 구문이 나오네요. 그런 다음 예를 든 것들을 보니 계속 둘 사이의 차이 속에서 다른 의미가 나온다는 것을 강조하는군요. 그럼 당연히 답은 ④번의 The Implications of Different Classification System이 되는 것이죠. 잘 이해하셨길 바라요.

한글 번역

예제 01 시험 공부를 할 때 세 가지 단계를 따라야 한다. 첫째 필요한 정보를 확실히 다 갖고 있어야 한다. 다음으로 그 정보들을 순서대로 정렬해야 한다. 마지막으로 가장 중요한 것의 목록을 작성해야 한다.

02 파라킷은 열대우림에 사는 작은 새이다. 이 앵무새는 파라킷과 비슷하지만 더 크다. 두 새 모두 가끔 단어를 말하는 법을 배운다.

03 어떤 종류의 새들은 날 수가 없다. 펭귄은 이런 새 중 하나이다. 펭귄은 대부분 아주 추운 남극 기후에서 산다. 날 수 없는 다른 종류의 새는 타조이다. 타조는 아프리카에 산다.

04 어떤 이들은 글을 쓸 때 컴퓨터를 쓰는 것을 좋아하지 않는다. 그들은 타자기를 쓰기를 선호한다. 그들은 컴퓨터가 더 빠르고 정확하다는 것을 알고 있지만 타자기가 더 편하다고 느낀다.

05 리프 에릭슨은 아마도 미국을 본 첫 번째 유럽인일 것이다. 그는 1000년경에 일부 북쪽 지방을 방문했다. 그 다음 미국을 본 유럽인은 1492년 크리스토퍼 콜럼버스이다.

06 콜라와 진저에일은 둘 다 일종의 음료수이다. 두 음료는 다 설탕이 많이 들어 있지만 콜라는 그 안에 카페인이 들었고 진저에일은 그렇지 않다.

07 일부 초기의 미국인들은 이 나라에 오고 싶지 않았다. 예를 들어 많은 아프리카인들이 노예로서 와야 했다. 일부 유럽인들은 종교적 자유 때문에 와야 했다.

08 리사는 올 여름에 유럽을 여행할 계획이다. 6월에 그녀는 시실리를 방문할 것이다. 7월에는 이태리 북부를 자전거 여행할 것이다. 8월에는 프랑스 전역을 여행할 것이다. 그녀는 9월까지는 파리에 있기를 바란다.

09 클램베이크는 뉴잉글랜드의 유명한 저녁 메뉴이다. 이 요리는 보통 여러 해산물이 들어간다. 조개는 클램베이크에서 가장 흔한 해산물 종류이다. 가재나 홍합이 들어갈 때도 있다.

10 많은 미국 인디언들이 유럽인들이 오고 나서 죽었다. 여기에는 아주 중요한 이유가 하나 있다. 유럽인들은 자신들과 더불어 신종 질병들을 가져왔다. 이 질병들은 단기간에 수천의 목숨을 앗아가는 원인이 되었다.

11 1970년대의 베트남 전쟁 기간 동안, 많은 마을이 파괴되었다. 집을 잃은 사람들은 도시로 이동했다. 나은 삶을 향한 작은 희망을 안은 사람들로 도시는 너무나 혼잡했다. 이것은 많은 사람들로 하여금 조국을 떠나 미국으로 이주하게 만들었다. 현재, 미국의 많은 학교와 대학들은 영어 프로그램을 확장하고 있다.

12 흑인 작가 마야 안젤루는 자라면서 매우 어려운 경험을 했다. 1929년, 캘리포니아의 롱비치에서 태어난 그녀의 원래 이름은 마가렛 존슨이었다. 그녀가 3살 때, 부모님은 별거했다. 그리고 그녀와 오빠는 아칸소주의 Stamps에 계시는 할머니 댁으로 갔다. 후에 그녀는 미주리주의 세인트루이스에서 잠시 동안 어머니, 할머니와 살았다. 18살이 되어서 마야는 어머니의 남자친구로부터 강간을 당했다. 어디에서 살든 간에, 그녀는 인종 차별로 인해 종종 부당한 취급을 받았다. 그러나 그녀의 삶은 강력한 사랑의 영향으로 발전되었다. 어린 시절, 그녀는 할머니와 오빠에게서 사랑을 배웠다. 성장하면서, 그녀는 문학을 사랑하기 시작했다. 중학교를 졸업한 뒤, 마야는 샌프란시스코에서 어머니와 함께 살았다. 1945년, 그곳에서 그녀는 고등학교를 졸업했다. 몇 달 후, 그녀는 자신의 삶의 핵심이 된 아들을 가졌다. 후에, 마야는 이런 모든 경험을 그녀의 소설과, 희곡, 시에 포함시켰다. 그녀는 작가이자 흑인을 위한 여성 대변인으로 존경을 받아왔다. 그러나 아마도 그녀에게 가장 명예로운 순간은 1993년이었을 것이다. 빌 클린턴 대통령은 그녀에게 그의 취임사를 써줄 것을 부탁했고, 그녀는 미국 대중들 앞에서 큰 소리로 낭독했다.

실전
문제
사회(공동체)는 (자신들이) 원하는 결과를 생산해내는 분류체계를 사실이라 간주한다. '사실'에 대한 과학적 검증은 사회적 검증과 마찬가지로 상당히 실용적이지만, 차이는 과학적 검증은 원하는 결과가 사회적 검증보다 훨씬 제한적이란 사실이다. 사회(공동체)가 바라는 결과는 비합리적이고, 미신적이고, 이기적이며, 또는 인간적이지만, 과학자들에 의해 행해지는 바라던 결과는 우리의 분류체계가 예측 가능한 결과를 만들어낸다는 것뿐이다. 분류는 분류된 대상이나 사건에 대한 우리들의 태도나 행동을 결정한다. 번개가 '신의 분노의 증거'라 분류됐을 땐, 그것을 피하기 위해 우리가 취해야 할 행동 양식은 기도밖에는 없게 된다. 하지만 벤자민 프랭클린이 번개를 '전기'라 분류한 이후로 번개를 컨트롤하는 조치는 피뢰침의 발명에 의해 해결되었다. 몇몇 육체적 질병은 예전엔 '악령에 사로잡힌' 것으로 분류되었기에, 따라서 여기에 적합한 조치는 우리가 생각할 수 있는 모든 주문을 통해서 악령을 몰아내는 것이었다. 그 결과는 불확실한 것이었다. 하지만, 그런 질병이 '세균 감염'으로 분류되었을 때, 더욱 예측 가능한 결과를 만들어내는 행동 조치가 제안되었다. 과학은 가장 일반적으로 유용한 분류체계만을 추구한다; 더욱 유용한 분류가 나올 때까지는, 당분간 과학은 그 가장 일반적으로 유용한 분류체계를 '사실'로 간주한다.

Main Idea & Supporting Details

Main idea요지란 무엇인가? 저자가 **topic을 통해서 독자에게 말하려고 하는 것**으로, 보통 **완전한 문장**으로 이루어져 있다. 이미 우리는 topic을 다루는 장에서 설명을 했다. 하지만, 다시 한번 살펴보자.

> 예 Topic : 의사
> Possible main ideas:
> ① 의사라는 직업은 힘들다.
> ② 의사는 환자와 가까이 지내야 한다.
> ③ 의사는 부자가 되는 지름길이다.

이상에서 보듯이 하나의 topic에는 무수히 많은 main ideas가 나올 수 있다. 이 세 가지 말고도 여러분은 더욱 많은 main ideas를 쓸 수가 있다. 하지만 한 문단paragraph에서는 단 하나의 요지 main idea만 가능하다는 점을 명심하자.

01 요지 혹은 주제문의 의미와 의의

다시 정리하면, 주제topic 혹은 화제話題가 필자가 진술하고자 하는 대상이라면 요지main idea 혹은 주제문topic sentence은 주제를 통해서 필자가 독자에게 말하고자 하는 핵심 주장 혹은 요점이라고 할 수 있다. 따라서 주제가 한 단어 혹은 간단한 어구로 표현된다면, 요지는 보통 완전한 문장으로 이루어진다. 요지를 찾는 것은 필자의 핵심 주장을 파악하는 것이므로 글을 읽는 궁극적인 목적이 될 뿐만 아니라, 세부적인 정보의 이해와 같은 여타의 글을 읽는 목적을 올바로 달성하기 위한 기본적인 전제가 된다. 또한 주제문의 파악이 정확해야 나머지 내용들에 대한 이해도 정교해진다. 올바른 주제문을 중심으로 해서 글을 구조화했을 때만 여타의 내용들이 주장을 뒷받침하는 논거인지, 부연설명인지, 세부적 정보를 제공하는지를 정확하게 가릴 수 있다.

02 2S2R과 요지 찾기

실제 글 읽기 과정에서 주제문의 파악은 '주제의 파악 → 주제문의 파악 → 글 전체의 구조화 및 논거와 세부 정보의 확인'과 같은 단선적인 방식으로 진행되지 않는다. 잠정적 주제와 주제문을 통해 글을 구조화하고 글의 나머지 정보를 이해해가는 과정에서 주제와 주제문은 끊임없이 정교하게 수정될 수밖에 없다. 이는 2S2R의 독해전략을 활용할 때도 마찬가지이다.

2S2R의 2단계인 Reading 단계에서 주장과 근거들을 도표나 도식으로 정리하면서 핵심 주장을 도출하게 되지만, 최종적으로 읽은 것을 요약하는 단계로 접어들면서, 잠정적으로 이해된 주제문은 더욱 명료한 형태로 수정되게 된다. 즉 잠정적으로 설정된 주제문을 중심으로 어떤 주제문일 때 글 전체가 가장 짜임새 있게 구조화되는지, 글 전체의 내용을 포괄하면서 요점을 가장 경제적으로 전달할 수 있는지의 여부를 확인한다. 이 과정을 거쳐서 글 읽기가 종료되는 시점에 주제문이 확정된다고 할 수 있다. 따라서 잠정적 주제문의 채택과 그 주제문을 통해 글을 구조적으로 이해하고 평가하는 과정은 순환적으로 반복되는 과정이다.

결국 주제문을 정확하게 파악하는 것은 잠정적 주제 및 주제문과 전체 글의 구조와 논거 supporting details를 끊임없이 일치시켜가는 과정이라고 할 수 있는데, 특히 이러한 노력은 긴 지문을 독해할 때 반드시 요구된다. 문장이 길고 내용이 난해할수록 주제문을 명료화하기 위한 반복적 읽기가 더 요구되는 것은 분명하다. 반복적 읽기의 횟수를 줄이고 주제문을 정확하게 찾기 위한 가장 단순한 방법은 글을 많이 읽는 것이다. 그러나 글 읽기 훈련을 위한 충분한 시간이 주어지지 않는다는 것을 논외로 하더라도, 글을 단순히 많이 읽는다고 해서 글을 구조적으로 독해하고 행간의 의미를 파악하는 대화적 독해의 능력이 향상된다는 보장은 주어지지 않는다는 것에 문제가 있다. 때로 저자들은 자신이 언급하고자 하는 것을 직접적으로 말하지 않는다. 왜냐하면 **독자 스스로 논리적 추론을 거쳐 핵심적 주장에 이르게 될 경우, 주장의 설득력과 독자의 공감이 더 커지게 되기 때문**이다. 즉 핵심적 주장을 명시적으로 되풀이되는 것보다 제시된 논거와 세부적 정보들을 통해서 자연스럽게 어떤 주장에 도달하게 될 때 독자의 공감이 커질 수 있다는 것이다. 따라서 고급 독해를 할수록 주제문을 찾기 위한 추론이 요구되며, 독자가 파악한 주제문이 과연 필자가 의도한 바인지가 쉽게 일치되지 않을 수도 있음을 명심해야 한다.

우리에게 주어진 시간과 달성해야 할 독해의 수준을 고려할 때, 읽기 훈련의 과정에서부터 스스로 주제문을 찾고 검증하는 방법을 사용하는 것이 필요하다. 앞서 제시한 2S2R의 읽기 훈련과 그 훈련의 일부라고 할 수 있는 주제문을 찾고 검증하는 노력들은 비록 귀찮고 더디게 가는 방법처럼 보이지만 탄탄한 읽기 내공을 쌓는 정도이자 지름길이다.

03 주제문을 찾고 검증하는 방법

주제문을 찾고 검증하는 방법은 앞서 이야기한 주제topic을 확인하는 방법과 밀접하게 연관되어 있다. 다음을 잊지 말자.

> 주제문(topic sentence) = 주제(topic) + 서술어(controlling idea)

1. 주제에 대한 서술 : 주제를 통한 검증

주제문이 주제에 대한 서술controlling idea인 이상 문단과 글 전체에서 가장 많이 언급되는 대상 혹은 개념을 찾고, 그 개념이 문단과 글 전체에서 진술된 내용을 일반적 수준에서 포괄하는지를 파악하는 것은 반드시 거쳐야 할 과정이다. 우선 이해를 쉽게 하기 위해 우리말로 된 예문을 보자.

다음 제시문을 읽고 글의 요지가 들어있는 문장이 무엇인지 생각해보자.

어떤 사람에게 세계 지도를 한 번 그려보라고 한다면? 결과는 매우 흥미롭다. ① 실제로 세계의 모습에 대해 매우 정확히 아는 사람은 많지 않다. ② 아마 당신조차도 나라들의 위치를 잘못 생각하고 있을 지도 모른다. ③ 이것은 뛰어난 기억력 등의 여러 가지 능력을 필요로 하는 일이다. ④ 그러나 많은 사람들이 대륙의 상대적인 크기에 대해서조차 알지 못한다. ⑤ 보통 사람들은 자신이 속한 나라의 대륙을 더 크게 그리는 경향이 있다. 예를 들면, 베트남 사람들이 아시아를 크게 그리는 반면, 브라질 사람들은 남아메리카의 면적을 더 크게 그린다.

위 글은 세계 지도를 그려보라고 했을 때 나타나는 현상에 대해서 기술하고 있다. 나라들의 위치를 잘못 생각하기 쉬운데 이는 뛰어난 기억력 등이 요구되는 일이라고 진술한다. 많은 사람들이 대륙의 상대적인 크기도 모르며, 보통 사람들은 자신의 대륙을 더 크게 그린다고 지적하고 있다. 이 모든 내용은 사람들이 세계 지도를 잘 그리지 못한다는 것, 즉 세계의 모습에 대해 정확히 아는 사람이 많지 않다는 것으로 모아질 수 있다. 글에서는 계속해서 세계 지도 그리기에 대해서 언급하고 있지만, 내용적으로 판단할 때 세계 지도 그리기는 곧 세계의 모습을 정확히 아는 것과 뜻이 같음을 알 수 있다. 따라서 제시문의 요지를 가장 잘 나타내고 있는 문장은 ①이다.

문제는 오히려 많은 사람들이 대륙의 상대적인 크기에 대해서조차 알지 못한다고 진술하고 있는 문장 ④에 있다. 문장 ④는 문장 ①의 내용을 구체화하면서 뒤에 부연설명까지 달고 있다. 문장 ①에 비해서 더 쉽게 기억되고 강한 인상을 가지게 되는 것이 구체성을 가진 문장 ④의 힘이다. 그래서 짧은 순간 독해를 마치고 지문의 요지를 찾게 될 경우 답으로 고르기 쉽다. 그러나 문장 ④는 문장 ②의 내용을 포괄하지 못할 뿐만 아니라, 문장 ①의 내용에 의해서 일반화될 수 있음에 주의해야 한다.

물론 항상 모든 글의 전체 내용을 포괄하는 진술이 주제문이 되는 것은 아니다. 도입부의 일반적 진술로 문장 ①의 내용과 같은 포괄적 진술을 하고, 정작 문장 ④와 같은 구체적인 내용을 핵심적으로 기술하거나 주장할 수 있다. 이러한 경우에는 글의 뒷부분이 구체적 내용에 대한 진술로 채워지고, 그러한 구체적 내용이 중요한 이유가 무엇인지가 글에서 명확히 언급될 경우에 한정되어 있다.

2. 문장관계를 통한 검증

각각의 문장들은 일정한 의미를 가지고 서로 연결되어 있다. 연결되는 문장이 동등한 내용을 담을 수도 있으며, 앞의 내용을 부연하거나 이유를 설명할 수도 있고, 일반화시켜 결론을 도출할 수도 있다. 문장 간의 내용이 서로 동등한 지위를 가지는 경우에도 앞의 문장과 논지가 동일하게 이어질 수도 있고 반대의 논지가 전개될 수도 있다. 이러한 문장 간의 관계는 궁극적으로 문장의 내용과 논지의 변화를 통해서 파악해야 하지만 연결어가 있는 경우 문장들 사이의 연결 관계를 이해하기가 수월해진다.

특히 요지나 주제문을 찾는 과정에서 유용한 것은 '그러나'와 같은 역접의 관계를 나타내는 연결어와 '그러므로/따라서'와 같이 원인과 결론을 이어주는 연결어라고 할 수 있다. 역접의 연결어의 경우 어떤 사물이나 현상, 사실에 대한 일반적인 이해를 진술한 뒤 그러한 일반적 상식을 뒤엎는 필자의 주장을 진술하게 된다. 따라서 필자가 강조하고 싶은 것은 '그러나' 뒤에 놓이기가 쉽고, 주제문과 밀접한 연관을 갖게 된다.

다음에 나오는 key ideas핵심생각를 찾는 훈련은 글의 요지나 주제문을 파악하는데 있어서 그 기초가 되는 훈련이므로 연습을 해두면 도움이 될 것이다.

■ Key Ideas를 찾는 방법

1. 이 글이 '누구who'에 관한 것인지 또는 '무엇what'에 관한 것인지를 묻는다.
2. 그 사람이나 대상이 무엇을 하고 있는지 또는 그 사람이나 대상에게 무슨 일이 일어나고 있는지를 질문한다.
3. when, what kind, where, why에 관련된 것은 details(세부사항)에 해당된다는 점을 염두해 두자. 즉 이것들은 key ideas가 아니다.

그러면 다음의 예문들에서 key ideas를 찾아보자.

A little boy in a green dress rushed away into the trees just beyond the gate to Yongsan Park.

번역 녹색 옷을 입은 작은 소년이 용산 공원 쪽 문 바로 지나서 있는 나무 쪽으로 질주했다.

위에서 나온 key ideas를 찾는 방법을 적용해보면,

① '누구'에 관한 것인지 ⇨ A boy

② 사람이나 대상object이 무엇을 하고 있는지 ⇨ rushed away

③ ①, ②를 제외한 나머지 것들은 세부사항details일 따름이다. in a green dress는 'what kind'에 해당하고, into the trees는 'where'에 해당하며, beyond the gate to Yongsan Park는 'where'에 해당한다. 따라서, key idea는 'A boy rushed away'가 된다.

Because of the new rules, most foreign automobiles in Korea now offer safety features at no extra charge.

번역 새로운 규칙 때문에, 한국의 대부분의 외국 자동차들은 현재 추가비용 없이 안전장치를 제공하고 있다.

① automobiles

② offer safety features

③ ①, ②를 제외한 나머지 것들은 세부사항details일 따름이다. Because of the new rules는 'why'에 해당, most foreign는 'what kind'에 해당, in Korea는 'where'에 해당, now는 'when'에 해당, at no extra charge는 'how'에 해당한다. 따라서, key idea는 'automobiles offer safety features'가 된다.

예제

[1-5] 다음 문장에서 key ideas를 찾아보시오.

01 Because of their busy lifestyles, Americans have less time to prepare and eat food at home.

Key ideas : _____

02 Inventions like the microwave oven dramatically reduce the amount of time necessary for cooking.

Key ideas : _____

03 Not only are Americans busier than ever before, but they frequently change houses, on an average of once every five years.

Key ideas : _____

04 Fast-food chains, which exist all over the country, provide a familiar place for Americans to eat, no matter where they go.

Key ideas : _____

05 Americans can even find fast-food chains in cities like Paris, Moscow, and Beijing.

Key ideas : _____

한글 번역

예제 | **01** 바쁜 생활방식 때문에 미국인들은 집에서 음식을 장만하고 먹을 시간이 적다.

02 전자레인지와 같은 것들의 발명은 조리에 필요한 시간을 현저하게 줄여주었다.

03 미국인들은 과거 어느 때보다 바쁠 뿐 아니라 또한 평균 5년에 한 번 정도, 자주 거주지를 바꾼다.

04 전국에 있는 패스트푸드 체인점들은 미국인들이 어딜 가든 친숙하게 먹을 수 있는 장소를 제공해준다.

05 미국인들은 심지어 파리나 모스크바, 베이징 같은 도시에 가도 패스트푸드 체인점을 찾을 수가 있다.

정답 | **01** Americans have less time to prepare and eat food.

02 Inventions reduce time cooking.

03 Americans change houses.

04 Fast-food chains provide a familiar place to eat.

05 Americans find fast-food chains.

04 Stated Main Ideas

글 안에 요지가 언급되어 있는 경우 그 요지가 있는 문장을 topic sentence주제문라 하는데, 크게 다음과 같이 나눌 수 있다.

참고로, 글 안에서 topic sentence를 찾아내는 방법은 다음과 같다.

1단계 : 주제 개념을 찾기 위해 전체 문단을 읽는다.

2단계 : 전체 문단의 전반적인 그림을 보여주는지 보기 위해 첫 문장을 읽는다. 그렇지 않다면 첫 문장이 개론적인 배경이나 대조적인 정보를 주기 위한 것일 수 있다. 또는 첫 문장이 그 뒤 두세 문장의 답이 되는 질문을 던지는 것일 수도 있다.

3단계 : 만약 첫 문장이 요지를 말하고 있지 않으면 전체 문단의 전반적인 그림을 제시하는지를 보기 위해 마지막 문장을 보라.

4단계 : 첫 문장이나 마지막 문장이 문단의 전체적인 개요, 즉 요지를 제시한다면 당신은 주제문을 찾은 것이다.

5단계 : 첫 문장이나 마지막 문장 둘 다 주제문이 아니라면 문단 중간의 문장들 중 하나가 개요나 요지를 말하고 있는지를 알기 위해 모든 문장을 평가해야 한다. 각 문장을 질문문으로 바꾸고 문단의 다른 문장들이 이 질문에 답변하는 것인지를 결정함으로써 각 가능성을 확인하라.

---

1. At the Beginning 글의 맨 앞에 오는 경우

Probably the most striking feature of Egyptian religion was its focus on the afterlife. Unlike the Mesopotamians, the Egyptians believed that death could be an extremely pleasant continuation of life on earth. Hence, they actively sought immortality. The wealthy placed great emphasis on building tombs, decorating them with paintings and inscriptions, and stocking them with cherished possessions for use in the world beyond. The most cherished possession of all, of course, was the body itself, and the Egyptians provided for its preservation through their mastery of the science of embalming—hence the Egyptian mummies. The Egyptians believed that a person's spirit could live on after death, but unlike later civilizations, they were not prepared to jettison the body altogether, believing instead that from time to time a person desired to return to the body after death. That belief made mummification necessary.

*embalming : (시체를) 약품 처리하여 썩지 않게 보존하기; 미라로 만들기
*immortality : 불멸, 불사
*inscription : 묘비에 새기는 글, 묘비명
*jettison : 버리다, 포기하다, (비행기에서 짐을) 낙하하다
*preservation : 보존
*striking : 놀라운, 눈에 띄는

번역 아마도 이집트 종교의 가장 눈에 띄는 특성은 사후세계를 중시한다는 점일 것이다. 메소포타미아 사람들과 달리 이집트 사람들은 죽음을 아주 즐거운 현생의 연속으로 믿었다. 따라서 그들은 능동적으로 영생을 추구했다. 부자들은 무덤을 만드는 일, 그림과 묘비글로 장식하는 일, 사후세계에 쓸 물건들로 무덤을 채우는 일에 아주 공을 들였다. 물론 이들 중 가장 칭송받는 소장품은 몸 그 자체로, 이집트인들은 시체 방부처리의 과학에 통달함으로써 보존하게 했는데, 이게 바로 이집트 미라다. 이집트인들은 사후에도 사람의 영혼은 살아있다고 믿었는데, 이후 문명들과는 달리 이들은 몸을 완전히 포기할 준비는 되어 있지 않았고 대신에 사람의 영혼이 사후에도 가끔은 몸으로 돌아오고 싶어 한다고 믿었다. 이 믿음 때문에 미라 만들기는 꼭 필요한 일이었다.

2. In the Middle 글의 중간에 오는 경우

Maria Luisa Martinez uses the same routine for her face every day. First, she washes it, then she uses a nonirritating toner, and finally she gently rubs in a light moisturizer. Most important, she recognizes some truths about the skin care industry : **Spending more money does not guarantee getting a better product for your skin.** So, instead of going out and buying an expensive brand, Maria Luisa follows the advice of Paula Begoun, a well-recognized skin care expert and author of the book *Don't Go to the Cosmetics Counter Without Me.* Maria Luisa's use of skin care products proves the point well. She knows that expensive soap by Erno Laszlo is not better for her skin than an inexpensive bar of Dove. And a toner by Neutrogena that doesn't have irritants in it is as good or perhaps better than an expensive toner by Orlane or La Prairie.

nonirritating : 무자극의

번역 마리아 루이자 마르티네즈는 얼굴을 위해 매일 같은 일을 반복한다. 첫째, 그녀는 얼굴을 씻고, 무자극의 스킨을 바르고, 마지막으로 가벼운 로션을 바른다. 가장 중요한 것은 그녀가 화장품 산업의 진실을 알고 있다는 점이다. 돈을 더 많이 들인다고 해서 당신 피부에 더 좋은 제품을 반드시 구하는 것은 아니라는 점이다. 그래서 그녀는 나가서 비싼 브랜드를 찾는 대신에 유명한 스킨케어 전문가이며 '나 없이 화장품 판매대에 가지 마세요'라는 유명한 책의 저자인 파울라 베건의 충고를 따른다. 마리아 루이자의 화장품 사용은 중요한 점을 잘 파악한 것이다. 그녀는 에르노 라즐로의 비싼 비누가 값싼 도브 비누보다 자기 피부에 더 좋지 않음을 알고 있다. 또 무극성 뉴트로지나 스킨은 비싼 올랑이나 라 프레리 스킨보다 충분히, 어쩌면 더 좋을 수 도 있음을 알고 있는 것이다.

먼저 이 글의 topic을 찾아보자. 즉 이 글은 무엇(또는 누구)에 관한 것인가?

① Maria Luisa Martinez

② the same routine for her face

③ skin care products

④ Paula Begoun, a well-recognized skin care expert

⑤ the skin care industry

이 다섯 가지 중에서 여러분은 어떤 것을 골랐는가?

우선, ① Maria Luisa Martinez가 topic이 되려면, Maria Luisa Martinez란 사람에 대한 이야기가 그 뒤에 supporting details로 쫙 언급이 되어야 한다. 예를 들어 Maria가 어떤 사람이고 어디에 살고 어떤 음식을 좋아하며 어떤 사람들과 어울리는지 등 그 개인에 대한 언급이 나와야 하는데 그런 것이 없다. 따라서 topic이 될 수 없다.

② the same routine for her face가 topic이 되려면, 얼굴을 위해 매일 같은 일을 하는 것에 대한 구체적인 예가 글 전체에 나와야 한다. 얼핏 보면, 바로 다음 문장 "첫째, 그녀는 얼굴을 씻고, 무자극의 스킨을 바르고, 마지막으로 가벼운 로션을 바른다." 등의 supporting details가 나와 있어 topic이 될 만한 소지는 있는 것처럼 보인다. 하지만, 거기서 끝이다. 그 다음에 이어지는 문장들이 더 이상 '얼굴을 위해 매일 같은 일을 하는 것'을 뒷받침support하는 세부사항들details이 아니기 때문이다. 이것은 다음에 나올 요지를 언급하기 위한 도입introduction 의 역할만을 할 따름이다.

③ skin care products가 topic이다. 왜냐하면, 그 다음 문장들에서 덜 비싼 화장품들이 더 비싼 것들만큼이나 좋다는 예들이 계속 언급되고 있기 때문이다.

④ Paula Begoun, a well-recognized skin care expert는 근거를 들기 위해 사용된 예일 따름이다.

⑤ the skin care industry은 너무 포괄적이어서(too broad) topic이 될 수 없다.

자, 이제 요지를 알아내보자. 우리는 다음과 같은 질문, 즉 '저자가 topic을 가지고 독자에게 말하려 하는 것이 무엇인가'라는 질문을 던져야 한다. skin care products가 topic이므로, 이 것을 가지고 저자가 말하려는 요점은, "더 비싼 화장품을 쓰는 것이 더 나은 효과를 보장하는 것은 아니다Spending more money does not guarantee getting a better product for your skin"가 되는 것이다.

3. At the End 글의 맨 끝에 오는 경우

때때로 글쓴이는 자신의 주장을 먼저 제기하기 전에 여러 사실들을 먼저 나열하여 자신의 주장의 설득력을 높이는 전략을 구사하기도 한다. 이럴 때 글의 요지는 맨 마지막에 오는 경우가 많다. 하지만 영어 구조에선 그렇게 흔한 것은 아니다.

Everybody uses words to persuade people of something without actually making a clear argument for it. This is called using loaded language. For example, a newspaper writer who likes a politician call him "Senator Smith"; if he doesn't like the politician, he refers to him as "right-wing or left-wing senator as Smith." If a writer likes an idea proposed by a person, he calls that person "respected"; if he doesn't like the idea, he calls the person "controversial." If a writer favors abortion, she calls somebody who agrees with her "prochoice" (choice is valued by most people); if she opposes abortion, she calls those who agree with her pro-life ("life," like "choice," is a good thing). **Recognizing loaded language in a newspaper article can give you important clues about the writer's point of view**.

번역 모든 사람들은 실제로 명확한 논거 없이 사람들을 설득하는 말을 한다. 이것을 유도적인 언어라고 부른다. 예를 들어, 어떠한 정치가를 좋아하는 신문기자는 그를 '스미스 상원의원'이라 부르고, 만약 그 정치가를 좋아하지 않는다면, '스미스와 같은 우파 또는 좌파 의원'이라고 부른다. 만약 글쓴이가 어떤 사람에 의해 제안된 아이디어를 좋아하면, 그 사람은 '존경받는' 이라 불리지만, 그가 그 아이디어를 좋아하지 않으면 그 사람은 '논란이 많은 사람'이라 지칭한다. 만약 글쓴이가 임신중절을 찬성한다면 그녀에게 동조하는 사람들은 '선택을 지지하는 사람'(선택은 대부분의 사람에 의해 가치 있게 여겨진다)이라고 부르 지만, 임신중절에 반대한다면 '생명을 지지하는 사람'(선택과 마찬가지로 생명은 좋은 것이다)으로 부른다. 신문기사의 유도적 인 언어는 기자의 견해에 관한 중요한 단서를 제공해준다.

4. In the First and Last 첫 번째 문장과 마지막 문장에 둘 다 오는 경우

Although holiday gift-giving to teachers can be stressful for parents of young children, research has found that **teachers prefer gifts from the children as opposed to fancy or expensive gifts.** In some affluent neighborhoods, parents seem to compete to give the fanciest item. They need to remember not to embarrass families with limited resources. "To appear with a $50 basket of fruit in the classroom would certainly make other children feel uncomfortable," says National PTA president Shirley Igo. Some schools' room mothers invite parents to chip in for a group gift or gift certificate so that teachers aren't awash in "World's Greatest Teacher" mugs. When in doubt, parents should give their children markers, construction paper, and glue. **What teachers appreciate most are handmade presents—such as artwork, cards, and cookies, says Igo. Gifts from the children themselves are always the best way to say thank you.**

affluent : 풍족한, 부유한   *PTA : Parent-Teacher Association*
invite 사람 to+동사원형 : 사람에게 to 이하 할 것을 권하다
chip in for : 각출하다   *awash in : ~로 홍수가 나다*

번역 선생님들께 명절 선물을 드리는 것이 어린 자녀를 둔 부모들에게는 스트레스일 수 있다 해도, 연구에 따르면, 교사들은 아이들에게 받는 선물을 고급스럽고 비싼 선물을 받는 것보다 더 좋아한다. 몇몇 부유한 지역에서는 부모들이 더 고급스러운 선물을 주기 위해 경쟁하는 것 같다. 그들은 경제적 여유가 없는 부모들을 당황시키지 말아야 할 필요가 있음을 기억해야 한다. "50달러짜리 과일 바구니를 들고 교실에 나타나는 것은 분명히 다른 아이들을 불편하게 할 수 있다."라고 전국 학부모-교사 연합(National PTA)의 대표인 셜리 이고는 말한다. 어떤 학교의 학부모 대표들은 학생들의 부모들이 돈을 조금씩 내서 단체 선물이나 상품권을 살 수 있도록 한다. 교사들이 '세계 최고의 교사' 머그컵으로 홍수가 나지 않게 말이다. 잘 모르겠으면, 부모 들은 아이들에게 마커나 만들기 종이, 풀을 주면 된다. 교사들이 가장 고마워하는 것은 수공예품이나 카드, 쿠키 같은 직접 만든 선물이라고 이고는 말한다. 아이들 본인들로부터 교사가 받을 수 있는 최고의 선물은 아이들로부터 '선생님 고맙습니다.' 라는 말을 듣는 것이다.

이 글의 topic은 holiday gift-giving to teachers이고, 요지는 teachers prefer gifts from the children to fancy or expensive gifts이다. 마지막 문장은 다시 한번 요지를 언급하여 강조를 하는 기능을 한다.

5. Two-Step Topic Sentence 두 개의 문장에서 찾아야 하는 경우

때때로 저자는 요지를 하나의 문장에 두는 대신에 요지의 각 부분들을 두 개의 서로 다른 문장에 넣기도 한다. 이때 독자는 이 둘을 하나로 통합하여 하나의 완전한 주제문으로 구성해야 한다.

> At one time, the right brain was regarded as the "minor" hemisphere. However, we now know that it has its own special talents. The right hemisphere is superior at recognizing patterns, faces, and melodies. It is also involved in detecting and expressing emotion. The right brain is also better than the left at visualization skills, such as arranging blocks to match a pattern, putting together a puzzle, or drawing a picture.

번역 한때, 우뇌는 '덜 중요한' 반구로 간주되었다. 하지만 지금 우리는 우뇌가 자기 자신만의 특별한 재질을 가지고 있음을 안다. 우뇌는 패턴이나 면, 멜로디 등을 인식하는 데 뛰어나다. 그것은 또한 감정을 인지하고 표현하는 데 연루되어 있다. 또한 우뇌는 모양을 맞추기 위해 블록을 정렬하거나, 퍼즐을 맞추거나, 그림을 그리는 등의 시각적 기술에 있어 좌뇌보다 뛰어나다.

첫 번째 문장은 글의 topic인 'the right brain'을 소개하고 있지만, topic sentence는 아니다. 이 글 전체가 우뇌가 '덜 중요한' 반구라는 점에 초점을 맞추고 있지 않기 때문이다. 첫 번째 문장은 도입 문장introductory sentence으로, 이 글의 요지인 '우뇌가 자기 자신만의 특별한 재질을 가지고 있음'을 말하는 두 번째 문장이 나오도록 단순히 길잡이 역할을 하고 있을 따름이다. 하지만, 두 번째 문장 'we now know that it has its own special talents.'은 it과 its가 무엇인지 명확하지 않기 때문에 완전한 주제문이 될 수 가 없다. 이 대명사를 명확히 언급을 해주어야만 완전한 주제문이 되기 때문이다. 따라서 첫 번째 문장과 두 번째 문장을 통합할 때만이 "the right brain has its own special talents."라는 완전한 주제문이 나오게 된다.

05 Unstated(Implied) Main Ideas

글 안에 요지가 있는 경우보다, 당연하게도 글 안에 없는 요지를 찾아내는 것은 어렵다. 따라서, 글 안에 없는 요지를 찾아내기 위해서 여러분은 체계적이면서도 꼼꼼하게 한 단계 한 단계씩 접근methodical and step-by-step approach하는 것이 필요하다. 이 과정은 기본적으로 ① supporting details에 있는 힌트clues를 찾고 ② 그것들을 함께 모아 ③ 그 근거에 기반하여 논리적 결론을 도출하는 것이다. 글 안에 없는 요지를 찾아내는 데 다음과 같은 방법이 도움이 될 것이다.

> Step 1. 글의 주제(subject)를 찾아낸다. (그러기 위해선 우선 각각의 문장 하나하나를 꼼꼼히 읽고, 반복되는 단어나 어구를 본다.)
> Step 2. topic과 관련이 있는 supporting details를 목록화한다.
> Step 3. 그 supporting details이 어떤 패턴으로 되어 있는지 알아낸다.
> Step 4. 그 supporting details의 공통 속성에 기반해서 an implied main idea를 결정한다.

01

다음 글의 요지를 찾아보자.

---

40 percent of Finns aged 24 to 65 have a college degree compared with twelve percent in the United States. Understandably, Finns are, per capita, the greatest consumers of literature in the world. School attendance is compulsory up to age 16, an earlier age than in Belgium, but schooling is rigorous. High school students attend classes 38 hours a week, compared with about 25 hours in the United States. Finnish students are also required to take more courses, including two foreign languages. All higher education is free, with most financial support coming from the state and the rest from private industries.

번역 24세에서 65세 사이의 핀란드인 40%가 대학 학위를 갖고 있으며 이는 미국의 12%와 비교된다. 알려진 대로 핀란드인들은 개인당 세계에서 문학작품을 가장 많이 읽는 사람들이다. 16세까지 학교 교육은 의무이며 이는 벨기에보다 이른 나이이긴 하지만 학교생활은 대단히 엄격하다. 고등학생들은 미국의 25시간에 비해 일주일에 38시간의 수업을 받는다. 핀란드 학생들은 두 개의 외국어 과정을 포함하여 더 많은 과목을 필수적으로 이수해야 한다. 모든 고등교육은 무료이며 대부분의 재정 지원은 국가에서 하고 나머지는 사기업들에서 한다.

자, 우선 첫 번째 질문을 던지자. 이 글은 무엇에 관한 것인가? 반복되어 나오는 단어들을 확인해 보자. 핀란드, 학교, 교육, 학비 등이다. 따라서 이것들을 정리해보면, Education in Finland라는 걸 알 수 있다. 이 글은 미국하고 핀란드를 비교하는 글이 아니다. 그렇다면, 중간에 벨기에가 나올 이유가 없다. 이 글은 벨기에와 미국을 언급해서 핀란드의 교육에 대해 말하고자 하는 것일 뿐이다.

그러면, 두 번째 단계로 가보자. 이 글에 나오는 **supporting details**을 목록화해보자.

① 40 percent of Finns have college degrees versus 12 percent in the United States.
② Finns consume the most literature (read the most) in the world.
③ School attendance is compulsory up to age 16.
④ High school students are in class 38 hours a week versus 25 in the United States. Finns take more courses.
⑤ All higher education is free.

이 글의 supporting details는 열거series의 패턴을 취하고 있다. 따라서 그것을 정리해보면 우선 ① 핀란드 국민의 대학 졸업율을 언급하며 ② 세계에서 가장 많이 읽는 사람들이란 것을 강조한다. 그런 다음 좀 더 구체적으로 열거를 하는데, 첫 번째로는 ③ 16살까지(즉, 고등학교 전까지) 학교가 요구하는 것이 많음을 말하고, 그다음에 ④ 고등학교 수업의 엄격함을, 그런 뒤엔 ⑤ 대학이 무상으로 제공된다는 점(즉, 누구나 대학에 갈 수 있음으로서 돈을 내고 다니는 나라의 학생들보다 훨씬 교육의 기회가 많음을 암시한다)을 설명한다.

따라서 이 5가지의 supporting details를 일반화시킨 다음, 앞에서 파악했던 topic(education in

Finland)과 연결하면, 이 글의 요지가 추출될 수 있다. 이 글은 열거의 패턴으로 되어 있으므로 나열된 것의 공통 속성을 찾는 것이 요지를 찾는 핵심 방법이 된다. 앞의 5가지 details의 공통 속성을 먼저 파악해보면 모두 핀란드 교육제도의 장점들만을 언급하고 있다. 따라서 이 글의 요지는 "Finland has an outstanding educational system핀란드는 우수한 교육제도를 가지고 있다."가 된다.

06 Supporting Details

Topic은 글쓴이가 읽는 이로 하여금 글을 다 읽었을 때, 알게끔 하거나 믿도록 하는 일반적인 특징이다. 그러나 이러한 특징은 읽는 이가 종종 더 많은 정보를 얻지 못하는 한 이해하거나 받아들일 수 없게 만드는 경우가 있다. 글의 뒷받침 내용은 이러한 정보를 제공해준다. Supporting details는 구체적인 사실과 통계, 예시, 단계, 일화, 이유, 묘사, 정의 등으로 주제문에 서술된 공통적인 main idea를 설명하고 증명하는 것이다. Supporting details는 이 main idea를 보충하거나 탄탄한 토대를 제공한다. Supporting details는 주제문에서 제시된 모든 문제에 답이 되어야 한다. 예를 들어, 다음 문장을 읽어보라.

> Female surgeons are treated differently from male surgeons by their colleagues, nurses, and patients.

이 문장은 즉각적으로 당신의 생각에 '어떻게, 왜'라는 질문들을 제기한다. 그 질문들에 답하기 위해서는 문단이 계속 이어져서 이 요점을 증명할 만한 이유와 기타 설명이 제시되어야 한다. 다음의 단락을 읽으면서, 어떻게 뒷받침 내용이 굵은 글씨체로 쓰인 main idea를 명료화시키는지 주시하고, 왜 참인지 설명해보라.

> **If you want to become rich, you must follow four important rules**. The first rule is to establish a reasonable income base. To reach and maintain that stable, middle-income base, you should earn a college degree, marry someone with an equal or higher education and stay married, and work as long as you are able to. The second rule for becoming rich is to avoid frivolous temptations. For example, don't drive expensive luxury cars; instead, buy medium-priced cars. Following rule #2 will allow you to save more money, which is rule #3. Average people who become rich often do so because they save more of their money, even if they must make sacrifices to do so. Finally, the fourth rule to become rich is take advantage of compound interest. If you invested $2,000 every year from age 22 to age 65 and that money earned 10 percent interest per year, you'd have over a million dollars when you retired.

번역 부자가 되고 싶다면, 다음의 중요한 4가지 법칙을 따르라. 첫 번째 법칙은 적당한 수입의 토대를 마련하는 것이다. 안정적인 중산층이 되고 이를 유지하기 위해서는 학사 학위를 취득하고, 동등하거나 또는 더 높은 수준의 교육을 받은 사람과 결혼하여 결혼 상태를 유지하고, 할 수 있는 한 계속 일을 해야 한다. 부자가 되기 위한 두 번째 법칙은 사소한 유혹을 피하는 것이다. 예를 들면, 사치스러운 차를 몰지 마라; 대신, 중간 가격대의 차를 구입하라. 두 번째 규칙을 따르는 것은 당신이 더 많은 돈을 절약하게 해줄 것이다. 그것이 바로 세 번째 규칙이다. 부자가 된 사람들의 대부분은 희생이 따르더라도 돈을 더 절약하기 위해 대개 그렇게 한다. 마지막으로, 부자가 되기 위해 필요한 네 번째 법칙은 복리를 이용하라. 만약 당신이 22세부터 65세까지 매년 2,000달러를 투자했다면 해마다 10%의 이자가 붙어서 은퇴 시에는 백만 달러 이상을 소유하게 될 것이다.

이 문단의 주제 문장에서는 '부자가 되는 네 가지 법칙들은 무엇인가'라는 질문을 제기한다. 이어서 재산을 불리기 위해 해야 할 네 가지를 설명하면서 그 질문에 답한다. 문단의 뒷부분에 나오는 세부사항을 읽지 않고는 주제 문장을 이해할 수 없을 것이다.

07 Major and Minor Details

Supporting details는 주요 세부사항major details과 부차적 세부사항minor details의 두 가지이다. 주요 세부사항은 글의 주요 내용으로 주제문에 있는 idea를 설명하고 보충한다. 부차적 세부사항은 main idea를 이해하기 위해 있어야 하는 필수적 이유와 기타 정보를 제공한다. 부차적 세부사항은 주요 세부사항을 부연 설명해준다. 부차적 세부사항은 main idea를 이해하는 데 항상 큰 영향을 끼치는 것은 아니어도, 더 구체적 정보를 제공해서 문단 내에서 요점을 한결 명료하게 해준다. 이 두 가지의 차이를 알아보기 위해, 다음의 문단을 읽어보라.

Many Americans believe in the supernatural. For one thing, they believe in supernatural beings. A recent Gallup poll revealed that 69 percent of people believe in angels, half of them believe they have their own guardian angels, and 48 percent believe that there are aliens in outer space. Americans also believe in the existence of supernatural powers. For example, over 10 million people have called the Psychic Friends Network to get advice about their present and future.

번역 많은 미국인들이 초자연주의를 믿는다. 하나의 예로, 그들은 초자연적인 존재를 믿는다. 최근 갤럽 투표에 따르면 69%의 사람들이 수호신을 믿고, 그들 중의 절반이 자신을 지켜주는 수호신이 있다고 믿으며, 48%는 외부 세계에 외계인이 존재한다고 믿는 것으로 나타났다. 미국인들은 또한 초자연적인 힘의 존재를 믿는다. 예를 들면, 천만 명이 넘는 사람들이 그들의 현재와 미래에 대한 조언을 얻기 위해 Psychic Friends 통신망에 전화를 걸고 있다.

굵은 글씨체의 문장이 이 문단의 주제 문장이다. '어떤 종류의 초자연적인 일을 믿는가?'라고 질문을 제기한다. 문단의 둘째, 넷째 문장에서는 미국인들이 초자연적 존재와 초자연적 힘을 믿는다고 말한다. 문단 내 다른 문장들은 작은 세부사항을 제공한다. 이 경우에, 작은 세부사항은 사람들이 실재한다고 믿는 존재나 힘의 종류를 예로 든다. 그러므로 작은 세부사항은 main idea를 좀 더 설명해주는 비필수적인 정보를 제공한다. 이런 기타 문장들supporting details은 또한 총체적으로나 구체적으로 서로 연관되어 있다.

Chapter 06 Main Idea & Supporting Details 83

	MAIN IDEA	
MAJOR DETAIL	MAJOR DETAIL	MAJOR DETAIL
Minor Detail	Minor Detail	Minor Detail

글을 읽을 때 이해를 돕기 위해, 문장들을 도표로 시각화하려 할 것이다. 이러한 관계를 구분해 보는 것은 문단을 이해하는 데 중요할 뿐만 아니라, 당신이 작가의 생각에 동의할 수 있는지의 여부를 결정하는 데에도 중요하다.

MAIN IDEA
MAJOR DETAIL
Minor detail
MAJOR DETAIL
Minor detail
MAJOR DETAIL
Minor detail

📑 예제

[1-3] 각 문장의 주제(subject)를 쓰시오.

01

> (1) Teachers, according to 79 percent of public high school students, are too easy on students when it comes to enforcing rules and assigning homework. (2) In addition, half of teens in public schools say their teachers and schools do not challenge them. (3) Too many disruptive students in classrooms, according to 70 percent of teenagers, are interfering with learning. (4) Schools' standards for graduation, say 70 percent of students, are too low. (5) According to three-fourths of students, diplomas are given to students even if they don't learn the required materials.

Sentence 1 subject _____

Sentence 2 subject _____

Sentence 3 subject _____

Sentence 4 subject _____

Sentence 5 subject _____

정답 | 01 Sentence 1 subject : teachers
Sentence 2 subject : teachers and schools
Sentence 3 subject : disuptive students
Sentence 4 subject : Schools' standards
Sentence 5 subject : diplomas

02

> (1) *Ladies' Home Journal* is a magazine that focuses on women's issues and is generally considered appropriate for women in their thirties, forties, and fifties. (2) *Glamour* is a magazine that devotes many pages to issues facing women in their twenties and early thirties. (3) *Mode* is a new magazine devoted entirely to issues affecting "plus-size" women. (4) *Allure* magazine has the most information on beauty products and is for women who are interested in the latest information on makeup and hairstyles. (5) For the most information on home life, however, the best magazine to buy is *Better Homes and Gardens*.

Sentence 1 subject _____

Sentence 2 subject _____

Sentence 3 subject _____

Sentence 4 subject _____

Sentence 5 subject _____

03

> (1) Thomas Jefferson, who wrote the Declaration of Independence, was lean, elegant, remote, and a bit sneaky. (2) John Adams, who contributed to the Declaration as well, was stout, cheap, and perhaps too honest about himself and everyone else. (3) Considered somewhat eccentric, or odd, Benjamin Franklin was a noted inventor and diplomat who was somewhat chubby and messy, but neither of those things interfered with his ability to help write the most important document in American history. (4) George Washington was a genius at lifting morale and knowing when to retreat to fight another day, so keeping the Founding Fathers agreeable and on task was his major contribution.

Sentence 1 subject _____

Sentence 2 subject _____

Sentence 3 subject _____

Sentence 4 subject _____

[4-6] 각각의 문장의 주제(subject)와 글의 패턴을 파악해보고, 이 글의 topic을 찾아내시오.

04

> (1) In today's busy world, do you have an understudy if something unexpected comes up? (2) First, organize a handful of friends, neighbors, or relatives and deputize one another; you look out for them, and they look out for you. (3) Second, pass out blank copies of the plan—a list with important names, numbers, and other contacts—to the people who've agreed to participate. (4) Third, share whatever medical information you feel comfortable sharing with the people you trust most. (5) The information you provide can help you feel more comfortable whether you are home or away from home.
>
> *understudy : 대역(대신 해줄 사람)

Sentence 2 subject　_____

Sentence 3 subject　_____

Sentence 4 subject　_____

Sentence 5 subject　_____

Pattern　_____

Topic　_____

정답 | **02** Sentence 1 subject : Ladies' Home Journal

Sentence 2 subject : Glamour

Sentence 3 subject : Mode

Sentence 4 subject : Allure

Sentence 5 subject : Better Homes and Gardens

03 Sentence 1 subject : Thomas Jefferson

Sentence 2 subject : John Adams

Sentence 3 subject : Benjamin Franklin

Sentence 4 subject : George Washington

04 Sentence 2 subject : organize and deputize friends, neighbors, or relatives

Sentence 3 subject : pass out copies of plan

Sentence 4 subject : share medical information

Sentence 5 subject : information help you feel comfortable

Pattern : time order

Topic : steps in creating understudies

05

(1) Judge Larry Standley of Harris County, Texas, required a man who slapped his wife to sign up for a yoga class as part of his punishment. (2) Municipal Judge Frances Gallegos in Santa Fe often sentences people convicted of domestic violence or fighting to a twice-a-week, New Age anger-management class, where offenders experience tai chi, meditation, acupuncture, and Eastern philosophy as means of controlling rage. (3) Municipal Judge David Hostetler of Coshocton, Ohio, ordered a man who had run away from police after a traffic accident to jog for an hour every other day around the block where the jail is located. (4) Hostetler also received worldwide attention in 2001 when he ordered two men to dress in women's clothing and walk down Main Street as a sentence for throwing beer bottles at a car and taunting a woman. (5) Judge Mike Erwin of Baton Rouge ordered a young man who hit an elderly man in an argument to listen to a John Prine song, "Hello in There," about lonely senior citizens and write an essay about it.

Sentence 1 subject _____

Sentence 2 subject _____

Sentence 3 subject _____

Sentence 4 subject _____

Sentence 5 subject _____

Pattern _____

Topic _____

06

(1) Do you miss the clothing of your youth? (2) Original Penguin, the geeky-chic brand, brought back their piped trench coats and pastel polos recently and opened a store last winter in New York City. (3) The women's collection, now in its second season, features shrunken tees and even bikinis. (4) Camp Beverly Hills, makers of 80s T-shirts and shorts, just thrilled twenty and thirty something by hauling out new versions of their kitschy wares this spring. (5) Now, Le Tigre, the feline version of Lacoste, which closed its doors in 1992, is offering its preppy duds again. (6) The spring collection—available at Bloomingdale's in New York City—features polo dresses, tanks, wristbands, and belts.

Original Penguin, the geeky-chic brand : 특이한 유행 브랜드 오리지널 펭귄

Sentence 2 subject _____

Sentence 3 subject _____

Sentence 4 subject _____

Sentence 5 subject _____

Sentence 6 subject _____

Pattern _____

Topic _____

07 다음 글의 Main idea를 쓰시오.

(1) Islam is centered on the Koran, the Islamic scriptures, which Muslims believe were revealed to the prophet Mohammed, which commands five basic devotional duties, called the "Five Pillars" : a declaration of belief that "there is no God but Allah [Arabic for "the God"] and Mohammed is his prophet"; prayers offered five times a day; daytime fasting during the month of Ramadan; charitable giving; and at least one pilgrimage to Mecca. (2) Muslims are forbidden to consume alcohol, illicit drugs, pork, or any meat that is not *halal,* the Islamic equivalent of kosher. (3) Premarital sex and extramarital sex are sternly prohibited, as are most forms of unchaperoned dating. (4) Emphasis on public modesty prompts many Muslims to cover themselves from the wrists to the ankles. (5) Muslims also may not gamble or pay or accept

interest on loans or savings accounts. (6) It is a regimen that often runs in conflict with the dominant culture. (7) Most American Muslims have no choice but to break the prohibition on usury to buy homes and automobiles, for example.

kosher : 율법에 맞는, 정결한 (음식)
unchaperoned : 보호자(chaperon) 없는
public modesty : 사람들 많은 데서 정숙함을 유지하는 것
regimen : 처방
usury : 고리대금, 이자

해설 이 글을 조직화해보면 다음과 같다.

Step 1. 각 문장의 주제 찾기
문장 1의 주제 : Five duties commanded by the Koran
문장 2의 주제 : Forbidden food, drugs, and drink
문장 3의 주제 : Prohibitions about sex and dating
문장 4의 주제 : Emphasis on public modesty
문장 5~7의 주제 : Prohibitions on gambling and usury

Step 2. 글의 패턴 : series
Step 3. 글의 topic : Duties and rules of Islam
Step 4. 각 문장의 핵심 내용 찾기
문장 1의 핵심 내용 : Many duties require personal sacrifices.
문장 2의 핵심 내용 : Regulations are strict and eliminate many substances from the diet.
문장 3의 핵심 내용 : Rules about sex and dating are old-fashioned and not permissive.
문장 4의 핵심 내용 : Modesty requires covering up the entire body.
문장 5~7의 핵심 내용 : Rules against gambling and paying interest make it hard to acquire expensive possessions.
Generalization : Islam's duties are numerous and strict.
따라서 이 글의 요지는 "The numerous duties and rules of Islam are strict and sometimes conflict with mainstream modern culture."가 된다.

정답 05 Sentence 1 subject : Judge Larry Standley
Sentence 2 subject : Judge Frances Gallegos
Sentence 3 subject : Judge David Hostetler
Sentence 4 subject : Judge David Hostetler
Sentence 5 subject : Judge Mike Erwin
Pattern : series
Topic : judges in the US who have imposed unusual sentences

06 Sentence 2 subject : Original Penguin
Sentence 3 subject : Original Penguin's women's collection
Sentence 4 subject : Camp Beverly Hills
Sentence 5 subject : Le Tigre
Sentence 6 subject : Le Tigre's spring collection
Pattern : series
Topic : clothing companies bringing back styles from the past

07 The numerous duties and rules of Islam are strict and sometimes conflict with mainstream modern culture.

예제 01 (1) 79%의 공립 고등학교 학생들에 의하면 교사들은 규칙을 강행하거나 숙제를 부과하는 데 있어 너무 너그럽다고 한다. (2) 게다가 공립학교를 다니는 십대의 절반이 그들의 교사와 학교가 그들이 도전하도록 하지 않는다고 말했다. (3) 수업에 방해를 주는 매우 많은 학생들이, 십대의 70퍼센트에 의하면, 학습을 방해한다. (4) 70%의 학생들은 학교의 졸업 기준이 너무 낮다고 말한다. (5) 학생들의 3/4에 따르면, 학위가 필수과목을 공부하지 않은 학생들에게도 주어진다고 한다.

02 (1) *Ladies' Home Journal*은 여성들과 관련된 이슈에 초점을 둔 잡지로 보통 30대, 40대, 50대 여성들에게 적합하다고 여겨지고 있다. (2) *Glamour*는 20대 및 30대 초반의 여성들이 직면한 이슈와 관련해 많은 페이지를 할애하고 있는 잡지다. (3) *Mode*는 전적으로 플러스 사이즈인 여성들과 관련된 이슈로 구성되어 있다. (4) *Allure*는 화장품과 관련된 최신 정보가 있어 메이크업과 헤어스타일에 관련된 최신 정보에 관심이 있는 여성들을 위한 잡지다. (5) 그러나 가정생활과 관련된 최고의 정보를 위해서는 *Better Homes and Gardens*를 구입하는 것이 가장 좋다.

03 (1) 독립 선언문을 쓴 토마스 제퍼슨은 야위었고 우아하며 쌀쌀맞고 조금은 엉큼한 사람이었다. (2) 또한 선언문에 기여한 존 애덤스는 통통하고 천박한 성격에 본인 스스로와 다른 모두에게 너무나 솔직한 사람이었다. (3) 별나고 기이한 것으로 따지면 저명한 발명가이자 외교관이었던 벤자민 프랭클린이 있는데, 그는 조금 통통하며 지저분한 성격이나 미국 역사상 가장 중요한 문서를 작성하는 능력에는 전혀 방해가 되지 않았다. (4) 조지 워싱턴은 사기를 높이고, 후일에 다시 싸우기 위해 언제 후퇴할지에 대해 잘 알고 있는 천재여서 (독립 선언문의) 창시자들의 동의를 얻어 과업을 넘기는 것이 그의 주요한 공헌이었다.

04 (1) 오늘날과 같은 바쁜 세상에 당신은 무슨 일이 생기면 자신의 대역을 해줄 사람이 있는가? (2) 첫째, 몇 명의 친구, 이웃, 또는 친척을 구성하고 상호간에 대리를 해주기로 설정해라; 당신도 그들을 찾고, 그들도 당신을 찾도록 말이다. (3) 둘째, 동의한 사람들에게 중요한 이름, 전화번호, 다른 연락처 리스트를 나누어 주어라. (4) 셋째, 당신이 가장 신뢰하는 사람들과 공유해도 좋은 모든 건강상의 정보를 공유하라. (5) 당신이 준 정보는 당신이 집에 있든 밖에 있든 간에 더 마음을 편하게 해줄 것이다.

05 (1) 텍사스주의 판사 래리 스탠드리는 와이프를 때린 남자에게 처벌의 일부로써 요가 클래스를 수강하도록 했다. (2) 산타페의 지방 판사 프랜시스 갤리고스는 가정 폭력이나 싸움으로 기소된 이들에게 종종 이주에 한 번 뉴 에이지 분노관리 수업을 듣도록 판결하는데 이 수업에서 범법자는 태극권이나 명상, 침술 그리고 동양 철학 등을 분노 조절의 수단으로 경험하게 된다. (3) 오하이오 코섹튼의 지방 판사 데이비드 호스틀러는 교통사고 이후 교통경찰로부터 도망간 남자에게 이틀에 한 번 감옥이 소재된 블록을 조깅하라는 명령을 내렸다. (4) 호스틀러는 2001년에도 세계적인 관심을 받았는데 그때 그는 차에 맥주병을 던지고 여성을 희롱한 두 사람에게 여자 옷을 입고 대로를 걸으라는 명령을 내리기도 했다. (5) 배턴 루지의 마이크 어윈 판사는 말다툼 끝에 노인을 때린 젊은 남성에게 외로운 노인에 대한 존 프라인의 노래 "Hello in There"을 듣고 거기에 대한 글을 써오라는 명령을 내리기도 했다.

06 (1) 젊었던 시절의 옷이 그리운가? (2) 특이한 유행 브랜드 오리지날 펭귄은 최근 파이프 모양의 트렌치 코트와 파스텔 톤의 폴로 셔츠를 재현하여 지난 겨울 뉴욕시에 점포를 열었다. (3) 두 번째 시즌의 여성 콜렉션은 줄어든 티셔츠와 심지어 비키니까지 갖고 있다. (4) 80년대 티셔츠와 반바지 브랜드인 캠프 비버리 힐즈는 이번 봄, 키치한 제품들의 새로운 형태를 끌어냄으로써 20대와 30대를 흥분케 했다. (5) 이제 라코스테의 고양이식 버전인 르 타이거(1992년 문을 닫았지만)는 다시 프레피 룩을 내놓고 있다. (6) 뉴욕 블루밍데일 백화점에서 구할 수 있는 봄 콜렉션은 폴로 원피스, 탱크탑, 손목밴드, 벨트 등이다.

07 (1) 이슬람은 이슬람 경전인 코란을 중심으로 하고 있는데, 무슬림들은 이 코란이 마호메드 예지자에 의해 나타났다고 믿으며, 코란은 '다섯 개의 기둥'이라고 하는 다섯 개의 기본적인 신앙 의무를 요구한다; (그 다섯은) "알라는 유일신이며 마호메드는 선지자이다."라는 신앙 고백과, 하루 다섯 번의 기도, 라마단 기간 중 낮 동안의 금식, 자선, 그리고 최소 메카로 한 번은 순례 여행을 가는 것이다. (2) 이슬람교도들은 알콜 섭취, 부정한 약물, 돼지고기 또는 이슬람 코셔 음식이라 할 수 있는 할랄이 아닌 고기류의 섭취가 금해져 있다. (3) 혼전 성교나 혼외 성교는 강력히 금해지고 보호자 없는 대부분의 데이트도 금지된다. (4) 사람들이 많은 곳에서 정숙하기 위해 손목부터 발목까지 자신을 가리게 된다. (5) 이슬람인들은 또한 도박을 하지 않아야 하며 빌려준 돈이나 은행계좌의 이자도 받지 않는다. (6) 이것은 자주 주류 문화와 충돌을 하는 처방이다. (7) 예를 들어, 대부분의 미국인 이슬람교도들은 집이나 차를 사기 위해 고리대금업을 금하는 율법을 어기게 되는 것이다.

CHAPTER 07

The Writer's Technique - Purpose and Tone

01 목적의 파악과 2S2R

글의 목적purpose을 파악하는 것은 글의 요지를 이해하고 그와 관련된 문제들을 추론하는 데 있어서 의미 있는 정보를 제공한다. 따라서 저자가 왜 글을 쓰는지를 파악하는 것은 2S2R Reading 단계에서 주제문을 파악하고, 주장main point과 논거supporting details를 구분하는 데 있어서 중요한 역할을 한다. 저자가 글을 쓸 때는 수많은 서로 다른 목적이 있을 것이기 때문에 매우 복잡할 수 있다. 하지만, 그렇게 복잡한 것은 한국에서 출제되는 시험의 영역 바깥에 있는 것이기 때문에, 여기서는 가장 일반적인 글의 목적 3가지를 제시하고자 한다. 보통 대다수의 글은 넓게 보아 다음의 3가지의 틀 안에 포함이 된다.

1. To Entertain

글을 읽는 독자 여러분을 즐겁게 하거나 미소 짓게 하기 위한 것. 주로 소설, 단편, 시, 드라마 등 문학작품들과 그냥 흥밋거리로 붓 가는 대로 글을 쓰는 수필 등이 여기에 해당한다. 흥미로운 이야기를 전함으로써 독자 여러분에게 **즐거움을 가져다주는 것**이 가장 큰 목적이다.

2. To Inform

글을 읽는 독자 여러분에게 글의 topic에 대해 더 많은 정보를 주기 위한 것. 학교 교재, 신문 기사, 백과사전과 같은 참고문헌 등이 여기에 해당하는데 주로 여러분에게 뭔가를 가르치는 것teach을 목적으로 한다.

① 주제, 사건, 이슈 등을 개인의 의견 없이 묘사한다.
② 객관적인 어조에 의존한다.
③ 사실을 진술하거나 다른 이의 의견을 자신의 관점을 드러냄 없이 진술한다.
④ 일인칭 단수나 복수(I, We 등)의 사용을 피하고 독자를 직접적으로 언급하지 않는다.
⑤ 어떤 이슈에 대해 양쪽 모두의 견해를 제공한다.

3. To Persuade

글을 읽는 독자 여러분이 가지고 있는 세상에 대한 태도, 신념, 혹은 행위를 변화시키기 위해 설득하기 위한 것 또는 저자 자신의 생각에 동의하도록 만들기 위한 것. 신문의 사설과 광고가 대표적인 예이다.

① 주제, 사건, 이슈 등을 개인의 의견을 가지고 표현한다.
② 감정이나 태도를 드러내는 어조를 사용한다.
③ 상대방의 의견을 언급하는데, 그 의견을 반박하기 위해서 그렇게 한다.
④ 한쪽의 관점을 편애하는 사실을 포함시킨다.
⑤ 자신의 의견이 다른 이들에 의해서 받아들여져야 하는 이유를 제공한다.

다음의 우리 글을 읽어보자.

> 타당한 논증이란 타당한 형식의 논증을 말한다. 타당한 형식의 논증이란 반례가 있을 수 없는 형식의 논증을 일컫는다. '반례'란 그 논증이 부당함을 보여주는 반박 사례의 준말로서, 전제들이 모두 참이면서 결론은 거짓인 논증의 사례를 말한다. 반례가 나올 수 있는 형식의 논증은 부당한 형식의 논증이다. 부당한 논증 형식과 동일한 형식의 논증은 설령 그 전제들과 결론이 모두 참이라 해도 부당한 논증으로 간주된다. 왜냐하면 그 형식의 논증 가운데는 반례가 있기 때문이다.

이 글은 읽는 이에게 즐거움을 주기 위한 것도 아니고, 읽는 이의 태도, 신념, 혹은 행위를 변화시키거나 읽는 이를 설득하기 위한 목적을 가지고 있지도 않다. 글의 주제와 관련하여 더 많은 **정보를 주는 것**이 목적이라고 할 수 있다.

이렇게 글의 목적을 나누는 것은 그에 따라서 글에서 제공하고 있는 정보를 수용할지의 여부와 정보를 수용하는 과정에서 필요한 비판적 검토의 정도가 달라지기 때문이다. 정보의 제공을 주된 목적으로 하는 글의 경우 관련된 학문 공동체에서 대체로 인정하는 **사실**을 바탕으로 하거나, 필자가 판단할 때 대부분의 사람들이 **사실이 아니라고 부인하기 어려운 내용들**을 토대로 하게 된다. 그러나 때로 논쟁적 주제에 관해서 사실을 설명하는 방식으로 자신의 주장을 진술할 수도 있다. 이때 필자가 드러내고 있는 글의 목적만을 가지고 판단할 경우 필요한 비판을 생략하고 글쓴이의 주장을 수용하게 될 위험이 있으므로 주의해야 한다. 따라서 정보의 제공을 주된 목적으로 삼는 글로 판단될 경우에도 배경지식의 검토와 필자의 설명과 배치되는 설명의 가능성을 검토함으로써 정보의 수용 여부를 결정해야 할 필요가 있다.

■ 글의 목적을 파악하는 데 도움이 될 만한 단서들

1. Main Point
즐거움(오락)을 위한 글은 요지가 없을 수도 있으며, 그 요지를 작가가 어떤 경험으로부터 배운 것에 초점을 둘지도 모른다. 정보를 주는 글의 요지는 대개 사실을 진술하거나 사건의 진술에 대한 어떠한 판단도 하지 않고 그것을 묘사할 것이다. 그러나 설득하는 글의 요지는 의견을 나타낼 것이다. 그러한 글의 목적은 should, must, 그리고 have to와 같은 단어들로 종종 지시된다. 왜냐하면 작가는 신념이나 행위를 변화시키거나 개조시키기 위해 독자를 설득하려고 하기 때문이다.

2. Supporting Details
오락을 위한 글에서 뒷받침하는 세부 내용은 종종 이야기나 묘사이고, 유머를 포함하고 있을지도 모른다. 정보를 제공하는 글에서 세부사항은 증명될 수 있는 사실의 형태를 취한다. 그리고 그것들은 그러한 사실들에 대한 작가의 의견을 제공하지 않는다. 설득하는 글 역시 사실들을 포함하지만 요지를 정당화하는 데 사용되는 의견들이 더 많을 수 있다.

3. Source of Information
오락을 위한 글에서는 대개 출처가 제공되지 않는다. 정보를 제공하는 글에서는 종종 출처를 인용하며, 그러한 출처들은 대개 특성상 정보를 제공한다. 설득하는 글도 출처를 인용하기는 하지만 그것들은 저자 자신의 관점에 매우 호의적인 것들일 수도 있다.

4. Author
지은이의 배경, 자격, 경험, 그리고 흥미에 관해서 얻을 수 있는 정보에도 관심을 집중해야 한다. 왜냐하면 이러한 특성들은 작가가 글을 쓰면서 의도하는 바를 당신이 평가하기 쉽도록 할 것이기 때문이다. 때때로 작가들은 그들의 약력을 고지하여 직접적으로 목적을 언급하기도 한다. 그들은 당신에게 그들이 그 주제에 관한 글을 쓰도록 이끈 배경에 대한 어떤 세부사항을 제공할 수도 있다. 그러나 본문에서 작가에 대해 거의 밝히지 않거나 아무것도 밝히지 않는다 하더라도 당신은 작가가 누구인지, 그가 무엇을 이루기 바라는지에 대한 관점을 얻을 수 있다. 작가가 사용하는 단어들과 그들이 문장을 조합하는 방식 또한 그들의 감정과 태도, 그리고 목표에 대해 많은 것을 밝혀줄 수 있다. 구체적으로 당신은 다음 부분에서 논의된 편견을 인식하고 본문, 주제의 어조를 결정하는 것을 습득할 수 있다. 당신은 그 글이 포함하고 있는 사상과 정보에 대하여 더 비판적인 사고로 시작하는 법을 터득하기 위해서 독서 선별의 이러한 면을 검토하는 습관을 가져야 한다.

📝 **예제**

[1-8] What is the author's primary purpose?

01 Since the 2000s, voting among young people has increased by about 10 percent in Korea.
  ① to entertain　　　　② to inform　　　　③ to persuade

02 If you don't serve your time as a juror, you can't expect our legal system to be fair.
  ① to entertain　　　　② to inform　　　　③ to persuade

03 The high rate of corporate crime prove that Korea needs to have much stricter law enforcement than now.

① to entertain 　　② to inform 　　③ to persuade

04

> Frankly, it seems pretty easy to come up with a new exercise. You just take something people are already doing—like eating—and add "exercise." Or say it's cardio-friendly. So how's about?
>
> R.C. Colaerobics : Soda shopping? Don't just grab a Coke. Stretch waaaaay down to reach the Royal Crown! Your abs will be glad—and so will your wallet!
>
> Karaoke Swim : Tired of singing on that stupid bike? Start singing as you swim across the pool! Pounds peel away as you struggle to clear your lungs and stay afloat. You go, gurgle!
>
> Lego Lifts : Step 1 : Invite a child to play with Legos on your rug. Step 2 : Have child leave after "cleaning up." Step 3 : Remove your socks and run around. Yeow! Ouch. There's another one he missed! You're hopping your way to health!

① to entertain 　　② to inform 　　③ to persuade

05

> Firefighters spend much of their time at fire stations, which usually have features common to a residential facility like a dormitory. When an alarm sounds, firefighters respond rapidly, regardless of the weather or hour. Firefighting involves risk of death or injury from sudden cave-ins of floors, toppling walls and exposure to flames and smoke. Firefighters may also come in contact with poisonous, flammable, or explosive gases and chemicals, as well as radioactive or other hazardous materials that may have immediate or long-term effects on their health. For these reasons, they must wear protective gear that can be very heavy and hot.

① to entertain 　　② to inform 　　③ to persuade

정답 | 01 ②　 02 ③　 03 ③　 04 ①　 05 ②

06

At least 12 women from the United States contracted bacterial infections after undergoing breast enlargement surgery or other cosmetic procedures in the Dominican Republic, the government said yesterday. The Centers for Disease Control and Prevention said the women developed soft tissue infections known as *mycobacterium abscesses* after traveling to Santo Domingo for procedures between May 2003 and February 2004. All have since recovered after being given antibiotics. Nine had to be hospitalized. An increasing number of Americans are getting cosmetic surgery abroad because it is cheaper. The CDC said that it has yet to establish the source of the infection but that previous outbreaks in other places have been attributed to contaminated surgical equipment.

① to entertain   ② to inform   ③ to persuade

07

Charter schools, indeed all public schools, must do more than make parents feel good. Fostering high academic standards and improving student achievement must be the primary goals. Those schools failing to do so cannot be tolerated. State officials, and we the public, must make sure they are not.

① to entertain   ② to inform   ③ to persuade

08

I'm a pretty good housekeeper. Ask anybody. No, wait : Don't ask my wife. She and I disagree on certain housekeeping issues, such as whether it's OK for a house to contain dirt. Also smells. If NASA scientists really want to know about life on Mars, instead of sending up robots that keep finding rocks, they need to send my wife and have her take a whiff of the Martian atmosphere. If there's a single one-celled organism anywhere on the planet, she'll smell it. And if the other astronauts don't stop her, she'll kill it with Lysol. This is why her approach to leftovers baffles me. I am opposed to leftovers. I believe the only food that should be kept around is takeout Chinese, which contains a powerful preservative chemical called "kung pao" that enables it to remain edible for several football seasons. All other leftover foods should be thrown away immediately.

① to entertain   ② to inform   ③ to persuade   ④ to praise

정답 | 06 ②   07 ③   08 ①

예제 | **01** 2000년대 이래로 한국에서 젊은 층의 투표율은 10% 정도 증가했다.

02 배심원으로서 봉사하는 시간을 내지 않는다면, 우리의 법적 제도가 공정하기를 바랄 수 없다.

03 높은 기업 범죄율은 한국이 훨씬 더 엄격한 법의 적용이 필요한 나라임을 보여준다.

04 솔직히, 새로운 운동을 생각해 내는 것은 아주 쉬운 것 같다. 사람들이 이미 하는 일들(먹는 일처럼)을 택해서 '운동'을 붙이기만 하면 된다. 아니면 그것이 심장에 좋다고 말하면 된다. 자 그러면 다음은 어떤가?
R.C. 콜라에어로빅 : 탄산음료를 사러 나왔는가? 그냥 콜라를 잡을 게 아니다. 로얄 크라운을 잡을 수 있도록 아래로 쭈우욱 몸을 펴라! 당신의 복근이 좋아할 것이고 당신의 지갑도 좋아할 것이다!
노래방 수영 : 멍청한 자전거 위에서 노래하기가 싫증나는가? 수영장을 헤엄치면서 노래하는 운동을 시작해보라! 폐를 비우면서도 물에 뜨는 것을 동시에 하려고 버둥거리면서 살들이 빠질 것이다.
레고 집어들기 : 1단계 : 어린이를 한 명 오게 해서 당신의 카펫 위에서 레고를 가지고 놀게 하라. 2단계 : 아이가 다 '치우기'를 한 다음 가게 하라. 3단계 : 양말을 벗고 뛰어다녀라. 아야! 아이가 못 찾은 게 또 있다! 당신은 건강으로 깡총깡총 뛰어가고 있는 것이다.

05 소방관들은 많은 시간을 소방서에서 보내며, 소방서는 보통 기숙사와 같은 주거시설과 유사한 특징을 지니고 있다. 경보음이 울리면 소방관들은 날씨나 시간에 상관없이 빠르게 대처한다. 소방 활동은 갑작스럽게 마루가 함몰하고, 벽이 무너지고, 화염과 연기에 노출되는 등의 부상과 사망의 위험을 수반한다. 소방관들은 그들의 건강에 즉각적인 혹은 장기적인 효과를 지닌 방사선이나 다른 위험 물질 뿐만 아니라 아마도 유독한 가연성의 혹은 폭발성 가스나 화학 물질에 노출될 수 있다. 이러한 이유로 소방관들은 매우 무겁고 뜨거운 보호복을 착용해야 한다.

06 적어도 12명의 미국 여성들이 도미니카 공화국에서 가슴 확대 수술이나 다른 미용 시술을 받은 이후에 박테리아성 질병에 감염되었다고 당국이 어제 밝혔다. 질병 통제 예방센터는 산토 도밍고로 2003년 5월에서 2004년 2월까지 수술 여행을 다녀온 여성들에게서 mycobacterium abscesses이라 알려진 연조직 감염이 발병하였다고 밝혔다. 그들은 모두 항생제 처방을 받은 이후에 회복되었지만, 아홉 명은 병원에 입원했어야만 했다. (수술) 비용이 저렴하기 때문에 점점 더 많은 수의 미국인들이 성형 수술을 받기 위해 외국에 나가고 있다. 질병 예방 통제센터는 아직 감염의 원천을 밝혀내지 못했지만, 이전의 다른 지역에서의 감염은 오염된 외과용 수술 도구 탓이었다.

07 차터 스쿨들, 아니 사실 모든 공립학교들이 학부모들을 기분 좋게 해주는 것 이상을 해야만 한다. 높은 학업기준을 배양하고 학생들의 학업 성적을 올리는 것은 첫 번째 목표이다. 이렇게 하지 못하는 학교들을 관대하게 봐주어서는 안 된다. 주 공무원들과 일반 대중들은 이것이 묵과될 수 없는 것임을 분명히 해야 한다.

08 나는 꽤 훌륭한 살림꾼이다, 누구에게든지 물어보라. 아니, 기다려보라 : 내 아내에게는 묻지 말라. 그녀와 나는 집에 먼지가 있거나 냄새가 나도 괜찮은지 아닌지와 같은 가사 문제에 있어서 의견의 불일치가 있다. NASA의 과학자들이 화성에 정말로 생물체가 있는지 없는지에 대해 알기를 원한다면 바위나 계속 찾는 로봇을 보내는 대신에 내 아내를 보내서 화성의 대기를 한 모금 마시게 할 필요가 있다. 그 행성의 어디엔가 단 하나의 세포를 가진 유기체라도 있다면 그녀는 그 냄새를 맡을 것이다. 그리고 다른 비행사가 그녀를 제지하지 않는다면, 리졸로 그것을 죽일 것이다. 이것이 남은 음식에 대한 그녀의 접근법이 나를 당황하게 만드는 이유이다. 나는 음식을 남기는 것을 반대한다. 나는 보존되어야 하는 유일한 음식은 여러 번의 축구 시즌 동안 남겨서 먹을 수 있도록 하는 '쿵파오'라고 불리는 강력한 보존 화학물을 보유한 포장 중국 음식이라고 믿는다. 다른 모든 남겨진 음식물들은 즉시 폐기되어야 한다.

02 | 어조의 파악과 2S2R

글의 어조tone를 파악하는 것은 글의 요지를 이해하고 그와 관련된 문제들을 추론하는 데 있어서 의미 있는 정보를 제공한다. 따라서, 글의 어조를 파악하는 것은 글의 목적과 더불어서 2S2R Reading 단계에서 주제문을 파악하고, 주장main point과 논거supporting details를 구분하는 데 있어서 중요한 역할을 한다.

　　어조란 **글쓴이가 서술 대상을 바라보는 태도와 느낌을 나타내는 언어적 표현 방식**이다. 어조는 글쓴이의 개성적인 **목소리**로 나타나거나 글을 지배하는 **분위기**로 나타남으로써 글의 의미 및 주제를 형성하는 데 이바지한다. 따라서 어조를 평가하는 것은 글의 주제와 글쓴이의 태도 및 관점을 정확히 짚어내는 데 이바지할 수 있다. 특히 **반어적인 어조**의 경우는 파악하기가 까다로울 뿐더러, 잘못 판단하면 글의 중심 내용까지도 잘못 독해할 수 있으므로 주의해야 한다. 저자가 글을 쓸 때는 수많은 서로 다른 어조를 사용할 수 있을 것이기 때문에 수많은 어조가 있을 수 있다. 하지만, 어쩔 수 없이, 여기선 가장 일반적인 글의 어조 10가지만 제시한다.

① Objective tone　　　　　② Sympathetic tone
③ Critical tone　　　　　　④ Ironical tone
⑤ Admiring tone　　　　　⑥ Angry (indignant) tone
⑦ Disgusted tone　　　　　⑧ Humorous tone
⑨ Sad (sorrowful) tone　　⑩ Worried tone

우리말로 된 다음의 네 가지 예문을 보자. 아래 예문들은 하나의 내용을 다른 어조로 표현한 것이다.

---

(1) 정부 관보에 실린 내용에 따르면, 이민귀화국은 최악으로 운영된 연방 기관 중 하나이다. 이민귀화국에서는 기본적인 문서 작업과 심지어 정보 제공용 전화에도 요금을 부과하고 있다. 게다가 이용자들이 충분히 이용할 만큼 넉넉한 시설을 갖추고 있지 않다.

(2) 최악으로 운영된 연방 기관 중의 하나로 정부 관보에 순위가 오른 이민귀화국을 평가하기에 가장 좋은 표현은 '관료제의 악몽'일 것이다. 그곳에서는 간단한 문서 작성에도 요금을 부과하고, 정보 제공 전화 요금을 지불하라고까지 요구해서 가난한 이민자들이 힘들게 번 돈을 착취한다. 게다가 민망하게도 설비는 기준 이하인데다가 이용자들이 충분히 이용할 정도로 시설을 넉넉히 갖추고 있지도 않다.

(3) 정보 관보에 의해 최악으로 운영된 연방 기관 중의 하나로 평가된 이민귀화국은 늘 열악한 환경에 시달리고 있다. 이민귀화국에서는 만성적인 예산 부족 때문에 간단한 문서 작업이나 정보 제공 전화에도 요금을 부과할 수밖에 없다. 오랫동안 주력 부서로 취급되지 않았던 기관이기 때문에 설비는 노후하고 이용자들이 충분히 이용할 만큼 넉넉한 시설을 갖추고 있지도 못하다.

글 (1)의 경우 '이민귀화국이 최악으로 운영된 연방 기관 중 하나'라는 것을 정부 관보를 인용해서 이야기하고 있다. 즉 필자 자신의 의견으로 제시하고 있지 않다. 과다한 요금 부과나 시설 부족에 대해서도 같은 시각으로 평가할 수 있다. 따라서 예문 중에서 글 (1)은 중립적인 어조를 가졌다고 할 수 있다. 그러나 글 (1)이 절대적 중립성을 가지고 있는지는 여전히 의문이다. 왜냐하면 정부 관보에 실린 내용이 이미 이민귀화국에 대해서 특정한 가치평가를 담고 있기 때문이다. 마치 자신의 의견이 아닌 것처럼 권위 있는 기관이나 학자의 의견을 이용해서 주장을 펴는 것은 자신의 주장에 설득력을 더하기 위한 고전적인 수법이라고 할 수 있다. 따라서 관련된 주제topic에 대해서 다양한 의견이 균형감 있게 제시되고 있는지를 살피는 것은 중립적 어조의 글을 평가할 때 반드시 필요한 일이다. 글 (2)의 경우 '관료제의 악몽', '착취', '민망하게도' 등의 단어를 사용함으로써 이민귀화국에 대한 비판적 시각을 직접적으로 드러내고 있다. 글 (3)의 경우 이민귀화국에 대한 동정 혹은 비판에 대해서 해명하는 어조를 보여주고 있다.

(1) Neutral Tone

The Immigration and Naturalization Service ranks among the worst managed federal agencies rated by Government Executive magazine. It charges immigrants for doing basic paperwork and even for some informational phone calls. Additionally, its facilities aren't equipped to handle the volume of people it serves.

(2) Critical Tone

The bureaucratic nightmare we call the Immigration and Naturalization Service ranks among the worst managed federal agencies rated by Governmen Executive magazine. It robs poor immigrants of their hard-earned money by charging them for basic paperwork, and it even has the nerve to require these people to pay for informational phone calls. Additionally, its embarrassingly substandard facilities aren't equipped to handle the volumes of people it serves.

(3) Sympathetic Tone

The overworked and struggling Immigration and Naturalization Service ranks among the worst managed federal agencies rated by Government Executive magazine. Its meager resources force it to charge immigrants for doing basic paperwork, and its pitiful lack of funding leaves it no choice but to charge people for informational phone calls. The agency has been ignored for so long that its cramped and outdated facilities just aren't equipped to handle the volumes of people it serves.

예제

[1-11] Read the passage and follow the directions.

01 What is the primary tone of the passage?

> If I talk about my own country, where the average person only has complaints about the corruption of the decision-makers, I must say that it is we citizens who voted for them. There are still intellectuals who support those decision-makers who will most likely win election again. But if we look across the general society, almost everybody is trying to cheat others—meters in taxis are changed if you do not know the fare, the shopkeeper will charge more, and the examples go on and on. So why do we only blame others? It is time that we as a whole society took the blame for the prevalence of corruption. We must improve the public's perception of right and wrong.

① ironic   ② sympathetic   ③ neutral
④ critical   ⑤ disgusted

02 What is the tone of the passage?

> I was brought up in Europe. I came to the United States at age 25 in 1963, and for the past 41 years, I have been disturbed by the eating habits of Americans. Americans have come to demand that an endless quantity of foods be available at all times. I have seen them pile food on their plates at buffet-style restaurants. However, seldom have I seen them eat all of the items they put on their plates. Some restaurants, in a smart move, have had to resort to posting signs such as, "You may take as much as you want, but please eat all that you take."

① disgusted   ② optimistic   ③ humorous
④ sad   ⑤ ironic

03 What is the primary tone of the passage?

A friend of mine was about to leave for a weekend ski trip and realized that he had forgotten to send in his motorcycle payment. It was due on Monday, but he was out of stamps. Moreover, the post office was closed. He taped a quarter to the upper right-hand corner of the payment envelope, wrote "PLEASE" underneath it, and dropped it into the mailbox. The next week he received a plain white envelope in the mail. Taped to the card inside the envelope was a nickel in change. Under it a postal employee had penned : "Just this once."

① humorous　　② optimistic　　③ worried
④ respectful　　⑤ sorrowful

04 What is the primary tone of the passage?

Like to go to the beach, do you? Swim? Surf? Fish? Snorkel? Scuba dive? Wait! What can you be thinking? Don't you read the papers? Watch TV? Don't you know sharks are massing along our coastlines, biting bathers, eating people? Should you risk an attack by these JAWS wanna-bes?

① critical　　② angry　　③ neutral
④ ironic　　⑤ alarmed

해설 글쓴이는 해변에 가는 위험에 대해 놀라서 염려하고 있다. alarmed는 "feel afraid or anxious(걱정하는)"의 뜻이다.

05 **What is the primary tone of the passage?**

In the past, curtailing information in wartime has had disastrous results. Recall the secret bombing of Cambodia in 1969, when President Nixon kept even Congress in the dark. The North Vietnamese, the ones who could put Americans at risk, were well aware of the attacks. Americans were left out of the equation, eventually adding to anger over the war. Today, the Bush administration is packaging its attempts to restrict information as a way to protect the war effort—when in fact they could do the opposite. The moves violated the very spirit of freedom that America is fighting for. They risk obliterating the checks on government decisions that come when lawmakers and the general public know what the administration is doing.

equation : (여러 고려해야 할) 상황
risk -ing : ~할 위험에 처하다

① critical   ② sympathetic   ③ neutral
④ ironic   ⑤ sorrowful

06 **What is the primary tone of the passage?**

Killing animals for their fur is wrong. Consider the cute mink, the cuddly raccoon, the lovable harp seal. These animals haven't hurt us, so why should we savagely murder these adorable creatures? Think of a puppy. Picture its soulful, trusting eyes. Would you want to wear spot's hide on your back? The answer, from any thoughtful individual, must be a resounding "No!"

① critical   ② sympathetic   ③ angry
④ ironic   ⑤ neutral

해설 critical도 어느 정도 답이 될 수 있지만, angry가 전체적인 어조엔 더 맞다. 글 전체의 어조는 모피를 사용하는 행위에 대한 분노가 스며들어 있다. "wrong" "why should" (도대체 왜) "savagely" "spot's hide" 등의 단어에서 저자의 분노가 묻어나고 있다.

07 What is the primary tone of the passage?

A boss was disturbed when he saw his employees loafing. "Look" he said, "everytime I come in here I see things I'd rather not see. Now, I'm a fair man, and if there are things that bother you, tell me. I'm putting up a suggestion box and I urge you to use it so that I'll never what I just saw!" At the end of the day, when the boss opened the box, there was only one little piece of paper in it. It read : "Don't wear rubber-soled shoes!"

① critical   ② sympathetic   ③ upset
④ ironic   ⑤ humorous

해설 마지막 구절에 힌트가 들어 있다. "고무창을 댄 신발을 신지 말아 주세요!"라는 말은 '제발 사장님이 올 때 구두 소리가 나서 자신이 빈둥거리는 것을 들키지 않길 바라는 마음'이 들어있다.

08 What is the primary tone of the passage?

It's not easy being a mother these days. Most work outside the home in addition to their parenting duties. Because of the high divorce rate, many are rearing their children alone or with only part-time help from fathers. In 2001, an ABC news columnist did some research that suggested if you paid mothers for all the things they do, they would draw down about $500,000 a year. Moms face a daunting task, whether they have other jobs or not.

daunting : 벅찬; 두려운

① admiring   ② ironic   ③ neutral
④ sympathetic   ⑤ worried

해설 엄마가 직면해 있는 많은 (힘든) 일들에 대해 동정적인 어조로 쓰여 있다.

정답 | 05 ①   06 ③   07 ⑤   08 ④

09 What is the tone of Wilde's response?

> Oscar Wilde was asked by a judge during his trial, "Are you trying to show contempt for this court?" and Wilde replied, "On the contrary, I'm trying to conceal it."

① critical　　　　② sympathetic　　　　③ neutral
④ ironic　　　　⑤ angry

해설 오스카 와일드는 자신에 대한 재판에서, 판사의 "그대는 본 법정에 대한 경멸을 **보이려고** 하는가?(Are you trying to **show** contempt for this court?)"라는 말에, "아니 반대로, 난 그것을 **숨기려 하고** 있지요(I'm trying to **conceal** it.)"라는 재치 있는 답변을 하고 있다. "show"와 대비되는 "conceal"이란 단어를 사용함으로써 아이러니하면서도 (뱉어진 말과 그것의 의미가 반대의 경우이므로) 유머러스한 어조를 만들어 내고 있는 것이다. 만일 그냥 평이하게 "Yes. I am."이라고 답했다면, 그 의미가 퍽 반감되면서 글의 맛이 사라지게 되었을 것이고, 글 전체의 어조도 바뀌게 되었을 것이다.

10 What is the tone of the passage?

> Seabiscuit was one of the most remarkable thoroughbred racehorses in history. From 1936 to 1940, Americans thronged to racetracks to watch the small, ungainly racehorse become a champion. He had an awkward gait but ran with dominating speed; he was mild-mannered yet fiercely competitive; and he was stubborn until he became compliant.

① admiring　　　　② sympathetic　　　　③ neutral
④ ironic　　　　⑤ worried

해설 "remarkable", "champion", "dominating speed", "fiercely competitive" 등의 단어들에서 알 수 있다.

11 **What is the primary tone of the passage?**

> It's really great to see the Bush family living off profitable trust funds and working hard to initiate government programs that will hit the wallets of hard-working people like my father.

① admiring　　　　② amused　　　　③ neutral

④ ironic　　　　　⑤ worried

해설 글쓴이는 to 이하의 내용에 대해, 실제로는 전혀 '멋진(great)'일이라고 생각하지 않는다. 다음 구절, 즉 "열심히 일하는 사람들의 호주머니를 털어가는(hit the wallets of hard-working people)"이 바로 아이러니한 어조의 핵심 힌트가 된다.

정답 | 09 ④　10 ①　11 ④

한글 번역

예제 **01** 보통 사람이 의사 결정자들의 부패에 대해 불평만 하는 우리나라에 대해 말하자면, 그들에게 찬성표를 던진 것은 바로 우리 시민들이다. 여전히 십중팔구 다시 선거에 승리할 것 같은 그러한 의사 결정자들을 옹호하는 지식인들이 있다. 그러나 만약 사회 일반을 살펴보면, 요금을 모르면 택시의 미터기가 변동되고 가게 종업원이 더 많은 비용을 청구하는 등 예는 많듯이, 거의 모든 사람들이 다른 사람들을 속이려고 한다. 그러면 왜 우리는 다른 사람들만 탓하는가? 사회 전체가 부패의 만연에 대한 비난을 받아야 할 시기이다. 우리는 대중의 옳고 그름에 대한 인식을 개선해야 한다.

02 나는 유럽에서 자랐다. 나는 1963년, 미국에 25살의 나이로 왔고, 지난 41년 동안 미국인들의 식습관에 심적으로 불편을 느꼈다. 미국인들은 무한한 양의 음식이 항상 있기를 요구하게 되었다. 나는 사람들이 뷔페 스타일의 식당에서 접시에 음식을 수북이 쌓는 것을 보아왔다. 영리한 움직임의 일환으로 일부 식당들은 "마음대로 가져가시되 가져간 것은 모두 드십시오."라는 문구를 붙여놓는 방법을 고안해야만 했다.

03 내 친구 하나가 주말 스키 여행을 떠나려고 하던 중 자신의 오토바이 할부금을 내지 않은 것이 기억났다. 월요일이 만기인데 자신은 우표가 없었다. 게다가 우체국은 문을 닫은 상태였다. 그래서 그는 할부금을 넣은 봉투의 우측 상단에 25센트 동전을 붙이고는 그 밑에 '제발 부탁드립니다.'라고 쓴 후 우체통에 넣었다. 다음 주에 내 친구는 흰 봉투 하나를 받았다. 봉투의 안쪽에 카드에 5센트 동전이 붙여져 있었고, 그 밑에 우체국 직원이 펜으로 '이번만 해드립니다.'라고 써둔 것이었다.

04 해변에 가는 것을 좋아하지, 그렇지? 수영? 파도타기? 낚시? 스노클링? 스쿠버 다이빙? 잠깐! 대체 무슨 생각을 하고 있는 거야? 신문도 안 보나? TV는 보나? 상어들이 해안가를 따라 떼 지어 다니고, 수영하는 사람들을 물고, 잡아먹기도 하는 거 몰라? 이 죠스가 되고 싶어 하는 놈들에게 공격당할지 모르는 위험을 감수해야 하겠어?

05 과거에, 전시에 정보를 제대로 공개하지 않는 것은 끔찍한 결과를 낳았다. 1969년에 있었던 캄보디아에 대한 비밀 폭탄 투하를 상기해보라. 대통령인 닉슨은 심지어 미 의회도 그걸 모르게 했다. 북베트남인들은 미국인들을 위험에 빠뜨릴 수 있었던 그 공격들을 잘 알고 있었다. 미국인들은 여러 고려해야 할 상황들로부터 배제되었고, 이것이 그 전쟁에 대한 분노를 증폭시켰다. 오늘날, 부시 정부는 전쟁을 하려는 자신의 노력을 방어하려는 하나의 방법으로 정보를 제한하는 일괄 프로그램을 만들고 있다. 그러한 조치들은 미국인들이 지키기 위해 그렇게 싸워왔던 바로 그 자유의 정신을 침해했다. 그것들은 정부가 하고 있는 것을 국회의원이나 일반 대중들이 알았을 때, 취하게 될 정부의 결정에 대한 견제를 무력화시킬 위험이 있다.

06 모피를 얻기 위해 동물을 죽이는 것은 잘못된 일이다. 귀여운 밍크와 꼭 껴안고 싶은 미국 너구리, 사랑스러운 하프 바다표범을 생각해 보라. 이 동물들은 우리를 해치지 않는다. 그런데 왜 우리는 이러한 사랑스런 동물들을 잔인하게 죽이는가? 강아지를 떠올려보라. 강아지의 영혼이 담긴 진심어린 눈을 그려보라. 당신은 자신의 몸에 오명의 가죽을 입기를 원하는가? 지각 있는 사람이라면 누구든 그 대답은 확실히 '아니오.'일 것이다.

07 한 사장이 직원들이 빈둥거리고 있는 것을 보자 심기가 불편했다. "내가 이곳에 올 때마다 보지 않았으면 하는 광경을 보게 되었습니다. 나는 공정한 사람이니 여러분들을 신경 쓰게 하는 것이 있다면 나에게 말하시오. 의견함을 놓겠으니 오늘처럼 내가 본 광경을 다시 보지 않게 하도록 이것을 이용해 주시기 바랍니다." 그날 밤 사장이 상자를 열었을 땐 단 하나의 쪽지만 들어 있었는데, "고무창을 댄 신발을 신지 말아 주세요!"라고 쓰여 있었다.

08 요즘 엄마가 된다는 것은 쉬운 일이 아니다. 대다수의 엄마들은 부모로서의 의무뿐 아니라 집 바깥에서도 일을 한다. 높은 이혼율로 인해서, 많은 엄마들은 자녀들을 홀로 키우거나 아이들의 아빠들로부터 시간제로 도움을 받아서 키우고 있다. 2001년, (미국의) ABC 방송의 한 뉴스 컬럼니스트는 연구를 했는데, 그것이 시사하는 바는 다음과 같다. 만일 엄마들이 하는 일들에 대해 임금을 지불한다면, 일 년에 약 50만 달러(6억 원 정도)를 지불해야 한다. 엄마들은 (집에서 하는 일이 아닌) 다른 직업이 있든 없든 간에, 벅찬 일에 직면해 있다.

09 오스카 와일드는 자신에 대한 재판에서, 판사가 "그대는 본 법정에 대한 경멸을 보이려고 하는가?"라고 묻자, "아니 반대로, 난 그것을 숨기려 하고 있지요."라고 대답했다.

10 씨비스킷은 역사상 가장 놀라운 순종 경주마 가운데 하나다. 1936년부터 1940년까지, 미국인들은 그 조그맣고 볼품 없는 경주마가 우승자가 되는 것을 보기 위해 경기장으로 몰려들었다. 그 말은 이상한 걸음걸이를 했지만, 압도적인 속도로 질주했다; 온유한 성품이었지만 놀랍도록 경쟁심이 강하였다; 말을 들을 때까진 자기 고집이 강했다.

11 부시 가족이 돈이 되는 신탁자금에 의지해서 (호의호식하며) 살아가며 내 아버지와 같이 열심히 일하는 사람들의 호주머니를 털어가는 정부 정책을 발의하는 것을 보는 것은 정말이지 멋진 일이다.

Summarizing

2S2R 전략적 독해의 3단계에 해당하는 요약하기summarizing는 요지를 정확하게 파악하는 데 도움이 되는데, 보통 100여 자 정도의 짧은 글의 요약은 요지와 유사하다. 따라서 요지를 잘 파악하려면 요약하기의 기술을 활용해야 한다. 좋은 요약은 작거나 반복되는 세부사항을 포함하지 않는다. 주제문은 일반적인 요약보다 더 짧은 요약이므로 핵심 주장만을 드러낼 뿐 논거와 부연설명을 포함하지 않는다. 정리해서 보자.

요악하기는 글의 중요한 부분을 **훨씬 짧은 형식**으로 다시 말하는 것으로, 좋은 요약을 하기 위한 방법은 다음과 같다.

① 요약할 글의 전 지문을 주의 깊게 읽는다.
② main idea와 major supporting points에 밑줄을 긋거나 리스트를 따로 체크한다.
③ 지문의 main idea를 요약의 가장 중요한 부분으로 포함시킨다. 이 main idea를 요약의 첫 번째 문장에 놓는다.
④ 원 지문에 있던 사실들과 개념들을 그것들 사이의 논리적 일관성을 보여주는 문장으로 재구성하여 쓴다. 이때 상호간의 논리적 연관관계가 명확해야 한다.
⑤ 원래 지문에 있던 불필요한 단어들을 반복하지 않는다. minor details, repeated details, the reader's opinion을 포함하지 않는다.
⑥ 요점과 요점 사이에 비약이 있어선 안 된다.
⑦ 한 문단의 요약은 그 문단의 요지와 동일하다. 하지만, 요지를 여러분 자신의 언어로 바꾸어 쓸rephrase; paraphrase수록 더욱 좋은 요약이 된다.
⑧ 원래의 지문을 4분의 1로 줄이는 것이 좋다.

■ **Summary할 때 자주 사용되는 연결사(Transitional Signal Words)**

Transition Signal	Common Terms		
To indicate addition to the original train of thought (원래 있던 것에 더 첨가하고자 할 때)	also further moreover too	in addition furthermore second	first last secondly

To indicate a change, challenge, or contradiction (이미 있던 것에 대해 변화, 도전, 또는 반박 등을 나타낼 때)	although by (in) contrast nevertheless rather yet	after all despite that fact on the other hand regardless	but however on the contrary still
To point out similarities (유사성을 강조할 때)	likewise in the same vein	by the same token similarly	
To introduce examples and/or illustrations (예시나 사례 따위를 도입할 때)	for example specifically	for instance that is	in other words
To introduce the effect of some cause (결과를 나타낼 때)	as a result in response	consequently therefore	hence thus
To help readers follow a time sequence (시간의 흐름을 나타낼 때)	afterward finally next then	after a while in the meantime of late thereafter	before in time soon
To repeat a point made before (반복, 정리할 때)	in brief in short to reiterate	in conclusion in summary to sum up	in other words on the whole to repeat

📝 예제

01 다음을 3단어로 요약하시오.

The small cowboy put the saddle on his horse, untied him from the fence, waved good bye and rode off the sunset.

Summary : _____

해설 위의 요약의 방법을 이용하여 보자. ④번의 원리, 즉, "원 지문에 있던 사실들과 개념들을 그것들 사이의 논리적 일관성을 보여주는 문장으로 재구성하여 쓴다. 이때 상호간의 논리적 연관관계가 명확해야 한다."를 응용해보면,
① put the saddle on his horse
② untied him from the fence
③ waved good bye
④ rode off the sunset
위의 4가지 사실들을 논리적 일관성의 측면에서 재구성해보면, 결국 그 카우보이가 '떠났다'라는 것을 뒷받침하는 것일 따름이다. 따라서 요약하면, "The cowboy left."가 되는 것이다.

02 다음을 5단어로 요약하시오.

Elena put her pens and pencils neatly in a row, turned on the radio, stacked her English books on the desk, got herself a soda, and sat down in her desk chair.

Summary : _____

해설 예제 1번에 썼던 요약의 방법을 다시 이용하여 보자. ④번의 원리, 즉, "원 지문에 있던 사실들과 개념들을 그것들 사이의 논리적 일관성을 보여주는 문장으로 재구성하여 쓴다. 이때 상호간의 논리적 연관관계가 명확해야 한다."를 응용해보면,

① **put** her pens and pencils neatly in a row
② **turned on** the radio
③ **stacked** her English books on the desk
④ **got** herself a soda
⑤ **sat down** in her desk chair

이 5가지의 문장—"펜과 연필을 깔끔히 일렬로 놓은" 다음, "라디오를 켜고" "책상에 영어책을 올려놓고" "소다를 준비해서" "의자에 앉았다"—을 읽고 무슨 생각이 드는가? 라디오를 틀어 놓았으니, 춤을 추려고 하는 것이라 생각할 수도 있고, 펜과 연필을 깔끔히 일렬로 놓은 뒤 연필로 (개그맨 최양락이 잘하던) 알까기를 하려고 하는 것이라 생각할 수도 있고, 소다를 준비하는 것을 보니 영화를 보려 하는 것이라 생각할 수도 있다. 하지만 각각의 생각들이 맞는다 하더라도 전체 글의 논리적 맥락에서 볼 때 위의 생각들은 각각의 사실들 사이의 논리적 일관성을 보여주지 못하고 있다. 즉, 다시 말하면, '춤을 추는' 사실과 '알까기를 하려는' 사실과 '영화를 보려는' 사실과 사이에는 그 어떠한 논리적 연관성이 없다는 것이다. 따라서 사실들 사이의 논리적 일관성을 고려할 때 위의 문장은 Elena가 공부하려고 준비 중이라는 내용으로 요약을 해야하는 것이다. 따라서 "Elena got ready to study."가 가장 좋은 요약이 된다.

03 다음을 한 문장으로 요약하시오.

Although several early societies experimented with paper currency—most notably the Chinese during the 1st millennium B.C.—Coins of silver and gold predominated as the major form of exchange over early experiences with paper currency. The reasons were understandable enough : coins were far more durable than paper and less likely to be destroyed by fire, and coins contained the very precious metals that made money worth its salt. It required a leap of both imagination and of courage to establish a form of currency that was only backed by a precious metal but of itself was intrinsically worthless.

Summary : _____

정답 | **01** The cowboy left.

02 Elena got ready to study.

03 Because silver and gold were more durable, less flammable, and more intrinsically valuable, they predominated over early paper money.

해설 2단계로 나누어 요약을 해보자.

Step 1. 다음의 A와 B 둘 중 더 타당한 요약을 골라보자.

A. Although several early societies experimented with paper currency—most notably the Chinese during the 1st millennium B. C.—Coins of silver and gold predominated as the major form of exchange over early experiences with paper currency.

B. Coins of silver and gold predominated as the major form of exchange over early experiences with paper currency.

당연히 문장 B가 더 적절하다. 하지만 이것만으로는 불충분하다. 다음의 2단계를 보자.

Step 2. 이 글의 핵심 정보는 '동전이 종이돈보다 주요 통화수단이었다.'는 것만이 아니라 '왜' 그렇게 됐는지에 대한 것도 포함하고 있다. 따라서 이 둘의 주요 핵심 내용이 들어가야 올바른 요약이 된다. 여기서 항상 유념할 것은 여러분 자신의 언어로 '바꾸어 써야(rephrase; paraphrase)'한다는 것이다.

다시 요약해보면, "Because silver and gold were more durable, less flammable, and more intrinsically valuable, they predominated over early paper money."가 적절한 요약이 된다.

[4-11] 다음의 문장들을 요약하시오.

04 As the bus rolled into his hometown, Sammy looked around at the familiar streets and shops which he had not seen for twenty years.

Summary : _____

05 Anthony put on his raincoat, picked up his umbrella from the table near the door, turned off the lights, put out the cat, and got ready for his twenty-minute walk to the bus stop.

Summary : _____

06 When the Kim family returned from their vacation, they found the back door broken open, the television set missing, and all the food in their freezer gone.

Summary : _____

07 In Anthony's library you can find mysteries, novels, biographies, travel books, how-to manuals, science fiction thrillers, and reference books.

Summary : _____

08 With her new credit card, Elena bought groceries at the supermarket, shoes at the department store, and a new set of tires for her sports car at the auto supply store.

Summary : _____

09 During the summer along the Charles River in Boston, you can go rollerblading, running, biking, or sailing, or you can have a picnic, listen to a concert, or watch a movie.

Summary : _____

10 After clearing away the old leaves and branches, Anthony dug up the hard ground, mixed in fertilizer and new soil, raked it all smooth, and planted the seeds.

Summary : _____

11 When he heard the weather forecast, Anthony closed the windows, put tape across the glass, moved all of his plants and chairs indoors, and stocked up on bottles of fresh water.

Summary : _____

정답 | **04** Sammy came home.
05 Anthony left the house.
06 The Kims were robbed.
07 Anthony has a variety of books.
08 Elena bought many things with her credit card.
09 You can do many things along the Charles in the summertime.
10 Anthony planted a garden.
11 Anthony prepared for the storm.

[12-16] 다음의 문단들을 요약하시오.

12

While shopping malls have changed American life, not all of their effects have been positive. Most of the shops and services found in malls are parts of large corporations. These businesses have taken away customers from smaller shops in the area and forced them to close. That has meant fewer individually owned businesses and less local control over jobs. In addition, malls are harmful to the environment. They have sometime been built on land that is important for the survival of birds and wild animals. Wherever they are built, they cover large areas with buildings and parking lots instead of trees or grass. Thus, they contribute to the general loss of nature. And finally, malls are usually far from any town center, so people must use cars to get there. This results in increased air pollution and heavy traffic on the roads near the mall.

Summary : _____

13

By 1984, NASA, the United States space program, had carried out many successful flights of the space shuttle. In fact, Americans were beginning to take the whole NASA program for granted. Then, the president announced that the next shuttle would carry a school teacher into space. Hundreds of teachers from all parts of the country applied for the job. They all wanted to be "the first teacher in space." During the next year, these adventurous educators were tested and examined and trained. At last, the choice was announced. A teacher from New Hampshire, Christa MacAuliffe, would be the first teacher-astronaut.

Summary : _____

14

Everyone knows what happened on that terrible day in January, 1986. Early in the morning, the Challenger crew had a good breakfast and discussed their plans. They made sure they understood all of the work they would be doing during the flight. Later, they boarded a special van which carried them to the shuttle. The weather was rather cold, and some NASA officials wondered if they should put off the flight. After some discussion, they decided to go ahead. The Challenger took off over the Atlantic Ocean in Florida. Minutes later, it exploded in the air. All of the crew members died in the crash.

Summary : _____

15

People who are looking for outdoor adventure often go to Maine. This state in the northeastern United States contains large areas of wilderness. There you can enjoy a new and exciting sport : white water rafting. In the past, this sport was practiced only in the western states. But now, several outdoor travel companies offer weekend rafting trips. They provide guide service, equipment, and even food and they invite people who have had no experience at all. Thus, city residents, too, can get a taste of wilderness. All they need to bring with them is a desire for adventure.

"White water" is the water of a river when it moves very fast over rocky areas. As the water fills with air bubbles, it looks white. The areas of white water are also the most exciting areas for rafters—and also the most dangerous. In fact, rafting guides must always be on the look for white water. And rafters must be ready to swim, because the raft can tip over in white water. For that reason, rafters should always wear special life vests that will keep them afloat.

Rafting is a sport that almost anyone can do. It does not require great physical strength. Sometimes, at very rocky parts of the river, rafters will need to walk for a while. They may also need to carry the rubber rafts at times, but these are very light. Paddling the boats is easy because they are going down river. The main activity is simply to enjoy the wonderful wild scenery.

Most rafting companies offer overnight trips that combine with camping. This kind of trip is ideal for a family with children over twelve. Several rafts of people will start out from a base camp. Their food supplies, sleeping bags, tents, and other necessities are sometimes packed onto the rafts. Or all the supplies might be brought by car to the next camp site. The guide often is also the cook for the group of rafters and may be quite a good chef. After a day of rafting, in any case, the food tastes good and sleep comes easily.

Write one sentence to summarize each paragraph.

Paragraph 1 : _____

Paragraph 2 : _____

Paragraph 3 : _____

Paragraph 4 : _____

Summary : _____

16 Summarize the passage in approximately 100 words.

In nineteenth-century America, most migrants went west because the region seemed to promise a better life. Railroad expansion made remote farming regions accessible, and the construction of grain elevators eased problems of shipping and storage. As a result of population growth, the demand for farm products grew rapidly, and the prospects for commercial agriculture—growing crops for profit— became more favorable than ever.

Life on the farm, however, was much harder than the advertisements and railroad agents suggested. Migrants often encountered shortages of essentials they had once taken for granted. The open prairies contained little lumber for housing and fuel. Pioneer families were forced to build houses of sod and to burn manure for heat. Water was sometimes as scarce as timber. Few families were lucky or wealthy enough to buy land near a stream that did not dry up in summer and freeze in winter. Machinery for drilling wells was scarce until the 1880s, and even then it was very expensive.

The weather was seldom predictable. In summer, weeks of torrid heat and parching winds often gave way to violent storms that washed away crops and property. In winter, the wind and cold from blizzards piled up mountainous snowdrifts that halted all outdoor movement. During the Great Blizzard that struck Nebraska and the Dakota Territory in January 1888, the temperature plunged to 36 degrees below zero, and the wind blew at 56 miles per hour. The storm stranded schoolchildren and killed several parents who ventured out to rescue them. In the spring, melting snow swelled streams, and floods threatened millions of acres. In the fall, a week without rain could turn dry grasslands into tinder, and the slightest spark could ignite a raging prairie fire.

Nature could be cruel even under good conditions. Weather that was favorable for crops was also good for breeding insects. Worms and flying pests ravaged corn and wheat. In the 1870s and 1880s swarms of grasshoppers virtually ate up entire farms. Heralded only by the din of buzzing wings, a mile-long cloud of insects would smother the land and devour everything : plants, tree bark, and clothes. As one farmer lamented, the "hoppers left behind nothing but the mortgage."

Summary : _____

_____

_____

_____

_____

정답 | **12** Malls can have negative effects on local business and on the environment.

13 In 1984, NASA chose Christmas Macauliffe, a school teacher, to be an astronaut.

14 The Challenger exploded in 1986.

15 Paragraph 1 : Many people go white-water rafting in Maine.

Paragraph 2 : White-water ratting, which is done on fast-moving rivers, is exciting but dangerous.

Paragraph 3 : Rafting is easy and enjoyable.

Paragraph 4 : Most rafting trips include an overnight stay with good food.

Summary : Many people can go white-water rafting in Maine. White-water rafting, which is done on fast-moving rivers, is easy and exciting but dangerous. Most trips include an overnight stay and a good dinner.

16 During the nineteenth century, countless men and women went west in the belief that farming was a way to make money and improve their lot in life but most found it harder and more rigorous than expected. Essentials like lumber and water were hard to come by. The weather was both harsh and unpredictable. In winter, the temperature might plunge as low as 36 degrees below zero while the wind could blow at 56 miles per hour. In summer, scorching heat and drought would suddenly be followed by slashing rainstorms. Insects were an additional problem and plagues of them could devour entire farms.

한글 번역

예제 **01** 그 키 작은 카우보이는 말에 안장을 얹고, 말뚝으로부터 말을 풀고, 작별 인사를 하고, 석양 속으로 말을 타고 갔다.

02 엘레나는 펜과 연필을 깔끔히 일렬로 늘어놓고, 라디오를 켜고, 책상에 영어책들을 올려놓고, 소다를 준비한 다음 의자에 앉았다.

03 비록 여러 초기 사회들이 지폐를 시험해보았지만―이것의 가장 주목할 만한 예로는 기원전 1000년 동안 중국인들이 있다―은화나 금화가 종이 화폐를 쓴 초기 경험을 뛰어넘고 주요한 교환수단으로 우세하게 자리 잡았다. 이유는 충분히 이해할 만하다. 동전은 종이보다 훨씬 내구성이 좋았고, 불에 파손될 우려가 적었으며, 제구실을 할 만한 귀금속을 가지고 있었다. 귀금속이 뒷받침만 해 줄 뿐 그 자체로는 내재적 가치가 없는 하나의 통화 형태를 만들기 위해서는 상상력과 용기 양쪽에서 도약을 해야 하는 일이었다.

04 고향마을로 버스가 들어가자 새미는 자신이 20년간 보아 왔던 익숙한 거리들과 상점들을 둘러보았다.

05 앤서니는 비옷을 걸치고 문가의 테이블에서 우산을 집어 들고, 불을 끄고, 고양이를 내보내고 버스 정류장을 향해 20분간의 산보를 위한 준비를 마쳤다.

06 김씨 가족이 휴가에서 돌아왔을 때, 그들은 뒷문이 부서져 열려 있고, 텔레비전이 없어졌으며, 냉장고의 음식이 모두 사라진 것을 발견했다.

07 앤서니의 서가에서 당신은 미스테리물, 소설, 전기, 여행 서적, 방법 매뉴얼, SF 소설, 그리고 참고 서적들을 볼 수 있다.

08 엘레나는 새 신용카드로 수퍼마켓에서 먹을 것들을 사고, 백화점에서 신발을 사고, 자동차 용품점에서 자신의 스포츠카에 넣을 새 타이어를 샀다.

09 보스톤의 찰스 강변에서 여름 동안 롤러블레이드를 탈 수도 있고, 달리기도 할 수 있고, 자전거 타기나 배 타기를 할 수도 있고, 아니면 소풍을 가거나 음악회를 듣거나 영화를 볼 수도 있다.

10 오래된 나뭇잎들과 나뭇가지들을 치운 후 앤서니는 단단한 땅을 파고 새 흙을 비료에 섞고, 전부 평평하게 갈퀴로 긁은 다음 씨를 뿌렸다.

11 기상예보를 들었을 때 앤서니는 창문을 닫고 유리창에 테이프를 두르고 화분들과 의자들을 집안으로 들여놓고 생수 병을 쌓아 비축해 놓았다.

12 쇼핑몰이 미국인의 생활을 변화시키고 있지만, 이러한 모든 결과가 긍정적인 것은 아니다. 쇼핑몰에 있는 대부분의 상점들과 서비스 업체들은 대기업에서 운영하는 것이다. 이러한 상점들은 지역에 있는 소규모 상점들로부터 손님을 빼앗아 가고 결국 문을 닫게 만든다. 이것은 더 적은 개인 사업자들과 지역민에게 더 적은 일자리가 주어짐을 의미한다. 게다가, 쇼핑몰은 환경에 해롭다. 그것들은 새나 야생동물들의 생존에 있어 중요한 지역 위에 건설된다. 그것들이 건설될 때마다, 나무나 잔디 대신 건물들이나 주차장으로 넓은 지역이 덮이게 된다. 따라서, 그것들은 자연의 전체적인 훼손에 책임이 있다. 마지막으로, 쇼핑몰은 대개 도시의 중심지와 멀리 떨어져 있어서, 사람들은 그 곳에 가기 위해 자동차를 이용해야 한다. 이것은 증가된 공기 오염과 근처에 있는 도로의 심한 정체를 유발시킨다.

13 1984년까지 미국 우주 프로그램은 많은 우주 비행선의 성공적인 항해를 이루어내고 있었다. 사실상, 미국인들은 모든 NASA의 프로그램들을 당연하게 여기기 시작했다. 그리고 나서, 대통령은 다음 비행선이 학교 교사들을 우주로 보낼 것이라고 발표했다. 전국의 수백 명의 교사들이 이 일에 지원했다. 그들은 모두 '우주로 가는 첫 번째 교사'가 되기를 원했다. 다음 해에, 이러한 모험적인 교육자들은 시험을 치르고 검사를 받고 훈련을 받았다. 결국, 선출자가 발표되었다. 뉴햄프셔의 교사인, 크리스타 맥아울리프가 첫 번째 교사―우주비행사가 될 것이다.

14 1986년 1월의 어느 끔찍한 날에 무슨 일이 발생했는지 누구나 알고 있다. 이른 아침, 챌린저호의 승무원들이 기분 좋게 아침 식사를 마치고 그들의 계획에 대해 논의했다. 그들은 비행 중 해야 할 임무들에 대해 모두 이해하고 있음을 확인했다. 그 후, 그들은 비행선으로 그들을 데려다줄 특별한 밴 차량에 탑승했다. 날씨는 약간 추운 편이었고, 몇몇 NASA 직원들은 항해를 연기해야 할 지를 의아해했다. 약간의 논의 후, 그들은 강행하기로 결정했다. 챌린저호는 플로리다에서 대서양 위로 이륙했다. 몇 분 후, 그것은 하늘 위에서 폭발했다. 모든 승무원들은 사고로 사망했다.

15 야외에서 즐기는 모험을 찾는 사람들은 자주 메인으로 간다. 미국의 동북부에 위치하고 있는 이곳은 드넓은 야생의 지역이다. 그곳에서 여러분들은 새롭고 흥미진진한 스포츠를 즐길 수 있는데, 그것은 급류타기이다. 과거에는, 서부에 있는 지역에서만 이 스포츠를 했었다. 그러나 현재, 몇 개의 야외 활동을 취급하는 여행사가 주말 급류타기 관광을 선보이고 있다. 그들은 가이드와 장비, 그리고 음식을 제공하기도 하고, 전혀 경험이 없는 사람들을 초대하기도 한다. 따라서, 도시 거주자들도 야생의 참맛을 맛볼 수 있다. 그들이 필요한 것은 모험을 하고자 하는 마음만 가지고 가면 되는 것이다.

'급류'는 강물이 암석 지역위로 빠르게 이동할 때 발생하는 것이다. 물이 공기 방울로 가득찰 때, 그것은 하얗게 보인다. 급류 지역은 또한 급류타기를 즐기는 사람들에게 가장 흥미진진한 지역이고, 가장 위험한 지역이기도 하다. 사실, 급류타기 가이드는 늘 급류를 주의 깊게 살피고 있어야 한다. 그리고 급류타기를 하는 사람들은 수영을 할 대비를 하고 있어야 하는데 보트가 급류로 들어갈 수 있기 때문이다. 이러한 이유로, 급류타기를 하는 사람들은 늘 물 위에 뜰 수 있도록 하는 특별한 구명조끼를 입어야 한다.

급류타기는 거의 누구나 할 수 있는 스포츠이다. 그것은 큰 물리적 힘을 필요로 하지 않는다. 때로는, 강의 암석 지역에서, 급류타기를 하는 사람들은 잠시 걸어야 할 필요가 있다. 그들은 또한 때때로 고무보트를 날라야 할 필요가 있지만, 이 보트는 매우 가볍다. 보트를 노 저으며 가는 것은 매우 쉬운데, 보트가 강 아래로 흘러 내려가기 때문이다. 주 활동은 야생의 멋진 경치를 즐기기만 하면 되는 것이다.

대부분의 급류타기 여행사들은 캠핑을 결합시킨 1박 2일의 관광상품을 내놓고 있다. 이러한 여행은 12세 이상의 아이들이 있는 가족에게 이상적이다. 몇몇 사람들은 베이스 캠프에서 시작할 것이다. 음식, 침낭, 텐트와 다른 필수품들은 그 보트에 함께 챙겨진다. 또는 모든 물품들을 자동차로 다음 캠프 지역으로 나를 수 있다. 대개 가이드는 급류타기 하는 사람들의 요리사가 되기도 하는데 꽤 훌륭한 요리사일 것이다. 급류타기를 하고 나면, 어쨌든 간에, 음식 맛이 좋고 잠도 쉽게 든다.

16 19세기 미국에서 대부분의 이민자들은 서부로 갔다. 그 이유는 그 지역이 더 나은 삶을 약속한 것처럼 보였기 때문이다. 철도의 확장은 거리가 먼 농장 지역을 접근하기 쉽게 만들었고, 양곡기의 건설은 수송과 저장의 문제를 완화시켰다. 인구 증가의 결과로써, 농작물 생산을 위한 수요는 빠르게 증가했고, 이윤을 위한 작물들 같은 상업적 농업의 전망은 그 어떤 때보다 더 유리해졌다.

그러나 농장에서의 삶은 광고나 철도청에서 제시한 것보다 훨씬 더 힘들었다. 이주민들은 이미 한번 그들이 양도 받았던 본질적 요소들의 결핍에 자주 직면하였다. 개방된 대초원은 집과 연료를 위한 적은 양의 제재들을 포함하였다. 개척자 가족들은 잔디에 집을 짓고, 열을 위해 거름을 태웠다. 물은 때때로 재목과 같이 부족하였다. 몇몇 일가는 운이 좋았는데, 여름에 메마르거나 겨울에 얼지 않는 개울이 있는 땅을 살 수 있는 충분한 부가 축적되어 있었기 때문이다. 씨를 잘 조파하기 위한 기계류는 1880년대까지 부족하였고, 매우 비싸기까지 했다.

날씨는 좀처럼 예측하기 어려웠다. 여름에 타는 듯한 열과 바싹 마르게 하는 바람이 있는 주기는 작물과 소유물들을 씻어 없애는 격렬한 폭풍에 의해 무너졌다. 겨울에는 눈보라로 인한 바람과 추위가 모든 외부의 움직임을 멈추게 하는 거대한 눈 더미를 쌓아올렸다. 1888년 1월, 네브래스카와 다코타 지역은 대폭풍설로 인해 갇히게 되었는데 그 당시 온도는 영하 36도로 급락했고, 바람은 시속 56마일이었다. 그 폭풍은 학생들을 오도 가도 못하게 했고, 아이들을 구하기 위해 위험을 무릅쓴 몇몇 학부모들을 죽이기도 했다. 봄에는 녹은 눈이 시냇물의 수위를 증가시켰고, 홍수가 100만 에이커를 위협했다. 가을에 비가 없는 주간에는 불이 붙기 쉽게 대초원이 건조해지고, 아주 미약한 불꽃이 격렬한 대초원의 불이 되어 태울 수 있었다.

자연은 좋은 조건 속에서도 무자비할 수 있다. 작물에게 유리한 날씨는 곤충을 번식시키기에도 좋은 조건이다. 애벌레나 파리 유해물들은 옥수수와 밀을 황폐화시켰다. 1870년대와 1880년대에 메뚜기 떼들은 전체 농작물을 사실상 먹어치웠다. 날개의 윙윙거리는 소음에 의한 포고로 1마일이나 떨어져 있는 곤충 떼는 땅을 완전히 덮어버리고, 작물 그리고 나무껍질, 직물 등 모든 것을 게걸스레 먹었다. 한 농부는 "메뚜기들은 저당 증서 빼고 모든 것을 앗아갔다."며 한탄하였다.

Summary : 19세기 동안, 무수한 남자와 여자는 농사만이 돈을 벌 수 있고, 그들의 삶에서 많은 것을 향상시킬 거란 믿음을 가지고 서부로 갔다. 하지만 농부의 삶은 그들이 예상했던 것보다 훨씬 어렵고 혹독하였다. 필수인 제재들과 물조차도 얻기 어려웠다. 날씨는 가혹하였고 예측하기도 힘들었다. 겨울에는 바람이 시속 56마일이 부는 동안 온도는 영하 36도까지 떨어졌다. 여름에는 통렬한 더위와 가뭄이 맹렬한 폭풍우에 의해 따라다녔다. 곤충들은 특별한 문제였는데 그들의 재해는 온 농장을 망쳐버릴 수 있었다.

유희태 일반영어 ①
2S2R
기본

2S2R 적용

01 Read the passage and follow the directions.

We crunch and chew our way through vast quantities of snacks and confectionaries and relieve our thirst with multicolored, flavored soft drinks, with and without calories, for two basic reasons. The first is simple: the food tastes good, and we enjoy the sensation of eating it. Second, we associate these foods, often without being aware of it, with the highly pleasurable experiences depicted in the advertisements used to promote their sale. Current television advertisements demonstrate this point: people turn from grumpiness to euphoria after crunching a corn chip. Others water ski into the sunset with their loved ones while drinking a popular soft drink. People entertain on the patio with friends, cook over campfires without mosquitoes, or go to carnivals with granddad munching away at the latest candy or snack food. The people portrayed in these scenarios are all healthy, vigorous, and good looking; one wonders how popular the food they convince us to eat would be if they would crunch or drink away while complaining about low back pain or clogged sinuses.

MEMO

Explain why people consume snacks and soft drinks. Second, describe how television advertisements portray people eating snack foods.

_____

_____

_____

NOTE

Step 1	Survey
Key Words	
Signal Words	
Step 2	**Reading**
Purpose	
Pattern of Organization	
Tone	
Main Idea	
Step 3	**Summary**
지문 요약하기 (Paraphrasing)	
Step 4	**Recite**
	요약문 말로 설명하기

Answer Key

We crunch and chew our way through vast quantities of **snacks** and confectionaries and relieve our thirst with multicolored, flavored **soft drinks**, with and without calories, for two basic reasons. The first is simple: the food tastes good, and we enjoy the sensation of eating it. Second, we associate these foods, often without being aware of it, with the highly pleasurable experiences depicted in **the advertisements** used to promote their sale. Current **television advertisements** demonstrate this point: people turn from grumpiness to euphoria after crunching a corn chip. Others water ski into the sunset with their loved ones while drinking a popular soft drink. People entertain on the patio with friends, cook over campfires without mosquitoes, or go to carnivals with granddad munching away at the latest candy or snack food. The people portrayed in **these scenarios** are all healthy, vigorous, and good looking; one wonders how popular the food they convince us to eat would be if they would crunch or drink away while complaining about low back pain or clogged sinuses.

→ key words

→ signal word

→ key words

모범답안

They eat it because of the flavor and also because of the positive lifestyle images in the commercial. Second, they portray them euphoric, with friends and loved ones doing pleasant things.

한글 번역

우리가 어마어마한 양의 스낵과 사탕과자를 오도독 부수고 씹으며, 칼로리가 있든지 말든지 간에 다양한 색깔의 맛이 들어간 음료수로 갈증을 해소하는 데는, 두 가지 기본적인 이유가 있다. 첫 번째는 간단하다; 음식의 맛이 좋고, 우리가 그것을 먹을 때 느껴지는 감각을 즐기기 때문이다. 두 번째, 우리는 의식하지 못한 채 광고에서 판매를 촉진하기 위해 묘사된 매우 즐거운 경험을 그 음식들과 연관시킨다. 현재 TV 광고는 이런 면을 입증한다: 사람들은 콘칩을 먹고 나서 기분이 언짢은 상태에서 행복한 상태로 바뀐다. 어떤 사람들은 인기 있는 음료수를 마시면서 저녁 노을 아래 사랑하는 사람들과 수상 스키를 탄다. 사람들은 파티오에서 친구들과 즐거운 시간을 보내며 모기가 없이 모닥불 위에서 요리를 하거나, 최신의 사탕 혹은 스낵을 우걱우걱 먹으며 할아버지와 축제에 간다. 이런 시나리오에 묘사된 사람들은 모두 건강하고, 활기차며, 잘생긴 외모를 지녔다; 만약 그들이 요통이나 코막힘을 호소하며 음식을 먹거나 음료를 마신다면, 그들이 우리로 하여금 먹도록 확신시키려는 그 음식이 얼마나 인기가 있을지에 대해서는 누군가 궁금해할지도 모른다.

NOTE

Step 1	Survey
Key Words	snacks; soft drinks; advertisements
Signal Words	two basic reasons; The first; Second
Step 2	**Reading**
Purpose	to explain why people eat junk food
Pattern of Organization	cause&effect
Tone	critical
Main Idea	There are two reasons people eat so much junk food.
Step 3	**Summary**
지문 요약하기 (Paraphrasing)	There are two reasons people eat so much junk food such as snacks and soft drinks. They eat it because of the flavor and the positive lifestyle images in the commercials.
Step 4	**Recite**
	요약문 말로 설명하기

02   Read the passage and follow the directions.

The earthquake shook down in San Francisco hundreds of thousands of dollars' worth of walls and chimneys. But the conflagration that followed burned up hundreds of millions of dollars' worth of property. There is no estimating within hundreds of millions the actual damage wrought. Not in history has a modern imperial city been so completely destroyed. San Francisco is gone! Nothing remains of it but memories and a fringe of dwelling houses on its outskirts. Its industrial section is wiped out. Its social and residential section is wiped out. The factories and warehouses, the great stores and newspaper buildings, the hotels and the palaces of the nabobs, are all gone. Remains only the fringe of dwelling houses on the outskirts of what was once San Francisco.

MEMO

What happened to the san Francisco industrial section? What were the only things that remained of San Francisco after the earthquake?

_____

_____

_____

NOTE

Step 1	Survey
Key Words	
Signal Words	
Step 2	Reading
Purpose	
Pattern of Organization	
Tone	
Main Idea	
Step 3	Summary
지문 요약하기 (Paraphrasing)	
Step 4	Recite
요약문 말로 설명하기	

02

💡 Answer Key

The earthquake shook down in San Francisco hundreds of thousands of dollars' worth of walls and chimneys. But **the conflagration** that followed burned up hundreds of millions of dollars' worth of property. There is no estimating within hundreds of millions the actual **damage** wrought. Not in history has a modern imperial city been so completely destroyed. San Francisco is gone! Nothing remains of it but memories and a fringe of dwelling houses on its outskirts. Its industrial section is wiped out. Its social and residential section is wiped out. The factories and warehouses, the great stores and newspaper buildings, the hotels and the palaces of the nabobs, are all gone. Remains only the fringe of dwelling houses on the outskirts of what was once San Francisco.

→ key words

모범답안

It was "wiped out", that is to say, destroyed. Second, the buildings at the edge of the city were the only still standing.

어휘

a fringe of 언저리에   conflagration 큰 불   dwelling house 주택
nabob 부유한 사람   wiped out 전멸하다   wrought 초래하다, 일으키다

한글 번역

지진은 샌프란시스코에서 수십만 달러 가치의 벽과 굴뚝들을 무너뜨렸다. 하지만 그것에 뒤따른 큰 불은 수억 원의 재산을 태워버렸다. 실제 피해 액수를 정확히 측정한 바는 없었다. 역사에서 현대 제국의 도시가 그렇게 완전히 파괴된 적이 없었다. 샌프란시스코가 사라진 것이다! 추억과 변두리에 있는 언저리의 주택 말고는 남은 것이 하나도 없었다. 샌프란시스코의 산업 구역은 완전히 전멸하였다. 사회지역과 거주지역도 완전히 전멸하였다. 공장과 창고, 대형마트, 신문사 빌딩, 호텔, 통치자의 궁전들은 모두 사라졌다. 변두리의 주변 주택만 남은 곳이 한때 샌프란시스코였다.

NOTE

Step 1	Survey
Key Words	The earthquake in San Francisco; conflagration; destroyed; wiped out
Signal Words	none
Step 2	**Reading**
Purpose	to describe the effects of the devastating San Francisco earthquake
Pattern of Organization	cause&effect
Tone	emotional
Main Idea	The earthquake in San Francisco caused the devastating damage.
Step 3	**Summary**
지문 요약하기 (Paraphrasing)	The earthquake in San Francisco caused the devastating damage.
Step 4	**Recite**
요약문 말로 설명하기	

03 Read the passage and follow the directions.

We did it. With less than two months to go until our second child is scheduled to arrive, my husband and I swallowed our pride, plundered our savings and joined the much ridiculed ranks of minivan owners. It had to be done. Neither of our old vehicles had what it takes to handle two car seats, two parents, the odd grandparent and the sheer tonnage of baby paraphernalia required for even quick trips to the grocery. Still, it took multiple visits to the dealership before I came to terms with the sociological enormity of what we were about to do. In America, you are what you drive. And as everyone knows, cruising around in a shiny new minivan definitively announces to your fellow road warriors, "I am an unabashed suburban breeder."

What is it that the writer and her husband did? What was the cause that made the writer and her husband take the action they did? Why do you think the writer resisted doing what she and her husband eventually did? What does the writer mean by "The sociological enormity" of what they did?

NOTE

02

Step 1	Survey
Key Words	
Signal Words	
Step 2	Reading
Purpose	
Pattern of Organization	
Tone	
Main Idea	
Step 3	Summary
지문 요약하기 (Paraphrasing)	
Step 4	Recite
요약문 말로 설명하기	

💡 Answer Key

We did it. With less than two months to go until our second child is scheduled to arrive, my husband and I swallowed our pride, plundered our savings and joined the much ridiculed ranks of minivan owners. It had to be done. Neither of our old vehicles had what it takes to handle two car seats, two parents, the odd grandparent and the sheer tonnage of baby paraphernalia required for even quick trips to the grocery. Still, it took multiple visits to the dealership before I came to terms with the sociological enormity of what we were about to do. In America, you are what you drive. And as everyone knows, cruising around in a shiny **new minivan** definitively announces to your fellow road warriors, "I am an unabashed **suburban breeder**."

→ key words

모범답안

They purchased a minivan. The practical necessity of the vehicle is to handle two children and their paraphernalia. The minivan is a cultural signal of a "suburban breeder" which they did not want to be seen in. By buying one, they are branding themselves with a new kind of identity.

한글 번역

우리는 해냈다. 둘째 아이가 태어날 때까지 두 달도 안 남은 상황에서 내 남편과 난 자존심을 굽히고, 저축한 것을 다 사용하여, 미니밴을 끄는 사람으로서 놀림 당하는 지위에 합류했다. 그래야만 했다. 우리의 예전 차 중 그 어떤 것도 두 개의 카시트와 두 명의 부모, 한 명의 조부모와, 잠깐 식료품을 사러 나갈 때조차 필요한 많은 양의 아기 용품들을 실을 수 없었다. 그러나, 우리가 하려는 일의 사회적인 심각성을 받아들이기까지 그 자동차 딜러샵을 여러 번 왔다 갔다 해야 했다. 미국에서, 당신이 운전하는 것이 당신을 의미한다. 그리고 모든 이들이 알고 있듯이, 빛나는 새 미니밴을 타고 일주를 하는 것은 당연히 너의 친구 용사들에게 "나는 부끄러움을 모르는 시골의 애 키우는 사람이다."라고 공표하는 것이다.

Step 1	Survey
Key Words	new minivan; suburban breeder
Signal Words	none

Step 2	Reading
Purpose	to explain why the narrator bought a new minivan
Pattern of Organization	cause&effect
Tone	subjective
Main Idea	The demands of a growing family led the narrator to buy a minivan. 또는 The practical necessity of the vehicle led the narrator to buy a minivan.

Step 3	Summary
지문 요약하기 (Paraphrasing)	The practical necessity of the vehicle to handle two children, their parents, the grandparent, and paraphernalia caused the narrator to buy a minivan, which she and her husband had refused.

Step 4	Recite
	요약문 말로 설명하기

04 Read the passage and follow the directions.

MEMO

Freckles are small brown spots in the skin. They are most common in people with fair skin. People are not born with freckles. Why do they suddenly appear? Cells in your skin produce a brown coloring called melanin. Melanin gives skin its color. Melanin is important because it protects skin from the harmful rays of the sun. The sunlight triggers the skin to produce more melanin. This is why you get a tan when you are in the sun. However, in some people, the melanin- producing cells work unevenly. The result is that the skin does not readily tan. Instead, the melanin appears in clumps, producing the brown spots called freckles. Between the freckles, there is little or no melanin to protect the skin from the sun's rays. Too much sunlight can damage that skin, causing it to burn. So, people with freckles are often easily sunburned. Making melanin is only one of the many functions of the skin.

What is the purpose of the passage? Write your answer by filling in the blank below with TWO words.

To explain _____ appear

02

NOTE

Step 1	Survey
Key Words	
Signal Words	
Step 2	Reading
Purpose	
Pattern of Organization	
Tone	
Main Idea	
Step 3	Summary
지문 요약하기 (Paraphrasing)	
Step 4	Recite

요약문 말로 설명하기

💡 Answer Key

Freckles are small brown spots in the skin. They are most common in people with fair skin. People are not born with freckles. Why do they suddenly appear? Cells in your skin produce a brown coloring called melanin. **Melanin** gives skin its color. Melanin is important because it protects skin from the harmful rays of the sun. The sunlight triggers the skin to produce more melanin. This is why you get a tan when you are in the sun. However, in some people, the melanin-producing cells work unevenly. The result is that the skin does not readily tan. Instead, the melanin appears in clumps, producing the brown spots called freckles. Between the freckles, there is little or no melanin to protect the skin from the sun's rays. Too much sunlight can damage that skin, causing it to burn. So, people with freckles are often easily sunburned. Making melanin is only one of the many functions of the skin.

➤ key words
➤ signal word

모범답안

To explain why freckles appear

한글 번역

주근깨는 피부에 있는 작은 갈색 반점이다. 그것들은 대부분 일반적으로 피부가 흰 사람에게 생긴다. 사람은 주근깨가 없이 태어난다. 왜 갑자기 나타나는 걸까? 피부의 세포들은 멜라닌이라 불리는 갈색의 색소를 생성한다. 멜라닌은 피부에 색소를 침착시킨다. 멜라닌은 태양의 해로운 광선으로부터 피부를 보호해주므로 중요하다. 햇빛은 피부가 더 많은 멜라닌을 생성하게 만든다. 이것이 바로 햇빛에 노출될 때 검게 그을리는 이유이다. 그러나 어떤 이들에겐 멜라닌이 만들어내는 세포가 균일하지 않게 작용한다. 그 결과 피부가 쉽게 타지 않는다. 대신에 멜라닌이 덩어리로 나타나며 주근깨라 불리는 갈색 반점을 생성한다. 주근깨 사이에는 햇빛으로부터 피부를 보호하는 멜라닌이 적거나 아예 없다. 지나친 햇빛은 화상을 유발하여 피부에 손상을 입힐 수 있다. 그래서 주근깨가 있는 사람들은 종종 쉽게 햇빛으로 인한 화상을 입는다. 멜라닌 생성은 피부의 많은 기능 중의 하나일 뿐이다.

02

NOTE ▶

Step 1	Survey
Key Words	freckles; melanin
Signal Words	why; because; result; causing; so

Step 2	Reading
Purpose	to explain why freckless appear
Pattern of Organization	definition; cause&effect
Tone	neutral
Main Idea	Freckles appear due to uneven work of melanin-producing cells.

Step 3	Summary
지문 요약하기 (Paraphrasing)	Freckles are the result of sunlight effecting melanin-producing cells unevenly in some people, meaning they are less protected from sun damage.

Step 4	Recite
	요약문 말로 설명하기

05 Read the passage and follow the directions.

Being unemployed creates many problems for my family and me. First of all, there are financial problems. We have cut back on the quality of groceries we purchase. We now buy two pounds of hamburger in place of two pounds of sirloin. This hamburger is also divided into quantities sufficient for three meals: one may be creole beef, one chili, and the other spaghetti. There is also less money for clothing. Dresses must be altered and made into blouses; pants make nice skirts after some alteration. I have two more very sticky problems. I've fallen behind in the rental payments for our apartment, and now I am experiencing difficulties trying to pay the back rent. The other sticky problem is my son's tuition payments. There does not seem to be any way that I can send a complete payment to his college. These are not the only problems I face. I also have psychological problems as a result of unemployment. Often I wonder why this has happened to me. Then depression and confusion take over, and I feel drained of all my abilities. The one question that fills my mind most often is the following: Why can't I get employment? This question evokes in me a lack of self-confidence and self-worth. I am haunted by an overall feeling of uselessness. My other problems center on trying to cope with the bureaucracy of the Employment Bureau. Once I get to the Employment Bureau, I stand in line to sign up. I then wait in another line to which I must report. Once I go through all of this, I am sent out for job interviews, only to find that the employer wants someone with more experience. To top everything off, I had to wait almost six months to receive my first unemployment check. As you can see, there is often a frustratingly long delay in receiving benefits. My family and I have suffered through many problems because of my unemployment.

What makes the writer feel "drained" of her abilities? What is the main idea of the passage?

_____

_____

_____

NOTE

Step 1	Survey
Key Words	
Signal Words	
Step 2	**Reading**
Purpose	
Pattern of Organization	
Tone	
Main Idea	
Step 3	**Summary**
지문 요약하기 (Paraphrasing)	
Step 4	**Recite**
요약문 말로 설명하기	

Answer Key

Being unemployed creates many **problems** for my family and me. First
of all, there are **financial** problems. We have cut back on the quality of   → key words
groceries we purchase. We now buy two pounds of hamburger in place
of two pounds of sirloin. This hamburger is also divided into quantities
sufficient for three meals: one may be creole beef, one chili, and the
other spaghetti. There is also less money for clothing. Dresses must be
altered and made into blouses; pants make nice skirts after some
alteration. I have two more very sticky problems. I've fallen behind in
the rental payments for our apartment, and now I am experiencing
difficulties trying to pay the back rent. The other sticky problem is my
son's tuition payments. There does not seem to be any way that I can
send a complete payment to his college. These are not the only problems
I face. I also have psychological problems as a result of unemployment.
Often I wonder why this has happened to me. Then depression and
confusion take over, and I feel drained of all my abilities. The one
question that fills my mind most often is the following: Why can't I get
employment? This question evokes in me a lack of self-confidence and
self-worth. I am haunted by an overall feeling of uselessness. My other
problems center on trying to cope with the **bureaucracy** of the
Employment Bureau. Once I get to the Employment Bureau, I stand in
line to sign up. I then wait in another line to which I must report. Once
I go through all of this, I am sent out for job interviews, only to find
that the employer wants someone with more experience. To top
everything off, I had to wait almost six months to receive my first
unemployment check. As you can see, there is often a frustratingly long
delay in receiving benefits. My family and I have suffered through many
problems because of my unemployment.

모범답안

Depression and confusion, which is caused by doubt as a result of not being able to get a job. The
main idea is that the speaker and her family have had many problems because of her
unemployment.

한글 번역

실직 상태에 있는 것은 나와 내 가족에게 많은 문제점을 안겨준다. 우선, 경제적인 어려움이다. 우리 집은 구입하는 식품품의 질을 낮추어야 했다. 우리는 2파운드 분량의 소 등심 대신 이제 2파운드의 햄버거용 고기를 사고 있다. 이 햄버거용 고기는 다시 세 끼에 맞는 양으로 나뉜다: 한 끼는 크리올 소고기, 다른 끼니는 칠리, 또 다른 끼니는 스파게티일지도 모른다. 옷에 쓰이는 돈도 더 줄었다. 드레스는 수선하여 블라우스로 만들어 입는다; 바지는 조금만 수선하면 멋진 스커트가 된다. 나에겐 매우 곤란한 문제가 두 가지 더 있다. 우리 아파트 임대 비용이 밀린 상태이고, 이것을 갚는 데 어려움을 겪고 있다. 또 다른 힘든 문제는 아들의 학비 문제이다. 아들의 대학교 학비를 완납할 방법이 없어 보인다. 내가 겪는 것은 이 문제들뿐만이 아니다. 난 실직의 영향으로 정신적 문제도 겪고 있다. 종종 왜 이런 일이 내게 일어났는지 궁금하다. 그러면 우울과 혼란이 날 덮치고 내 모든 능력이 소진된 것처럼 느낀다. 가끔 내 마음을 사로잡고 있는 한 가지 의문은 다음과 같다: 왜 나는 직업을 구할 수 없을까? 이 질문은 내게 자신감과 자부심 결여를 불러일으킨다. 내 자신이 무능한 존재라는 전반적인 생각이 나를 괴롭혔다. 나의 또 다른 문제는 고용관리국의 관리들을 상대하는 데에 있다. 일단 고용관리국에 가면, 나는 등록하기 위해 줄을 선다. 그 다음 신고하기 위해 다른 줄에 서야 한다. 이 모든 것을 끝마치고 나면, 나는 구직 인터뷰를 하러 보내지는데, 고용주는 나보다 경험이 더 많은 다른 이를 원한다는 사실을 발견하게 될 뿐이다. 다른 것들은 제쳐두고, 나는 첫 실직 수당을 받는 데 거의 6개월을 기다려야 했다. 여러분도 알다시피, 혜택을 받는 데는 종종 절망스러울 정도로 긴 기다림이 필요하다. 나와 나의 가족은 내 실직으로 인해 많은 고초를 겪었다.

NOTE

Step 1	Survey
Key Words	being unemployed; problems; financial; psychological; bureaucracy
Signal Words	creates; First of all; also; as a result of; other problems; because of
Step 2	Reading
Purpose	to explain how unemployment creates many problems
Pattern of Organization	cause&effect; series
Tone	critical; angry
Main Idea	The narrator and her family have had many problems due to her unemployment.
Step 3	Summary
지문 요약하기 (Paraphrasing)	The narrator's unemployment causes a lot of problems for the narrator and her family. First, it creates financial problems such as curtailment of the quality of groceries, less money for clothing, difficulties of rental payment and tuition. Second, the narrator suffers from psychological problems such as depression and confusion. Finally, the bureaucracy of government makes the narrator frustrated.
Step 4	Recite
요약문 말로 설명하기	

06   Read the passage and follow the directions.

MEMO

Over the years Halloween has shown an enduring malleability and a terrierlike tenacity to survive religious persecution, class prejudice, Victorian politesse, and consumerist inflation. Still, all the adaptability and advertising and marketing in the world couldn't keep Halloween alive if Americans weren't yearning for what it has to offer. Candy Day, energetically touted in the early part of the twentieth century, never sent the nation out to buy boxes of sweets for loved ones on the second Saturday in October. Why have Americans, so admirably skeptical and adamantly opposed to adopting other holidays, taken to their hearts this originally scary, often silly festival? Many say it reminds them of their childhood, which baby boomers are notoriously reluctant to relinquish. And maybe it reminds some others of the childhood they wish they'd had. Since people don't go home for Halloween as they do for Thanksgiving and Christmas, there is less likelihood of parental disappointment, sibling squabbles, free-floating depression, and the other symptoms of the disquiet we are told afflict America's families. Moreover, though recently cornered by adults, Halloween is still identified with children, and while our society may quarrel over the expensive realities of raising children, like health care and education, it cherishes the idea of childhood. But perhaps the greatest attraction of the holiday is that it no longer has any reason for being. It is not a night to worship the God of our choice, honor the dead, celebrate the nation's past, take stock for the future, or woo a loved one. It is simply an occasion for fun. Costumes camouflage identity, blur status, and change gender. Men can be women, children adults, milquetoasts heroes, good girls bad, devils saints, and vice versa.

What is the main purpose of the passage? Write your answer in 5 words or so.

To discuss _____

NOTE

Step 1	Survey
Key Words	
Signal Words	
Step 2	**Reading**
Purpose	
Pattern of Organization	
Tone	
Main Idea	
Step 3	**Summary**
지문 요약하기 (Paraphrasing)	
Step 4	**Recite**
요약문 말로 설명하기	

💡 Answer Key

Over the years **Halloween** has shown an enduring malleability and a terrierlike tenacity to survive religious persecution, class prejudice, Victorian politesse, and consumerist inflation. **Still**, all the adaptability and advertising and marketing in the world couldn't keep **Halloween alive if Americans weren't yearning for what it has to offer.** Candy Day, energetically touted in the early part of the twentieth century, never sent the nation out to buy boxes of sweets for loved ones on the second Saturday in October. **Why have Americans, so admirably skeptical and adamantly opposed to adopting other holidays, taken to their hearts this originally scary, often silly festival?** Many say it reminds them of their childhood, which baby boomers are notoriously reluctant to relinquish. And maybe it reminds some others of the childhood they wish they'd had. **Since** people don't go home for Halloween as they do for Thanksgiving and Christmas, there is less likelihood of parental disappointment, sibling squabbles, free-floating depression, and the other symptoms of the disquiet we are told afflicts America's families. **Moreover**, though recently cornered by adults, Halloween is still identified with children, and while our society may quarrel over the expensive realities of raising children, like health care and education, it cherishes the idea of childhood. **But** perhaps the greatest attraction of the holiday is that it no longer has any reason for being. It is not a night to worship the God of our choice, honor the dead, celebrate the nation's past, take stock for the future, or woo a loved one. **It is simply an occasion for fun**. Costumes camouflage identity, blur status, and change gender. Men can be women, children adults, milquetoasts heroes, good girls bad, devils saints, and vice versa.

→ key word

question

answers
①

②

③

④

모범답안

To discuss the enduring popularity of Halloween

어휘

corner (시장을) 장악하다; 몰아넣다
malleability 유연성; 순응성
over the years 수년간, 오랜 세월 동안
relinquish 포기 · 단념하다
take ~ to one's heart ~를 따뜻이 맞이하다
tenacity 끈질김; 강인함

disquiet 불안
milquetoasts 《미》 대가 약한 남재[사람], 변변치 못한 남자
politesse (특히 형식적으로) 예의 바름, 품위 있음
squabble 옥신각신, 아웅다웅(하다)

terrierlike (사냥개) 테리어처럼

free-floating 걷잡을 수 없는

take stock ~을 고려하다; 자세히 조사하다
woo 구애하다

한글 번역

오랜 세월 동안 할로윈은 지속적인 적응력과 테리어(사냥개)같은 끈질김을 보여주며 종교적 박해, 계층 편견, 빅토리아 시대의 품위와 걷잡을 수 없는 소비자중심주의를 견뎌냈다. 하지만, 할로윈이 주는 것을 갈망하는 미국인들이 없었더라면, 그 모든 적응력, 세상의 광고와 마케팅만으로는 할로윈을 살아남게 하지는 못했을 것이다. 20세기 초반 열심히 홍보되었던 '사탕 주고 받는 날'(10월 둘째 주 토요일–할로윈 이전의 사탕에 관한 공휴일)에 사람들은 더 이상 사랑하는 사람들을 위해 사탕을 사러 나가지 않았다. 왜 미국인들은 다른 공휴일을 받아들일 때는 너무나 회의적이고 강하게 반대하면서, 원래는 무섭고 가끔은 바보 같은 이 축제를 따뜻하게 맞이해왔는가? 많은 이들은 할로윈이 베이비 붐 세대 사람들이 포기하기 꺼려했던 그들의 어린 시절을 떠올리게 한다고 말한다. 또한 어떤 이에게는 그들이 이랬으면 하고 소망했던 어린 시절을 떠올리게 할 수도 있다. 사람들은 추수감사절이나 크리스마스에 집에 가는 것처럼, 할로윈에는 집에 가지 않기 때문에, 부모의 실망, 형제자매 간의 말다툼, 걷잡을 수 없는 우울함과 미국 가정을 위협하는 다른 불안의 징후들이 덜할 가능성이 있다. 게다가, 비록 최근에는 성인들에 의해 시장이 장악되었지만, 할로윈은 여전히 아이들과 동일시된다. 우리 사회가 의료 서비스나 교육과 같이 아이들을 양육하는 값비싼 현실에 언쟁을 높이는 동안에도, 할로윈은 어린시절이라는 아이디어를 소중히 여긴다. 그러나 할로윈의 가장 큰 매력은 존재를 위한 어떤 이유도 가지고 있지 않다는 것이다. 할로윈은 우리가 선택한 신을 숭배하거나, 죽은 사람을 기리거나, 국가의 과거를 찬양하거나, 미래를 고려하거나, 사랑하는 사람에게 구애를 하는 밤이 아니다. 할로윈은 단지 재미를 위한 날이다. 할로윈 의상은 자신의 정체를 위장하고, 신분을 흐릿하게 하며, 성을 바꾼다. 남자는 여자가, 아이는 어른이, 겁쟁이는 영웅이, 착한 소녀가 나쁜 소녀로, 악마가 성인이 될 수 있으며 그 반대도 마찬가지다.

NOTE

Step 1	Survey
Key Words	Halloween; enduring
Signal Words	why; since; moreover; reason
Step 2	**Reading**
Purpose	to discuss the reasons for the enduring popularity of Halloween in America
Pattern of Organization	cause&effect; question&answer
Tone	neutral
Main Idea	Halloween has retained its mass appeal through many years in America because of several of the holiday's characteristics.
Step 3	**Summary**
지문 요약하기 (Paraphrasing)	Halloween has retained its mass appeal through many years in America for the following reasons: it reminds people of childhood; it doesn't induce conflict between family members; it celebrate childhood; and it is fun.
Step 4	**Recite**
요약문 말로 설명하기	

07 Read the passage and follow the direction.

MEMO

Violence is defined as the intentional use of force to harm a human being. Its outcome is injury (whether physical or psychological, fatal or non-fatal). Violence among teenagers is on the rise, and has been since the early 1980s. In my opinion this is due to the increase of violence in the media, the astounding availability of firearms and the lack of proper guidance in the home. Northeastern University's College of Criminal Justice reports that from 1985 to 1993 murders committed by people over the age of 25 dropped an impressive 20%; meanwhile they increased 65% for people between the ages of 18-24 and an astounding 165% growth for teenagers 14 to 17. According to the National Center for Injury Prevention and Control, in 1996, 6548 young people 15-24 years old were victims of homicides. This amounts to an average of 18 youth homicides per day in the US. It also states that homicide is the second leading cause of death for persons 15-24 and is the leading cause of death for African-American and Hispanic youths in this age group. There are a few things that we can do to stunt this problem, and it starts with the home. By focusing on the home first, we can drastically reduce the amount of violent crime committed in the US. _____ is getting way out of hand. Hollywood realizes that the more violence that it shows in its movies, the more likely it will have a larger box office draw. We have the rating (NC-17) but it seems as though the only reason it is there is for pornography.

Fill in the blank in FOUR words from the passage.

NOTE

Step 1	Survey
Key Words	
Signal Words	
Step 2	Reading
Purpose	
Pattern of Organization	
Tone	
Main Idea	
Step 3	Summary
지문 요약하기 (Paraphrasing)	
Step 4	Recite

요약문 말로 설명하기

💡 **Answer Key**

Violence is defined as the intentional use of force to harm a human being. Its outcome is injury (whether physical or psychological, fatal or non-fatal). **Violence among teenagers** is on the rise, and has been since the early 1980s. In my opinion this is due to the increase of ① violence in the media, the ② astounding availability of firearms and the ③ lack of proper guidance in the home. **Northeastern University's College of Criminal Justice reports that from 1985 to 1993 murders committed by people over the age of 25 dropped an impressive 20%; meanwhile they increased 65% for people between the ages of 18-24 and an astounding 165% growth for teenagers 14 to 17. According to the National Center for Injury Prevention and Control, in 1996, 6548 young people 15-24 years old were victims of homicides. This amounts to an average of 18 youth homicides per day in the US. It also states that homicide is the second leading cause of death for persons 15-24 and is the leading cause of death for African-American and Hispanic youths in this age group.** There are a few things that we can do to stunt this problem, and it starts with the home. By focusing on **the home** first, we can drastically reduce the amount of violent crime committed in the US. violence in the media is getting way out of hand. **Hollywood** realizes that the more violence that it shows in its movies, the more likely it will have a larger box office draw. We have the rating (NC-17) but it seems as though the only reason it is there is for pornography.

➤ key words

Topic

key words

객관적 현실

대안
③

①

※ ②에 대한 논의는
없음

모범답안

Violence in the media

한글 번역

폭력은 인간에게 해를 주는 의도적인 힘의 사용으로서 정의된다. (육체적으로거나 심리적으로거나, 치명적이거나 치명적이지 않거나 간에) 그 결과는 상처이다. 10대들 사이의 폭력은 증가 추세에 있고, 1980년대 초 이래로부터 계속되어 왔다. 내 생각에는, 이것은 대중 매체에서의 폭력성의 증가와 놀라울 정도로 총기를 사용하기가 쉽다는 것과 가정에서의 적절한 지도가 결핍되었기 때문이다. 노스이스턴대학교의 응용범죄학부는 1985년부터 1993년까지 25세 이상의 성인들에 의해 저질러진 살인은 20%나 되는 괄목할 만한 하락률을 보인 반면에, 18-24세 사이의 사람들에 의한 살인은 65% 증가했고, 14-17세의 청소년들의 살인 범죄율은 놀랍게도 165%가 증가했다고 보고했다. 국립 피해 예방·관리 센터에 따르면, 1996년에 6548명의 15-24세 젊은이들이 살해를 당했다. 이 수치는 미국에서 하루에 평균적으로 18건의 청년 살인이 벌어진다는 것이다. 이것은 또한 살인이 15-24세 사이 젊은이들의 죽음의 두 번째 주요 원인이고, 이 나이 또래의 아프리카계와 중남미계 미국인 사망의 주요 원인이라고 말한다. 우리가 이 문제를 막을 수 있는 몇 가지 방법이 있는데, 이것은 가정에서부터 시작된다. 가정에 먼저 집중함으로써 미국에서 발생하는 폭력적인 범죄량을 철저하게 감소시킬 수 있다. 대중매체에서의 폭력성은 걷잡을 수 없어지고 있다. 할리우드는 영화에서 더 많은 폭력성을 보여줄수록, 인기를 끌기가 더욱 쉽다는 것을 알고 있다. 우리는 NC-17(17세 이하 관람 불가) 등급이 있지만 마치 이것은 오직 포르노그래피가 있기 때문에 존재하는 이유에 지나지 않는 것처럼 보인다.

NOTE	
Step 1	**S**urvey
Key Words	Violence; violence among teenagers
Signal Words	due to; a few things
Step 2	**R**eading
Purpose	to explain why violence has risen among young people in the US
Pattern of Organization	cause&effect; series
Tone	critical
Main Idea	Violence has risen among teenagers because of the prevalence of violence in the mass media and lack of proper guidance in the home.
Step 3	**S**ummary
지문 요약하기 (Paraphrasing)	Violence has risen among the youth(teenagers) due to the influence of the violent media available and the lack of appropriate guidance in the home. If there were more restrictions around the inclusion of violence in films and more appropriate care in the home, it could be an important first step to reduce the rising youth homicides.
Step 4	**R**ecite
	요약문 말로 설명하기

08 Read the passage and fill in the blank with ONE or TWO word(s) from the passage. If necessary, change the word form.

MEMO

> If you want to get a sense of how pervasive corporate influence in U.S. education is, just take a tour of your neighborhood school. Enter the cafeteria and you'll probably find wrappers from Taco Bell, Arby's, and Subway, fast food chains that provide school lunches. The third grade class may be learning math by counting Tootsie Rolls. Science curricula might well come from Dow Chemical, Dupont, or Exxon. It doesn't end there. Education in the U.S. has become big business. The 'education industry', a term coined by EduVentures, an investment banking firm, is estimated to be worth between $630 and $680 billion in the U.S. The stock value of publicly traded educational companies is growing twice as fast as the Dow Jones Average. Brokerage firms like Lehman Brothers and Montgomery Securities have specialists seeking out venture capital for the _____ⓐ_____.
>
> Analysts at the conservative think tanks, like the Heritage Foundation, Hudson and Pioneer Institutes, tell us that the problems in education stem from inefficient, bloated school bureaucracies. Conservatives talk about 'school choice,' referring to vouchers and other public/private schemes. Free marketeers strike a chord with many parents when they point out that families do not have the choices they deserve, especially in urban school districts.
>
> However, according to progressive school activists, the problems in education have their roots on decades of unequal school funding. They say that as long as school districts are financed through property taxes, kids in poor, urban districts will never receive a(n) _____ⓑ_____ education with suburban school kids. Wide disparities in school resources open the door for corporations to fill the gap (and their pockets), especially in inner city schools.

NOTE

Step 1	Survey
Key Words	
Signal Words	
Step 2	Reading
Purpose	
Pattern of Organization	
Tone	
Main Idea	
Step 3	Summary
지문 요약하기 (Paraphrasing)	
Step 4	Recite
요약문 말로 설명하기	

💡 Answer Key

If you want to get a sense of **how pervasive corporate influence in U.S. education is**, just take a tour of your neighborhood school. Enter the cafeteria and you'll probably find wrappers from Taco Bell, Arby's, and Subway, fast food chains that provide school lunches. The third grade class may be learning math by counting Tootsie Rolls. Science curricula might well come from Dow Chemical, Dupont, or Exxon. It doesn't end there. **Education in the U.S. has become big business**. The 'education industry', a term coined by EduVentures, an investment banking firm, is estimated to be worth between $630 and $680 billion in the U.S. The stock value of publicly traded educational companies is growing twice as fast as the Dow Jones Average. Brokerage firms like Lehman Brothers and Montgomery Securities have specialists seeking out venture capital for the education industry

Analysts at the **conservative** think tanks, like the Heritage Foundation, Hudson and Pioneer Institutes, tell us that the **problems in education** stem from inefficient, bloated school bureaucracies. **Conservatives** talk about 'school choice,' referring to vouchers and other public/private schemes. **Free marketeers** strike a chord with many parents when they point out that families do not have the choices they deserve, especially in urban school districts.

However, according to **progressive school activists**, the **problems in education** have **their roots** on decades of **unequal** school funding. They say that as long as school districts are financed through property taxes, kids in poor, urban districts will never receive a(n) equal education with suburban school kids. **Wide disparities in school resources open the door for corporations to fill the gap (and their pockets), especially in inner city schools.**

key words

key words

signal words

모범답안

ⓐ education industry　　ⓑ equal

어휘

brokerage firm 종합 증권회사(투자 은행업, 주식 매매 중개, 투자 운용 등 증권 업무 전반을 취급)
voucher 쿠폰(바우처 제도란 정부가 수요자에게 쿠폰을 지급하여 원하는 공급자를 선택하도록 하고, 공급자가 수요자로부터 받은 쿠폰을 제시하면 정부가 재정을 지원하는 방식을 말하는데, 이때 지급되는 쿠폰을 바우처라고 한다. 일종의 상품이나 서비스를 구매할 수 있는 증서와 같다.)
wrapper 포장지

02

만약 미국 교육계에 기업의 영향이 얼마나 널리 퍼져있는지 알고 싶다면, 동네에 있는 학교를 한번 둘러보면 된다. 학교 카페테리아에 들어서면 아마도 타코벨이나 아비스, 서브웨이와 같은 학교에 점심을 제공하는 패스트푸드 업체의 포장지를 발견할 것이다. 3학년 학급에서는 아마도 Tootsie Roll을 세며 수학을 배우고 있을 것이다. 과학 교과 과정들은 다우 케미컬이나 뒤퐁 또는 엑슨에서 제공받았을 것이다. 하지만 여기서 그치지 않는다. 미국에서의 교육은 거대한 사업이 되어가고 있다. '교육산업'이라는 용어는 EduVentures라는 투자은행에 의해 고민된 용어로, 이 교육산업은 미국에서 6300~6800억 달러의 가치가 있는 것으로 추정된다. 상장된 교육기업의 주가는 다우존스 평균보다 2배나 빠르게 성장하고 있다. 리먼 브라더스나 몽고메리 시큐리티스 같은 증권회사들은 교육산업을 위한 투기자본을 찾아내기 위한 전문가들까지 두고 있는 실정이다.

헤리티지 재단과 허드슨 인스티튜트, 그리고 파이오니아 인스티튜트 같은 보수파 두뇌집단의 애널리스트들은 교육계의 문제들이 비효율적이고 지나치게 비대한 학교 관료주의에서 비롯된다고 말한다. 보수주의자들은 '학교 선택권'에 대해 주장한다. 이는 바우처나 그 밖의 정부나 민간의 프로그램을 지칭한다. 자유 시장 경제 옹호자들은 응당 있어야 할 학교 선택권이 특히 도심지역의 학군에 없다는 사실을 지적해 많은 부모들의 공감을 얻고 있다.

하지만 진보적인 학교 운동가들에 따르면, 교육계의 문제는 수십 년 동안 지속된 불공평한 학교의 운영자금 제공 방식에 뿌리를 두고 있다. 그들은 학군이 재산세를 통해 지원되는 한 도시 빈민가의 가난한 아이들이 교외지역의 아이들과 동등한 교육을 받을 수는 없을 것이라고 말한다. 학교 재정의 극심한 격차가 기업들에게 격차를 줄이기 위한 (그리고 기업들의 주머니를 채우기 위한) 문을 열어주도록 했으며, 특히 도심 빈민가의 학교에서 이런 상황이 심각한 실정이다.

NOTE

Step 1	Survey
Key Words	Corporate influence; education industry; unequal school funding
Signal Words	stem from; their roots; However
Step 2	**Reading**
Purpose	to explain concerns about the presence of corporations in schools and the causes for their presence
Pattern of Organization	cause&effect; contrast
Tone	critical
Main Idea	The problems in education come from corporate influence as a result of unequal funding.
Step 3	**Summary**
지문 요약하기 (Paraphrasing)	The problems in education come from corporate influence as a result of unequal funding. Conservative criticism cites bad organization and points out options available for parents, which free marketeers believe aren't plentiful. On the other hand, progressive activists argue that the unfair history of funding creates a wealth gap that corporations are taking advantage of.
Step 4	**Recite**
요약문 말로 설명하기	

09 Read the passage and follow the directions.

The greatest of all Greek scientific discoveries was the discovery—
or rather, the invention—of nature itself. The Greeks defined nature
as the universe minus human beings and their culture. Although this
seems to us to be the most obvious sort of distinction, no other
civilization came upon it. A plausible account of how the Greeks
happened to invent _____ⓐ_____ is that they came to make a
distinction between the external, objective world and the internal,
subjective one. And this distinction came about because the Greeks,
unlike everyone else, had a clear understanding of subjectivity
arising from the tradition of debate. It makes no sense for you to try
to persuade me of something unless you believe that there is a
reality out there that you apprehend better than I do. You may be
able to force me to do what you want and even into saying that I
believe what you do. But you will not _____ⓑ_____ me until I
believe that your subjective interpretation of some state of affairs is
superior to mine. So, in effect, objectivity arose from subjectivity—
the recognition that two minds could have different representations
of the world and that the world has an existence independent of
either representation.

MEMO

Fill each blank with ONE word from the passage.

NOTE

Step 1	Survey
Key Words	
Signal Words	
Step 2	**Reading**
Purpose	
Pattern of Organization	
Tone	
Main Idea	
Step 3	**Summary**
지문 요약하기 (Paraphrasing)	
Step 4	**Recite**
요약문 말로 설명하기	

💡 **Answer Key**

The greatest of all Greek scientific discoveries was the discovery—or rather, the invention—of nature itself. The Greeks defined **nature** as the universe minus human beings and their culture. Although this seems to us to be the most obvious sort of **distinction**, no other civilization came upon it. A plausible account of **how the Greeks happened to invent nature is that they came to make a distinction between the external, objective world and the internal, subjective one.** And this distinction came about because the Greeks, unlike everyone else, **had a clear understanding of subjectivity arising from the tradition of debate.** It makes no sense for you to try to persuade me of something unless you believe that there is a reality out there that you apprehend better than I do. You may be able to force me to do what you want and even into saying that I believe what you do. But you will not persuade me until I believe that your subjective interpretation of some state of affairs is superior to mine. So, in effect, **objectivity arose from subjectivity**—the recognition that two minds could have different representations of the world and that the world has an existence independent of either representation.

key words

key words
main idea

main idea
→ key word

모범답안

ⓐ nature   ⓑ persuade

한글 번역

그리스인들의 과학적 발견 중 가장 위대한 것은 자연 그 자체의 발견, 혹은 발명이었다. 그리스인들은 자연을 세상에서 인간과 그들의 문화를 뺀 것으로 정의했다. 물론 이 같은 정의는 우리에게는 뻔한 종류의 구분이라고 생각할 수 있지만, 그리스 이외의 그 어느 문명도 이 같은 정의에 이르지 못했었다. 그리스인들이 어떻게 자연을 발명하기에 이르렀는지 그럴듯한 설명을 생각해 본다면 아마도 그들이 외적이고 객관적인 세계와 내적이며 주관적인 세계를 구분할 수 있었기 때문일 것이다. 이 같은 구분이 나온 것은 그리스인들이 다른 이들과는 달리 전통적인 토론 문화에서 유래한 주관성에 대한 명확한 이해가 있었기 때문이다. 만약 당신이 나보다 더 잘 이해하고 이것이 현실임을 믿지 못한 상태에서는, 나를 무언가에 대해 설득하려 노력하는 것은 말이 되지 않는다. 당신이 원하는 것을 내가 하도록 강요할 수도 있고 심지어 당신이 하는 일을 내가 믿는다고 말하도록 할 수도 있다. 하지만 만일 내가 당신의 어떤 현상에 대한 주관적인 해석이 나의 해석보다 더 뛰어나다고 믿기 전까지는 나를 설득할 수 없을 것이다. 따라서 사실상 객관화란 주관화에서 나왔다. 즉 두 사람이 세상에 대해 서로 다른 설명을 할 수 있으나 그 세계는 각각의 설명과는 별개의 존재라는 자각이 바로 그것이다.

Step 1	Survey
Key Words	Greeks; nature; subjectivity; objectivity; debate
Signal Words	accont; because; So; in effect

Step 2	Reading
Purpose	to explain what led the Greeks to an understanding of objectivity and nature
Pattern of Organization	definition; cause&effect
Tone	persuasive
Main Idea	The debate tradition of the Greeks led them to discover the concepts of subjectivity and nature.

Step 3	Summary
지문 요약하기 (Paraphrasing)	The Greeks invented the concept of nature as something separate from human beings and their culture by realizing that there is a difference between the internal subjective world and the external world. In debate, they probably noticed that two minds would differently describe the same external reality, in other words, nature.

Step 4	Recite
	요약문 말로 설명하기

10 Read the passage and follow the directions.

MEMO

Why do people value gold and precious stones? Not simply because of their rarity: there are a number of elements called "rare earths" which are much rarer than gold, but no one will give a penny for them except a few men of science. There is a theory, for which there is much to be said, that gold and gems were valued originally on account of their supposed magical properties. The mistakes of governments in modern times seem to show that this belief still exists among the sort of men who are called "practical." At the end of the last war, it was agreed that Germany should pay vast sums to England and France, and they in turn should pay vast sums to the United States. Every one wanted to be paid in money rather than goods; the "practical" men failed to notice that there is not that amount of money in the world. They also failed to notice that money is no use unless it is used to buy goods. As they would not use it in this way, it did no good to anyone. There was supposed to be some superstitious virtue about gold that made it worth while to dig it up in the Transvaal and put it underground again in bank vaults in America. In the end, of course, the debtor countries had no more money, and, since they were not allowed to pay in _____, they went bankrupt. The Great Depression was the direct result of the surviving belief in the superstitious properties of gold.

Fill in the blank with the ONE most appropriate word from the passage.

_____

NOTE

Step 1	Survey
Key Words	
Signal Words	
Step 2	**Reading**
Purpose	
Pattern of Organization	
Tone	
Main Idea	
Step 3	**Summary**
지문 요약하기 (Paraphrasing)	
Step 4	**Recite**
요약문 말로 설명하기	

💡 Answer Key

Why do people value gold and precious stones? Not simply because of their rarity: there are a number of elements called "rare earths" which are much rarer than gold, but no one will give a penny for them except a few men of science. There is a theory, for which there is much to be said, that gold and gems were valued originally on account of their supposed **magical properties**. The mistakes of governments in modern times seem to show that this belief still exists among the sort of men who are called "practical." At the end of the last war, it was agreed that Germany should pay vast sums to England and France, and they in turn should pay vast sums to the United States. Every one wanted to be paid in money rather than goods; the "practical" men failed to notice that there is not that amount of money in the world. They also failed to notice that money is no use unless it is used to buy goods. As they would not use it in this way, it did no good to anyone. There was supposed to be some superstitious virtue about gold that made it worth while to dig it up in the Transvaal and put it underground again in bank vaults in America. In the end, of course, the debtor countries had no more money, and, since they were not allowed to pay in goods, they went bankrupt. **The Great Depression was the direct result of the surviving belief in the superstitious properties of gold**.

question

➤ key word

모범답안

goods

한글 번역

사람들은 왜 금과 보석을 소중하게 여길까? 그저 드물기 때문만은 아니다: 세상에는 금보다 훨씬 더 드문 '희토류'라는 원소가 몇 가지 있는데 몇 안 되는 과학자들 말고는 아무도 여기에 관심을 갖지 않는다. 논의할 여지가 많은 다음과 같은 이론도 있다. 즉, 금과 보석은 원래 마술적 성질을 지니고 있기 때문에 소중하게 여겨진다는 것이다. 현대의 각국 정부가 저지르는 실수를 보면 이러한 믿음은 이른바 '실용주의자'들 사이에도 여전히 존재하는 듯하다. 제1차 세계대전이 끝날 무렵에 독일은 영국과 프랑스에 막대한 배상금을 지불하기로 합의했고, 뒤이어 두 나라 또한 미국에 막대한 채무를 갚기로 합의했다. 그들 모두 물건이 아닌 돈으로 지급받기를 원했다: '실용주의자'들은 그토록 많은 돈이 이 세상에 없다는 사실을 알아차리지 못했던 것이다. 게다가 그들은 물건을 사는 데 쓰지 않는 한 돈은 아무것도 아니라는 사실도 알아차리지 못했다. 그들이 돈을 이런 식으로(물건을 사는 식으로) 사용하려 하지 않았기 때문에 그 돈은 누구에게도 도움이 되지 못했다. 남아프리카의 트란스발에서 캐낸 금을 다시 미국에 있는 은행의 지하 금고에 묻은 것을 보면 그들은 금에 틀림없이 어떤 신비한 가치가 있다고 생각했을 것이다. 물론 채무국들은 결국 돈이 남아나지 않았고, 물건으로 지불하도록 허락받지 못한 탓에 파산하고 말았다. 대공황은 금의 마술적 성질을 끝끝내 믿으려 한 데서 비롯된 직접적인 결과였던 것이다.

Step 1	Survey
Key Words	Gold; money; magical; superstitious
Signal Words	because of; on account of; result

Step 2	Reading
Purpose	to show the risks of attaching superstitious value to gold
Pattern of Organization	cause&effect
Tone	cautioning; critical
Main Idea	The superstitious value attached to gold and money is impractical and creates problems.

Step 3	Summary
지문 요약하기 (Paraphrasing)	The superstitious value that is attached to gold and money instead of real, practical goods has led to many mistakes, including creating bankruptcy after WWI and causing the Great Depression.

Step 4	Recite
요약문 말로 설명하기	

11 Read the passage and follow the directions.

Society is losing its odor integrity. Some enterprising souls are actually marketing aerosol cans filled with the aromas of pizza, new cars, anything that might enhance people to buy something they would otherwise not. From the inexhaustible engine of commerce have come Aroma Discs, which when warmed in a special container (only $22.60) emit such scents as Passion, Fireplace and After Dinner Mints. And, in what may be the odor crime of the century, a company in Ohio is selling a cherry-scented garden hose. I may seem like a weird curmudgeon looking for something new to complain about, but it's only the fake smells I don't like, the ones that are meant to fool you. This is a dangerous business because the human nose is emotional and not very bright. Inside the brain, smell seems snuggled right up to the centers for cooking, sex and memory. I recently discovered a substance whose odor stimulates my memory of childhood like nothing else: Crayola crayons. I don't expect you to experience the effect of this odor memory just by thinking about crayons, since most people can't recall smells the way they can recall pictures or sounds. But once you get a good whiff of waxy crayon odor, the bells of childhood will ring. Go out and buy a box. Get your nose right down on the crayons and inhale deeply. Pull that crayon smell right up into the old reptile brain. You'll be flooded with a new-crayon, untouched-coloring-book feeling—you're young, the world is new, the next thing you know your parents may bring home a puppy. The smell is part of our culture in the same class as the Howdy Doody song. Long after my daughters have stopped drawing with crayons, they will have in their brains, as I do now, the subconscious knowledge that if you smell stearic acid—the major component in the smell of Crayola crayons—you're able to have a good time. We're responsible for what posterity will smell, and like to smell. If we're not careful, we may end up with a country in which everyone thinks garden hoses are supposed to smell like cherries.

*Howdy Doody : a famous American children's television program
*stearic acid : a saturated fatty acid with an 18-carbon chain

MEMO

Describe the main idea of the passage and explain why the writer believes "we may end up with a country in which everyone thinks garden hoses are supposed to smell like cherries." When you answer each question, do not copy more than SIX consecutive words from the passage.

_____

_____

_____

_____

_____

NOTE

Step 1	Survey
Key Words	
Signal Words	
Step 2	**Reading**
Purpose	
Pattern of Organization	
Tone	
Main Idea	
Step 3	**Summary**
지문 요약하기 (Paraphrasing)	
Step 4	**Recite**
요약문 말로 설명하기	

💡 Answer Key

Society is losing its odor integrity. Some enterprising souls are actually → main idea
marketing aerosol cans filled with the **aromas** of pizza, new cars, anything
that might enhance people to buy something they would otherwise not.
From the inexhaustible engine of commerce have come Aroma Discs,
which when warmed in a special container (only $22.60) emit such scents
as Passion, Fireplace and After Dinner Mints. And, [**in what may be the
odor crime of the century**], a company in Ohio is selling a cherry-scented → tone : critical
garden hose. I may seem like a weird curmudgeon looking for something
new to complain about, but it's only **the fake smells** I don't like, the ones → key word
that are meant to fool you. **This is a dangerous business because the
human nose is emotional and not very bright**. Inside the brain, smell
seems snuggled right up to the centers for cooking, sex and memory. I
recently discovered a substance whose **odor** stimulates my **memory** of → key word
childhood like nothing else: Crayola crayons. I don't expect you to
experience the effect of this odor memory just by thinking about crayons,
since most people can't recall smells the way they can recall pictures or
sounds. But once you get a good whiff of waxy crayon odor, the bells
of childhood will ring. Go out and buy a box. Get your nose right down
on the crayons and inhale deeply. Pull that crayon smell right up into the old
reptile brain. You'll be flooded with a new-crayon, untouched-coloring-book
feeling—you're young, the world is new, the next thing you know your
parents may bring home a puppy. **The smell is part of our culture in the
same class as the Howdy Doody song**. Long after my daughters have
stopped drawing with crayons, they will have in their brains, as I do now,
the subconscious knowledge that if you smell stearic acid—the major
component in the smell of Crayola crayons—you're able to have a good
time. We're responsible for what posterity will **smell**, and like to smell. ⎫ opinion
If we're not careful, we may end up with a country in which everyone ⎬
thinks garden hoses are supposed to smell like cherries. ⎭

모범답안

First, the main idea of the passage is that artificial aromas, which are sold by businesses, are too
commonplace and causes a lack of odor integrity. Second, the writer believes that if businesses (or
companies) are allowed to market fake odors, people will lose their ability to recognize real odors
and, ultimately, society's odor memories will be distorted.

어휘

curmudgeon 괴팍한 사람	end up with 결국 ~하게 되다	posterity 후손
snuggle up to ~에 바짝 달라붙다	stearic acid 스테아르산	whiff (잠깐 동안) 훅 풍기는 냄새

02

사회는 향기의 온전함을 잃어가고 있다. 몇몇 기업들은 사람들이 그렇게 하지 않으면 사지 않을 것들을 사게끔 강화할지도 모르는 피자, 새로운 차들과 같은 향으로 가득 찬 에어로졸 캔들을 판매하고 있다. 지칠지 모르는 상업의 엔진으로부터 애로마 디스크가 나왔는데 그것들은 특별한 용기 (22.60달러) 안에서 따뜻해질 때 열정, 벽난로, 그리고 애프터 디너 민트(식후 입가심용 민트향 사탕)와 같은 향들을 내뿜는다. 그리고, 세기의 향기 범죄인 오하이오주의 한 회사는 체리향의 정원 호스를 판매하고 있다. 나는 불평할만한 새로운 것을 찾고 있는 괴팍한 사람처럼 보일지 모르지만, 내가 싫어하는 것은 단지 당신을 속이려고 의도된 가짜 냄새이다. 인간의 코는 감정적이지만 매우 똑똑하지는 않기 때문에 이것은 위험한 사업이다. 뇌 속에서, 향기는 요리, 성, 그리고 기억의 중심부에 바짝 달라붙어 있는 것처럼 보인다. 나는 최근에 한 물체를 발견했는데, 그것의 향기는 다른 것들과 같지 않게 나의 어린 시절 기억을 자극했다: 크래욜라 크레파스이다. 나는 당신이 크레파스들을 단지 생각함으로써 이러한 향기 기억 효과를 경험하기를 바라지 않는다, 왜냐하면 대부분의 사람은 사진이나 소리를 회상하는 것처럼 냄새를 회상할 수 없기 때문이다. 하지만 당신이 왁스 크레파스의 좋은 냄새를 한번 맡아본다면, 어린 시절의 벨이 울릴 것이다(추억이 회상될 것이다). 나가서 박스를 사라. 크레파스에 코를 갖다 대고 깊게 숨을 들여 마셔봐라. 크레파스 냄새를 파충류 뇌로 곧바로 집어넣어라. 당신은 새로운 크레파스로 감정이 벅찰 것인데, 당신은 어리고, 세상은 새롭고, 당신의 부모에 대해 당신이 알고 있는 다음의 것은 강아지를 집으로 데려오는 것이다. 그 냄새는 하우디 두디의 노래와 같은 분류의 우리 문화의 한 부분이다. 나의 딸들이 크레파스로 그림그리기를 멈춘 한참 뒤로, 내가 지금 그렇듯, 나의 딸들도 그들의 크레파스 냄새에 대한 추억이 그들의 뇌에 있을 것인데, 이것은 만약 당신이 크래욜라 크레파스의 냄새의 주요한 요소인 스테아르산을 맡는다면, 당신도 좋은 시간을 보낼 것이라고 생각하는 잠재의식이다. 우리는 후손들이 냄새를 맡고, 냄새 맡길 좋아하는 것에 대한 책임이 있다. 만약 우리가 주의하지 않는다면, 우리는 결국 모두가 정원 호스가 체리향이라고 생각하는 나라에 살게 될 것이다.

NOTE

Step 1	Survey
Key Words	society; odor integrity; fake smells
Signal Words	because, since
Step 2	Reading
Purpose	to explain why society is losing its odor integrity
Pattern of Organization	cause&effect
Tone	critical
Main Idea	Artificial aromas, which are sold by businesses, are too banal and causes a lack of odor integrity.
Step 3	Summary
지문 요약하기 (Paraphrasing)	Artificial aromas, which are sold by businesses, are too commonplace and causes a lack of odor integrity. Recently it is common to be able to purchase products with fake smells like a cherry-smelling garden hose. Since our noses are prone to strong sense memories, like a Crayola crayon which will evoke childhood feelings vividly, these fake smells might cause us to hold inaccurate memories.
Step 4	Recite
요약문 말로 설명하기	

12   Read the passage and follow the directions.

All young children, whatever their culture, are alike in their charm and innocence—in being a clean slate on which the wonders and ways of the world are yet to be written. But during the three years I worked in a school in Milan, I learned that American and Italian children are different in several ways. First, young American children tend to be active, enthusiastic, and inquisitive. Italian children, on the other hand, tend to be passive, quiet, and not particularly inquisitive. They usually depend on their parents to tell them what to do. Second, American children show their independence while their Italian counterparts are still looking to their parents and grandparents to tell them what to do or not do. Third, and most important to those who question the influence of environment on a child, the American children generally surpass their Italian schoolmates in math, mechanical, and scientific abilities. But American children are overshadowed by their Italian counterparts in their languages, literature, art, and music courses. Perhaps the differences, which those of us at the school confirmed in an informal study, were to be expected. After all, what priority do Americans give to the technological skills? And what value do Italians—with the literature of poets and authors like Boccaccio, the works of Michelangelo, and the music of the world-famous La Scala opera at Milan—place on the cultural arts?

inquisitive : curious

MEMO

Describe the main idea of the passage in 30 words or less.

_____

_____

_____

NOTE

Step 1	Survey
Key Words	
Signal Words	
Step 2	Reading
Purpose	
Pattern of Organization	
Tone	
Main Idea	
Step 3	Summary
지문 요약하기 (Paraphrasing)	
Step 4	Recite
요약문 말로 설명하기	

02

💡 Answer Key

All young **children**, whatever their culture, are **alike** in their charm and innocence—in being a clean slate on which the wonders and ways of the world are yet to be written. But **during the three years I worked in a school in Milan, I learned that American and Italian children are different in several ways.** First, young American children tend to be active, enthusiastic, and inquisitive. Italian children, **on the other hand**, tend to be passive, quiet, and not particularly inquisitive. They usually depend on their **parents** to tell them what to do. Second, American children show their independence while their Italian counterparts are still looking to their parents and grandparents to tell them what to do or not do. Third, and most important to those who question the **influence** of **environment** on a child, the American children generally surpass their Italian schoolmates in math, mechanical, and scientific abilities. But American children are overshadowed by their Italian counterparts in their languages, literature, art, and music courses. Perhaps the **differences**, which those of us at the school confirmed in an informal study, were to be expected. // After all, what priority do Americans give to the technological skills? And what value do Italians—with the literature of poets and authors like Boccaccio, the works of Michelangelo, and the music of the world-famous La Scala opera at Milan—place on the cultural arts?

→ key words

topic sentence

topic sentence

모범답안

There are some differences between Italian children and American children. American children are independent and focus on technology while Italian kids are dependent on their parents and focus on culture.

한글 번역

모든 어린이들은, 그들이 어떤 문화에 처해 있더라도, 모두 사랑스럽고 순수하다. 마치 세상의 경이로운 일들과 살아가는 방식들이 아직 쓰여 있지 않은 빈 서판과 같은 것이다. 하지만 밀라노의 학교에서 3년간 일하는 동안, 나는 미국인 어린이와 이탈리아 어린이들의 다른 점들을 몇 가지 발견했다. 첫째로, 미국인 어린이들은 적극적이고 열정적이고 탐구심이 많은 경향을 보였다. 반면에, 이탈리아 어린이들은 수동적이고 조용하고 딱히 호기심을 내비치지 않았다. 그들은 대개 부모님들에게 의존했고 부모님들이 시키는 대로 움직였다. 둘째로, 미국인 어린이들은 독립적인 성향을 보인 반면, 이탈리아 어린이들은 여전히 부모님과 할아버지, 할머니께서 하라는 대로 혹은 하지 말라는 대로 따르는 성향을 드러냈다. 셋째로, 아이에게 가장 큰 영향을 주는 환경적 요인이 무엇이냐를 묻는 답변으로, 미국인 학생들은 일반적으로 이탈리아 학생들보다 수학, 기술, 과학적 능력이 뛰어나다. 하지만 미국인 학생들은 언어, 문학, 예술, 음악 과정에서는 이탈리아 학생들보다 뒤처진다. 아마도 그 차이점은, 학교에서 행해졌던 비공식적인 조사를 통해, 일부 예상할 수 있다. 결국, 무엇이 미국인이 과학기술을 우선시하도록 만드는가? 그리고 무엇이 이탈리아인이(보카치오와 같은 시인과 작가의 문학, 미켈란젤로의 작품, 밀라노에 있는 세계적으로 유명한 라 스칼라 오페라를 가지고 있는 이탈리아인) 문화 예술에 높은 가치를 부여하도록 만드는가?

NOTE

Step 1	Survey
Key Words	children; parents; culture; differences; influence; environment
Signal Words	first; second; third; after all
Step 2	**Reading**
Purpose	to point out differences between American children and Italian children
Pattern of Organization	comparison&contrast
Tone	subjective
Main Idea	There are some important differences between Italian children and American children in several ways.
Step 3	**Summary**
지문 요약하기 (Paraphrasing)	There are some important differences between Italian children and American children in several ways. While American kids are more independent and are more active and inquisitive about such things as science and math, Italian children are quieter and more dependent on family members. At the same time, Italian children surpassed American children in culture and the arts.
Step 4	**Recite**
	요약문 말로 설명하기

13 Read the passage and follow the direction.

I learned, that if A is standing on a street corner and B wants his spot, B is within his rights if he does what he can to make A uncomfortable enough to move. In Beirut only the hardy sit in the last row in a movie theater, because there are usually standees who want seats and who push and shove and make such a nuisance that most people give up and leave. Another silent source of friction between Americans and Arabs is in an area that Americans treat very informally—the manners and rights of the road. In general, in the United States we tend to defer to the vehicle that is bigger, more powerful, faster, and heavily laden. While a pedestrian walking along a road may feel annoyed, he will not think it unusual to step aside for a fast-moving automobile. He knows that because he is moving, he does not have the right to the space around him that he has when he is standing still. It appears that the reverse is true with the Arabs who apparently take on rights to space as they move. For someone else to move into a space an Arab is also moving into is a violation of his rights. It is infuriating to an Arab to have someone else cut in front of him on the highway. It is the American's cavalier treatment of moving space that makes the Arab call him aggressive and pushy.

MEMO

What is the main idea of the passage above? Write your answer in 15 words or so.

_____

NOTE

Step 1	Survey
Key Words	
Signal Words	
Step 2	Reading
Purpose	
Pattern of Organization	
Tone	
Main Idea	
Step 3	Summary
지문 요약하기 (Paraphrasing)	
Step 4	Recite
요약문 말로 설명하기	

02

💡 **Answer Key**

I learned, that if A is standing **on a street corner** and B wants his spot, B is within his rights if he does what he can to make A uncomfortable enough to move. **In Beirut** only the hardy sit in the last row in **a movie theater**, because there are usually standees who want seats and who push and shove and make such a nuisance that most people give up and leave. Another **silent source of friction between Americans and Arabs** is in **an area** that **Americans** treat very informally — the manners and rights of **the road**. In general, **in the United States** we tend to defer to the vehicle that is bigger, more powerful, faster, and heavily laden. While a pedestrian walking along a road may feel annoyed, he will not think it unusual to step aside for a fast-moving automobile. He knows that because he is **moving**, he does not have the right to the space around him that he has when he is standing still. It appears that the reverse is true with **the Arabs** who apparently take on rights to space as they **move**. For someone else to move into a space **an Arab** is also moving into is a violation of his rights. It is infuriating to **an Arab** to have someone else cut in front of him on the highway. It is **the American's** cavalier treatment of **moving space** that makes **the Arab** call him aggressive and pushy.

➤ key word
➤ key word
➤ key word
➤ key word

모범답안

There are cultural differences between Arabs and Americans concerning the concept of space.

한글 번역

만약 A가 길모퉁이에 서 있고 B가 그 자리를 원한다면, B는 A가 불편해서 자리를 옮기게 하기 위해 어떤 짓을 하든지 간에 그 권리를 가지고 있다. 베이루트에서는 강한 자만이 영화관 마지막 줄에 앉는데, 왜냐하면 거기엔 주로 앉고 싶어 하는 입석 관람객들이 있어서, 그들이 밀고 밀치며 성가시게 하여 대부분 관람객들이 포기하고 떠나게 만들기 때문이다. 미국인과 아랍인 사이의 또 다른 암묵적 마찰의 근원은 미국인들의 공간에 대한 격식에 얽매이지 않는 태도이다. 즉, 그들의 도로에 대한 매너와 권리에 관련하여. 일반적으로 미국에서 사람들은 더 크고, 강력하고, 빠르며, 짐이 많은 차를 따르는 경향이 있다. 길을 걸어가 던 보행자가 짜증날 수도 있지만 그는 빠르게 이동하는 차를 위해 비켜주는 것을 당연하다고 생각할 것이다. 그는 움직이고 있기 때문에 가만히 있었다면 차지할 수 있었던 그의 주변 공간에 대한 권리가 없다는 것을 알고 있다. 움직여도 그 공간에 대한 권리를 분명히 가질 수 있는 아랍에서는 정반대가 진리이다. 아랍인이 이동하고자 하는 공간으로 누군가가 이동하는 것은 그 아랍인 권리의 침해이다. 아랍인에게 고속도로에서 누군가가 자신의 앞을 가로막는 일은 매우 분노할 일이다. 이동 공간에 대한 미국인의 무신경한 태도는 아랍인들이 그들을 공격적이고 지나치게 밀어붙이는 사람들이라고 부르게 만든다.

NOTE

Step 1	Survey
Key Words	Arabs; Americans; space; moving; road
Signal Words	friction between A and B; the reverse is true
Step 2	**Reading**
Purpose	to describe cultural differences between Arabs and Americans concerning the concept of space
Pattern of Organization	contrast
Tone	subjective
Main Idea	There are cultural differences between Arabs and Americans in terms of the rights of space.
Step 3	**Summary**
지문 요약하기 (Paraphrasing)	There are cultural differences between Arabs and Americans in terms of the rights of space. An Arab believes he has the right to make another still person uncomfortable in order to take his place, while Americans believe someone in place has the right to be there. In terms of rights of the road, Arabs perceive that a person in motion has rights to the space as they move, while Americans do not.
Step 4	**Recite**
요약문 말로 설명하기	

14 Read the passage and follow the directions.

She was my best friend, and hard as it may have been to figure by the looks of us, she was the good girl, I the bad. I suppose everyone has at least one friendship like this in their lives. We were dialectical, she the thesis, I the antithesis. She was direct, trustworthy, kind, and naive; I was manipulative, selfish, and clever. She laughed at all my jokes, took part in all my schemes, told everyone that I was the smartest and the funniest and the best. Like a B movie of boarding school life, we stole peanut butter from the refectory, short-sheeted beds, called drugstores and asked them if they had Prince Albert in a can. Whenever I hear a mother say, "If so-and-so told you to jump off the Brooklyn Bridge, would you do it?" I think of her. On my order, she would have jumped.

What words does the writer use to describe herself? Second, what simile does the author use to describe the friendship?

NOTE

Step 1	Survey
Key Words	
Signal Words	
Step 2	**Reading**
Purpose	
Pattern of Organization	
Tone	
Main Idea	
Step 3	**Summary**
지문 요약하기 (Paraphrasing)	
Step 4	**Recite**
요약문 말로 설명하기	

Answer Key

She was **my best friend**, and hard as it may have been to figure by the looks of us, she was **the good girl**, I the **bad**. I suppose everyone has at least one friendship like this in their lives. We were dialectical, she the thesis, I the antithesis. She was direct, trustworthy, kind, and naïve; I was manipulative, selfish, and clever. She laughed at all my jokes, took part in all my schemes, told everyone that I was the smartest and the funniest and the best. Like a B movie of boarding school life, we stole peanut butter from the refectory, short-sheeted beds, called drugstores and asked them if they had Prince Albert in a can. Whenever I hear a mother say, "If so-and-so told you to jump off the Brooklyn Bridge, would you do it?" I think of her. On my order, she would have jumped.

→ key words

→ signal words

모범답안

She describes herself as bad, manipulative, selfish and clever. Her friend thinks she is the funniest and smartest person in school. Second, the simile is "Like a B movie of boarding school life."

한글 번역

그녀는 나의 가장 친한 친구였고, 외모만으로 판단하기에는 힘들겠지만 그녀는 착한 소녀였고 나는 나쁜 소녀였다. 모든 사람들이 자신의 인생에서 이런 종류의 친구 관계를 하나쯤은 갖고 있을 거라 생각한다. 우린 모두 변증법적인데, 즉 그녀가 정립이면 나는 반정립이다. 그녀는 단도직입적이고 신뢰할만 하고 상냥하고 순진한 반면 나는 교묘하고 이기적이며 똑똑했다. 그녀는 나의 모든 농담에 웃어줬고 내 계획에 참여하였고 모든 사람들에게 내가 가장 똑똑하고 웃기며, 최고라고 얘기했다. 기숙학교 인생의 B급 영화처럼 우리는 식당에서 땅콩버터를 훔쳤고, 침대 시트로 장난을 쳤고, 약국에 전화하여 캔 속에 앨버트 왕자가 있는지를 물어보았다. 엄마가 "아무개가 너에게 브루클린 다리에서 뛰어내리라고 하면 할 거야?"라고 물어볼 때마다 나는 그녀를 떠올린다. 내 명령이라면 그녀는 뛰어내릴 것이다.

Step 1	Survey
Key Words	best friend; good girl; bad girl
Signal Words	dialectical; thesis; antithesis
Step 2	Reading
Purpose	to provide a candid assessment of an unbalanced friendship from the speaker's days at a boarding school for girls
Pattern of Organization	comparison&contrast
Tone	humorous
Main Idea	Though the speak is different from her friend in many ways, they can have a good friendship.
Step 3	Summary
지문 요약하기 (Paraphrasing)	Though the speak is different from her friend in many ways, they can have a good friendship. As children, the speaker was selfish and bad while her friend was good, and the speaker led her friend to misbehave along with her.
Step 4	Recite
	요약문 말로 설명하기

15 Read the passage and follow the directions.

Only two animals have entered the human household otherwise than as prisoners and become domesticated by other means than those of enforced servitude: the dog and the cat. Two things they have in common, namely, that both belong to the order of carnivores and both serve man in their capacity of hunters. In all other characteristics, above all in the manner of their association with man, they are as different as the night from the day. There is no domestic animal that has so radically altered its whole way of living, indeed its whole sphere of interests, that has become domestic in so true a sense as the dog; and there is no animal that, in the course of its centuries-old association with man, has altered so little as the cat. There is some truth in their assertion that the cat, with the exception of a few luxury breeds, such as Angoras, Persians and Siamese, is no domestic animal but a completely wild being. Maintaining its full independence it has taken up its abode in the houses and outhouses of man, for the simple reason that there are more mice there than elsewhere. The whole charm of the dog lies in the depth of the friendship and the strength of the spiritual ties with which he has bound himself to man, but the appeal of the cat lies in the very fact that she has formed no close bond with him, that she has the uncompromising independence of a tiger or a leopard while she is hunting in his stables and barns, that she still remains mysterious and remote when she is rubbing herself gently against the legs of her mistress or purring contentedly in front of the fire.

What do a dog and a cat have in common? Second, how do a dog and a cat differ in their association with their owners? Third, describe what main idea of the passage is.

_____

_____

_____

_____

_____

NOTE

Step 1	Survey
Key Words	
Signal Words	
Step 2	Reading
Purpose	
Pattern of Organization	
Tone	
Main Idea	
Step 3	Summary
지문 요약하기 (Paraphrasing)	
Step 4	Recite
	요약문 말로 설명하기

02

💡 **Answer Key**

Only two animals have entered the human household otherwise than as prisoners and become domesticated by other means than those of enforced servitude: **the dog** and **the cat**. Two things they **have in common**, namely, that both belong to the order of carnivores and both serve man in their capacity of hunters. In all other characteristics, above all in the manner of their association with man, **they are as different as the night from the day**. There is no domestic animal that has so radically altered its whole way of living, indeed its whole sphere of interests, that has become domestic in so true a sense as **the dog**; and there is no animal that, in the course of its centurics-old association with man, has altered so little as **the cat**. There is some truth in their assertion that **the cat**, with the exception of a few luxury breeds, such as Angoras, Persians and Siamese, is no domestic animal but a completely wild being. Maintaining its full independence it has taken up its abode in the houses and outhouses of man, for the simple reason that there are more mice there than elsewhere. The whole charm of **the dog** lies in the depth of the friendship and the strength of the spiritual ties with which he has bound himself to man, but the appeal of **the cat** lies in the very fact that she has formed no close bond with him, that she has the uncompromising independence of a tiger or a leopard while she is hunting in his stables and barns, that she still remains mysterious and remote when she is rubbing herself gently against the legs of her mistress or purring contentedly in front of the fire.

➤ key words

➤ key words

모범답안

They are both carnivores and both serve in the capacity of hunters, and are the only animals tamed in domestic life with humankind. Second, cats remain independent while dogs form deep friendships and spiritual ties. Third, it is that while both dogs and cats are similar in several ways, cats are more independent as pets while dogs are more in-touch and involved with people.

포로나 강제적인 노예 상태 외의 방법들로 길들여진 것이 아닌 오직 두 동물만이 인간의 가정집으로 들어왔다. 바로 강아지와 고양이다. 다시 말해, 두 동물은 공통점이 있는데, 즉 이들은 둘 다 육식 동물 계열에 속하고 사냥꾼으로서의 능력을 통해 인간을 돕는다는 것이다. 다른 특징으로는 무엇보다도 인간과의 관계에서, 밤과 낮이 다르듯, 서로 차이가 있다. 개처럼 진정한 개로서 가정용이 되기 위하여, 자신의 전체 생활 방식, 그의 전체적인 관심사 자체를, 그렇게 급진적으로 바꿔버린 애완 동물은 없다. 그리고 고양이처럼 수 세기나 된 인간과의 관계에서 이렇게 변하지 않은 동물은 없다. 몇 개의 고급 종—앙고라, 페르시안, 샴—을 제외한 고양이는 애완동물이 아니라 완전히 야생 동물이라는 주장에는 어느 정도 진실성이 있다. 고양이는 자신의 완전한 독립심을 유지하면서 단지 다른 곳보다 쥐가 더 많다는 이유로 인간의 집안과 별채에 자신의 거주지를 차지한다. 개의 온전한 매력은 우정의 깊이와 자신이 직접 인간과 형성하는 정신적 교감의 힘에 있다. 하지만 고양이의 매력은 주인과 깊은 유대는 형성하지 않고 마구간과 헛간에서 사냥하면서 호랑이나 표범의 단호한 독립성을 가지고 있다는 데에 있다. 또한 주인의 다리에 부드럽게 부빌 때와 만족스럽게 가르랑거릴 때에도 여전히 신비스러우며, 거리를 유지한다는 데에 고양이의 매력이 있다.

NOTE

Step 1	Survey
Key Words	dogs; cats
Signal Words	have in common; different

Step 2	Reading
Purpose	to describe what dogs and cats have in common and how they differ
Pattern of Organization	comparison&contrast
Tone	subjective
Main Idea	Dogs and cats have some similarities and differences.

Step 3	Summary
지문 요약하기 (Paraphrasing)	While both dogs and cats have been domesticated by man, cats remain independent while dogs are deeply bonded with man. Cats have altered themselves very little over time in its relationship with people and remain appealing mysterious. On the other hand, dogs have been completely altered and have deep friendships with man.

Step 4	Recite
	요약문 말로 설명하기

16 Read the passage and follow the directions.

MEMO

In T'ai Chi class Dr. Young talked about yin and yang. In the beginning square form, each movement is followed by a pause : the movement is yin, the pause yang. To my Western ears this smacks of sexism; the masculine principle acting, the feminine doing nothing. But I eventually begin to learn the pause is not nothing. Given its proper weight, gravity, and time, the pause does its work, its stretch, its subtle modification of the quality of the move before and the one to come. Later in the round form, the movement is continuous. Yin and yang, though still opposite, are inscrutably simultaneous, engaged in an ancient abstract intercourse.

What is a yin and what is yang in the beginning square form of T'ai Chi? Second, why does the writer think the notion of yin and yang "smacks of sexism"? Third, describe what the main idea of the passage is.

NOTE

Step 1	Survey
Key Words	
Signal Words	
Step 2	Reading
Purpose	
Pattern of Organization	
Tone	
Main Idea	
Step 3	Summary
지문 요약하기 (Paraphrasing)	
Step 4	Recite
요약문 말로 설명하기	

02

🔍 Answer Key

In T'ai Chi class Dr. Young talked about **yin** and **yang**. In the beginning **square form**, each movement is followed by a pause: the **movement** is yin, the **pause** yang. To my Western ears this smacks of sexism; the masculine principle acting, the feminine doing nothing. But I eventually begin to learn the pause is not nothing. Given its proper weight, gravity, and time, the pause does its work, its stretch, its subtle modification of the quality of the move before and the one to come. Later in the **round form**, the movement is continuous. Yin and yang, though still opposite, are inscrutably simultaneous, engaged in an ancient abstract intercourse.

→ key words

모범답안

The yin is pause, and the yang is movement in the beginning square form. Second, the concept analogizes the male as active and the female being passive. Third, the concepts of the yin and the yang seemed problematic at first, but came to be appreciated.

한글 번역

태극권 수업에서 Young 박사는 음과 양에 대해서 얘기했다. 처음에 네모 형태 자세에서, 각 움직임 이후에 정지가 뒤따른다. 움직임 뒤에는 음이 따라오고, 정지 뒤에는 양이 따라온다. 서양인인 나의 입장에서, 이것은 성차별주의의 기미가 보인다. 남성스러움의 원칙은 행동을 취하는 것이고, 여성스러움은 아무것도 하지 않는 것이다. 그러나 나는 결국 멈춰 있는 것이 아무것도 아닌 것은 아니라는 사실을 배우기 시작하였다. 정지의 적절한 무게, 중력, 시간을 고려해보았을 때, 정지는 그것의 수행, 당기기, 이전 동작과 앞으로 올 동작의 질에 대한 미묘한 수정의 일을 하고 있다. 그리고 나서 원의 형태로 그 동작이 계속된다. 음과 양은 여전히 정반대이지만, 고대의 추상적인 소통에 참여하며, 불가사의하게도 동시에 일어난다.

NOTE

Step 1	Survey
Key Words	yang; yin; pause; movement; square form; round form
Signal Words	But; opposite
Step 2	Reading
Purpose	to explain what yang is and what yin is
Pattern of Organization	contrast
Tone	neutral
Main Idea	In T'ai Chi, yin and yang, though opposite, are simultaneous and important.
Step 3	Summary
지문 요약하기 (Paraphrasing)	In T'ai Chi, yin and yang, though opposite, are simultaneous and important.
Step 4	Recite
요약문 말로 설명하기	

17 Read the passage and follow the directions.

Physically and psychologically women are by far the superior to men. The old chestnut about women being more emotional than men has been forever destroyed by the facts of two great wars. Women under blockade, heavy bombardment, concentration camp confinement, and similar rigors withstand them vastly more successfully than men. The psychiatric casualties of civilian populations under such conditions are mostly masculine, and there are far more men in our mental hospitals than there are women. The steady hand at the helm is the hand that has had the practice at rocking the cradle. Because of their greater size and weight, men are physically more powerful than women—which is not the same thing as saying that they are stronger. A man of the same size and weight as a woman of comparable background and occupational status would probably not be any more powerful than a woman. As far as constitutional strength is concerned, women are stronger than men. Many diseases from which men suffer can be shown to be largely influenced by their relation to the male Y-chromosome. More males die than females. Deaths from almost all causes are more frequent in males of all ages. Though women are more frequently ill than men, they recover from illnesses more easily and more frequently. Women, in short, are fundamentally more resistant than men. With the exception of the organ systems subserving the functions of reproduction, women suffer much less frequently than men from the serious disorders which affect mankind. With the exception of India, women everywhere live longer than men.

MEMO

Describe the main idea of the passage in 10 words or less.

_____

NOTE

Step 1	Survey
Key Words	
Signal Words	
Step 2	Reading
Purpose	
Pattern of Organization	
Tone	
Main Idea	
Step 3	Summary
지문 요약하기 (Paraphrasing)	
Step 4	Recite
요약문 말로 설명하기	

02

💡 Answer Key

Physically and psychologically women are by far the superior to men. The old chestnut about women being more emotional than men has been forever destroyed by the facts of two great wars. Women under blockade, heavy bombardment, concentration camp confinement, and similar rigors withstand them vastly **more successfully than men.** The psychiatric casualties of civilian populations under such conditions are mostly masculine, and there are far more men in our mental hospitals than there are women. The steady hand at the helm is the hand that has had the practice at rocking the cradle. // Because of their greater size and weight, men are physically more powerful than women—which is not the same thing as saying that they are stronger. **A man of the same size and weight as a woman of comparable background and occupational status would probably not be any more powerful than a woman.** As far as constitutional strength is concerned, **women are stronger than men.** Many diseases from which men suffer can be shown to be largely influenced by their relation to the male Y-chromosome. **More males die than females.** Deaths from almost all causes are more frequent in males of all ages. Though women are more frequently ill than men, they recover from illnesses more easily and more frequently. **Women, in short, are fundamentally more resistant than men.** With the exception of the organ systems subserving the functions of reproduction, women suffer much less frequently than men from the serious disorders which affect mankind. With the exception of India, women everywhere live longer than men.

topic sentence

psychologically

physically

모범답안

Women are superior to men both physically and psychologically.

육체적으로 그리고 심리적으로 여성은 남성들보다 훨씬 우월하다. 여성이 남성들보다 더 감정적이라는 케케묵은 이야기는 두 건의 큰 전쟁에 대한 사실들로 인해 영원히 깨졌다. 봉쇄와 집중 포격, 강제 수용소 감금, 그리고 또 다른 비슷한 고초하에 있는 여성들은 남성들보다 그런 고초들을 훨씬 더 성공적으로 이겨낸다. 그러한 상황하에 있는 시민들 중 정신질환을 가지고 있는 피해자들은 대부분 남성들이고, 정신병원에는 여자보다 남자가 훨씬 더 많이 있다. 안정적인 손은 요람을 흔든 경험을 가진 손이다. 그들의 큰 덩치와 무게 때문에 남자들은 여자들보다 힘이 넘친다. 이 말은 남자들이 강하다고 말하는 것과는 다르다. 비슷한 배경과 직업적 지위를 가진 여성과 같은 크기와 무게를 가진 남자는 아마도 여자보다 힘이 강하지 않을 것이다. 체질적인 힘이 고려되는 한, 여자들은 남자보다 더 강하다. 남자들이 고통스러워 하는 많은 질병들은 남성의 Y염색체의 영향을 크게 받은 것으로 보일 수 있다. 여성보다 많은 남성들이 죽는다. 온갖 원인에 의한 죽음은 모든 연령대의 남자들에게 더 빈번하다. 여자들은 남자들보다 더 자주 아픔에도 불구하고 더 쉽게, 더 자주 아픔을 회복한다. 즉 여자들은 남성들보다 근본적으로 내성이 더 강하다. 생식의 기능을 하는 장기 기관을 제외하고는 여자들은 인류에 영향을 미치는 심각한 장애로부터 남자들보다 덜 빈번하게 고통을 겪는다. 인도를 제외하면 여자들은 어디에서나 남자들보다 오래 산다.

NOTE

Step 1	Survey
Key Words	women; men; physical; psychiatric; strength
Signal Words	superior to; more··· than; because of; in short; with the exception of
Step 2	**Reading**
Purpose	to support the claim that women are superior to men both physically and psychologically
Pattern of Organization	comparison&contrast
Tone	subjective
Main Idea	Women are superior to men both physically and psychologically.
Step 3	**Summary**
지문 요약하기 (Paraphrasing)	Women are superior to men both physically and psychologically. They hold up better in stressful situations and recover more quickly from disease. Death from all causes, including disease, violence, and accidents, is more prevalent among men. Women live longer on the average.
Step 4	**Recite**
요약문 말로 설명하기	

18 Read the passage and follow the directions.

Who talk more—men or women? Most people believe that women talk more. However, this is a stereotype. Women are more verbal—talk more—in private situations, where they use conversation as the "glue" to hold relationships together. But men talk more in public situations, where they use conversation to exchange information and gain status. We can see these differences even in children. Little girls often play with one best friend; their play includes a lot of conversation. Little boys often play games in groups; their play usually involves more doing than _____ⓐ_____. A recent study at Emory University helps to shed light on the roots of communication style differences. Researchers studied conversation between children age 3-6 and their parents. They found evidence that parents talk very _____ⓑ_____ to their sons than they do to their daughters. The startling conclusion was that parents use far more language with their girls. Specifically, when parents talk with their daughters, they use more descriptive language and more details. There is also far more talk about emotions, especially sadness, with daughters than with sons. Most parents would be surprised to learn this. They certainly don't plan to talk more with one child than with another. They don't even realize that this is happening. So why do they do it? Interestingly, it begins when the children are newborn babies.

Fill in each blank with the ONE most appropriate word from the passage. If necessary, change the word form.

NOTE

Step 1	Survey
Key Words	
Signal Words	
Step 2	**Reading**
Purpose	
Pattern of Organization	
Tone	
Main Idea	
Step 3	**Summary**
지문 요약하기 (Paraphrasing)	
Step 4	**Recite**
요약문 말로 설명하기	

02

💡 Answer Key

Who talk more—men or women? Most people believe that women talk more. However, **this is a stereotype**. Women are more verbal—talk more —in **private** situations, where they use conversation as the "glue" to hold relationships together. But men talk more in **public** situations, where they use conversation to exchange information and gain status. We can see **these** differences even in children. Little girls often play with one best friend; their play includes a lot of conversation. Little boys often play games in groups; their play usually involves more doing than talking. A recent study at Emory University helps to shed light on **the roots of communication style** differences. Researchers studied conversation between children age 3-6 and their parents. They found evidence that parents talk very differently to their sons than they do to their daughters. The startling conclusion was that parents use far more language with their girls. Specifically, when parents talk with their daughters, they use more descriptive language and more details. There is also far more talk about emotions, especially sadness, with daughters than with sons. Most parents would be surprised to learn this. They certainly don't plan to talk more with one child than with another. They don't even realize that this is happening. So why do they do it? Interestingly, it begins when the children are newborn babies.

question

key words

key words

모범답안

ⓐ talking ⓑ differently

어휘

gain status 지위를 얻다
shed light on ~을 밝히다

glue 붙이다
specifically 특히, 분명하게

hold together 단결하다; 뭉치게 하다
startling 아주 놀라운

한글 번역

누가 더 수다를 많이 떠는가? 남자인가 여자인가? 대부분의 사람들은 여자들이 더 많이 수다를 떤다고 생각한다. 그러나 그것은 고정관념이다. 여자들은 그들이 서로 관계를 유지하기 위해 '접착제'로 대화를 하는 사적인 상황에서 더 말이 많다. 그러나 남자들은 정보를 교환하거나 지위를 획득하기 위해 대화를 하는 공적인 상황에서 더 말이 많다. 우리는 심지어 이러한 차이점들을 아이들에게서도 발견할 수 있다. 어린 여자아이들은 종종 한 명의 가장 친한 친구와 어울리며, 그들의 놀이는 많은 대화를 포함한다. 어린 남자아이들은 종종 무리를 지어 게임을 하며 논다; 그들의 놀이는 말보다 행동을 더 많이 포함한다. 에모리 대학교의 최근 연구는 대화 방법의 차이점의 근원을 밝혀내는 데 일조를 했다. 연구자들은 3세부터 6세의 아이들과 그들의 부모 사이의 대화를 연구했다. 그들은 부모들이 딸들에게 하는 것에 비해 아들들에게는 다르게 이야기한다는 증거를 발견했다. 아주 놀라운 결과는 부모는 자신들의 딸에게 훨씬 더 많은 언어를 사용한다는 것이었다. 특히, 부모들이 그들의 딸과 대화했을 때, 그들은 더 서술적이고 자세한 언어를 사용한다는 것이었다. 또한 아들보다 딸에게 더 많은 감정들, 특히 슬픔을 이야기한다는 것이다. 대부분의 부모는 이 사실을 알고는 놀랄 것이다. 그들은 분명 다른 자녀보다 어느 한 자녀와 더 많이 이야기하려고 하지는 않기 때문이다. 그들은 심지어 이러한 사실이 일어나리라고는 생각지도 못한다. 그들은 왜 그러는가? 흥미롭게도 그것은 아이들이 갓난아이일 때부터 시작한다.

NOTE

Step 1	Survey
Key Words	Talk; men; women; private; public
Signal Words	However; differences; differently than; more; more··· than
Step 2	**Reading**
Purpose	to outline the differences between the development of boys and girls, particularly in regard to their use of speech
Pattern of Organization	comparison&contrast; cause&effect
Tone	informative
Main Idea	Men and women have different styles of speaking which are influenced unconsciously from birth by their parents.
Step 3	**Summary**
지문 요약하기 (Paraphrasing)	Men and women have different styles of speaking which are influenced unconsciously from birth by their parents. Girls develop their language ability through differing influential factors such as socialization with other girls and language treatment by parents. Parents unknowingly use different, more verbal communication with girls than with boys from birth, nurturing this difference later in life.
Step 4	**Recite**
요약문 말로 설명하기	

19 Read the passage and follow the directions.

MEMO

America's juvenile population live in a society that glorifies aggressive behavior. Even if children are not influenced to commit violence themselves, they may live in fear of violent acts by their schoolmates, friends, and neighbors. At the same time, children are desensitized to these violent realities. There are two ways to go about changing this situation. One plan is to make all parents and grandparents in America aware of the fact that media violence is a huge and growing problem that must be addressed now. Another plan is to give parents and grandparents some helpful guidelines for helping children to live happy, secure, and safe lives. There are many ways for parents to combat the negative effects of media violence in their home. First, provide a Media Free zone in your home where children can read, talk, and play games. Second, do not put a television in your child's bedroom. Third, read to your children. Fourth, refuse to expose younger children to violence content in movies, television shows, and video games. Fifth, check Moviereports.org. Movieports.org is a Web site run by the Center for Successful Parenting that has reviews of movies and video games for parents to look at before they take their children to a movie or buy them a video game. The reviews are done by experts who look at content in movies and games. The Web site is an excellent resource for those parents who wish to become informed about a movie or game.

What is the main idea of the passage? Write your answer in 20 words or so.

_____

_____

_____

NOTE

Step 1	Survey
Key Words	
Signal Words	
Step 2	Reading
Purpose	
Pattern of Organization	
Tone	
Main Idea	
Step 3	Summary
지문 요약하기 (Paraphrasing)	
Step 4	Recite
요약문 말로 설명하기	

💡 Answer Key

America's juvenile population live in a society that glorifies **aggressive** →key word
behavior. Even if children are not influenced to commit **violence** →key words
themselves, they may live in fear of **violent acts** by their schoolmates,
friends, and neighbors. At the same time, children are desensitized to these
violent realities. There are two ways to go about changing this situation. →signal words
One plan is to make all parents and grandparents in America aware of the
fact that **media violence** is a huge and growing problem that must be →key words
addressed now. Another plan is to give parents and grandparents some
helpful guidelines for helping children to live happy, secure, and safe lives.
**There are many ways for parents to combat the negative effects of media
violence in their home.** First, provide a Media Free zone in your home
where children can read, talk, and play games. Second, do not put a →signal words
television in your child's bedroom. Third, read to your children. Fourth,
refuse to expose younger children to violence content in movies, television
shows, and video games. Fifth, check Moviereports. org. Movieports.org is
a Web site run by the Center for Successful Parenting that has reviews of
movies and video games for parents to look at before they take their
children to a movie or buy them a video game. The reviews are done by
experts who look at content in movies and games. The Web site is an
excellent resource for those parents who wish to become informed about a
movie or game.

모범답안

Media violence has adverse effects on the children and with conscientious and active parenting,
these effects can be countermanded.

구문분석

There are many ways for parents to help combat the negative effects of media violence in their home
⇨ to부정사의 의미상 주어 for＋목적격. to help combat하는 것은 parents이다.
⇨ help는 곧장 뒤에 동사원형이 올 수도 있고, to부정사가 올 수도 있다. 여기선 동사원형(combat)이 왔는
데 help의 목적어 역할을 한다.
⇨ effect of와 effect on의 차이를 구별하자.
   effect of A : A의 영향(즉, A가 영향을 주는 것을 의미), effect on A: A에 대한 영향(즉, A가 영향을
   받는 것을 의미)
   예 **The effect of A on B** : B에 대한(B에 끼치는) A의 영향
      the negative effects of media violence on teen age boys 10대 소년들에게 끼치는 미디어 폭력의 부정적 영향

어휘

adverse 나쁜, 불쾌한, 도움이 되지 않는   go about ~을 착수하다, 끊임없이 ~하다
make available 공개하다, 내놓다

02

한글 번역

미국의 어린이들은 공격적인 행위를 찬양하는 사회에서 살고 있다. 심지어 아이들이 직접 폭력적인 행동을 저지르도록 영향을 받지 않는다 해도 이들은 자신의 학교 친구나 이웃의 폭력 행위에 대한 공포감을 가지고 살아야 할지 모른다. 동시에 아이들은 이러한 폭력적인 현실에 둔감해진다. 이 상황을 변화시키기 위해 두 가지 방법이 있다. 첫째는 모든 부모들과 조부모들이 미디어 폭력이 지금 다루어져야 할 큰 문제라는 사실을 인지하는 것이다. 또 다른 계획은 부모들과 조부모들에게 아이들이 행복하고 안정감 있고 안전하게 살 수 있도록 돕는 가이드라인을 제공하는 것이다. 부모들이 미디어 폭력의 부정적인 영향과 집에서 싸울 수 있는 여러 방법이 있다. 첫째, 집에서 아이들이 읽고 말하고 놀이를 할 수 있는 미디어에 노출되지 않을 만한 공간을 만들어라. 둘째, 아이들 방에 텔레비전을 놓지 마라. 셋째, 아이들에게 책을 읽어 주어라. 넷째, 어린 아이들에게 영화, 텔레비전, 쇼, 비디오 게임에서 폭력적인 내용을 보여주지 않도록 하라. 다섯째, Moviereports.Org 사이트를 체크하라. 이는 성공적인 부모 센터에서 운영하는 웹사이트로 부모들이 영화에 데려가거나 비디오 게임을 사주기 전에 볼 수 있는 영화와 비디오 게임에 대한 리뷰를 제공한다. 리뷰는 영화와 비디오 게임을 본 전문가들이 한다. 이 웹사이트는 영화와 게임에 대해 정보를 얻고 싶은 부모들에게 훌륭한 자료가 된다.

NOTE

Step 1	Survey
Key Words	media violence; juvenile population; home
Signal Words	ways; First; Second; Third; Fourth; Fifth; one plan; another plan
Step 2	Reading
Purpose	to explain the effects of media violence on children and give parents advice about it
Pattern of Organization	series
Tone	informative; cautioning
Main Idea	Media violence has adverse effects on children and with conscientious, active parenting, these effects can be countermanded.
Step 3	Summary
지문 요약하기 (Paraphrasing)	The harmful effects of media violence on the juvenile population of the States are serious. America's children live in a society that glorifies violence. Such active ways as providing a Media Free zone in the home; no TV in children's rooms; reading; prohibition of violent content; and using Moviereports.org are helpful for parents in combating the detrimental consequences of media violence.
Step 4	Recite
요약문 말로 설명하기	

20   Read the passage and follow the directions.

On ten Santa Fe walls, the history of the Chicanos, both mythical and actual, is depicted in brilliant colors and disproportionate figures. Aztec medicine figures dance and gods protect peasants, all for the glory of the Chicano in the present. On some walls, the chains of bondage are being broken and the Lady of Justice, depicted as an Indian Maiden, watches over both Indians and Chicanos. On others, Pancho Villa and Father Hidalgo lead the Mexican peasants to freedom. But the clenched fist at the end of the grotesquely muscled arms is the most predominant image. It symbolizes unity, determination, ambition, and pride, all traits that Los Artes believe should be a part of Chicano psychology. The figures they paint are bold, upright, strong, and grasping far from the stereotype of the Mexican-American with drooping moustache and floppy sombrero lying in the shade of a stucco building.

Describe what the purpose of the paintings is. Second, what does the clenched fist in the paintings symbolize? Third, how do the figures in the paintings differ from the stereotypes the author describes at the end of the passage? Fourth, describe what the main idea of the passage is.

NOTE

Step 1	Survey
Key Words	
Signal Words	
Step 2	Reading
Purpose	
Pattern of Organization	
Tone	
Main Idea	
Step 3	Summary
지문 요약하기 (Paraphrasing)	
Step 4	Recite
요약문 말로 설명하기	

02

💡 Answer Key

On ten **Santa Fe walls**, the history of **the Chicanos**, both mythical and actual, is depicted in brilliant colors and disproportionate figures. Aztec medicine figures dance and gods protect peasants, all for the glory of **the Chicano** in the present. On some walls, the chains of bondage are being broken and the Lady of Justice, depicted as an Indian Maiden, watches over both Indians and Chicanos. On others, Pancho Villa and Father Hidalgo lead the Mexican peasants to freedom. But **the clenched fist at the end of the grotesquely muscled arms is the most predominant image. It symbolizes unity, determination, ambition, and pride, all traits that Los Artes believe should be a part of Chicano psychology.** The figures they paint are bold, upright, strong, and grasping far from the stereotype of **the Mexican-American** with drooping moustache and floppy sombrero lying in the shade of a stucco building.

→ key words

모범답안

The purpose is to communicate the cultural richness and strength of Chicano people. Second, it symbolizes unity, determination, dignity and pride. Third, they are strong and lack the moustaches and sombreros, and not lying down lazy. Fourth, the wall paintings of the barrios presents a strong cultural image to inspire the Chicano community.

한글 번역

산타페의 열 개의 벽에 치카노의 신화적 역사와 실제적 역사가 화려한 색채와 균형이 안 맞는 모습으로 묘사되어 있다. 아즈텍의 의술을 다루는 사람들은 춤을 추고, 신들은 소작농들을 보호하는데, 그 모든 것이 현재의 치카노의 영광을 위한 것이다. 어떤 벽에는 구속하는 사슬이 부러져 있고 정의의 여신이 인디언 아가씨로 묘사되어 인디언과 치카노 모두를 보살펴준다. 다른 벽에는 판초 비야와 이달고 신부가 멕시코 농부들에게 자유를 준다. 하지만 괴상하게 생긴 근육이 있는 팔의 끝에 꽉 쥔 주먹은 가장 압도적인 이미지이다. 그것은 로스 아르테스가 치카노 정신에 반드시 일부분이 되어야 한다고 믿었던 특징들, 즉 단합, 결심, 야망, 자부심을 상징한다. 그들이 그린 인물들은 대담하고 꼿꼿하고 강하고 소유욕이 강한 모습으로 멕시코계 미국인에 대한 고정관념인 치장벽토로 된 건물의 그늘 아래서 축 늘어져 누워 있는, 늘어진 콧수염이 있고 헐렁한 솜브레로(챙 넓은 모자)를 쓰고 있는 모습과 거리가 멀다.

NOTE

Step 1	Survey
Key Words	ten Santa Fe walls; the Chicanos; symbolizes
Signal Words	On some walls; On others
Step 2	**Reading**
Purpose	to communicate the cultural richness and strength of Chicano people
Pattern of Organization	series
Tone	objective
Main Idea	The paintings in Santa Fe illustrating Chicano history are intended to provide an alternative to stereotypical images of the culture.
Step 3	**Summary**
지문 요약하기 (Paraphrasing)	The paintings in Santa Fe illustrating Chicano history are intended to provide an alternative to stereotypical images of the culture. Some feature mythological figures and others real history, with the primary symbol of a clenched fist highlighting empowering traits for Chicanos.
Step 4	**Recite**
	요약문 말로 설명하기

21 Read the passage and follow the directions.

Researchers note three frequent attitudes among mothers of
_____(a)_____ children. The first attitude is reflected by those
mothers who reject their child or are unable to accept the child as
a handicapped person. Complex love-hate and acceptance-rejection
relationships are found within this group. Rejected children not only
have problems in adjusting to themselves and their disabilities, but
they also have to contend with disturbed family relationships and
emotional insecurity. Unfortunately, such children receive even less
encouragement than the normal child and have to absorb more
criticism of their behavior. A second relationship involves mothers
who overcompensate in their reactions to their child and the
disorder. They tend to be unrealistic, rigid, and overprotective.
Often, such parents try to compensate by being overzealous and
giving continuous instruction and training in the hope of establishing
superior ability. The third group consists of mothers who accept their
children along with their defects. These mothers have gained the
ability to provide for the special needs of their handicapped
children while continuing to live a normal life and tending to family
and home as well as civic and social obligations. The child's
chances are best with parents who have accepted both their child and
the _____(b)_____.

MEMO

Fill in each blank with the ONE most appropriate word from the passage.

NOTE

Step 1	Survey
Key Words	
Signal Words	
Step 2	Reading
Purpose	
Pattern of Organization	
Tone	
Main Idea	
Step 3	Summary
지문 요약하기 (Paraphrasing)	
Step 4	Recite

요약문 말로 설명하기

💡 Answer Key

Researchers note three frequent attitudes among mothers of handicapped children. The first attitude is reflected by those mothers who reject their child or are unable to accept the child as a handicapped person. Complex love-hate and acceptance-rejection relationships are found within this group. Rejected children not only have problems in adjusting to themselves and their disabilities, but they also have to contend with disturbed family relationships and emotional insecurity. Unfortunately, such children receive even less encouragement than the normal child and have to absorb more criticism of their behavior. // A **second** relationship involves mothers who overcompensate in their reactions to their child and the disorder. They tend to be unrealistic, rigid, and overprotective. Often, such parents try to compensate by being overzealous and giving continuous instruction and training in the hope of establishing superior ability. // The **third** group consists of mothers who accept their children along with their defects. These mothers have gained the ability to provide for the special needs of their handicapped children while continuing to live a normal life and tending to family and home as well as civic and social obligations. The child's chances are best with parents who have accepted both their child and the defects.	topic sentence category 1 : rejection category 2 : compensation category 3 : acceptance

모범답안

ⓐ handicapped　　ⓑ defects

한글 번역

연구자들은 장애 아동을 둔 어머니들의 세 가지의 흔한 태도에 대해 주목한다. 첫 번째는 그들의 자녀가 장애인이라는 것 자체를 거절하거나 용납할 수 없는 태도를 보이는 어머니들이다. 복잡한 (자식들에 대한) 사랑-증오와 인정-거부의 관계는 이러한 그룹 내에서 발견된다. 이렇게 거부당한 아이들은 그들 스스로와 그들의 장애에 대해 적응하는 것에 있어서 문제가 있을 뿐만 아니라, 잘못된 가족 관계와 감정적인 불안정과도 맞서 싸워야만 한다. 불행하게도, 그러한 아이들은 비장애인 아동들보다 적은 격려를 받으며, 그들의 행동에 대하여 더 많은 비난을 받아내야만 한다. 두 번째 관계는 그들의 아이와 장애에 대하여 과잉보호를 하는 엄마들을 포함한다. 그들은 비현실적이고, 완고하며, 과보호하는 경향이 있다. 종종, 그러한 부모들은 과다하게 열정적이거나 지속적인 지시를 주고, 우수한 능력을 가질 수 있다는 희망을 가지고 훈련시킴으로써 보상하려고 한다. 세번째 그룹은 아이들의 장애에 대해 인정하는 어머니로 구성된다. 이러한 어머니들은 평범한 삶을 지속하고, 가족과 집에서 뿐만 아니라 시민으로서의 사회적인 의무를 지면서 그들의 장애 아동의 특별한 요구에 대해 제공할 능력을 가지고 있다. 장애아들의 기회는 아이들 자체와 그 부족함을 받아들이는 부모님들과 있을 때 가장 극대화된다.

NOTE

Step 1	Survey
Key Words	mother; handicapped children; attitude
Signal Words	three; not only··· but also; first; second; third

Step 2	Reading
Purpose	to describe the three frequent attitudes among mothers of handicapped children
Pattern of Organization	series
Tone	neutral
Main Idea	There are three common attitudes among mothers of handicapped children.

Step 3	Summary
지문 요약하기 (Paraphrasing)	Three attitudes are common among mothers of handicapped children: rejection, overcompensation, and acceptance. Children who face rejection or are overcompensated for have trouble adjusting to life, while those whose defects are accepted and worked with are able to live a more normal life both in the family and in society.

Step 4	Recite
	요약문 말로 설명하기

22 Read the passage and follow the directions.

MEMO

In the sixteenth century, Cardinal Wolsey's greyhound Urian forced King Henry VIII to begin the English Reformation. Wolsey had gone to Pope Clement VII to ask for an annulment of Henry's marriage, but when Urian bit the pope's foot, negotiations ended; consequently, Henry had no choice but to declare himself head of the Church of England so that he could have his divorce. Another dog may have contributed to the American Revolution and the creation of the United States. Had Scotland's Robert Bruce not been saved from death by one of his dogs, his family would not have taken over the English throne. The Stuarts' hereditary mental disorder would not have influenced the English king's treatment of the American colonies. Likewise, several other dogs saved the lives of great people who went on to influence history. A Newfoundland rescued nineteenth-century explorers Lewis and Clark from a charging buffalo, a greyhound saved Alexander the Great from a rampaging elephant, another Newfoundland dove off the deck of a boat and rescued Napoleon Bonaparte from a stormy sea, and Abraham Lincoln's mixed-breed dog alerted passersby when her eleven-year-old master fell into a dark cave.

What is the main idea of the passage? Write your answer in 10 words or so.

_____

NOTE

Step 1	Survey
Key Words	
Signal Words	
Step 2	Reading
Purpose	
Pattern of Organization	
Tone	
Main Idea	
Step 3	Summary
지문 요약하기 (Paraphrasing)	
Step 4	Recite
요약문 말로 설명하기	

💡 Answer Key

In the sixteenth century, Cardinal Wolsey's greyhound Urian forced King Henry VIII to begin the English Reformation. Wolsey had gone to Pope Clement VII to ask for an annulment of Henry's marriage, but when Urian bit the pope's foot, negotiations ended; consequently, Henry had no choice but to declare himself head of the Church of England so that he could have his divorce. Another dog may have contributed to the American Revolution and the creation of the United States. Had Scotland's Robert Bruce not been saved from death by one of his dogs, his family would not have taken over the English throne. The Stuarts' hereditary mental disorder would not have influenced the English king's treatment of the American colonies. Likewise, several other dogs saved the lives of great people who went on to **influence history**. A Newfoundland rescued nineteenth-century explorers Lewis and Clark from a charging buffalo, a greyhound saved Alexander the Great from a rampaging elephant, another Newfoundland dove off the deck of a boat and rescued Napoleon Bonaparte from a stormy sea, and Abraham Lincoln's mixed-breed dog alerted passersby when her eleven-year-old master fell into a dark cave.

key words

Series

①

②

③

key words

모범답안

Several dogs have actually helped determine the course of human history.

구문분석

Had Scotland's Robert Bruce not been saved from death by one of his dogs, his family would not have taken over the English throne.

⇨ 가정법 과거완료 구문으로, if가 생략되면서 도치 일어남

Had Scotland's Robert Bruce not been ⇨ If Scotland's Robert Bruce had not been

어휘

a charging buffalo 화난, 공격태세를 갖춘 버팔로

dove dive의 과거형; (물에) 뛰어내리다

annulment 무효화

rampaging 광분한

16세기 울시 추기경의 그레이 하운드 우리언은 헨리 8세가 영국 개혁을 시작하도록 만들었다. 울시는 헨리의 결혼을 무효화하기 위해 교황 클레멘트 7세에게 갔지만 우리언이 교황의 발을 물었을 때 협상은 끝나버렸다. 결과적으로 헨리는 이혼을 하기 위해서 영국 교회의 수장이 스스로 되기로 선언하는 것 외에는 선택의 여지가 없었다. 다른 개는 아마도 미국 혁명과 미합중국의 탄생에 공헌을 했을 터이다. 만약 스코틀랜드의 로버트 브루스가 그의 개들 중 한 마리 덕에 죽음을 면하지 못했다면 그의 가족들은 영국의 왕좌를 차지하지 못했을 것이다. 스튜어트 가의 유전적인 정신병이 영국 왕의 미국 식민지에 대한 처우에 영향을 끼치는 일도 없었을 것이다. 마찬가지로 몇몇 다른 개들은 계속해서 역사에 영향을 미친 위인들의 생명을 구했다. 한 뉴펀들랜드 종은 19세기의 탐험가 루이스와 클락을 화난 버팔로에게서 구했고, 한 그레이하운드 종은 화난 코끼리로부터 알렉산더 대왕을 구했다. 또 다른 뉴펀들랜드 종은 보트에서 뛰어내려 폭풍 치는 바다에서 나폴레옹 보나파르트를 구했다. 그리고 에이브러햄 링컨의 한 잡종견은 11살짜리 주인이 어두운 동굴에 떨어졌을 때 지나가는 사람에게 짖어 주인을 살렸다.

NOTE

Step 1	Survey
Key Words	dogs; influenced; history
Signal Words	Another; Likewise; several other

Step 2	Reading
Purpose	to explain how dogs have influenced the course of human history
Pattern of Organization	series
Tone	neutral
Main Idea	Several dogs have actually helped determine the course of human history.

Step 3	Summary
지문 요약하기 (Paraphrasing)	Dogs have had an influence on human history on several occasions involving the British court, figures in American history, Alexander the Great, and so on.

Step 4	Recite
요약문 말로 설명하기	

23 Read the passage and follow the directions.

MEMO

We're used to taking the car everywhere we go. Three blocks to the store? We just hop in the car and go. However, if you stop and consider it for a moment, you'll realize there are lots of good alternatives. You can walk, bike, or crawl! And there are other benefits, besides saving money on gas. When you walk, you'll get exercise and live longer. When you bike, you can stop and meet that new, single neighbor down the street. When you crawl, you could pick up loose change! If you live in a town or city with decent public transportation, leave your car home and use the bus or train. Even if you use public transit just once or twice a week, you'll save wear and tear on your car, you won't be shelling out for all that gas, and you won't have to dodge cell-phone-addicted rush-hour commuters. Plus you get to people—an underappreciated activity. For more information on public transportation in your' hood, check out the directory at the American Public Transportation Association website. Time to buy a new car? Do the math and see what it'll cost you if gas costs, say, $5 a gallon in six years. If you're like most Americans, and drive about 20,000 miles a year, increasing your car's fuel efficiency by 10 MPG can save you over a thousand bucks a year—not to mention countless stops at the gas station where you breathe fumes and stand in the rain. Our advice? Get the smallest, most efficient vehicle that makes sense for your daily driving. There are more hybrids on the market every year. And, when you really do need that Giganotosaurus SUV for loading up the family and hauling the 24-foot cabin cruiser to the beach, rent it for two weeks.

Complete the summary of the passage by filling in the blanks below. In the blank ⓐ, start the letter "a".

We should all consider _____ⓐ_____ to driving everywhere. Public transportation is cheap and readily available in most cities. When buying a car, drivers should consider _____ⓑ_____ vehicles.

NOTE

Step 1	Survey
Key Words	
Signal Words	
Step 2	**Reading**
Purpose	
Pattern of Organization	
Tone	
Main Idea	
Step 3	**Summary**
지문 요약하기 (Paraphrasing)	
Step 4	**Recite**
	요약문 말로 설명하기

💡 Answer Key

We're used to taking **the car** everywhere we go. Three blocks to the store? We just hop in the car and go. However, if you stop and consider it for a moment, you'll realize there are **lots of good alternatives**. You can walk, bike, or crawl! And there are other **benefits**, besides **saving money on gas**. When you walk, you'll get exercise and live longer. When you bike, you can stop and meet that new, single neighbor down the street. When you crawl, you could pick up loose change! // If you live in a town or city with decent public transportation, leave your car home and use the bus or train. Even if you use public transit just once or twice a week, you'll save wear and tear on your car, you won't be shelling out for all that gas, and you won't have to dodge cell-phone-addicted rush-hour commuters. **Plus** you get to people—an underappreciated activity. For more information on public transportation in your' hood, check out the directory at the American Public Transportation Association website. // Time to buy a new car? Do the math and see what it'll cost you if gas costs, say, $5 a gallon in six years. If you're like most Americans, and drive about 20,000 miles a year, increasing your **car's fuel efficiency** by 10 MPG can save you over a thousand bucks a year—not to mention countless stops at the gas station where you breathe fumes and stand in the rain. Our advice? **Get the smallest, most efficient vehicle that makes sense for your daily driving.** There are more hybrids on the market every year. And, when you really do need that Giganotosaurus SUV for loading up the family and hauling the 24-foot cabin cruiser to the beach, rent it for two weeks.

▶ key word

▶ key word
main idea ①

▶ key word
tone : humorous

main idea ②

▶ tone : casual /
humorous
neighborhood의 축약

▶ key word

tone : humorous
main idea ③

모범답안

ⓐ alternatives
ⓑ cheaper or more efficient (또는 the most efficient and smallest)

어휘

dodge 피하다	get to ~ (사람)을 괴롭히다(영향을 미치다)
plus 게다가	shell out for ~에 대해 거액을 지불하다
underappreciated 인정을 덜 받는	wear and tear 마모

한글 번역

우리는 가고자 하는 곳 어디든 자동차로 가곤 한다. 상점까지 3블럭인가? 우리는 자동차에 그냥 올라타서 가기만 하면 된다. 하지만 당신이 멈춰서 잠시 동안 생각을 한다면 여기에는 좋은 대안책이 많이 있음을 알게 될 것이다. 당신은 걷거나 자전거를 타거나 기어갈 수 있다. 그리고 여기에는 주유비를 절약하는 것 외에 다른 이점들이 있다. 당신이 걸어갈 때는 운동도 할 수 있고 더 오래 살 수 있게 된다. 자전거를 타게 되면 길을 따라 가다 멈춰서 미혼인 새로 이사 온 이웃을 만날 수도 있다. 그리고 기어갈 때는 떨어진 동전을 주울 수도 있다. 만일 당신이 대중교통 수단이 잘 갖춰진 마을이나 도시에 산다면 차는 집에 두고 버스나 지하철을 이용하라. 일주일에 한두 번 대중교통 수단을 이용한다면 차가 닳는 것도 줄일 수 있고 주유비도 줄일 수 있으며 휴대전화에 중독된 출근하는 직장인들을 피해 다닐 필요도 없을 것이다. 게다가, 덜 인정받는 활동인, 타인에게 영향을 끼칠 수도 있다. 대중교통 수단에 대해 더 정보가 필요하다면 미국 대중교통 수단 협회 사이트에서 주소록을 확인해보라. 새 자동차를 살 때인가? 6년 동안 주유비가 1갤런에 5달러라고 한다면 얼마나 들지 따져보라. 당신이 미국인이라면 일 년에 2만 마일은 운전을 한다. 당신의 자동차 연료 효율을 10MPG까지 올리는 것은 일 년에 천 달러 이상을 절약하는 셈이다. 주유소에서 당신이 담배를 피우거나 비 오는 중에 잠시 서 있는 등의 정차는 언급하지 않았다. 우리의 조언은? 당신이 운전하는 데 적합한 가장 작으면서도 가장 효율적인 자동차를 가져라. 매년 시장에서는 하이브리드 자동차가 많이 나온다. 가족을 태우고 24피트의 캐빈 크루저를 실을 수 있는 Giganotosaurus SUV가 정말 필요하다면 2주 동안 렌트를 하라.

NOTE

Step 1	Survey
Key Words	cars; public transportation; gas; efficient vehicles
Signal Words	lots of alternatives; benefits
Step 2	**Reading**
Purpose	to recommend alternatives to using personal automobiles and explain the benefits of the alternatives
Pattern of Organization	series; comparison&contrast
Tone	entertaining; humorous
Main Idea	We should all consider alternatives to driving everywhere. People can benefit by walking, biking, or using public transportation or by driving the smallest, most efficient vehicle.
Step 3	**Summary**
지문 요약하기 (Paraphrasing)	We should all consider alternatives to driving everywhere. People can benefit by walking, biking, or using public transportation. Public transportation is cheap and readily available in most cities. When buying a car, drivers should consider cheaper, more efficient vehicles.
Step 4	**Recite**
	요약문 말로 설명하기

24 Read the passage and follow the directions.

MEMO

It is role of the Federal Reserve, known simply as the Fed, to control the supply of money in the U.S. through its system of twelve regional Federal Reserve Banks, each with its own Federal Reserve Bank. Many commercial banks belong to the Federal Reserve System and as members must follow the Fed's reserve requirements, a ruling by the Fed on the percentage of deposits that a member bank must keep either in its own vaults or on deposit at the Fed. If the Fed wants to change the money supply, it can change reserve requirements to member banks; for example, an increase in the percentage of deposits required to be kept on hand would reduce the available money supply. Member banks can also borrow money from the Fed, and an additional way that Fed can control the money supply is to raise or lower the discount rate, the interest rate at which commercial banks borrow from the Fed. An increase in the discount rate would reduce the funds available to commercial banks and thus shrink the money supply. In addition to using _____ and the discount rate to control the money supply, the Fed has another powerful tool, open-market operations.

Fill in the blank with the TWO most appropriate consecutive words from the passage.

NOTE

Step 1	Survey
Key Words	
Signal Words	
Step 2	Reading
Purpose	
Pattern of Organization	
Tone	
Main Idea	
Step 3	Summary
지문 요약하기 (Paraphrasing)	
Step 4	Recite
요약문 말로 설명하기	

💡 Answer Key

It is **role of the Federal Reserve**, known simply as the Fed, to control **the supply of money** in the U.S. through its system of twelve regional Federal Reserve Banks, each with its own Federal Reserve Bank. Many commercial banks belong to the Federal Reserve System and as members must follow the Fed's reserve requirements, a ruling by the Fed on the percentage of deposits that a member bank must keep either in its own vaults or on deposit at the Fed. If the Fed wants to change the money supply, it can change **reserve requirements** to member banks; for example, an increase in the percentage of deposits required to be kept on hand would reduce the available money supply. Member banks can also borrow money from the Fed, and an **additional** way that Fed can control the money supply is to raise or lower **the discount rate**, the interest rate at which commercial banks borrow from the Fed. An increase in the discount rate would reduce the funds available to commercial banks and thus shrink the money supply. **In addition to** using **reserve requirements** and the discount rate to control the money supply, the Fed has another powerful tool, **open-market operations**.

➤ key words

①

②

③

모범답안

reserve requirements

구문분석

1. If the Fed wants to change the money supply, it can change reserve requirements to member banks; **for example, an increase in** the percentage of deposits required **to be kept on hand /would** reduce the available money supply.

   만일 연준이 통화 공급량을 바꾸고 싶으면 회원 은행의 준비 요구액을 바꾸면 된다. 예를 들어 상시 준비시킬 예탁금의 비율을 증가시키면 가용한 통화 공급량은 줄어들 것이다.

2. an additional way that Fed can control the money supply is to raise or lower the discount rate, the interest rate at which commercial banks borrow from the Fed.

   ➪ 이 문장의 주어는 an additional way이고 동사는 단수동사인 is이며, that은 관계부사 대용으로 사용되었다. **명사 다음에 comma(,)가 나오고 관사+명사가 나오면 동격일 확률이 매우 높다.** 따라서 거기에 맞는 해석을 적용해야 한다. 이 때 comma는 '즉'으로 해석하는 것이 좋다. 여기서, the discount rate 다음에 나오는 comma(,)는 동격의 역할을 하여 the interest rate at which commercial banks borrow from the Fed.와 같은 것이 된다. 해석하면, '할인율, 즉, 시중 은행들이 연준으로부터 돈을 빌리는 금리'가 된다.

   ➪ at which commercial banks borrow from the Fed.
   = commercial banks borrow from the Fed at the interest rate.

어휘

a commercial bank 시중 은행; 상업은행

reserve requirements 지급준비 요구

the discount rate 할인율

on hand 가지고 있는; 수중에 있는

ruling 판정, 재정규정

vault (은행의) 금고; 지하 납골당

한글 번역

'연준'이라고도 하는 연방 준비 제도의 역할은 각기 자체 연방 준비 지방 은행을 가지고 있는 12개 지역의 연방 준비 은행 제도를 통해 미국의 통화 공급을 통제하는 것이다. 많은 시중 은행들이 연방 준비 제도에 속해 있으며 회원으로서 연준의 준비 요구를 따라야 하는데, 이것은 다름 아닌 회원 은행이 자신의 금고나 연준 예탁고에 확보하고 있어야 하는 예탁금의 비율에 관한 규정이다. 만일 연준이 통화 공급량을 바꾸고 싶으면 회원 은행의 준비 요구액을 바꾸면 된다. 예를 들어 상시 준비시킬 예탁금의 비율을 증가시키면 가용한 통화 공급량은 줄어들 것이다. 회원 은행은 연준으로부터 돈을 빌릴 수도 있으며 연준이 통화 공급량을 조절할 수 있는 또 하나의 방법은 할인율을 높이거나 낮추는 것인데, 이는 시중 은행들이 연준으로부터 돈을 빌리는 금리를 말한다. 할인율의 증가는 시중 은행의 가용 자금을 감소하게 만들어 통화 공급을 위축시키게 된다. 지급준비 요구와 할인율을 통하여 통화 공급을 조절하는 일 외에도 연준은 공개시장 조작(중앙은행이 금융을 조절하는 것)이라고 하는 또 하나의 강력한 수단을 가지고 있다.

NOTE

Step 1	Survey
Key Words	role of the Federal Reserve; the money supply; reserve requirements; the discount rate; open-market operations
Signal Words	for example; another
Step 2	Reading
Purpose	to explain the functions of the Federal Reserve
Pattern of Organization	definition; series
Tone	neutral; objective
Main Idea	The Federal Reserve employs various methods to control the supply of money in the U.S.
Step 3	Summary
지문 요약하기 (Paraphrasing)	The Federal Reserve controls the flow of money in the U.S. through a variety of methods such as reserve requirements, adjusting discount rates, and open-market operations.
Step 4	Recite
	요약문 말로 설명하기

25 Read the passage and follow the directions.

MEMO

Among creators, there are two principal types: those who are constantly rejecting what they and others have done and who move almost compulsively in new directions; and those who accept what others have done and work hard with ever greater skill and finesse over the course of a life. Without question, Mozart belongs to the second group: while impatient with others and constantly challenging himself, he showed little inclination to create new genres, preferring instead to realize to perfection the genres of his time. In part this tendency reflects the era in which he lived. In the seventeenth and eighteenth centuries, composers were craftsmen who worked in a well-recognized domain, creating works for their patrons. Certainly this is how Bach and Haydn—Mozart's greatest predecessors—thought of themselves, and what Leopold Mozart wished for his son. The tendency also reflects temperament. Though sympathetic to the political trends that were sweeping Europe, Mozart was hardly revolutionary. He might well have been horrified by the French Revolution, even as Beethoven was stimulated by it. Paradoxically, however, Mozart set the stage for musical revolution. He did so much in the way that Shakespeare, Goethe, and Keats did in their respective eras and genres—by so exhausting the existing lines of creation as to make it essentially impossible for those who succeeded them to follow in their footsteps. By being Mozart, he laid the groundwork for Beethoven and the Romantics, just as Brahms and Wagner stimulated the _____ of Stravinsky and Schoenberg a century later.

Fill in the blank with TWO words from the passage.

_____

NOTE

Step 1	Survey
Key Words	
Signal Words	
Step 2	**Reading**
Purpose	
Pattern of Organization	
Tone	
Main Idea	
Step 3	**Summary**
지문 요약하기 (Paraphrasing)	
Step 4	**Recite**
요약문 말로 설명하기	

💡 **Answer Key**

Among **creators**, there are **two principal types**: those who are constantly rejecting what they and others have done and who move almost compulsively in new directions; and those who accept what others have done and work hard with ever greater skill and finesse over the course of a life. Without question, **Mozart** belongs to the second group: while impatient with others and constantly challenging himself, he showed little inclination to create new genres, preferring instead to realize to perfection the genres of his time. // In part this tendency reflects the era in which he lived. In the seventeenth and eighteenth centuries, composers were craftsmen who worked in a well-recognized domain, creating works for their patrons. Certainly this is how Bach and Haydn—Mozart's greatest predecessors— thought of themselves, and what Leopold Mozart wished for his son. The tendency also reflects temperament. Though sympathetic to the political trends that were sweeping Europe, Mozart was hardly revolutionary. He might well have been horrified by the French Revolution, even as Beethoven was stimulated by it. // Paradoxically, however, Mozart set the stage for **musical revolution**. He did so much in the way that Shakespeare, Goethe, and Keats did in their respective eras and genres—by so exhausting the existing lines of creation as to make it essentially impossible for those who succeeded them to follow in their footsteps. By being Mozart, he laid the groundwork for Beethoven and the Romantics, just as Brahms and Wagner stimulated the muscial revolution of Stravinsky and Schoenberg a century later.

➤ key word

➤ key word

➤ key word

모범답안

musical revolution

한글 번역

창조적인 사람들 중에는 두 가지의 주된 전형이 있다: 본인 및 다른 이들이 이뤄놓은 것을 끊임없이 부정하며 거의 강박적으로 새로운 방향을 추구하는 이들과 다른 이들이 이뤄놓은 것을 받아들이고 보다 더 훌륭한 솜씨와 기교로 일생에 걸쳐 이를 개선하기 위해 노력하는 사람들이 바로 그것이다. 물어볼 것도 없이 모차르트는 두 번째 그룹에 해당한다: 비록 사람들과의 관계에 있어서는 참을성이 부족했고, 스스로에게는 끊임없이 도전적이었지만, 새로운 장르를 창조하기보다는 자신이 살던 시대의 장르에 완벽함을 실현하는 것을 더 선호했다. 어떤 면에서 이런 경향은 그가 살았던 시대를 반영한다. 17~18세기의 작곡가들은 장인이었다. 그들은 잘 알려진 특정 영역에서 일했으며, 자신들의 후원자를 위한 작품들을 만들었다. 이것이 모차르트의 대선배였던 바흐와 하이든이 그들 스스로에 대해 가졌던 생각이며, 레오폴드 모차르트가 그의 아들에게 바라던 것이기도 했다. 이런 경향은 또한 성격을 반영한다. 유럽을 휩쓸고 있었던 정치적 동향에 동조하는 마음이 있었음에도 불구하고, 모차르트는 혁명을 꿈꾸는 그런 인물은 아니었다. 베토벤이 프랑스 혁명에 자극을 받았던 바로 그 순간에, 모차르트는 프랑스 혁명을 보고 겁에 질렸을 것으로 추측된다. 하지만 모차르트는 역설적이게도 음악적 혁명의 장을 마련했다. 마치 셰익스피어나 괴테 혹은 키츠가 자신들의 시대와 장르에서 그랬던 것처럼 모차르트도 그러했다. 즉 자신들의 뒤를 따르는 그 누구도 사실상 이들의 발자취를 쫓을 수 없을 정도로 기존부터 존재했던 모든 구절(및 음절)들을 철저히 다루었다. 모차르트는 스스로의 존재를 통해서 베토벤과 낭만주의를 위한 초석을 마련했으며, 이것은 브람스나 바그너가 스트라빈스키와 쇤베르크의 음악적 혁명을 약 한 세기 이후에 고무시킨 것과 같다고 할 수 있다.

02

NOTE

Step 1	Survey
Key Words	Creators; Mozart; genres; groundwork
Signal Words	Among creators; In the seventeenth and eighteenth centuries; Paradoxically

Step 2	Reading
Purpose	to describe two different types of creators and the results of their ways of working
Pattern of Organization	series
Tone	subjective
Main Idea	Mozart was the type of creator to work in the established domain to its utmost potential rather than seek any new direction.

Step 3	Summary
지문 요약하기 (Paraphrasing)	Mozart was the type of creator to work in the established domain to its utmost potential rather than seek any new direction. Thus, he would find revolutionary ideas revolting but also contribute to inspiring new musical revolution by having maximized the existing forms.

Step 4	Recite
	요약문 말로 설명하기

26 Read the passage and follow the directions.

That all men are equal is a proposition to which, at ordinary times, no sane human being has ever given his assent. A man who has to undergo a dangerous operation does not act on the assumption that one doctor is just as good as another. Editors do not print every contribution that reaches them. And when they require civil servants, even the most democratic governments make a careful selection among their theoretically equal subjects. At ordinary times, then, we are perfectly certain that men are not equal. But when, in a democratic country, we think or act politically we are no less certain that men are equal. Or at any rate—which amounts to the same thing in practice—we behave as though we were certain of men's _____. Similarly, the pious mediaeval nobleman who, in church, believed in forgiving enemies and turning the other cheek, was ready, as soon as he had emerged again into the light of day, to draw his sword at the slightest provocation. The human mind has an almost infinite capacity for being inconsistent.

MEMO

Fill in the blank with ONE word from the passage. If necessary, change its word form.

NOTE

Step 1	Survey
Key Words	
Signal Words	
Step 2	**Reading**
Purpose	
Pattern of Organization	
Tone	
Main Idea	
Step 3	**Summary**
지문 요약하기 (Paraphrasing)	
Step 4	**Recite**
요약문 말로 설명하기	

💡 Answer Key

That **all men are equal** is a proposition to which, **at ordinary times**, no sane human being has ever given his assent. A man who has to undergo a dangerous operation does not act on the assumption that one doctor is just as good as another. Editors do not print every contribution that reaches them. And when they require civil servants, even the most democratic governments make a careful selection among their **theoretically** equal subjects. **At ordinary times**, then, we are perfectly certain that **men are not equal**. But when, in a democratic country, we think or act politically we are no less certain that men are equal. Or at any rate—which amounts to the same thing in practice—we behave as though we were certain of men's equality. <u>Similarly,</u> the pious mediaeval nobleman who, in church, believed in forgiving enemies and turning the other cheek, was ready, as soon as he had emerged again into the light of day, to draw his sword at the slightest provocation. **The human mind has an almost infinite capacity for being inconsistent.**

→ main idea

모범답안

equality

한글 번역

모든 인간이 평등하다는 것은, 평상시에는 정상적인 사람이라면 아무도 동의한 적이 없는 명제이다. 위험한 수술을 받아야 하는 사람은 이 의사나 저 의사나 매한가지라는 가정하에 행동하지 않는다. 편집자는 기고되는 원고를 모두 활자화하지 않는다. 공무원을 채용 모집할 때, 가장 민주적인 정부라도, 이론상으로는 평등하다고 하는 국민들을 신중히 선택하는 것이다. 따라서, 평상시에 우리는 인간이 평등하지 않다는 것을 완전히 확신하고 있는 것이다. 하지만, 민주 국가에서 우리가 정치적으로 생각하고 행동할 때는, 인간이 평등하다는 사실을 이와 마찬가지로 확신하는 것이다. 혹은, 어쨌든 간에—그것은 실제상으로 마찬가지지만—우리는 인간의 평등을 확신하는 것처럼 행동한다. 이와 비슷하게, 예배당 안에서는 적을 용서하고 다른 쪽 뺨도 내놓는 것을 믿는 독실한 중세의 귀족은, 예배당 밖으로 나오자마자 아주 사소한 도발에도 칼을 뽑을 준비가 되어 있다. 인간의 마음은 거의 무한한 모순의 가능성을 갖고 있다.

02

NOTE

Step 1	Survey
Key Words	the human mind; inconsistent
Signal Words	at ordinary times; Similarly

Step 2	Reading
Purpose	to point out human beings' inconsistent thoughts
Pattern of Organization	series
Tone	cynical
Main Idea	Human beings have a high capacity to think inconsistent thoughts.

Step 3	Summary
지문 요약하기 (Paraphrasing)	We have a high capacity to think inconsistent thoughts such that all men are equal at some times, but that they aren't at other times.

Step 4	Recite
요약문 말로 설명하기	

27   Read the passage and follow the directions.

The democratic doctrine of freedom of speech and of the press, whether we regard it as a natural and inalienable right or not, rests upon certain assumptions. One of these is that men desire to know the truth and will be disposed to be guided by it. Another is that the sole method of arriving at the truth in the long run is by the free competition of opinion in the open market. Another is that, since men will inevitably differ in their opinions, each man must be permitted to urge, freely and even strenuously, his own opinion, provided he accords to others the same right. And the final assumption is that from this mutual toleration and comparison of diverse opinions the one that seems the most rational will emerge and be generally accepted.

Describe the main idea of the passage in TEN words or more.

_____

NOTE

Step 1	Survey
Key Words	
Signal Words	
Step 2	Reading
Purpose	
Pattern of Organization	
Tone	
Main Idea	
Step 3	Summary
지문 요약하기 (Paraphrasing)	
Step 4	Recite
요약문 말로 설명하기	

💡 Answer Key

The democratic doctrine of freedom of speech and of the press, whether we regard it as a natural and inalienable right or not, rests upon **certain assumptions**. One of these is that men desire to know the truth and will be disposed to be guided by it. Another is that the sole method of arriving at the truth in the long run is by the free competition of opinion in the open market. Another is that, since men will inevitably differ in their opinions, each man must be permitted to urge, freely and even strenuously, his own opinion, provided he accords to others the same right. And the final assumption is that from this mutual toleration and comparison of diverse opinions the one that seems the most rational will emerge and be generally accepted.

→key words

모범답안

The freedom of speech and press is based on several important assumptions.

한글 번역

언론과 출판의 자유의 민주적인 원리는, 우리가 그것을 타고날 때부터의 양도할 수 없는 권리로 간주하든 아니든 간에, 어떤 가정들 위에 토대를 두고 있다. 이런 가정들의 하나는, 인간은 진실을 알고 싶어 하며 진실에 의해 인도되고 싶어 한다는 것이다. 또 다른 가정은, 진실에 도달하는 유일한 방법은 결국에는 공개 토론장에서 의견을 자유롭게 경쟁시키는 것이라는 것이다. 또 다른 가정은, 사람들이란 어쩔 수 없이 의견이 다르기 마련이므로, 각자가 똑같은 권리를 남에게 주는 한 자신의 의견을 자유롭게 심지어 열렬히 주장하는 것이 허용되어야 한다는 것이다. 그리고 마지막 가정은, 이와 같은 상호 아량과 다양한 의견의 비교로부터 가장 합리적으로 보이는 의견이 나타나서 일반적으로 인정된다는 사실이다.

NOTE

Step 1	Survey
Key Words	democratic doctrine of freedom of speech and of the press; certain assumptions
Signal Words	One of; Another; Another; the final
Step 2	Reading
Purpose	to explain several assumptions that freedom of speech and of the press is based on
Pattern of Organization	series
Tone	neutral
Main Idea	The freedom of speech and press is based on several important assumptions.
Step 3	Summary
지문 요약하기 (Paraphrasing)	The freedom of speech and press is based on several important assumptions. These are: men should seek the truth; free competition of opinion should drive at the truth; each man is free to urge his opinion; and through competition of these opinions the most rational will be generally accepted.
Step 4	Recite
	요약문 말로 설명하기

28 Read the passage and follow the directions.

In the 1840s, students protested and acted in violent ways. Students at Yale, for example, objected to their mathematics course and burned their books in the streets. Some captured their tutor and kept him tied up all night, and others shot a cannon through the tutor's bedroom window. In the 1940s and 1950s, students were a fun-loving, game-happy lot. They swallowed live goldfish, took part in dance marathons, and held contests to see how many people could crowd into a phone booth. The more daring males broke into women's rooms in panty raids and then festooned their own rooms with the ill-gotten silks. Then, in the 1960s, students repeated the activities of the 1840s. They objected to their courses, littered the campuses with their books and papers, and locked teachers inside college buildings. They protested against all forms of social injustice, from war to the food in the cafeteria. The more violent threw rocks at the police, and a few planted bombs in college buildings. In the 1970s students repeated the fun and games of the forties and fifties. They held contests to see how many people could squeeze into a phone booth. They had dance marathons. The more daring ran naked across campuses, in a craze called "streaking." The slightly less daring did their streaking with brown paper bags over their heads. History does seem to repeat itself, even in the sometimes violent and sometimes fun-and-games behavior of the students on college campuses.

MEMO

Describe the main idea of the passage in ONE sentence.

NOTE

Step 1	Survey
Key Words	
Signal Words	
Step 2	Reading
Purpose	
Pattern of Organization	
Tone	
Main Idea	
Step 3	Summary
지문 요약하기 (Paraphrasing)	
Step 4	Recite
요약문 말로 설명하기	

🔎 Answer Key

In the 1840s, **students protested and acted in violent ways.** Students at Yale, for example, **objected** to their mathematics course and **burned** their books in the streets. Some captured their tutor and kept him tied up all night, and others shot a cannon through the tutor's bedroom window. In the 1940s and 1950s, **students were a fun-loving, game-happy lot.** They swallowed live goldfish, took part in dance marathons, and held contests to see how many people could crowd into a phone booth. The more daring males broke into women's rooms in panty raids and then festooned their own rooms with the ill-gotten silks. Then, in the 1960s, **students repeated the activities of the 1840s.** They **objected to** their courses, **littered** the campuses with their books and papers, and **locked** teachers inside college buildings. They **protested against** all forms of social injustice, from war to the food in the cafeteria. The more violent threw rocks at the police, and a few planted bombs in college buildings. In the 1970s **students repeated the fun and games of the forties and fifties.** They held contests to see how many people could squeeze into a phone booth. They had dance marathons. The more daring ran naked across campuses, in a craze called "streaking." The slightly less daring did their streaking with brown paper bags over their heads. **History does seem to repeat itself, even in the sometimes violent and sometimes fun-and-games behavior of the students on college campuses.**

▶ key word

▶ key word

▶ key word

main idea

모범답안

Students on college campuses sometimes repeat the same behavior as college students of earlier eras.

한글 번역

1840년대에 학생들은 폭력적인 방식으로 저항하고 행동했다. 예를 들어 Yale의 학생들은 그들의 수학 강의에 반기를 들고 거리에서 교과서를 태웠다. 몇몇은 그들의 강사를 잡아 그를 하룻밤 내내 묶어두기도 했고, 다른 이들은 강사의 침실 창문으로 대포를 쏘기도 했다. 1940년대와 1950년대에 학생들은 꽤나 유희를 즐겼고, 게임하는 것을 좋아했다. 그들은 살아 있는 금붕어를 삼키거나 댄스 마라톤(장시간에 걸친 무도회)에 참가하거나, 얼마나 많은 사람이 공중전화 부스 안으로 들어갈 수 있는지 보기 위한 대회를 열기도 했다. 보다 대담한 남자들은 여자들의 방에 침입해 '팬티를 탈취하기 위한 급습'을 감행했고, 그들의 방을 부정하게 얻은 실크로 꾸몄다. 그리고 1960년대에, 학생들은 1840년대의 운동을 반복했다. 그들은 그들의 강의에 반대하여 책과 리포트를 캠퍼스 내에 흩뿌렸고, 학교 건물 안에 선생님들을 가두었다. 그들은 전쟁에서부터 학생 식당의 음식에까지, 모든 종류의 사회적인 부당함에 저항했다. 더 폭력적인 학생들은 경찰에게 돌을 던지고, 몇몇은 학교 건물 내에 폭탄을 설치하기도 했다. 1970년대에 학생들은 40년대와 50년대에 유희와 게임을 즐기던 방식을 반복했다. 그들은 얼마나 많은 사람이 공중전화 부스 안으로 밀려들어갈 수 있는지 보기 위한 대회를 개최했고 댄스 마라톤에 참가했다. 더 대담한 학생들은 '스트리킹'이라 불리는 유행으로서 벌거벗은 채 캠퍼스를 질주했다. 그 중에서 다소 덜 대담한 이들은 머리에 누런 종이 봉투를 뒤집어쓰고 뛰었다. 어떤 때는 폭력적이고 어떤 때는 게임을 즐기는 듯한 대학교 학생들의 행동에서조차 역사는 반복되는 것 같다.

02

NOTE

Step 1	Survey
Key Words	students; protests; fun; games; violent; repeated
Signal Words	in the 1940s and 1950s; then

Step 2	Reading
Purpose	to show that college students of different eras may behave in the same way
Pattern of Organization	time order; series
Tone	informative
Main Idea	Students on college campuses sometimes repeat the same behavior as college students of earlier eras.

Step 3	Summary
지문 요약하기 (Paraphrasing)	When it comes to the behavior of students on college campuses, history sometimes repeats itself. Students in the 1960s carried out protests that were very similar to those made by students in the 1840s, and in the 1970s, students repeated some of the fun and games that students used to do 20 to 30 years before.

Step 4	Recite
요약문 말로 설명하기	

29 Read the passage and follow the directions.

Recently I was unfortunate enough to be in a store when a robbery took place. I learned from that experience that a pointed gun makes people obey. I had stopped at the store on my way home from work to get a loaf of bread. I was at the checkout counter when a man standing nearby pulled out a gun and yelled, "Everyone on the floor and away from the cash register!" My first reaction was fear. Around me, people dropped to the floor, but I felt frozen where I stood. As I hesitated, the robber pointed his gun at me and yelled again, "On the floor!" Then I felt angry. I was bigger and stronger than he was. I was sure I could put him on the floor in a fair fight. But the gun, small enough to be cradled in the palm of my hand, was bigger and stronger than I was. I sank obediently to the floor. All of us watched silently as the robber scooped money out of the cash register into a paper bag. Then he ran out the door, jumped into a car that was waiting, and raced away. Everyone stood up and started talking. A clerk called the police, who asked if anyone could describe the robber or the car. No one could. Then one man, blustering defensively, told the clerk just what I was thinking. "Listen. Tell them when a gun is pointed at me, it's all I'm looking at. One look and I'm going to do whatever I'm told."

MEMO

Describe the main idea of the passage in ONE sentence.

_____

NOTE

Step 1	Survey
Key Words	
Signal Words	
Step 2	**Reading**
Purpose	
Pattern of Organization	
Tone	
Main Idea	
Step 3	**Summary**
지문 요약하기 (Paraphrasing)	
Step 4	**Recite**
요약문 말로 설명하기	

💡 Answer Key

Recently I was unfortunate enough to be in a store when a robbery took place. **I learned from that experience that a pointed gun makes people obey.** // I had stopped at the store on my way home from work to get a loaf of bread. I was at the checkout counter when a man standing nearby pulled out a gun and yelled, "Everyone on the floor and away from the cash register!" // My first reaction was fear. Around me, people dropped to the floor, but I felt frozen where I stood. // As I hesitated, the robber pointed his gun at me and yelled again, "On the floor!" Then I felt angry. I was bigger and stronger than he was. I was sure I could put him on the floor in a fair fight. // But the gun, small enough to be cradled in the palm of my hand, was bigger and stronger than I was. I sank obediently to the floor. // All of us watched silently as the robber scooped money out of the cash register into a paper bag. Then he ran out the door, jumped into a car that was waiting, and raced away. // Everyone stood up and started talking. A clerk called the police, who asked if anyone could describe the robber or the car. No one could. // Then one man, blustering defensively, told the clerk just what I was thinking. "Listen. Tell them when a gun is pointed at me, it's all I'm looking at. One look and I'm going to do whatever I'm told."

- thesis statement
- incidents arranged as they occurred in time
- frozen in place
- gun pointed
- sank to the floor
- robbery took place
- after robbery
- dialogue— significance of narrative restated

모범답안

When threatened by a pointed gun, one tends to focus only on the weapon.

한글 번역

최근에 나는 강도 사건이 일어나는 상점에 있는 불운을 만났다. 그 경험으로부터 나는 사람들이 자신에게 겨누어지는 총에 복종하게 된다는 것을 알게 되었다. 나는 빵 한 덩어리를 사기 위해서 퇴근하는 길에 상점에 들렀다. 내가 계산대에 서 있을 때 근처에 서 있던 어떤 남자가 총을 꺼내며 "모두 바닥에 엎드리고 계산대로부터 떨어져!"라고 소리쳤다. 나의 첫 반응은 두려움이었다. 내 주변의 사람들은 모두 바닥에 엎드렸다. 그러나 나는 선 채로 얼어붙었다. 내가 망설였을 때, 강도는 총을 나에게 겨눈 채 "엎드려!"라고 다시 소리쳤다. 그러자 나는 화가 치밀었다. 나는 강도보다 더 몸집이 크고 강했다. 내가 강도와 정정당당하게 싸운다면 강도를 바닥으로 내쳐버릴 수 있는 것은 확실했다. 그러나 내 손바닥에 잡힐 만큼 작은 총이 나보다 더 크고 강했다. 나는 고분고분하게 바닥에 엎드렸다. 우리 모두는 조용히 강도가 계산대에서 돈을 퍼내어 종이 봉지로 옮기고 있는 것을 지켜보았다. 그런 다음, 강도는 문을 나서 기다리고 있던 차에 뛰어 올라탄 후, 떠나버렸다. 모든 사람들은 일어났고, 말을 꺼내기 시작했다. 점원은 경찰에 전화했고, 경찰은 강도의 모습이나 강도가 타고 떠나간 차를 설명할 수 있는 사람이 있는지 물었다. 그러자 한 남성이 방어적으로 몰아붙이며 점원에게 마침 내가 생각하고 있었던 것을 그대로 말했다. "이봐요, 총이 나에게 겨눠지면, 총밖에 보이지 않습니다. 그러면 단번에 나는 나에게 명령된 어떤 것이라도 바로 하게 될 것입니다."

NOTE	
Step 1	**Survey**
Key Words	robbery; gun; weapon; fear
Signal Words	recently; when; then
Step 2	**Reading**
Purpose	to recount what it is like to be threatened with a gun
Pattern of Organization	time order (narrative)
Tone	emotional
Main Idea	When threatened by a pointed gun, one tends to focus only on the weapon.
Step 3	**Summary**
지문 요약하기 (Paraphrasing)	The narrator experienced being threatened by a man with a gun during a robbery at a store. Although the narrator was bigger and stronger than the robber, fear of the weapon made him obey the robber. None of the witnesses could describe the robber, because they were focused only on the gun itself.
Step 4	**Recite**
	요약문 말로 설명하기

30 Read the passage and follow the directions.

Preparing food for the saute line at the restaurant where I work is a hectic two-hour job. I come to work at 3:00 p.m. knowing that everything must be done by 5:00 p.m. The first thing I do is to check the requisition for the day. Then I have to clean and season five or six prime rib roasts and place them in the slow-cooking oven. After this, I clean and season five trays of white potatoes for baking and put them in the fast oven. Now I have two things cooking, prime ribs and potatoes, at different times and temperatures, and they both have to be watched very closely. In the meantime, I must put three trays of bacon in the oven. The bacon needs very close watching. Next, I make popovers, which are unseasoned rolls. These also go into an oven for baking. Now I have prime ribs, baking potatoes, bacon, and popovers cooking at the same time and all of them needing to be closely watched. With my work area set up, I must make clarified butter and garlic butter. The clarified butter is for cooking liver, veal, and fish. The garlic butter is for stuffing escargots. I have to make ground meat stuffing also. Half of the ground meat will be mixed with wild rice and will be used to stuff breasts of chicken. The other half of the ground meat mixture will be used to stuff mushrooms. I have to prepare veal, cut and season scampi, and clean and saute mushrooms and onions. In the meantime, I check the prime ribs and potatoes, take the bacon and the popovers out of the oven, and put the veal and chicken into the oven. Now I make au jus, which is served over the prime ribs, make the soup for the day, and cook the vegetables and rice. Then I heat the bordelaise sauce, make the special for the day, and last of all, cook food for the employees. This and sometimes more has to be done by five o'clock. Is it any wonder that I say preparing food for the saute line at the restaurant where I work is a very hectic two-hour job!

escargots : snails

MEMO

Describe the main idea of the passage in ONE sentence.

_____

NOTE

Step 1	Survey
Key Words	
Signal Words	
Step 2	**Reading**
Purpose	
Pattern of Organization	
Tone	
Main Idea	
Step 3	**Summary**
지문 요약하기 (Paraphrasing)	
Step 4	**Recite**
요약문 말로 설명하기	

02

💡 **Answer Key**

Preparing food for the saute line at the restaurant where I work is a **hectic** two-hour job. I come to work at 3:00 p.m. knowing that everything must be done by 5:00 p.m. The first thing I do is to check the requisition for the day. Then I have to clean and season five or six prime rib roasts and place them in the slow-cooking oven. After this, I clean and season five trays of white potatoes for baking and put them in the fast oven. Now I have two things cooking, prime ribs and potatoes, at different times and temperatures, and they both have to be watched very closely. In the meantime, I must put three trays of bacon in the oven. The bacon needs very close watching. Next, I make popovers, which are unseasoned rolls. These also go into an oven for baking. Now I have prime ribs, baking potatoes, bacon, and popovers cooking at the same time and all of them needing to be closely watched. With my work area set up, I must make clarified butter and garlic butter. The clarified butter is for cooking liver, veal, and fish. The garlic butter is for stuffing escargots. I have to make ground meat stuffing also. Half of the ground meat will be mixed with wild rice and will be used to stuff breasts of chicken. The other half of the ground meat mixture will be used to stuff mushrooms. I have to prepare veal, cut and season scampi, and clean and saute mushrooms and onions. In the meantime, I check the prime ribs and potatoes, take the bacon and the popovers out of the oven, and put the veal and chicken into the oven. Now I make au jus, which is served over the prime ribs, make the soup for the day, and cook the vegetables and rice. Then I heat the bordelaise sauce, make the special for the day, and last of all, cook food for the employees. This and sometimes more has to be done by five o'clock. Is it any wonder that I say **preparing food for the saute line at the restaurant where I work is a very hectic two-hour job!**

▶ key words

▶ repeltition

모범답안

Preparing food at a restaurant where the speaker works is a very busy job.

내가 일하는 레스토랑에서 볶음 라인 음식을 준비하는 것은 정신없이 바쁜 두 시간짜리 일이다. 난 다섯 시까지 모든 일이 완료되어야 한다는 것을 알고 있기에 3시에 직장에 온다. 내가 가장 먼저 하는 일은 여섯 개의 주문된 최고급 갈비구이를 확인하고 느리게 조리되는 오븐에 넣는 것이다. 그 후 구워야 하는 다섯 쟁반의 하얀 감자들을 씻고 양념을 하여, 빨리 조리되는 오븐에 넣는다. 이제 두 가지, 최상등품 소갈비와 감자는 다른 시간과 온도에 맞춰져서 요리되고 있고, 두 가지 모두 주의 깊게 지켜봐야 한다. 그동안 오븐에 세 쟁반의 베이컨을 넣어야 한다. 베이컨은 아주 세밀한 관찰이 요구된다. 다음 양념이 안 된 롤빵인 팝오버를 만든다. 이것도 굽기 위해 오븐에 넣는다. 이제 갈비구이, 구운 감자, 베이컨, 팝오버가 동시에 구워지고 있고 모든 요리를 주의 깊게 지켜봐야 한다. 내 근무 구역을 준비하면서 나는 속을 채운 식용 달팽이를 위한 녹인 버터와 마늘 버터를 만들어야 한다. 다진 고기 속도 만들어야 한다. 다진 고기의 절반은 줄풀과 섞어 닭가슴살을 채워 넣기 위해 사용될 것이다. 다진 고기의 또 다른 절반은 버섯 속을 채우기 위해 사용될 것이다. 송아지 고기를 준비하고 자르고 새우튀김을 양념하고 버섯과 양파를 씻고 볶아야 한다. 그러는 동안 소갈비와 감자를 확인하고 베이컨과 팝오버를 오븐에서 꺼내고 송아지 고기와 치킨을 오븐에 넣는다. 이제 소갈비 위에 뿌릴 고기 육즙을 만들고 그날의 수프를 만들고 야채와 쌀을 요리한다. 그리고 보르돌레즈 소스를 데우고 그날의 스페셜 요리를 만들고 마지막으로 직원들을 위한 요리를 한다. 이만큼의, 가끔은 더 많은 양의 일이 다섯 시 정각까지 끝나야 한다. 내가 일하는 레스토랑에서 볶음 라인을 위한 음식을 준비하는 것이 눈코 뜰 새 없이 바쁜 두 시간짜리 일이라고 말하는 것이 이제 놀라운가!

NOTE

Step 1	Survey
Key Words	Preparing food for the saute line at a restaurant; hectic
Signal Words	The first thing; Then; After this; Now; In the meantime; Next; With my work area set up; In the meantime; Now; Then; last of all; by five o'clock
Step 2	Reading
Purpose	to describe the hectic job of preparing food for the saute line
Pattern of Organization	time order (process)
Tone	informative
Main Idea	Preparing food at a restaurant where the speaker works is a very busy job.
Step 3	Summary
지문 요약하기 (Paraphrasing)	Preparing food for the saute line is a very hectic two-hour job. There is a large variety of foods that need to be readied, including prime ribs, butters, and sauces, among many more.
Step 4	Recite
	요약문 말로 설명하기

31 Read the passage and follow the directions.

Since that day, I've had the chance to visit another bomb museum of a different kind: the one that stands in Hiroshima. A serene building set in a garden, it is strangely quiet inside, with hushed viewers and hushed exhibits. Neither ideological nor histrionic, the displays stand entirely without editorial comment. They are simply artifacts, labeled: china saki cups melted together in a stack. A brass Buddha with his hands relaxed into molten pools and a hole where his face used to be. Dozens of melted watches, all stopped at exactly eight-fifteen. A white eyelet petticoat with great, brown-rimmed holes burned in the left side, stained with black rain, worn by a schoolgirl named Oshita-chan. She was half a mile from the hypocenter of the nuclear blast, wearing also a blue short-sleeved blouse, which was incinerated except for its collar, and a blue metal pin with a small white heart, which melted. Oshita-chan lived for approximately twelve hours after the bomb.

MEMO

Why do you think the displays in the museum "stand entirely without editorial comment"? Second, explain why the museum visitors are "hushed". Third, what is the significance of all the watches being "stopped at exactly eight-fifteen"?

_____

_____

_____

_____

_____

NOTE

Step 1	Survey
Key Words	
Signal Words	
Step 2	**Reading**
Purpose	
Pattern of Organization	
Tone	
Main Idea	
Step 3	**Summary**
지문 요약하기 (Paraphrasing)	
Step 4	**Recite**
요약문 말로 설명하기	

💡 Answer Key

Since that day, I've had the chance to visit another **bomb museum of a different kind: the one that stands in Hiroshima**. A serene building set in a garden, it is strangely quiet inside, with hushed viewers and **hushed exhibits**. Neither ideological nor histrionic, **the displays** stand entirely without editorial comment. They are simply artifacts, labeled: china saki cups **melted** together in a stack. A brass Buddha with his hands relaxed into **molten** pools and a hole where his face used to be. Dozens of melted watches, all stopped at exactly eight-fifteen. A white eyelet petticoat with great, brown-rimmed holes burned in the left side, stained with black rain, worn by a schoolgirl named **Oshita-chan**. She was half a mile from the hypocenter of the nuclear blast, wearing also a blue short-sleeved blouse, which was incinerated except for its collar, and a blue metal pin with a small white heart, which **melted**. Oshita-chan lived for approximately twelve hours after the bomb.

➤ key word

➤ key word

➤ key word

모범답안

To maintain a direct connection to the viewer (that resonates on each person's own terms). Second, they are hushed to show respect toward the event and loss, and also because they might be deep in introspection. Third, this was the moment the bomb was detonated(exploded), and broke them.

한글 번역

그 날 이후, 히로시마에 있는 다른 종류의 폭탄 박물관을 방문할 기회가 있었다. 고요한 건물이 정원에 세워져 있고 조용한 관람객들과 전시로 안은 이상하게 조용했다. 이념적이지도 과장적이지도 않게 전시는 편집된 코멘트 없이 온전하게 서 있었다. 그것들은 단순히 인공물이었고 중국의 사키 컵이 산더미로 녹았다는 라벨이 붙어 있었다. 부처상의 손이 녹은 웅덩이에 풀려 있고 얼굴이 있던 자리에 구멍이 있었다. 수십 개의 녹은 시계들은 정확히 8시 15분에 멈춰져 있었다. 커다란 갈색 테두리의 구멍이 왼쪽에 그슬려져 있고 까만 비로 인해 얼룩이 져 있는 오시타 짱이라는 여학생이 입었던 하얀색 구멍이 난 속치마가 있다. 그녀는 카라를 제외하고 다 타버린 파란색 반팔 블라우스를 입고 녹아버린 하얀색 작은 하트 모양의 파란색 메탈 핀을 한 상태로 핵 폭발의 진원지로부터 0.5마일 떨어져 있었다. 오시타 짱은 폭발 이후 대략 12시간 동안 살아 있었다.

02

Step 1	Survey
Key Words	The bomb museum at Hiroshima; the displays; melted
Signal Words	

Step 2	Reading
Purpose	to depict the bomb museum at Hiroshima
Pattern of Organization	description
Tone	solemn
Main Idea	The bomb museum at Hiroshima shows people the horror of an atomic bomb explosion.

Step 3	Summary
지문 요약하기 (Paraphrasing)	The bomb museum at Hiroshima shows us the horror of an atomic bomb explosion. It presents ruined objects without editorial comment to make an impact. Among the objects is a petticoat that is partially burned and was worn by a schoolgirl who died shortly after the bombing.

Step 4	Recite
요약문 말로 설명하기	

32 Read the passage and follow the directions.

I walk into the gym, and there they are, the cardio-bots, half human, half machine, eyes fixed on banks of televisions and ears glued to iPods as they scale imaginary mountains or jog down simulated country roads. How driven they seem, how profoundly self-conscious. Digital monitors strapped around their biceps register their blood pressures and heart rates as their tissues absorb L-glutamine-laced protein drinks that taste like the sort of thing computers would drink if computers got thirsty. And though there must be 30 cardio-bots, lifting their sinewy thighs in unison as their StairMasters and treadmills tick off the number of calories they've burned, each one of them seems to exist in his or her own universe, oblivious to the rest.

What is the writer's opinion of the "Cardio-bots" in the gym? Second, why does the writer describe the cardio-bots as being "half human, half machine"?

_____

_____

_____

_____

_____

NOTE

Step 1	Survey
Key Words	
Signal Words	
Step 2	**Reading**
Purpose	
Pattern of Organization	
Tone	
Main Idea	
Step 3	**Summary**
지문 요약하기 (Paraphrasing)	
Step 4	**Recite**
요약문 말로 설명하기	

02

💡 Answer Key

I walk into the gym, and there they are, **the cardio-bots, half human, half machine,** eyes fixed on banks of televisions and ears glued to iPods as they scale imaginary mountains or jog down simulated country roads. How driven they seem, how profoundly self-conscious. Digital monitors strapped around their biceps register their blood pressures and heart rates as their tissues absorb L-glutamine-laced protein drinks that taste like the sort of thing computers would drink if computers got thirsty. And though there must be 30 cardio-bots, lifting their sinewy thighs in unison as their StairMasters and treadmills tick off the number of calories they've burned, each one of them seems to exist in his or her own universe, oblivious to the rest.

➤ key words
: definition

모범답안

They act exactly as robots, autonomous, unresponsive, which is a metaphorically-suggested judgment of the humans exercising. Second, as the people sitting on the machine do exercise, the two work together as a combined whole.

한글 번역

내가 체육관 안으로 걸어 들어가면, 거기에는 그들이 있다. 반쯤은 인간이고, 반쯤은 기계와 같으며, 눈은 방둑처럼 길게 늘어선 텔레비전에 고정되어 있고 귀에는 아이팟이 딱 붙어있는 채 상상의 산을 오르거나 가상의 시골길을 조깅하며 내려가는 심근 강화 운동 로봇들이 말이다. 그들은 얼마나 의욕 넘쳐 보이며, 얼마나 엄청나게 자의식이 강해 보이는가. 컴퓨터가 목마르면 마실 만한 맛이 나는, L-글루타민이 가미된 단백질 음료를 그 로봇들의 세포 조직이 흡수할 때, 그들의 이두박근에 묶여있는 디지털 모니터들은 그들의 혈압과 심장 박동을 기록한다. 그리고 거기엔 자신들이 태워 온 열량의 숫자를 계단 오르기 기계와 트레드밀이 세어주는 동안 근육질로 된 자기 허벅지를 일제히 들어 올리는 30개의 심근 강화 로봇들이 있음이 분명하지만, 각각의 로봇은 그 혹은 그녀 자신만의 우주 안에서, 나머지 로봇들은 망각한 채 존재하는 것처럼 보인다.

02

NOTE ▶

Step 1	Survey
Key Words	the cardio-bots; half human, half machine
Signal Words	
Step 2	Reading
Purpose	to describe the cardio-bots in a gym
Pattern of Organization	definition
Tone	critical
Main Idea	The practice of exercising at the gym is a very inhuman (in both action and consumption).
Step 3	Summary
지문 요약하기 (Paraphrasing)	The practice of exercising is a very inhuman in both action and consumption. The cardio-bots at the gym are fully focused on their exercise with machine-like focus.
Step 4	Recite
요약문 말로 설명하기	

33   Read the passage and follow the directions.

A creative person, first, is not limited in his thinking to "what everyone knows." "Everyone knows" that trees are green. The creative artist is able to see that in certain lights some trees look blue or purple or yellow. The creative person looks at the world with his or her own eyes, not with the eyes of others. The creative individual also knows his or her own feelings better than the average person. Most people don't know the answer to the question, "How are you? How do you feel?" The reason they don't know is that they are so busy feeling what they are supposed to feel, thinking what they are supposed to think, that they never get down to examining their own deepest feelings.

MEMO

According to the writer, how does the creative person look at the world? Second, why do most people not know the answer to "how are you? How do you feel?" Third, what is the writer's definition of a creative person?

_____

_____

_____

_____

_____

NOTE

Step 1	Survey
Key Words	
Signal Words	
Step 2	**Reading**
Purpose	
Pattern of Organization	
Tone	
Main Idea	
Step 3	**Summary**
지문 요약하기 (Paraphrasing)	
Step 4	**Recite**
요약문 말로 설명하기	

💡 Answer Key

> **A creative person**, first, is not limited **in his thinking** to "what everyone knows." "Everyone knows" that trees are green. The creative artist is able to see that in certain lights some trees look blue or purple or yellow. The creative person looks at the world with his or her own eyes, not with the eyes of others. **The creative individual also** knows **his or her own feelings better than the average person**. Most people don't know the answer to the question, "How are you? How do you feel?" The reason they don't know is that they are so busy feeling what they are supposed to feel, thinking what they are supposed to think, that they never get down to examining **their own deepest feelings**.

➤ key words

➤ key word

모범답안

They see the world uniquely, without accepting the conventional perception of things. Second, they usually think about the answer they are expected to give about what they are thinking or feeling. Third, a creative person is one who looks at the world with her/his own thinking and knows her/his own deepest feelings.

한글 번역

창의적인 사람은 우선 자신의 사고를 '모두가 아는 것'으로 제한시키지 않는다. "모든 사람은 안다", 나무가 초록색이라는 것을. 창의적인 예술가는 어떤 빛에서는 나무가 파란색으로, 보라색 혹은 노란색으로 보이는 것을 알 수 있다. 창의적인 사람은 남의 눈이 아닌 자신의 눈으로 세상을 바라본다. 창의적인 사람은 또한 보통 사람보다 자신의 감정을 더 잘 안다. 대부분의 사람들은 "어떻게 지내? 기분이 어때?"라는 질문에 대한 대답을 모른다. 모르는 이유는 그들 자신이 느끼기로 되어 있는 것을 느끼고, 그들이 사고해야 하는 것에 대하여 사고하기에도 너무 바빠서 그들 자신의 가장 깊은 감정을 진단하는 것에 결코 관심을 기울이지 않기 때문이다.

NOTE

Step 1	Survey
Key Words	a creative person; thinking; feelings
Signal Words	is; also knows

Step 2	Reading
Purpose	to define what a creative person is
Pattern of Organization	definition
Tone	subjective
Main Idea	A creative person is one who looks at the world with her thinking and knows her own deepest feelings.

Step 3	Summary
지문 요약하기 (Paraphrasing)	A creative person is one who looks at the world with her thinking and knows her own deepest feelings. (or The creative person is able to see with their own eyes, which offers unique and truthful perception of the outside world and their own feelings.)

Step 4	Recite
요약문 말로 설명하기	

34 Read the passage and follow the directions.

What is likely to be the development of the family during the next two centuries? We cannot tell, but we can note certain forces at work which are likely, if unchecked, to have certain results. There are certain things in modem civilized communities which are tending to weaken the family; the chief of them is humanitarian sentiment toward children. More and more people come to feel that children should not suffer more than can be helped through their parents' misfortunes or even sins. In the Bible the lot of the orphan is always spoken of as very sad, and so no doubt it was; nowadays he suffers little more than other children. There will be a growing tendency for the state or charitable institutions to give fairly adequate care to neglected children, and consequently children will be more and more neglected by unconscientious parents or guardians. Gradually the expense of caring for neglected children out of public funds will become so great that there will be a very strong inducement for all who are not well off to avail themselves of the opportunities for giving their children over to the state; probably this will be done, in the end, as now with schooling, by practically all who are below a certain economic level.

MEMO

Identify the main class of people criticized in the above passage. Second, explain the changes in policy the writer is implying should be made.

_____

_____

_____

_____

_____

NOTE

Step 1	Survey
Key Words	
Signal Words	
Step 2	Reading
Purpose	
Pattern of Organization	
Tone	
Main Idea	
Step 3	Summary
지문 요약하기 (Paraphrasing)	
Step 4	Recite
요약문 말로 설명하기	

💡 Answer Key

What is likely to be the **development** of the **family** during the next two ————▸ key words
centuries? We cannot tell, but we can note certain forces at work which
are likely, if unchecked, to have certain results. There are certain things
in modem civilized communities which are tending to weaken the
family; the chief of them is **humanitarian** sentiment toward children. ————▸ key word
More and more people come to feel that children should not suffer more
than can be helped through their parents' misfortunes or even sins. In
the Bible the lot of the orphan is always spoken of as very sad, and so
no doubt it was; nowadays he suffers little more than other children.
There will be a growing tendency for the state or charitable institutions
to give fairly adequate care to **neglected** children, and consequently ————▸ key word
children will be more and more neglected by unconscientious parents or
guardians. Gradually the expense of caring for neglected children out of
public funds will become so great that there will be a very strong
inducement for all who are not well off to avail themselves of the
opportunities for giving their children over to the state; probably this
will be done, in the end, as now with schooling, by practically all who
are below a certain **economic level**. ————▸ key word

모범답안

Humanitarian sympathy(또는 emotion; sentiment) toward neglected children. Second, it is implied
that state and charitable institutions should not increase their support for neglected children so as
to discourage parents from relying on these.

어휘

at work 작용하는, (영향이) 미치는
inducement 유인; 동기
unchecked 억제하지(손을 쓰지) 않고 놔 둔

avail oneself of ~을 이용하다, ~을 적절히 사용하다
note 주목하다, 알아차리다
unconscientious 비양심적인; 지조가 없는

한글 번역

앞으로 200년 동안 가족은 어떻게 발달할 것 같은가? 우리는 알 수 없으나, 만일 내버려둔다면 어떤 결과를 낳을 수 있는 어떤 힘들이 작용하고 있음을 알아차릴 수는 있다. 현대 문명 사회에는 가족을 약화시키는 경향이 있는 어떤 것들이 있다; 이 가족을 약화시키는 것들 중에서 으뜸가는 것은 아이들에 대한 박애주의적인 감정이다. 부모에게 닥친 불행한 일이나 죄로 인하여 아이들이 도움을 받을 수 있는 것보다 더 많은 고통을 겪어서는 안 된다고(겪는 고통보다 더 많은 도움을 받아야 한다고) 느끼게 되는 사람들이 점점 더 많아지고 있다. 성경에서 고아의 운명은 항상 매우 비참하게 그려지며, (과거에는) 의심할 여지 없이 매우 비참했다; 그러나 오늘날 고아는 다른 아이들과 마찬가지로 고통을 겪지 않는다. 국가나 자선단체가 방치된 아이들에게 상당히 충분할 정도의 돌봄을 제공하는 경향이 증가할 것이며, 결과적으로 아이들이 (국가와 자선단체가 돌봐서 돌볼 필요가 없다고 생각하는) 비양심적인 부모나 후견인에 의해 점점 더 방치될 것이다. 공적자금에서 지출되는 방치된 아이들을 돌보는 비용은 점차적으로 막대해져서, 경제적으로 넉넉하지 않은 부모들에게는 아이를 국가에 맡길 기회를 활용하게 할 매우 강력한 유인책이 될 것이다. 아마도 이것은, 현재 학교 교육과 마찬가지로, 결국에는 특정 경제 수준 이하에 있는 거의 모든 사람들에게 이루어지게 될 것이다.

NOTE

Step 1	Survey
Key Words	family; development; humanitarian; neglected; economic level
Signal Words	more and more; nowadays; gradually; in the end
Step 2	**Reading**
Purpose	to predict changes that may take place in the family during the next two centuries
Pattern of Organization	series
Tone	speculative
Main Idea	Humanitarian sympathy toward neglected children could lead to the weakness of the family.
Step 3	**Summary**
지문 요약하기 (Paraphrasing)	Humanitarian sympathy toward neglected children could lead to the weakening of the family. State or charitable institutions tend to take over caring for neglected children. Consequently unconscientious parents, especially poor parents, will more and more come to turn the care of their children over to the state.
Step 4	**Recite**
요약문 말로 설명하기	

35 Read the passage and follow the directions.

Every day more than 100 million people hear the sound of background music. They hear it while they are working in offices, shopping in stores, and eating in restaurants. They even hear it while they are sitting in the dentist's chair. Why is background music played in so many places? The answer is easy. Music is such a powerful force that it can affect people's behavior. Studies show that background music can affect _____. Ronald Milliman, a marketing professor, measured the effects that fast music, slow music, and no music had on customers in a supermarket. He found that fast music did not affect sales very much when compared with no music. However, slow music made a big difference. Listening to music played slowly made shoppers move more slowly. When slow music was played, shoppers bought more and sales increased 38 percent. Milliman also found that restaurant owners can use music to their advantage. In the evening, playing slow music lengthened the amount of time customers spend in the restaurant. At lunch time, restaurants want people to eat more quickly so that they can serve more customers. Playing lively music at lunchtime encourages customers to eat quickly and leave.

MEMO

What is the title for the passage? Write down your answer in 5 words or more. Second, fill in the blank with the ONE word from the passage.

NOTE

Step 1	Survey
Key Words	
Signal Words	
Step 2	**Reading**
Purpose	
Pattern of Organization	
Tone	
Main Idea	
Step 3	**Summary**
지문 요약하기 (Paraphrasing)	
Step 4	**Recite**
요약문 말로 설명하기	

💡 Answer Key

Every day more than 100 million people hear the sound of **background music**. They hear it while they are working in offices, shopping in stores, and eating in **restaurants**. They even hear it while they are sitting in the dentist's chair. Why is **background music** played in so many places? The answer is easy. Music is such a powerful force that it can affect people's behavior. Studies show that **background music** can affect sales. Ronald Milliman, a marketing professor, measured the effects that fast music, **slow music**, and no music had on customers in a supermarket. He found that fast music did not affect sales very much when compared with no music. However, slow music made a big difference. Listening to music played slowly made shoppers move more slowly. When **slow music** was played, shoppers bought more and sales increased 38 percent. Milliman also found that **restaurant** owners can use music to their advantage. In the evening, playing **slow music** lengthened the amount of time customers spend in the **restaurant**. At lunch time, **restaurants** want people to eat more quickly so that they can serve more customers. Playing lively music at lunchtime encourages customers to eat quickly and leave.

→ key words

→ key word

모범답안

The title is "The Effect of Background Music on Human Behavior". The word is "sales".

한글 번역

매년 1억 명 이상의 사람들이 배경음악을 듣고 있다. 이들은, 사무실에서 일을 할 때, 상점에서 쇼핑을 할 때, 음식점에서 식사를 할 때 배경음악을 듣는다. 그들은 심지어 치과의사의 의자에 앉아 있을 때도 배경음악을 듣는다. 왜 배경음악이 그렇게 많은 장소에서 틀어지는가? 해답은 간단하다. 음악은 강력한 힘을 가지고 있어서 사람들의 행동에 영향을 줄 수 있기 때문이다. 연구 결과들은 배경음악이 사업상의 매출에 영향을 줄 수 있다는 것을 보여준다. 마케팅 교수인 로널드 밀리먼은 상점에서 빠른 음악, 느린 음악, 그리고 음악을 틀지 않는 것이 각각 고객들에게 미치는 영향을 알아보았다. 그는 음악을 틀지 않는 것과 비교할 때 빠른 음악이 판매에 그리 크게 영향을 미치지는 못한다는 것을 알아냈다. 하지만, 느린 음악은 아주 큰 효과가 있었다. 천천히 연주되는 음악을 듣는 것은 쇼핑객들이 보다 천천히 걷도록 하였다. 느린 음악이 틀어져 있을 때 쇼핑객들은 보다 많은 물건을 구입하였고 이에 따라 매출은 38% 증가하였다. 밀리먼은 또한 음식점 주인들이 음악을 그들에게 유리하도록 이용할 수 있다고 말한다. 저녁에, 느린 음악을 연주하는 것은 고객들이 음식점에서 보내는 시간을 연장시킨다. 점심시간에, 음식점들은 보다 많은 고객을 유치하기 위하여 사람들이 보다 빨리 식사하기를 원한다. 점심시간에 경쾌한 음악을 틀어주는 것은 고객들로 하여금 빨리 식사하고 떠나도록 자극한다.

NOTE

Step 1	Survey
Key Words	background music; slow music; restaurant
Signal Words	studies show; however; when
Step 2	Reading
Purpose	to explain the efficacy of background music
Pattern of Organization	
Tone	informative
Main Idea	Background music is prevalent and can have a strong effect on people, which can be useful for influencing business.
Step 3	Summary
지문 요약하기 (Paraphrasing)	Background music is common in everyday life because it has been proven to influence consumers. Slow music encourages more shopping or longer stays in a restaurant, while fast music can move along the lunchtime crowd at eateries.
Step 4	Recite
	요약문 말로 설명하기

36   Read the passage and follow the directions.

In spite of all its positive aspects, the Internet has its detractors. Some attack the use of the Internet as being time-consuming and addictive. In reality, research has shown that 90 percent of people who get on the Internet do what they need to do and then get off. It's the other 10 percent who are problem users. Early research stated that "although the new electronic media are frequently criticized for their so-called addictive qualities, little empirical evidence has been found to support the assertion that heavy media use is psychologically or physiologically addictive." Newer findings indicate that cyberaddiction—compulsive preoccupied usage of the Internet and chatrooms—can be a major negative aspect of Net usage. It is now believed that an Internet user can become addicted to the point of neglecting personal and work responsibilities, and becoming socially isolated. A study of college students, for example, found that 73 percent of students accessed the Internet at least once a week, and 13 percent of students indicated that their computer use interfered with personal functioning. Typically the computer addicts are bright, creative individuals who also feel lonely and isolated. They also can be bored, depressed, angry, or frustrated. About 71 percent were diagnosed as suffering from bipolar disorder, commonly called manic depression. The results of cyberaddiction can include lost jobs, college expulsions, emotional breakdowns, pedophilies stalking youngsters, marriages destroyed, domestic violence, unchecked deepening depression, heightened anxiety, mounting debts, broken trust, lies, and cover-ups. Symptoms of cyberaddiction include lying about or hiding the level of Internet usage, being preoccupied with using the Internet, and neglecting everything else in one's life. It's like a craving that you continue to satisfy despite the problems it's causing. On the other hand, spending time online may be more positive than excessive time in front of a television or playing video games. The key question to ask might be "Is your online time disrupting your face-to-face relationships, allowing you to hide from participating in face-to-face interactions, or forcing you to put other elements of your life on hold?" If you are an addict or think you are overdoing cyberconnectedness, ask yourself what you would do instead of spending so much time online. Some people who are addicted may need mental health therapy.

MEMO

Summarize the passage above in approximately 70 words.

_____

_____

_____

_____

_____

NOTE

Step 1	Survey
Key Words	
Signal Words	
Step 2	Reading
Purpose	
Pattern of Organization	
Tone	
Main Idea	
Step 3	Summary
지문 요약하기 (Paraphrasing)	
Step 4	Recite
요약문 말로 설명하기	

💡 Answer Key

In spite of all its positive aspects, **the Internet** has its detractors. Some attack the use of the Internet as being time-consuming and addictive. In reality, research has shown that 90 percent of people who get on **the Internet** do what they need to do and then get off. It's the other 10 percent who are problem users. Early research stated that "although the new electronic media are frequently criticized for their so-called addictive qualities, little empirical evidence has been found to support the assertion that heavy media use is psychologically or physiologically addictive." Newer findings indicate that **cyberaddiction**—compulsive preoccupied usage of the Internet and chatrooms—can be a major negative aspect of Net usage. It is now believed that **an Internet** user can become addicted to the point of neglecting personal and work responsibilities, and becoming socially isolated. A study of college students, for example, found that 73 percent of students accessed **the Internet** at least once a week, and 13 percent of students indicated that their computer use interfered with personal functioning. Typically the computer addicts are bright, creative individuals who also feel lonely and isolated. They also can be bored, depressed, angry, or frustrated. About 71 percent were diagnosed as suffering from bipolar disorder, commonly called manic depression. The results of **cyberaddiction** can include lost jobs, college expulsions, emotional breakdowns, pedophilies stalking youngsters, marriages destroyed, domestic violence, unchecked deepening depression, heightened anxiety, mounting debts, broken trust, lies, and cover-ups. Symptoms of **cyberaddiction** include lying about or hiding the level of Internet usage, being preoccupied with using the Internet, and neglecting everything else in one's life. It's like a craving that you continue to satisfy despite the problems it's causing. On the other hand, spending time online may be more positive than excessive time in front of a television or playing video games. The key question to ask might be "Is your online time disrupting your face-to-face relationships, allowing you to hide from participating in face-to-face interactions, or forcing you to put other elements of your life on hold?" If you are an addict or think you are overdoing cyberconnectedness, ask yourself what you would do instead of spending so much time online. Some people who are addicted may need mental health therapy.

▶ key word

▶ cyberaddiction

모범답안

Research indicates that cyberaddiction, which is obsessive use of the Internet and chatrooms, is a serious problem for some users. Recent research has shown that cyberaddicts are so attached to the Internet that they neglect their professional and personal lives. Symptoms of Internet addiction include lying about the level of usage and craving more and more time on the Internet. Users should question their own usage honestly and, if they are addicted, possibly seek therapy.

인터넷의 모든 긍정적인 면에도 불구하고, 인터넷을 비난하는 많은 사람들이 있다. 일부는 인터넷을 시간 소모가 크고 중독성이 있다고 공격한다. 하지만 사실 연구에 따르면 인터넷을 하는 사람들의 90%가 그들이 해야만 하는 일을 하고 인터넷 사용을 자제할 수 있다고 한다. 문제가 있는 사용자들은 10%이다. 초기 연구들은, "새로운 전자 미디어가 이른바 그들의 중독적인 특성을 가지고 있는 것 때문에 빈번하게 비판받고 있지만, 미디어를 과다 사용하는 것이 심리학적으로 혹은 생리학적으로 중독적이라는 주장을 뒷받침하는 실증적인 증거를 찾기는 힘들다"라고 주장했었다. 최신의 연구는 사이버 중독(충동적으로 인터넷과 채팅을 하는)이 인터넷 사용의 주요한 부정적인 면이 될 수 있음 보여준다. 인터넷 사용자는 자신의 개인적인 또는 업무 책임성을 무시하고, 사회적으로 소외될 정도로 중독이 될 수도 있다. 예를 들어 대학생들에 관한 어떤 연구를 보면 학생들의 73%는 적어도 일주일에 한 번은 인터넷에 접근했고 13%는 그들의 컴퓨터 사용이 개인적인 일을 하는 데 지장을 주는 것으로 나타났다. 대체적으로 컴퓨터 중독자들은 명석하지만 외로움을 느끼고 고립된 창의적인 개인들이다. 그들은 또한 지루해지거나 우울해지고 화가 나고 혹은 좌절하기도 한다. 약 71%가 조울증, 흔히 불리는 광적 우울증으로 고통받고 있다고 진단받았다. 사이버 중독의 결과는 실직, 퇴학, 신경쇠약, 소아성애자, 결혼 파탄, 가정폭력, 확인되지 않은 우울증, 고조된 불안, 늘어나는 빚, 깨진 신뢰, 거짓말, 은폐가 있다. 사이버 중독의 증상은 인터넷 사용의 정도를 숨기거나 혹은 사용에 대해 거짓말을 하면서 인터넷 사용에 정신이 팔려서 삶에서 다른 모든 것을 무시하는 것을 포함한다. 그것은 마치 그것이 야기하는 문제에도 불구하고 당신이 만족하기 위해 계속하는 갈망과도 같은 것이다. 한편, 온라인에서 시간을 쓰는 것은 비디오 게임을 하거나 텔레비전 앞에서 과도한 시간을 보내는 것보다는 긍정적일지도 모른다. 질문해야 할 핵심적 사항은 이것일지도 모른다. "온라인에서 보내는 시간이 당신의 타인과의 면대면 관계에 방해가 되는지, 당신이 면대면 상호작용에 참여하는 것을 피하도록 만드는지, 혹은 당신이 인생의 다른 요소들을 연기된 상태로 놔두도록 강요하는지"에 대해 물어야 할 것이다. 만약 당신이 중독자라면 혹은 사이버 유대를 지나치게 하고 있는 것으로 생각한다면, 온라인에서 많은 시간을 보내는 대신에 무엇을 할 것인지 당신 스스로에게 물어라. 사이버 중독인 어떤 사람들은 심리 치료가 필요할지도 모른다.

Step 1	Survey
Key Words	Internet; cyberaddiction
Signal Words	in spite of; in reality; typically; on the other hand
Step 2	**Reading**
Purpose	to point out the potential problems of cyberaddiction
Pattern of Organization	time order; series
Tone	informative
Main Idea	Cyberaddiction can cause serious damage in the lives of those who allow it to go unchecked.
Step 3	**Summary**
지문 요약하기 (Paraphrasing)	Cyberaddiction, which is obsessive use of the Internet and chatrooms, is a serious problem for some users. Recent research has shown that cyberaddicts are so attached to the Internet that they neglect their professional and personal lives. Symptoms of Internet addiction include lying about the level of usage and craving more and more time on the Internet. Users should question their own usage honestly and, if they are addicted, possibly seek therapy.
Step 4	**Recite**
	요약문 말로 설명하기

37 Read the passage and follow the directions.

Human beings no longer thrive under the water from which their ancestors emerged, but their relationship with the sea remains close. Over half the world's people live within 100 kilometers (62 miles) of the coast; a tenth are within 10 kilometers. On land at least, the sea delights the senses and excites the imagination. The sight and smell of the sea inspire courage and adventure, fear and romance. Though the waves may be rippling or mountainous, the waters angry or calm, the ocean itself is eternal. Its moods pass. Its tides keep to a rhythm. It is unchanging. Or so it has long seemed. Appearances deceive, though. Large parts of the sea may indeed remain unchanged, but in others, especially in the surface and coastal waters where 90% of marine life is to be found, the impact of man's activities is increasingly plain. This should hardly be a surprise. Man has changed the landscape and the atmosphere. It would be odd if the seas, which he has for centuries used for food, for transport, for dumping rubbish and, more recently, for recreation, had not also been affected.

The evidence abounds. The fish that once seemed an inexhaustible source of food are now almost everywhere in _____: 90% of large predatory fish (the big ones such as tuna and sharks) have gone. In estuaries and coastal waters, 85% of the large whales have disappeared, and nearly 60% of the small ones. Many of the smaller fish also decline. Indeed, most familiar sea creatures, from albatrosses to walruses, from seals to oysters, have suffered huge losses.

MEMO

Describe the main idea of the passage. Second, fill in the blank with the ONE most appropriate word from the passage.

_____

_____

_____

NOTE

Step 1	Survey
Key Words	
Signal Words	
Step 2	**Reading**
Purpose	
Pattern of Organization	
Tone	
Main Idea	
Step 3	**Summary**
지문 요약하기 (Paraphrasing)	
Step 4	**Recite**
	요약문 말로 설명하기

02

💡 Answer Key

Human beings no longer thrive under the **water** from which their ancestors emerged, but their relationship with the sea remains close. Over half the world's people live within 100 kilometers (62 miles) of the coast; a tenth are within 10 kilometers. On land at least, the sea delights the senses and excites the imagination. The sight and smell of the sea inspire courage and adventure, fear and romance. Though the waves may be rippling or mountainous, the **waters** angry or calm, the ocean itself is eternal. Its moods pass. Its tides keep to a rhythm. It is unchanging. Or so it has long seemed. Appearances deceive, though. Large parts of the sea may indeed remain unchanged, but in others, especially in the surface and coastal **waters** where 90% of marine life is to be found, the impact of man's activities is increasingly plain. This should hardly be a surprise. Man has changed the landscape and the atmosphere. It would be odd if the seas, which he has for centuries used for food, for transport, for dumping rubbish and, more recently, for recreation, had not also been **affected**.

→ key words

→ key word

The evidence abounds. The fish that once seemed an inexhaustible source of food are now almost everywhere in decline : 90% of large predatory fish (the big ones such as tuna and sharks) have gone. In estuaries and coastal **waters**, 85% of the large whales have disappeared, and nearly 60% of the small ones. Many of the smaller fish also decline. Indeed, most familiar sea creatures, from albatrosses to walruses, from seals to oysters, have suffered huge losses.

모범답안

The main idea is that the oceans have been an important part of human life and are being drastically damaged by human influence. Second, the word is "decline".

한글 번역

인간은 더 이상, 자신의 조상들이 나왔던, 바다 속에서 번창할 수는 없지만 바다와의 관계는 여전히 긴밀하다. 전 세계 인구의 절반 이상이 해안으로부터 100km 이내에 거주하고 있으며, 전 세계 인구의 1/10이 해안으로부터 10km 이내에 거주하고 있다. 적어도 육지에서, 바다는 인간의 감각을 만족시키며 그들의 상상을 자극시킨다. 바다의 모습과 바다의 냄새는 용기, 모험, 두려움 그리고 낭만을 고취시킨다. 파도가 물결치고 산처럼 높이 일어날지라도, 바다가 사납게 일렁거리거나 잔잔할지라도, 바다 그 자체는 영원하다. 바다의 기분은 변화한다. 바다의 밀물과 썰물은 규칙적으로 변화한다. 하지만 바다는 변화하지 않는다. 아니, 바다는 오랫동안 변화하지 않는 것처럼 보였다. 하지만, 겉모습은 본질을 속이는 법이다. 바다의 많은 부분이 여전히 변화하지 않는 것처럼 보인다. 하지만 다른 부분, 특히 해양생물의 90%가 생존하고 있는 바다 표면과 연근해에 있어서, 인간의 활동으로 인한 충격은 점점 더 분명하게 드러나고 있다. 이 사실은 결코 놀라운 일이 아니다. 인간은 경관과 대기를 변화시켰다. 인간이 수 세기에 걸쳐 식량과 교통과 쓰레기 처리장으로 그리고 최근에는 여가생활을 위한 목적으로 사용해온 바다가 전혀 영향을 받지 않았다고 생각하는 것이야말로 이상한 것이다.

증거는 많다. 한때 무궁한 식량자원처럼 보였던 물고기가 거의 모든 곳에서 지금은 줄어들고 있다: 참치나 상어 같은 대형 포식어류의 90%가 사라졌다. 하구나 연해에선, 큰 고래들이 85%나 사라졌고, 작은 고래들도 60%가 사라졌다. 더 작은 물고기 다수도 줄어들고 있다. 실제로 알바트로스에서 해마, 바다표범에서 굴까지 대부분의 친숙한 해양생물이 막대한 손실을 입었다.

NOTE

Step 1	Survey
Key Words	human beings; water; affected
Signal Words	though; indeed
Step 2	**Reading**
Purpose	to highlight the effects man has had on the sea
Pattern of Organization	description
Tone	concerned; critical
Main Idea	The oceans have been an important part of human life and are being drastically damaged by human influence.
Step 3	**Summary**
지문 요약하기 (Paraphrasing)	The ancestors of came from the ocean, and we have remained deeply connected with it, which has resulted in major damage caused to the proximal marine ecology. There has been a steep decline in the populations of sea life as a result of human influence.
Step 4	**Recite**
요약문 말로 설명하기	

38 Read the passage and follow the directions.

Who am I?

For Asian-American students, the answer is a diligent, hardworking and intelligent young person. But living up to this reputation has secretly haunted me. The labeling starts in elementary school. It's not uncommon for a teacher to remark, "You're Asian and you're supposed to do well in math." The underlying message is, "You're Asian and you're supposed to be smarter." Not to say being labeled intelligent isn't flattering, because it is, or not to deny that basking in the limelight of being top of my class isn't ego-boosting, because frankly it is. But at a certain point, the pressure became crushing. I felt as if doing poorly on my next spelling quiz would stain the exalted reputation of all Asian students forever. So I continued to be an academic overachiever, as were my friends. By junior high school I started to believe I was indeed smarter. I became condescending toward non-Asians. I was a bigot; all my friends were Asians. The thought of intermingling occurred rarely if ever. My elitist opinion of Asian students changed, however, in high school. As a student at what is considered one of the nation's most competitive science and math schools, I found that being on top is no longer an easy feat. I quickly learned that Asian students were not smarter. How could I ever have believed such a thing? All around me are intelligent, ambitious people who are not only Asian but white, black and Hispanic. Superiority complexes aside, the problem of social segregation still exists in the schools. With a few exceptions, each race socializes only with its "own kind." Students see one another in the classroom, but outside the classroom there remains distinct segregation. Racist lingo abounds. An Asian student who socializes only with other Asians is believed to be an Asian Supremacist or, at the very least, arrogant and closed off. Yet an Asian student who socializes only with whites is called a "twinkie," one who is yellow on the outside but white on the inside. A white teenager who socializes only with whites is thought

MEMO

of as prejudiced, yet one who socializes with Asians is considered an "egg," white on the outside and yellow on the inside. These culinary classifications go on endlessly, needless to say, leaving many confused, and leaving many more fearful than ever of social experimentation. Because the stereotypes are accepted almost unanimously, they are rarely challenged. Many develop harmful stereotypes of entire races. We label people before we even know them. Labels learned at young age later metamorphose into more visible acts of racism. For example, my parents once accused and ultimately fired a Puerto Rican cashier, believing she had stolen $200 from the register at their grocery store. They later learned it was a mistake. An Asian shopkeeper nearby once beat a young Hispanic youth who worked there with a baseball bat because he believed the boy to be lazy and dishonest. We all hold misleading stereotypes of people that limit us as individuals in that we cheat ourselves out of the benefits different cultures can contribute. We can grow and learn from each culture whether it be Chinese, Korean or African American. Just recently some Asian boys in my neighborhood were attacked by a group of young white boys who have christened themselves the Master Race. Rather than being angered by this act, I feel pity for this generation that lives in a state of bigotry. It may be too late for our parents' generation to accept that each person can only be judged for the characteristics that set him or her apart as an individual. We, however, can do better.

How did it affect the writer to be labeled as intelligent? Second, what did the writer learn about other students when she went to the competitive high school? Third, what is an "Asian supremacist", a "twinkie" and an "egg"? How do the culinary classifications influence people's behavior? According to the writer, how should we judge people?

NOTE

Step 1	Survey
Key Words	
Signal Words	
Step 2	**Reading**
Purpose	
Pattern of Organization	
Tone	
Main Idea	
Step 3	**Summary**
지문 요약하기 (Paraphrasing)	
Step 4	**Recite**
요약문 말로 설명하기	

🔆 Answer Key

Who am I?

For **Asian-American students**, the answer is **a diligent, hardworking and intelligent young person**. But living up to this reputation has secretly haunted me. **The labeling** starts in elementary school. It's not uncommon for a teacher to remark, "You're Asian and you're supposed to do well in math." The underlying message is, "You're Asian and you're supposed to be smarter." Not to say being labeled intelligent isn't flattering, because it is, or not to deny that basking in the limelight of being top of my class isn't ego-boosting, because frankly it is. But at a certain point, the pressure became crushing. I felt as if doing poorly on my next spelling quiz would stain the exalted reputation of all Asian students forever. So I continued to be an academic overachiever, as were my friends. By junior high school I started to believe I was indeed smarter. I became condescending toward non-Asians. I was a bigot; all my friends were Asians. The thought of intermingling occurred rarely if ever. My elitist opinion of Asian students changed, however, in high school. As a student at what is considered one of the nation's most competitive science and math schools, I found that being on top is no longer an easy feat. I quickly learned that Asian students were not smarter. How could I ever have believed such a thing? All around me are intelligent, ambitious people who are not only Asian but white, black and Hispanic. Superiority complexes aside, the problem of social segregation still exists in the schools. With a few exceptions, each race socializes only with its "own kind." Students see one another in the classroom, but outside the classroom there remains distinct segregation. **Racist lingo** abounds. An Asian student who socializes only with other Asians is believed to be an Asian Supremacist or, at the very least, arrogant and closed off. Yet an Asian student who socializes only with whites is called a "**twinkie**," one who is yellow on the outside but white on the inside. A white teenager who socializes only with whites is thought of as prejudiced, yet one who socializes with Asians is considered an "egg," white on the outside and yellow on the inside. **These culinary classifications** go on endlessly, needless to say, leaving many confused, and leaving many more fearful than ever of social experimentation. Because the stereotypes are accepted almost unanimously, they are rarely challenged. Many develop harmful stereotypes of entire races. We **label** people before we even know them. **Labels** learned at young age later metamorphose into more visible acts of racism. For example,

➤key words

➤key word

➤key word

02

my parents once accused and ultimately fired a Puerto Rican cashier, believing she had stolen $200 from the register at their grocery store. They later learned it was a mistake. An Asian shopkeeper nearby once beat a young Hispanic youth who worked there with a baseball bat because he believed the boy to be lazy and dishonest. We all hold **misleading stereotypes** of people that limit us as individuals in that we cheat ourselves out of the benefits different cultures can contribute. We can grow and learn from each culture whether it be Chinese, Korean or African American. Just recently some Asian boys in my neighborhood were attacked by a group of young white boys who have christened themselves the Master Race. Rather than being angered by this act, I feel pity for this generation that lives in a state of bigotry. **It may be too late for our parents' generation to accept that each person can only be judged for the characteristics that set him or her apart as an individual. We, however, can do better.**

→key word

main point

모범답안

It put a lot of pressure on her to perform better to not ruin the Asian stereotype. Second, she learned that Asian students were not more intelligent, as her classmates were from all other races. Third, an "Asian supremacist" is an Asian who only associates with other Asian students. While a "twinkie" is an Asian on the outside (appearance), but white on the inside—like the snack food, a twinkie. An "egg" is yellow on inside but white by outward appearances. Fourth, they confuse people and make them self-conscious about who they associate with. Fifth, we should judge them by their true nature, and not via any stereotypes, just as individuals.

한글 번역

나는 누구인가? 아시아계 미국 학생들에게 그 정답은 근면하고, 열심히 일하고, 똑똑한 젊은이다. 하지만 이러한 기대에 부응하는 것은 비밀스럽게 나를 괴롭혔다. (그러한) 규정은 초등학교에서 시작한다. 선생님들이 "너는 아시아인이니 수학을 잘하겠지"라고 말하는 것은 특별한 상황이 아니다. 그 기저에 숨어 있는 의미는 "너는 아시아인이니 똑똑해야 해"라는 말이다. 똑똑하다는 낙인이 기분 좋지 않다는 말은 아닌 것이, 사실 기분 좋기 때문이다. 또한, 우리 반에서 상위권이라는 각광을 누리는 것에 대하여 자신감이 드높아지는 것에 대하여 부인하는 것은 아닌 것이, 실제 그리하기 때문이다. 하지만 어떤 면에서 그러한 압박은 치명적이다. 나는 마치 내 다음 스펠링 시험을 잘 못 치르는 것이 모든 아시아 학생의 높은 명성을 영원히 더럽히는 것처럼 느껴졌다. 그래서 나는 나의 친구들이 그랬던 것처럼 계속해서 학업의 과잉성취자가 되었다. 중학교 시절 즈음에 나는 내가 실제로 남들보다 똑똑하다고 믿기 시작했다. 나는 비아시아 학생들에게 거들먹거리게 되었다. 나는 편견이 아주 심한 사람이었는데, 내 모든 친구들이 아시아인들이었다. 섞여서 어울린다는 생각은 거의 하지도 않았다. 하지만 나의 아시아 학생에 대한 엘리트주의적인 생각은 고등학교에서 바뀌었다. 국가에서 가장 경쟁이 치열한 과학, 수학 학교들 중 한 곳의 학생으로서, 나는 일등을 하는 것이 더 이상 쉬운 일이 아니라는 것을 깨달았다. 나는 아시아 학생들이 특별히 더 똑똑하지 않다는 것을 빨리 깨달았다. 어떻게 그런 것을 믿어왔을까? 내 주변의 모든 이들은 똑똑하고 야망이 있었으며, 그들은 아시아인뿐 아니라 백인, 흑인, 그리고 히스패닉계 사람들까지 포함하였다. 우월 콤플렉스를 제쳐두고, 사회적 차별의 문제는 여전히 학교에 존재하였다. 몇 경우를 제외하고, 각 인종들은 '자신의 인종' 안에서만 사교활동을 하였다. 학생들은 서로 교실에서 보지만 교실 밖에서는 뚜렷한 분리가 존재하였다. 인종차별적인 말들이 아주 많았다. 아시아인들과만 어울리는 아시아 학생들은 아시아인 우월주의자 혹은 적어도 오만하고 단절되어 있다고 생각되었다. 하지만 백인들이랑만 어울리는 아시아 학생들은 바깥은 노랗지만 안은 하얀 "트윙키"라고 불린다. 백인들과만 어울리는 백인들은 편견이 있다고 생각되지만 아시아인들과 어울리는 백인들은 바깥은 하얗고 안은 노란 "달걀"로 간주된다. 이러한 음식의 분류는 말할 필요도 없이 많은 이들에게 혼란을 남기고 사회적 실험보다 더 많은 공포를 남기며 끝없이 지속된다. 왜냐하면 고정관념은 거의 만장일치로 받아들여지기 때문에, 도전 받지 않는다. 많은 이들이 전 인종에 대한 해로운 고정관념을 생성하였다. 우리는 사람들을 알기도 전에 낙인을 찍는다. 꼬리표는 어린 나이에 배워지고 나중에 더 가시적인 인종차별 행위로 탈바꿈된다. 예를 들어 나의 부모님은 푸에르토리코인 계산원이 그 식료품 가게의 현금등록기에서 200달러를 훔쳤다고 생각하여 그 직원을 신고하여 결국에는 해고하였다. 그들은 나중에 그것이 실수였다는 것을 알았다. 근처의 한 아시아인 가게 주인이 한때 그 곳에서 일하는 젊은 히스패닉계 젊은이를 게으르고 정직하지 않다는 이유로 야구 방망이로 때렸다. 우리 모두는 다른 문화가 가지고 올 수 있는 이점들에 대해 우리 자신을 속이면서 우리에게 제한을 가하는 잘못된 고정관념을 가지고 있다. 우리는 중국인, 한국인, 아프리카계 미국인이든지 간에 서로의 문화로부터 배우고 성장할 수 있다. 최근 우리 동네에 살고 있는 몇몇의 아시아 학생들이, 스스로에게 우월 민족이라고 칭하는 한 무리의 젊은 백인 소년들에게 공격받았다. 나는 이러한 행동에 화가 나기보다는 심한 편견 속에서 살아가는 이러한 세대들에게 동정을 느낀다. 우리의 부모 세대들은 모든 사람들이 그나 그녀 자신의 특징들로만 판단될 수 있다는 사실을 받아들이기에는 아마도 너무 늦을 것이나, 우리는 더 잘 할 수 있다.

NOTE

Step 1	Survey
Key Words	Asian-American students; labeling; Racist lingo; twinkie; egg; misleading stereotypes
Signal Words	For example
Step 2	Reading
Purpose	to persuade people to discard racial stereotypes
Pattern of Organization	series (classification&division)
Tone	critical
Main Idea	The holding of stereotypes is ongoing and keeps racism and its effects alive.
Step 3	Summary
지문 요약하기 (Paraphrasing)	The holding of stereotypes is ongoing and keeps racism and its effects alive. For the writer, stereotypes influenced surrounding her Asian identity influenced her life through school. Likewise, outside of the classroom, the way races intermix can bring about judgements from peers for students. Stereotypes lead to greater acts of violence and avoidance of other cultures we could benefit from, so should be unlearned for a better future.
Step 4	Recite
	요약문 말로 설명하기

39   Read the passage and follow the directions.

MEMO

The time to harvest honey is summer's end, when it is hot. The temper of the bees requires that we wear protective clothing: a full set of overalls, a zippered bee veil and leather gloves. Even a very strong young man works up a sweat wrapped in a bee suit in the heat, hustling 60-pound supers while being harassed by angry bees. It is a hard job, harder even than haying, but jobs are scarce here and I've always been able to hire help.

This year David, the son of a friend of mine, is working for me. He is big and strong and used to labor, but he was nervous about bees. After we had made the job arrangement I set about desensitizing him to bee stings. I put a piece of ice on his arm to numb it and then, holding a bee carefully its head. I put it on the numbed spot and let it sting him. A bee stinger is barbed and stays in the flesh, pulling loose from the body of the bee as it struggles to free itself. The bulbous poison sac at the top of the stinger continues to pulsate after the bee has left, pumping the venom and forcing the stinger deeper into the flesh.

The first day I wanted David to have only a partial dose of venom, so after a minute I scraped the stinger out. A few people are seriously sensitive to bee venom; each sting they receive can cause a more severe reaction than the one before—reactions ranging from hives, breathing difficulties, accelerated heart beat and choking to anaphylactic shock and death. I didn't think David would be allergic in that way, but I wanted to make sure. We sat down and had a cup of coffee and I watched him. The spot where the stinger went in grew red and began to swell. That was a normal reaction, and so was the itching that he felt later on. The next day I coaxed a bee into stinging him again, repeating the procedure, but I left the stinger in place for 10 minutes, until the venom sac was empty. Again the spot was red, swollen and itchy but had disappeared in 24 hours. By that time David was ready to catch a bee himself and administer his own sting. He also decided that the ice cube was a

bother and gave it up. I told him to keep to one sting a day until he had no redness or swelling and then to increase to two stings. He was ready for them the next day. The greater amount of venom caused redness and swelling for a few days, but soon his body could tolerate it without reaction and he increased the number of stings once again.

Today he told me he was up to six stings. His arms look as though they have track marks on them, but the fresh stings are having little effect. I'll keep him at it until he can tolerate 10 a day with no reaction and then I'll not worry about taking him out to the bee yard.

When is the honey harvested? Second, how much do the supers that hold the honey weigh? Third, how many stings per day does the beekeeper want her helper to tolerate before taking him out to the bee yard?

_____

_____

_____

NOTE

Step 1	Survey
Key Words	
Signal Words	
Step 2	**Reading**
Purpose	
Pattern of Organization	
Tone	
Main Idea	
Step 3	**Summary**
지문 요약하기 (Paraphrasing)	
Step 4	**Recite**
요약문 말로 설명하기	

02

The time to harvest honey is summer's end, when it is hot. The temper of the bees requires that we wear protective clothing: a full set of overalls, a zippered bee veil and leather gloves. Even a very strong young man works up a sweat wrapped in a bee suit in the heat, hustling 60-pound supers while being harassed by angry bees. It is a hard job, harder even than haying, but jobs are scarce here and I've always been able to hire help.

This year **David**, the son of a friend of mine, is working for me. He is big and strong and used to labor, but he was nervous about bees. After we had made the job arrangement I set about **desensitizing** him to **bee stings**. I put a piece of ice on his arm to numb it and then, holding a bee carefully its head. I **put it on the numbed spot** and let it sting him. A bee stinger is barbed and stays in the flesh, pulling loose from the body of the bee as it struggles to free itself. The bulbous **poison sac** at the top of the stinger continues to pulsate after the bee has left, pumping the venom and forcing the stinger deeper into the flesh.

The first day I wanted David to have only a partial dose of venom, so after a minute I scraped the stinger out. A few people are seriously sensitive to bee venom; each sting they receive can cause a more severe reaction than the one before—reactions ranging from hives, breathing difficulties, accelerated heart beat and choking to anaphylactic shock and death. I didn't think David would be allergic in that way, but I wanted to make sure. We sat down and had a cup of coffee and I watched him. The spot where the stinger went in grew red and began to swell. That was a normal reaction, and so was the itching that he felt later on. The next day I coaxed a bee into stinging him again, repeating the procedure, but I left the stinger in place for 10 minutes, until the venom sac was empty. Again the spot was red, swollen and itchy but had disappeared in 24 hours. By that time David was ready to catch a bee himself and administer his own sting. He also decided that the ice cube was a bother and gave it up. I told him to keep to one sting a day until he had no redness or swelling and then to increase to two stings. He was ready for them the next day. The greater amount of venom caused redness and swelling for a few days, but soon his body could tolerate it without reaction and he increased the number of stings once again.

Today he told me he was up to six stings. His arms look as though they have track marks on them, but the fresh stings are having little effect. I'll keep him at it until he can tolerate 10 a day with no reaction and then I'll not worry about taking him out to the bee yard.

Summer's end. Second, they weigh 60-pounds. Third, she wants a helper who can handle 10 stings a day.

한글 번역

꿀을 수확하는 때는 여름의 끝자락으로, 날씨가 덥다. 벌들의 성질이 우리로 하여금 보호복―작업복 풀 세트, 지퍼로 된 복면포와 가죽장갑―을 입게 한다. 심지어 매우 건장한 젊은 남성도 화난 벌들에게 공격을 당하며 60파운드의 벌통과 씨름하며, 더위에 작업복 안에 갇혀 땀을 흘린다. 이것은 어려운 일이고 건초 만들기보다 더 어렵지만 이곳에서 일자리는 흔하지 않고 나는 항상 일손을 고용할 수 있었다.

올해는 내 친구의 아들인 데이빗이 나를 도와 일하고 있다. 그는 크고 강하며 노동을 하는 것엔 익숙하나 벌을 무서워했다. 일에 대한 조율을 한 뒤 나는 그를 벌침에 둔감하게 만드는 작업을 시작했다. 그의 팔 위에 얼음 한 조각을 올려놓고 팔의 감각을 없애면서, 벌의 머리를 쥐었다. 그 감각이 없어진 부위에 벌을 놓은 뒤 그를 쏘게 했다. 벌침이 낚시 바늘처럼 되어 빠지기 쉽지 않게 되어 살 속에 머무르게 되는데, 그것은 벌이 빠져나가려 몸부림을 치면 칠수록 벌의 몸으로부터 벌침이 더욱 느슨하게 되기 때문이다. 벌침 위에 있는 둥글 납작한 독낭은 벌이 떠나자 계속 진동하고 독을 펌프질하며 독침이 살 속에 더 깊이 파묻히게 한다.

첫 날, 나는 데이빗이 독의 아주 적은 양만 맞길 원했기에 1분 뒤에 벌침을 긁어냈다. 어떤 사람들은 벌의 독에 심각하게 민감하다: 각 쏘임은 그 이전의 것보다 더 심각한 반응을 야기시킬 수 있는데, 두드러기부터, 호흡곤란, 심장박동수 가속화, 과민성의 쇼크, 사망으로 이어지는 질식까지의 반응들이 있다. 데이빗은 그렇게까지 알러지 반응이 있진 않을 것이라고 생각했으나 확실히 하고 싶었다. 우리는 앉아서 커피를 마시며 그를 쳐다봤다. 벌침이 쏜 부위는 점점 빨개지고 부풀어 오르기 시작했다. 그것은 보통 반응이었고 그가 그 후에 느낀 가려움도 마찬가지였다. 다음날 나는 벌을 구슬려 그를 다시 쏘게 했고 그 과정을 반복했지만, 이번에는 독낭이 텅 빌 때까지 벌침을 10분 동안 놔두었다. 또 다시 그 부위는 빨개졌고, 부어 올랐으며, 가려웠지만 24시간 안에 그 증상들이 사라졌다. 그때쯤 데이빗은 자기 혼자 벌을 잡고 자신의 쏘임을 집행할 준비가 되었다. 그는 또한 얼음덩이가 귀찮아서 사용하지 않기로 결정했다. 난 그에게 빨개지는 현상이나 부어오르는 현상이 없어질 때까지 하루에 한 번의 벌침만 쏘고 그리고 나서 두 번으로 늘리라고 말했다. 그 다음날 그는 두 벌침을 맞을 준비가 되었다. 더 많아진 독의 양은 몇 일 동안 빨개짐과 부어오름을 유발했지만 그의 몸은 곧 이상 현상 없이 그것을 견뎌냈고, 그는 그 벌침의 횟수를 다시 한번 늘렸다.

오늘 그가 여섯 번의 벌침까지 맞았다고 말했다. 그의 팔은 마치 팔 위에 길자국이 난 것처럼 보였지만 신선한 벌침에 대한 반응 현상은 거의 없었다. 난 그가 하루에 이상 현상 없이 10회 벌침을 견뎌낼 때까지 계속 하게 할 것이고 그리고 나면 그를 양봉장에 데려가는 데에 염려하지 않을 것이다.

NOTE

Step 1	Survey
Key Words	time to harvest honey; desensitizing; bee stings
Signal Words	After; The first day; The next day; By that time; Today

Step 2	Reading
Purpose	to give information about the process of harvesting honey
Pattern of Organization	time order (process)
Tone	neutral
Main Idea	Preparing for a job as a beekeeper is a painstaking process that actually requires taking pain.

Step 3	Summary
지문 요약하기 (Paraphrasing)	Preparing for a job as a beekeeper is a painstaking process that actually requires taking pain. A new worker David built up a resistance to bee stings as an important first step to harvest honey. The process starts with icing the arm and causing a bee to sting on purpose. With the sting, a little venom was released, and each day the process repeated with more venom and stings as David had less reaction to them. He is now up to six stings and when he can handle 10 in a day he can begin harvesting.

Step 4	Recite
	요약문 말로 설명하기

40 Read the passage and follow the directions.

He slammed the door angrily behind him, and she heard the squeal of the tires as he raced off in the car. For a moment, she felt her usual fear. She knew he shouldn't drive after he'd been drinking heavily. But then she turned, went to the linen closet, and took out a clean towel. She spread the towel out on her neatly made bed. Next, she got her overnight bag and a larger suitcase from the closet and put them carefully on the towel on her bed. Methodically, she took neatly folded underwear, stockings, and nightgowns from her drawers and packed them in neat rows in the two bags. One set in the overnight bag, and five in the larger suitcase. She laid aside a nightgown with a matching robe to pack last. Next, she lifted dresses and suits, carefully hung on the hangers and buttoned up so they wouldn't wrinkle, from her closet and folded them into the larger suitcase. Two extra blouses and a dress went into the overnight bag. She'd wear the suit she had on. She brought plastic bags from the kitchen and put her shoes into them. One pair went into the overnight bag; two pairs, one for the dresses and one for the suits, went into the larger bag. Then she put her bedroom slippers and the nightgown with the matching robe on top of the other clothes in the overnight bag. She would take only the overnight bag into her parents' house, at least at first. No need for them to know right away that this time was for more than one night. They'd always said that she wasn't going to change him and that the marriage wouldn't last. She sighed again, closed the suitcases, carried them out to her car, and then went back into the house for one last look around. Almost ready, she took her coat from the hall closet, folded it carefully over her arm, and took a last look at his shoes and socks left beside his chair and the newspaper flung across the couch where it would leave stains on the upholstery. She left the shoes and socks but couldn't resist folding the newspaper and putting it on a table. Finally, she went out, closed the door silently behind her, got into her car, and drove quietly and slowly away.

Summarize the passage in 60-80 words.

NOTE

Step 1	Survey
Key Words	
Signal Words	
Step 2	**Reading**
Purpose	
Pattern of Organization	
Tone	
Main Idea	
Step 3	**Summary**
지문 요약하기 (Paraphrasing)	
Step 4	**Recite**
요약문 말로 설명하기	

💡 **Answer Key**

He slammed the door angrily behind him, and she heard the squeal of the tires as he raced off in the car. **For a moment**, she felt her usual fear. She knew he shouldn't drive after he'd been drinking heavily. // But **then** she turned, went to the linen closet, and took out a clean towel. She spread the towel out on her neatly made bed. // **Next**, she got her overnight bag and a larger suitcase from the closet and put them carefully on the towel on her bed. Methodically, she took neatly folded underwear, stockings, and nightgowns from her drawers and packed them in neat rows in the two bags. One set in the overnight bag, and five in the larger suitcase. She laid aside a nightgown with a matching robe to pack last. // **Next**, she lifted dresses and suits, carefully hung on the hangers and buttoned up so they wouldn't wrinkle, from her closet and folded them into the larger suitcase. Two extra blouses and a dress went into the overnight bag. She'd wear the suit she had on. She brought plastic bags from the kitchen and put her shoes into them. One pair went into the overnight bag; two pairs, one for the dresses and one for the suits, went into the larger bag. **Then** she put her bedroom slippers and the nightgown with the matching robe on top of the other clothes in the overnight bag. She would take only the overnight bag into her parents' house, at least at first. No need for them to know right away that this time was for more than one night. They'd always said that she wasn't going to change him and that the marriage wouldn't last. // She sighed again, closed the suitcases, carried them out to her car, and then went back into the house for one last look around. Almost ready, she took her coat from the hall closet, folded it carefully over her arm, and took a last look at his shoes and socks left beside his chair and the newspaper flung across the couch where it would leave stains on the upholstery. She left the shoes and socks but couldn't resist folding the newspaper and putting it on a table. **Finally**, she went out, closed the door silently behind her, got into her car, and drove quietly and slowly away.

introduction – narrative	
step 1 : preparation	
step 2 : finding suitcases	
step 3 : packing suitcases	
step 4 : final check and look around	

모범답안

Having decided to leave her husband, who is a heavy drinker, the woman in the story methodically packs an overnight bag and a large suitcase with her clothing and shoes. She takes one last look around the house and then gets in her car and drives away. She is going to go to stay with her parents, who have always predicted that the marriage would not last.

한글 번역

그는 화가 나서 문을 세게 쾅 닫았다. 그녀는 그가 차를 타고 내달릴 때, 타이어가 끼익 하는 소리를 들었다. 그 순간 그녀는 두려움을 느꼈다. 그녀는 그가 술을 진탕 마시고 운전하지 말아야 했음을 알고 있었다. 하지만 그리고 나서 그녀는 되돌아와 리넨 벽장에서 깨끗한 타월을 꺼내 깔끔하게 정돈된 침대에 펼쳐놓았다. 다음으로, 그녀는 벽장에서 작은 여행 가방과 더 큰 여행용 가방을 꺼내고, 침대에 깔아 놓은 타월 위에 놓았다. 그녀는 참으로 질서정연하게도 속옷, 스타킹, 나이트 가운들을 서랍에서 꺼내서, 깔끔하게 접고 두 개의 가방에 열 맞춰서 담았다. 한 세트는 작은 가방에, 그리고 다섯 세트는 더 큰 여행용 가방에 담았다. 나이트 가운과 겉옷은 맨 나중에 싸기 위해 그 옆에 두었다. 그리고 나서, 그녀는 원피스와 바지 정장이 구겨지지 않도록 단추를 모두 잠그고 옷걸이에 걸려 있는 채로 조심스럽게 벽장에서 꺼내 큰 여행용 가방에 넣었다. 두 개의 여분의 블라우스와 나머지 옷은 작은 가방에 넣었고, 이미 입고 있는 정장은 그대로 입고 나갈 것이다. 그녀는 주방에서 플라스틱 봉지를 가져와서 신발을 그 안에 넣었다. 한 켤레는 작은 가방에 들어갔고 두 켤레(하나는 원피스용, 다른 하나는 바지 정장용)는 여행용 가방에 들어갔다. 그리고 침실용 슬리퍼와 나이트 가운과 겉옷은, 작은 가방 맨 위 다른 옷들 위에 올려놓았다. 부모님 집에 처음 들어갈 때엔 작은 가방만을 들고 갈 것이다. 이번에는 하룻밤 이상 묵을 것이라는 것을 부모님이 바로 알 필요가 없기 때문이다. 부모님은 그녀가 그를 변하게 만들지 못할 것이며 결혼은 오래 가지 못할 것이라고 항상 말하곤 했다. 그녀는 또 한 번 한숨을 쉬고 여행용 가방을 닫고 차에 갖다 놓았다. 그리고 나서 다시 집으로 돌아와 집안을 마지막으로 휘익 둘러보았다. 이제 거의 다 준비가 됐다. 그녀는 복도 벽장에서 코트를 꺼내 팔에 조심스럽게 걸쳤다. 남편의 의자 옆에 남겨진 그의 신발 양말, 소파 위에 흩뿌려진 신문-소파 덮개에 잉크 자국을 남긴-을 마지막으로 휙 보았다. 남편의 신발과 양말은 그냥 내버려두었는데, 신문은 결국 접어서 테이블 위에 올려놓고 말았다. 마침내, 집에서 나와서 문을 소리 없이 닫고, 차에 탄 뒤 소리 없이 천천히 떠났다.

NOTE

Step 1	Survey
Key Words	angrily; methodically; carefully; quietly
Signal Words	for a moment; but then; next; Almost ready; finally
Step 2	**Reading**
Purpose	to show how a woman methodically prepared to leave her husband and the home they shared
Pattern of Organization	time order (process); description
Tone	emotional
Main Idea	Having decided to leave her marriage, the woman in the story methodically packs, takes a last look around, and drives away.
Step 3	**Summary**
지문 요약하기 (Paraphrasing)	Having decided to leave her husband, who is a heavy drinker, the woman in the story methodically packs an overnight bag and a large suitcase with her clothing and shoes. She takes one last look around the house and then gets in her car and drives away. She is going to go to stay with her parents, who have always predicted that the marriage would not last.
Step 4	**Recite**
	요약문 말로 설명하기

41 Read the passage and follow the direction.

In one form, women's history goes back to Plutarch, who composed little studies of virtuous women. Works such as these, known as "women worthies," celebrated the various capacities and talents of exceptional women. Although this kind of history established a record of some female activity in the past, its approach was _____ ⓐ _____, treating women apart from the consequences of class and gender in social life and historical change. A later form of women's history was the biography of the individual woman—the religious or political luminary. The study of individual lives had the advantage over "women worthies" in that such a study could embed a woman more carefully in her culture and society. Yet such studies were still inattentive to the role of gender in shaping women's lives. It was not until the early twentieth century in Europe that historical approaches similar to our own began to be utilized in the study of women. In her *Working Life of Women in the Seventeenth Century*(1919), Alice Clark departed in many particulars from the methods of her _____ ⓑ _____. In the first place, she went to the sources—not just to the pamphlets on the female sex and memoirs of aristocratic women, but also to archival materials: financial and administrative records as well as marriage contracts and wills. In addition, Clark, unlike her predecessors, developed a theory to account for the changing relations of women to power and work. She argued that, in the centuries before industrial capitalism and the commercialization of agriculture on a large scale, most women were contributing essential support to their families, both within and outside of the home. The widely accepted belief in the subjection of the wife to the husband did not lead to serious oppression, so Clark argued, as long as husband and wife made up a community in which work and wages were shared.

MEMO

Fill in blanks ⓐ and ⓑ in one word from the passage respectively. If necessary, change the word form.

NOTE

Step 1	Survey
Key Words	
Signal Words	
Step 2	Reading
Purpose	
Pattern of Organization	
Tone	
Main Idea	
Step 3	Summary
지문 요약하기 (Paraphrasing)	
Step 4	Recite
요약문 말로 설명하기	

In one form, **women's history** goes back to Plutarch, who composed little studies of virtuous women. Works such as these, known as "**women worthies**," celebrated the various capacities and talents of exceptional women. Although this kind of history established a record of some female activity in the past, its approach was ahistorical, treating women **apart from the consequences of class and gender in social life and historical change**. // A later form of **women's history** was the biography of the individual woman—the religious or political luminary. The study of individual lives had the advantage over "women worthies" in that such a study could embed a woman more carefully in her culture and society. // Yet such studies were still inattentive to **the role of gender in shaping women's lives**. It was not until the early twentieth century in Europe that historical approaches similar to our own began to be utilized in the study of women. In her *Working Life of Women in the Seventeenth Century*(1919), Alice Clark departed in many particulars from the methods of her predecessors. In the first place, she went to the sources—not just to the pamphlets on the female sex and memoirs of aristocratic women, but also to archival materials: financial and administrative records as well as marriage contracts and wills. In addition, Clark, unlike her predecessors, developed a theory to account for the changing relations of women to power and work. She argued that, in the centuries before industrial capitalism and the commercialization of agriculture on a large scale, most women were contributing essential support to their families, both within and outside of the home. The widely accepted belief in the subjection of the wife to the husband did not lead to serious oppression, so Clark argued, as long as husband and wife made up a community in which work and wages were shared.

key words
①
②
③
ⓐ
ⓑ

모범답안

ⓐ ahistorical   ⓑ predecessors

어휘

ahistorical 몰역사적인, 역사에 무관심한　apart from ~은 별문제로 하고　archival 기록의, 고문서의
compose ~을 쓰다　depart from ~에서 벗어나다　embed 끼워 넣다
luminary 유명인　predecessor 전임자　subjection 종속
virtuous 덕이 있는, 정숙한

한글 번역

한 가지 형태로, 여성사는 플루타르크까지 거슬러 가는데, 그는 훌륭한 여성에 대해 사소한 연구들을 하였다. '존경할 만한 여성들'로 알려진 이와 같은 작품들은 비범한 여성들의 다양한 능력이나 재능을 찬양했다. 비록 이런 종류의 역사가 과거 몇몇 여성의 활동에 대한 기록을 하기는 했지만, 그런 접근법은 몰역사적이었고, 여성을 계급의 결과, 사회생활에서의 성, 역사적인 변화와 분리시켜 취급하였다. 이후의 여성사의 형태는 종교적으로나 정치적으로 유명한 개인 여성의 전기였다. 개인적인 삶의 연구는 여성을 그 문화와 사회에 더욱 주의 깊게 끼워 넣는다는 점에서 '존경할 만한 여성들'보다 유리한 점이 있다. 하지만 이런 연구는 여성의 삶을 조형하는 성역할을 여전히 등한시했다. 20세기 초가 되어서야 유럽에서 우리의 것과 유사한 역사적 접근이 여성 연구에 활용되기 시작하였다. "17세기 여성의 노동생활"(1919)에서 앨리스 클락은 많은 부분에서 그녀의 선배들의 방식에서 벗어났다. 우선 그녀는 자료에 있어서—단순히 여성의 성이나 귀족 여성들의 회고록에 관한 소책자가 아니라 기록보관소의 자료들까지(결혼서약서나 유언장 뿐 아니라 재정적, 행정적 기록까지) 사용하였다. 게다가 그녀는 권력과 직업에 있어 여성의 변화된 관계를 설명하는 이론을 정립하였다. 그녀는 산업 자본주의와 대규모의 농업의 상업화 이전 시대에 대부분의 여성이 자신의 가족들에게 집 안팎으로 필수적 지원을 제공했다고 주장하였다. 그래서 남편과 아내가 노동과 임금이 공유되는 공동체를 만드는 한, 아내가 남편에게 종속된다는 널리 받아들여지는 믿음은 심각한 차별을 초래하지 않았다고 클락은 주장했다.

NOTE

Step 1	Survey
Key Words	Women's history; Clark
Signal Words	Plutarch; A later form; the early twentieth centruy; In the first place; In addition
Step 2	**Reading**
Purpose	to outline the way in which women were spoken of over time and to identify the contributions made by Alice Clark
Pattern of Organization	time order; series
Tone	neutral
Main Idea	Alice Clark, as opposed to her predecessors who lacked historical approaches, could develop a theory to reflect the changing relations of women to power and work.
Step 3	**Summary**
지문 요약하기 (Paraphrasing)	The historical study of women evolved over time, moving first from dealing primarily with notable women to deeper studies of individuals, then finally on to the influencing factors of gender and society. Alice Clark began this in her 1919 book, which took into account financial and social research to theorize that women were not subjugated prior to the industrial era but shared equally in wages and work.
Step 4	**Recite**
요약문 말로 설명하기	

42 Read the passage and follow the directions.

All Americans know that their country began as a British colony, but fewer realize that an American colony went on to become an independent nation. Africa's Liberia began its existence as an American colony established by free African Americans. Then it followed in the footsteps of its parent nation to declare independence and become a separate republic. In 1816, a group of white Americans created the American Colonization Society (ACS). The founders of the ACS wanted to establish an African settlement so that America's 200,000 free blacks, as well as newly emancipated slaves, could return to the continent of their ancestors. The society's motives were humanitarian, social, and religious. Members believed that an American colony like the one they imagined could help end the slave trade, correct the injustices done to enslaved blacks, and aid the spread of Christianity to the African continent. Others, however, advocated the return of free blacks for a different reason. They feared a revolt similar to the one that had occurred in Haiti, where slaves had overthrown their masters and set up a republic. In 1818, with $100,000 of seed money from the U.S. Congress, the ACS sent two representatives to Africa to purchase suitable territory. It wasn't until 1821, however, that a permanent place of settlement was found and bought. According to records, the earliest inhabitants arrived in 1822. In 1824, the colony was officially named Liberia, a name that suggests its purpose as a land of liberty and freedom for black Americans. By 1840, Liberia boasted a population of about 2,500 American expatriates and 28,000 African tribespeople. In 1847, the Liberian government proclaimed its independence from the United States. However, just as Britain had denied America its independence years before, the United States did not immediately recognize Liberia as a separate nation. Many lawmakers were also slaveholders who feared the consequences of acknowledging Liberia's independence. Not until 1862, during the Civil War, did President Abraham Lincoln formally recognize Liberia as an independent republic.

Describe the purpose of the passage by filling in the blank with THREE words.

The purpose of the passage is to describe the history of the _____ as an independent nation.

02

NOTE

Step 1	Survey
Key Words	
Signal Words	
Step 2	**Reading**
Purpose	
Pattern of Organization	
Tone	
Main Idea	
Step 3	**Summary**
지문 요약하기 (Paraphrasing)	
Step 4	**Recite**
요약문 말로 설명하기	

All Americans know that their country began as a British colony, but fewer realize that an American colony went on to become an independent nation. **Africa's Liberia** began its existence as an American colony established by free African Americans. Then it followed in the footsteps of its parent nation to declare independence and become a separate republic. In 1816, a group of white Americans created **the American Colonization Society (ACS)**. The founders of the ACS wanted to establish an African settlement so that America's 200,000 free blacks, as well as newly emancipated slaves, could return to the continent of their ancestors. The society's motives were **humanitarian, social, and religious**. Members believed that an American colony like the one they imagined could help end the slave trade, correct the injustices done to enslaved blacks, and aid the spread of Christianity to the African continent. Others, however, advocated the return of free blacks for a different reason. They feared a revolt similar to the one that had occurred in Haiti, where slaves had overthrown their masters and set up a republic. // In 1818, with $100,000 of seed money from the U.S. Congress, the ACS sent two representatives to Africa to purchase suitable territory. It wasn't until 1821, however, that a permanent place of settlement was found and bought. According to records, the earliest inhabitants arrived in 1822. In 1824, the colony was officially named Liberia, a name that suggests its purpose as a land of liberty and freedom for black Americans. By 1840, Liberia boasted a population of about 2,500 American expatriates and 28,000 African tribespeople. In 1847, the Liberian government proclaimed its independence from the United States. However, just as Britain had denied America its independence years before, the United States did not immediately recognize Liberia as a separate nation. Many lawmakers were also slaveholders who feared the consequences of acknowledging Liberia's independence. Not until 1862, during the Civil War, did President Abraham Lincoln formally **recognize Liberia as an independent republic**.

key words

time order

모범답안
formation of Liberia

한글 번역

미국인 중 자신의 모국이 영국 식민지에서 출발했다는 사실을 모르는 사람은 없다. 하지만 미국의 식민지에서 독립 국가로 변모한 나라가 있다는 사실을 아는 미국인은 거의 없다. 아프리카의 라이베리아는 미국 식민지로 시작했으며, 노예제도에서 풀려나 자유의 몸이 된 흑인들에 의해 세워졌다. 그런 후 라이베리아는 모국의 발자취를 쫓아 독립을 선언하고 독자적인 공화국을 형성하게 된다. 1816년, 한 무리의 미국 백인들이 ACS(American Colonization Society: 미국식민협회)를 설립했다. ACS의 설립자들은 아프리카에 정착지 설립을 희망했으며, 이를 통해 미국에 있는 20만 명의 자유의 몸이 된 흑인들뿐만 아니라 새롭게 노예제도에서 해방된 이들까지도 자신들의 선조가 있던 아프리카 대륙으로 되돌아갈 수 있도록 하고자 했다. ACS의 동기는 인도주의적이고, 사회적이며, 종교적이었다. ACS 회원들은 자신들이 구상한 것과 같은 미국 식민지가 노예 교역을 종식시키고, 흑인 노예들에게 가해졌던 불의를 바로잡으며, 아프리카 대륙에 기독교를 전파하는 데 일조할 것으로 믿었다. 하지만 다른 이들은 자유의 몸이 된 흑인들의 귀환을 이와는 다른 이유로 지지했다. 그들은 아이티에서 일어난 것과 같은 반란을 두려워했는데, 아이티의 노예들은 지배층을 뒤엎고, 공화국을 세웠었다. 1818년, 미국 의회로부터 받은 10만 달러의 초기자본과 함께, ACS는 두 명의 대표를 아프리카로 보내 적당한 영토를 구입하도록 했다. 그러나 1821년이 되어서야 영구적으로 정착할 장소를 찾아 구입할 수 있었다. 기록에 의하면, 초기의 거주민들은 1822년에 도착했다고 한다. 그리고 1824년, 그 식민지가 공식적으로 라이베리아라고 명명되었으며, 이 명칭은 미국 흑인들을 위한 자유와 평화의 땅을 목적으로 한다는 사실을 암시하고 있다. 1840년에 이르러서는 라이베리아에 미국에서 2,500명에 달하는 이들이 건너왔고, 아프리카 원주민들은 28,000명에 달하게 됐다. 1847년에는 라이베리아 정부가 미국으로부터 독립을 선언했다. 그러나 이전에 영국이 미국의 독립을 반대했던 것처럼, 미국도 라이베리아를 곧바로 독립국가로 인정하지 않았다. 많은 미국 의원들 또한 노예 소유자들이었기 때문에, 라이베리아를 독립국가로 인정하게 될 경우 일어날 여파에 대해 우려했다. 남북전쟁 중이던 1862년에 이르러서야 에이브러햄 링컨 대통령이 공식적으로 라이베리아를 독립국가로 승인했다.

NOTE

Step 1	Survey
Key Words	American Colonies; Liberia; independent republic
Signal Words	Then it followed; in 1816; in 1818; It wasn't until 1821; in 1822; in 1824; By 1840; in 1847; Not until 1862
Step 2	**Reading**
Purpose	to describe the formation of Liberia and how it gained its independence
Pattern of Organization	time order
Tone	informative
Main Idea	Liberia, which began as a U.S. colony, struggled for independence from the United States in much the same way as the United States did from Britain.
Step 3	**Summary**
지문 요약하기 (Paraphrasing)	Liberia began as an American colony before achieving its status as an independent nation. It was first formed primarily for freed blacks with the hopes of creating social justice and peace in order to end the slave trade. Later, it finally became recognized as an independent nation in 1862.
Step 4	**Recite**
요약문 말로 설명하기	

43   Read the passage and follow the directions.

It's really not a striking house, nor is it an old charming house. It is, in fact, very plain—just like the houses on each side of it. As I climb up the hilly driveway, its whiteness stares blankly back at me, reminding me that I am not the owner but just a temporary, unwanted trespasser. There are flowers lining the driveway, which push their faces toward the sun as they lie in their bed perfectly spaced, not too close and not too far apart, perfectly coordinated to reflect all the colors of the spectrum. Through the windows of the house nothing but my reflection can be seen. They are like the house, clean and tinted, allowing no one a look in, keeping life in the house shut off from the rest of the world, uninviting of intrusion, only interested in cleanliness, only leading the people inside to a feeling of loneliness. Upon entering the house the smell of Pine-Sol and disinfectant engulfs my nostrils and shoots directly to my brain, anesthetizing any emotions that might surface. Like the windows, the kitchen floor reflects the cleanliness of the house with its spotless white surface, scrubbed and shined, casting off reflections from the bright lights overhead. There is wallpaper on the walls of the kitchen, but it is void of any pattern and lends very little color to the whiteness of the room. Only items of importance for the duties of the kitchen are displayed, all in their properly appointed places, with the appropriate covers placed over them to hide them from prying eyes. The only personality the kitchen portrays is a cold, calculating, suspicious one, wary of intruders who may cause unnecessary filth to enter. Around the corner from the kitchen lies the dining room. An elegant, dark, formal table sits in the center of the room, the surface of which is smooth as glass under my fingertips. A white centerpiece is carefully placed at the table's center, with two white candles that have never been lit standing erect at the centerpiece's ends.

The chairs around the table are hard, providing support for the back but lending the body no comfort. Above hangs a crystal chandelier expensive, elegant, giving the room an artificial brightness. It is made up of many dangling, teardrop-shaped crystals, all cleaned and polished, and is the only object in the dining room that speaks clearly of conspicuous consumption. The drapes covering the tinted windows are a dark color and keep out the sun of the day. This room is often cleaned, often walked through, but never used. Having walked through the dining room, I enter the living room. Although this is the only room in the house where the family can all converge to spend time together, it is not a cheerful place. The walls are white, like the rest of the house, with the same drapery as the dining room, and the couch and loveseat are velvet, stiff, uncomfortable, and well maintained. A television set is placed in the corner but lies blank with disuse. The air of coldness here seems to hold tension though at the same time it gives the impression of ossification. I have heard it said that a person's home is a reflection of that person, a sentiment that, with few exceptions, is true of this home. Cleanliness is a priority of the owner, and socializing with people in this house is considered a nuisance that only causes more work because of the dirt that people carry in with them. The walls are kept white because it looks clean and repainting is made easy. And the smell of disinfectant pleases the owner, as it proves to the few who do enter that the house is clean. This house, the place I am calling home for this period of my life, offers me no comfort but does provide shelter and quiet. And with the dark stillness in its rooms, I can think, read, and plan my escape.

Describe the main idea of the passage in ONE sentence. Then fill in the blank in the box with ONE word from the passage.

The narrator depicts the house in spatial order from the outside and then as she walks through its rooms. The descriptive details provide the reader with an image of both the house and its _____.

NOTE

Step 1	Survey
Key Words	
Signal Words	
Step 2	Reading
Purpose	
Pattern of Organization	
Tone	
Main Idea	
Step 3	Summary
지문 요약하기 (Paraphrasing)	
Step 4	Recite
요약문 말로 설명하기	

02

🔆 Answer Key

It's really not a striking house, nor is it an old charming house. It is, in fact, very plain—just like the houses on each side of it. As I climb up the hilly driveway, its **whiteness** stares blankly back at me, reminding me that I am not the owner but just a temporary, unwanted trespasser. — view of the outside of the house

There are flowers lining the driveway, which push their faces toward the sun as they lie in their bed **perfectly spaced**, not too close and not too far apart, **perfectly coordinated** to reflect all the colors of the spectrum. — details : preciseness of the landscaping

Through the windows of the house nothing but my reflection can be seen. — thesis statement

They are like the house, clean and tinted, allowing no one a look in, keeping life in the house shut off from the rest of the world, uninviting of intrusion, only interested in cleanliness, only leading the people inside to a feeling of loneliness. // **Upon entering the house** the — entering the house

smell of Pine-Sol and disinfectant engulfs my nostrils and shoots directly to my brain, anesthetizing any emotions that might surface. Like the windows, the kitchen floor reflects the **cleanliness** of the house with its **spotless white surface, scrubbed and shined**, casting off reflections from the **bright lights** overhead. There is wallpaper on the walls of the kitchen, but it is **void of any pattern** and lends **very little color** to the **whiteness** of the room. — details : cleanliness and coldness of kitchen

Only items of importance for the duties of the kitchen are displayed, all in their properly appointed places, with the appropriate covers placed over them to hide them from prying eyes. The only personality the kitchen portrays is a cold, calculating, suspicious one, wary of intruders who may cause unnecessary filth to enter. // **Around the corner from the kitchen lies the dining room. An elegant, dark, formal table** sits in the center of the room, the surface of which — moving to dining room

is smooth as glass under my fingertips. A **white centerpiece** is carefully placed at the table's center, with two **white candles that have never been lit** standing erect at the centerpiece's ends. The chairs around the table are hard, providing support for the back but lending the body no comfort. Above hangs a crystal chandelier expensive, elegant, giving the room an artificial brightness. — details : formality and whiteness of room

It is made up of many dangling, teardrop-shaped crystals, all **cleaned and polished**, and is the only object in the dining room that speaks clearly of conspicuous consumption. The drapes covering the tinted windows are a dark color and **keep out the sun of the day.** This room is **often cleaned, often walked through**, but **never used.** // **Having walked through the dining room, I enter the living room.** Although this is the only room in the house where the family can — entering the living room

all converge to spend time together, it is not a cheerful place. The walls are **white**, like the rest of the house, with the same drapery as the dining room, and the couch and loveseat are velvet, **stiff, uncomfortable, and well maintained**. A television set is placed in the corner but **lies blank with disuse**. The **air of coldness** here seems to hold tension though at the same time it gives the impression of ossification. // I have heard it said that a person's home is a reflection of that person, a sentiment that, with few exceptions, is true of this home. **Cleanliness** is a priority of the owner, and socializing with people in this house is considered a nuisance that only causes more work because of the dirt that people carry in with them. The walls are kept white because it looks clean and repainting is made easy. And the smell of disinfectant pleases the owner, as it proves to the few who do enter that the house is clean. This house, the place I am calling home for this period of my life, offers me no comfort but does provide shelter and quiet. And with the **dark stillness** in its rooms, I can think, read, and plan my escape.

> details :
> impersonality
> of living room

> thesis statement
> (conclusion)

모범답안

The main idea is that the house in which the narrator is currently living is clean yet too austere and uninviting, reflecting the character of its owner. Second, the appropriate word for the blank is "owner".

이 집은 눈에 띄지도, 오래된 멋스러움을 풍기지도 않는다. 이는 사실상 양 옆에 놓인 집들처럼 매우 평범하다. 언덕진 진입로를 오르는 동안, 이 집의 하얀색은 내가 이곳의 주인이 아닌 그저 임시의, 달갑지 않은 무단 침입자임을 상기시키며 멍하니 나를 응시한다. 진입로를 따라 꽃들이 심어져 있는데, 사이사이의 간격이 너무 좁지도 너무 멀지도 않은 완벽한 상태로, 또 스펙트럼의 모든 색깔을 반영하는 듯 완벽히 조화된 상태로, 태양을 바라보고 있다. 집의 창문을 통해 보이는 건 반사된 내 모습을 제외하곤 아무것도 없다. 집과 같이 깔끔하고 착색된 유리는 그 누구도 안을 들여다보지 못하게, 침입으로부터 보호된 채 안에서의 삶을 바깥 세상과 단절시키고, 오로지 깔끔에만 집착하며 외로움의 감정이 도사리는 실내의 공간으로 사람들을 유도한다. 집에 들어서는 순간, 파인솔과 살균제의 냄새는 나의 코끝을 찌르고 머리를 멍하게 만들며 온갖 감정을 마비시킨다. 창문처럼 부엌의 바닥도 문질러지고 광택을 내 티끌 하나 없이 깨끗한 하얀 표면을 통해 '깔끔'함을 보이고 천장의 밝은 불을 반사시킨다. 부엌 벽에는 벽지가 붙어있지만 아무런 무늬도 없고, 순백의 공간에 어떠한 색도 가미하지 못한다. 부엌일에서 없어서 안 될 도구들만 각각의 지정된 자리에, 주변을 살피는 시선으로부터 보호받도록, 알맞은 덮개로 가려진 채 진열되어 있다. 부엌이 주는 유일한 인상은 차갑고 계산적이며 의심하는 것으로, 들어올 때 불필요한 불결함을 안길 수 있는 침입자들에게 대해 매우 경계적인 태세를 취한다. 부엌의 한 모퉁이를 돌아서면 다이닝 룸이 있다. 방 가운데에는 하나의 우아하면서 어둡고 격식을 차린 테이블이 놓여 있는데 그 표면을 만지면 마치 내 손끝에서 유리처럼 매끄럽다. 흰 중앙부 장식은 양 옆에 한 번도 켜지지 않은 곧게 솟은 촛불과 함께 조심스럽게 놓여 있다. 테이블을 둘러싼 의자는 딱딱하여 등을 받쳐줄지라도 안락함을 주지 못한다. 위로는 비싸고 우아하며 방 안을 인공적인 빛으로 채우는 수정 유리로 만들어진 샹들리에가 걸려 있는데, 깔끔하고 윤이 나는 눈물 모양의 수정 유리가 주렁주렁 달려있다. 방 안에 있는 물건 중에서 과시적 소비를 명백히 드러내는 것이라고는 이것뿐이다. 착색된 창문을 덮는 커튼은 어두운 색깔이며 방 안으로 들어오는 햇빛을 차단한다. 이 방은 종종 청소되고 지나쳐지지만 한 번도 사용된 적이 없다. 다이닝 룸을 지나 나는 거실에 도착한다. 이곳만이 온가족이 함께 모여 시간을 보낼 수 있는 유일한 공간임에도 불구하고 유쾌한 곳이 아니다. 집의 다른 곳과 같이 벽은 하얗고, 다이닝 룸에 걸려있는 커튼과 동일한 커튼이 있으며, 소파와 2인용 의자는 모두 벨벳으로 덮여져 있고, 딱딱하고 불편하되 잘 유지되고 있다. TV 세트는 구석에 오랜 시간 사용되지 않은 상태로 놓여 있다. 이곳의 차가운 공기는 긴장감을 자아내는 것 같음과 동시에 골화의 인상을 남기기도 한다. 집은 주인을 반영한다고들 말하는데 아주 소수의 몇 가지를 제외한다면 이 집과 일치하는 견해라고 본다. '깔끔'을 유지하는 것이야 말로 이 집주인의 우선순위이며 이곳에서 사교란 사람들이 가지고 들어오는 더러움으로 인해 더 많은 노동을 요구하는 골칫거리일 뿐이다. 벽들은 흰색으로 유지되는데 보기에도 깔끔하고 개칠이 용이하기 때문이다. 또한 살균제의 향은 주인을 기쁘게 하고 집을 들어서는 거의 몇 안 되는 이들에게 깔끔함을 증명한다. 지금 이 시기 동안은 내가 집이라 부르는 이 저택은 내게 안식을 주지 못하지만 적어도 단순 주거지와 고요함은 제공한다. 또한 집 안의 어둠 속에서 나는 생각하고, 읽고, 탈출을 계획한다.

NOTE

Step 1	Survey
Key Words	house; windows; kitchen; dining room; living room; reflection; clean; white
Signal Words	as I climb; upon entering; Around the corner; Having walked through

Step 2	Reading
Purpose	to describe the look and atmosphere of a clean, quiet but austere house where the narrator lives temporarily
Pattern of Organization	description
Tone	subjective
Main Idea	The house the narrator is visiting is austere and uninviting, reflecting the character of its owner.

Step 3	Summary
지문 요약하기 (Paraphrasing)	The house the narrator is visiting is austere and uninviting, reflecting the character of its owner. Everything about the house is clean and in perfect order. Inside everything is spotless and shines, with a cleanliness and lack of color that is oddly featureless. The order and cleanliness gives an impression that is cold and unwelcoming. Attributing to this impression is the uncomfortable and harsh furniture. Although the writer thinks and reads in the quiet of her room, she does not like it there and is planning to escape.

Step 4	Recite
	요약문 말로 설명하기

44 Read the following and answer the question.

There comes a time in each person's life when they reach the point where they are no longer children, but adults. The transition from a child into a young adult is often referred to as the "coming of age," or growing up. The time when this transition occurs is different in everyone, since everyone is an individual and no two people are alike. Certain children reach this stage through a tragic, painful event which affects them to such extent that they are completely changed. Other children reach this time by simply growing older and having a better understanding of the world around them. The _____ⓐ_____ really is indefinite and cannot be defined in a general way. This stage in life is one of the most important and most popular themes in literature. Although many people are only aware of the coming of age theme through literature and other forms of entertainment, there is also a very realistic part to this event in a person's life which is often ignored. The coming of age is an event which is often celebrated in many different cultures, through rituals or ceremonies. The rituals, also known as passage rites, mark the passing of a person from one stage of life to the next: birth, infancy, childhood, adulthood, old age, and death. The coming of age is celebrated along with birth and death because they are known as universal life crises. Evoking anxiety, these crises often elicit _____ⓑ_____.

All passage rituals serve certain universal functions. Passage rituals have three steps: separation from society; inculcation-transformation; and return to society in a new status. They work to dramatize the encounter of new responsibilities, opportunities, dangers. They alleviate disruption in the equilibrium of the community. They affirm community solidarity, and the sacredness of common values.

MEMO

Fill in the blanks ⓐ and ⓑ with appropriate words from the passage respectively.

NOTE

Step 1	Survey
Key Words	
Signal Words	
Step 2	**Reading**
Purpose	
Pattern of Organization	
Tone	
Main Idea	
Step 3	**Summary**
지문 요약하기 (Paraphrasing)	
Step 4	**Recite**
요약문 말로 설명하기	

💡 Answer Key

There comes a time in each person's life when they reach the point where they are no longer children, but adults. The **transition** from a child into a young adult is often referred to as the "coming of age," or growing up. The time when this **transition** occurs is different in everyone, since everyone is an individual and no two people are alike. Certain children reach this stage through a tragic, painful event which affects them to such extent that they are completely changed. Other children reach this time by simply growing older and having a better understanding of the world around them. **The coming of age** really is indefinite and cannot be defined in a general way. This stage in life is one of the most important and most popular themes in literature. Although many people are only aware of the **coming of age** theme through literature and other forms of entertainment, there is also a very realistic part to this event in a person's life which is often ignored. // **The coming of age** is an event which is often celebrated in many different cultures, through rituals or ceremonies. The rituals, also known as passage rites, mark the passing of a person from one stage of life to the next: birth, infancy, childhood, adulthood, old age, and death. **The coming of age** is celebrated along with birth and death because they are known as universal life crises. Evoking anxiety, these crises often elicit **passage rites**. All passage rituals serve certain universal functions. **Passage rituals** have three steps: separation from society; inculcation-transformation; and return to society in a new status. // They work to dramatize the encounter of new responsibilities, opportunities, dangers. They alleviate disruption in the equilibrium of the community. They affirm community solidarity, and the sacredness of common values.

key word 1

Introduction to the "coming of age"

▼

coming of age as a literary theme

main idea
key word 2

the role of passage rituals

모범답안

ⓐ coming of age   ⓑ passage rituals (또는 passage rites)

구문분석

1. There comes a time in each person's life (when they reach the point) (where they are no longer children, but adults).

   ⇨ there : 부사, comes : 동사, a time : 주어 (동사＋주어의 도치구문)
   ⇨ 관계부사절인 when they reach the point는 앞에 있는 선행사인 a time을 수식
   ⇨ 관계부사절인 where they are no longer children, but adults는 앞에 있는 선행사인 the point를 수식

2. Certain children reach this stage / through a tragic, painful event (which affects them to such extent (that they are completely changed)).

   ⇨ 관계대명사절 안에 또 하나의 관계대명사절이 있는 구조
   ⇨ 관계대명사절 1 : 관계대명사절인 which affects them to such extent that they are completely changed가 앞에 있는 선행사인 a tragic, painful event를 수식
   ⇨ 관계대명사절 2 : 관계대명사절인 that they are completely changed는 선행사인 extent를 수식

어휘

be referred to as A A라고 불리다(정의되다)
coming of age 성인이 됨
elicit 이끌어내다, 유도하다
evoke 일깨우다, 재현하다
mark 나타내다, 표시하다
transformation 변형, 변환

disruption 붕괴, 분열, 혼란
equilibrium 평형 상태, 균형
inculcation 설득함, 터득함, 배움
passage rite 통과의례
transition 이행, 과도(기), 변화

한글 번역

각 개인의 삶에는 그들이 더 이상 아이가 아니라 어른이 되는 순간에 도달하는 때가 있다. 아이에서 청년으로 변하는 것을 '성년' 즉 '성장'이라고 말한다. 모든 이들이 개별적이고 그 누구도 똑같지 않기 때문에 이러한 변화가 일어나는 시기는 모두가 다르다. 어떤 아이들은 그들이 완전히 변할 정도로 그들에게 영향을 주는 비극적이고 고통스러운 사건들을 겪으며 이 단계에 도달한다. 또 어떤 아이들은 단순히 나이가 들고 세상에 대한 이해력을 발달시키며 이러한 시기에 도달한다. 성숙은 분명하게 규정되기가 어렵고 일반적인 방식으로 정의될 수 없다. 삶의 이러한 단계는 문학에서 가장 중요하고 가장 인기 있는 주제 중의 하나이다. 많은 이들이 단지 문학이나 다른 오락의 형태를 통해 성년이란 주제를 알게 되지만, 종종 간과되는 것은 이것이 한 인간의 삶에서 나타나는 아주 현실적인 부분이라는 사실이다. 성년은 다양한 문화에서 종교적인 행사나 의식을 통해 축복을 받는 사건이다. 통과의례로서 알려진 종교적인 의식은 삶의 한 단계에서 다음 단계, 즉 출생, 유아기, 아동기, 성인기, 노년기, 그리고 죽음과 같은 단계로 한 인간의 경과를 나타낸다. 성숙은 출생, 죽음과 함께 축하되는데, 그것은 출생과 죽음이 보편적인 생의 위기라 알려져 있기 때문이다. 불안감을 재현시키며, 이러한 위기는 통과의례를 이끌어낸다. 모든 통과의례는 특정한 보편적 기능을 담당한다. 통과의례는 3가지 단계를 가지는데, 사회에서의 분리, 이해와 변화, 그리고 새로운 상태가 되어 사회로 복귀하는 것 등이 그것이다. 이는 새로운 책임감, 기회, 위험과의 만남을 극적으로 만드는 작용을 한다. 그것은 사회의 균형 상태가 깨지는 것을 완화시킨다. 또한 공동체의 견고함과 공동의 가치의 신성힘을 확고하게 한다.

NOTE

Step 1	Survey
Key Words	coming of age; passage rituals(rites)
Signal Words	be referred as; known as; series
Step 2	**Reading**
Purpose	to explain what the coming of age is and its function
Pattern of Organization	definition
Tone	neutral
Main Idea	The coming of age, the transition from a child to a young adult, is celebrated in a rite of passage in many cultures.
Step 3	**Summary**
지문 요약하기 (Paraphrasing)	The coming of age, the transition from a child to a young adult, is celebrated in a rite of passage in many cultures. The rite of passage serves certain universal functions and has three steps: separation from society, inculcation-transformation, and return to society in a new status. At the core of this rite of passage is the solidarity of the community.
Step 4	**Recite**
요약문 말로 설명하기	

MEMO

유희태 일반영어 ①
2S2R
기본

2S2R 심화

01 Read the passage and follow the directions.

The complete control of impulse by will, which is sometimes preached by moralists, and often enforced by economic necessity, is not really desirable. A life governed by purposes and desires, to the exclusion of impulse, is a tiring life; it exhausts vitality, and leaves a man, in the end, indifferent to the very purposes which he has been trying to achieve. When a whole nation lives in this way, the whole nation tends to become feeble, without enough grasp to recognize and overcome the obstacles to its desires. Industrialism and organization are constantly forcing civilized nations to live more and more by purpose rather than _____. In the long run such a mode of existence, if it does not dry up the springs of life, produces new impulses, not of the kind which the will has been in the habit of controlling or of which thought is conscious. These new impulses are apt to be worse in their effects than those that have been checked. Excessive discipline, especially when it is imposed from without, often issues in impulses of cruelty and destruction; this is one reason why militarism has a bad effect on national character. Either lack of vitality, or impulses which are oppressive and against life, will almost always result if the spontaneous impulses are not able to find an outlet. A man's impulses are not fixed from the beginning by his native disposition: within certain wide limits, they are profoundly modified by his circumstances and his way of life.

Fill in the blank with ONE word from the passage. Then describe the main idea of the passage in ONE sentence.

NOTE

Step 1	Survey
Key Words	
Signal Words	
Step 2	**Reading**
Purpose	
Pattern of Organization	
Tone	
Main Idea	
Step 3	**Summary**
지문 요약하기 (Paraphrasing)	
Step 4	**Recite**
요약문 말로 설명하기	

The complete control of impulse by will, which is sometimes preached by moralists, and often enforced by economic necessity, **is not really desirable.** A life governed by **purposes and desires,** to the exclusion of **impulse,** is **a tiring life**; it exhausts vitality, and leaves a man, in the end, **indifferent to the very purposes** which he has been trying to achieve. When a whole nation lives in this way, the whole nation tends to become feeble, without enough grasp to recognize and overcome the obstacles to its desires. Industrialism and organization are constantly forcing civilized nations to live **more and more by purpose rather than impulse. In the long run such a mode of existence,** if it does not dry up the springs of life, produces new impulses, not of the kind which the will has been in the habit of controlling or of which thought is conscious. **These new impulses** are apt to be worse in their effects than those that have been checked. Excessive discipline, especially when it is imposed from without, often issues in impulses of cruelty and destruction; this is one reason why militarism has a bad effect on national character. Either lack of vitality, or impulses which are oppressive and against life, will almost always result if the **spontaneous impulses** are not able to find an outlet. **A man's impulses are not fixed from the beginning by his native disposition**: within certain wide limits, they are profoundly modified by his circumstances and his way of life.

모범답안

The appropriate word for the blank is "impulse". Second, the main idea of the passage is that the excessive suppression of impulses can lead to a loss of vitality and the surfacing of even worse impulses.

한글 번역

도덕론자들은 흔히 의지를 통해서 충동을 완전히 억제하라고 훈계하고 이 훈계는 경제적 필요에 의해서 지지를 받는 경우가 적지 않다. 하지만 이는 결코 바람직스럽지 않다. 충동은 완전히 배제된 채 목적과 요구에 의해서 좌우되는 인생은 지루하다. 그런 생활은 생명력을 고갈시키고 결국에는 자신이 달성하려던 목적 그 자체에 대해 무관심하게 만든다; 온 국민이 이런 식으로 생활한다면 그 나라는 욕구를 방해하는 장애물을 파악하고 이를 극복할 능력이 충분하지 않은, 나약한 나라가 되기 쉽다. 산업주의와 조직은 문명 국가의 국민들에게 충동이 아니라 목적에 의거해서 생활하라고 끊임없이 강요한다. 장기적으로 볼 때 이런 생활 방식은 생명력의 원천을 고갈시키지는 않는다 해도 새로운 충동을 만들어내는데, 이는 의지가 통제하는 종류도, 사유가 이미 알고 있는 것도 아닌 것이다. 이런 새로운 충동은 자칫 지금까지 억제되어온 충동보다 훨씬 나쁜 영향을 미치기 쉽다. 과도한 규율, 특히 외부에서 강요되는 과도한 규율은 종종 잔학과 파괴의 충동을 야기한다; 바로 이런 이유에서 군국주의는 민족성에 악영향을 미친다. 자연스러운 충동이 출구를 찾지 못하면 그 사람은 대개 활력을 잃어버리거나 생명에 반하는 포악한 충동을 지니게 된다. 인간의 충동은 타고난 기질에 의해서 날 때부터 고정된 것이 아니라 환경과 생활 방식에 따라서 크게 달라지는 것이다.

Step 1	Survey
Key Words	Control of impulse; vitality; feeble; new
Signal Words	leaves; in the end; In the long run; effect; result
Step 2	**Reading**
Purpose	to warn against disregarding or suppressing impulses
Pattern of Organization	cause&effect
Tone	subjective; persuasive
Main Idea	The excessive suppression of impulses can lead to a loss of vitality and the surfacing of even worse impulses.
Step 3	**Summary**
지문 요약하기 (Paraphrasing)	Trying to control impulses can lead to a tiring life with a lack of vitality for both the individual and nation as a whole. Likewise, new impulses that are not thwarted by the will can arise, resulting in even more damaging conscquences.
Step 4	**Recite**
	요약문 말로 설명하기

02 Read the passage and follow the directions.

The use of a specific type of clothing—the T-shirt—to communicate other types of information began in the 1940s, when faces and political slogans appeared on T-shirts and, in the 1960s, with commercial logos and other designs. Technical developments in the 1950s and 1960s, such as plastic inks, plastic transfers, and spray paint, led to the use of colored designs and increased the possibilities of the T-shirt as a means of communication. Approximately one billion T-shirts are purchased annually in the United States. The T-shirt performs a function formerly associated with the hat, that of identifying an individual's social location instantly. Unlike the hat in the nineteenth century, which signaled social class status, the T-shirt speaks to issues related to ideology, difference, and myth: politics, race, gender, and leisure. The variety of slogans and logos that appear on T-shirts is enormous. Much of the time, people consent to being co-opted for "unpaid advertising" for global corporations selling clothes, music, sports, and entertainment in exchange for the social cachet of being associated with certain products. Some of the time, people use T-shirts to indicate their support for social and political causes, groups, or organization to which they have made a commitment. Occasionally, the T-shirt becomes a medium for grass-roots resistance. Bootlegged T-shirts representing characters on the television show The Simpsons appeared in response to T-shirts marketed by the network that produced the show. The bootlegged T-shirts represented the Simpson family as African Americans. Bart Simpson was shown as Rastabart, with dreadlocks and a red, green, and gold headband, as Rasta-dude Bart Marley, and as Black Bart, paired with Nelson Mandela. Using clothing behavior as a means of making a statement, the T-shirts appeared to be intended as an affirmation of African Americans as an ethnic group and as a commentary on the narrow range of roles for black characters in the show. Victims of gender-related violence, such as rape, incest, battering, and sexual harassment, have used T-shirts as venues for statements about their experiences that are exhibited in clotheslines in public plazas.

cachet : an indication of approved or superior status
bootlegged : pirated

MEMO

Summarize the above passage in a well-formed paragraph. Your summary must contain the main idea and all major supporting ideas expressed by the author and must not contain any of your own ideas. Do not copy more than EIGHT consecutive words from the passage. [Approximately 100 words, (4-6 lines)]

_____

_____

_____

_____

_____

NOTE

Step 1	Survey
Key Words	
Signal Words	
Step 2	Reading
Purpose	
Pattern of Organization	
Tone	
Main Idea	
Step 3	Summary
지문 요약하기 (Paraphrasing)	
Step 4	Recite
요약문 말로 설명하기	

Answer Key

The use of a specific type of clothing—the **T-shirt**—to **communicate other types of information** began in the 1940s, when faces and political **slogans** appeared on T-shirts and, in the 1960s, with commercial logos and other designs. Technical developments in the 1950s and 1960s, such as plastic inks, plastic transfers, and spray paint, led to the use of colored designs and increased the possibilities of the T-shirt as **a means of communication**. Approximately one billion T-shirts are purchased annually in the United States. The T-shirt performs **a function** formerly associated with the hat, that of identifying an individual's social location instantly. Unlike the hat in the nineteenth century, which signaled social class status, the T-shirt speaks to issues related to **ideology**, **difference**, and **myth**: politics, race, gender, and leisure. // The variety of slogans and logos that appear on T-shirts is enormous. Much of the time, people consent to being co-opted for **"unpaid advertising"** for global corporations selling clothes, music, sports, and entertainment in exchange for the social cachet of being associated with certain products. Some of the time, people use T-shirts to indicate their support for social and political causes, groups, or organization to which they have made a commitment. // Occasionally, the T-shirt becomes a medium for **grass-roots resistance**. **Bootlegged T-shirts** representing characters on the television show The Simpsons appeared in response to T-shirts marketed by the network that produced the show. **The bootlegged T-shirts** represented the Simpson family as African Americans. Bart Simpson was shown as Rastabart, with dreadlocks and a red, green, and gold headband, as Rasta-dude Bart Marley, and as Black Bart, paired with Nelson Mandela. Using clothing behavior **as a means of making a statement,** the T-shirts appeared to be intended as an affirmation of African Americans as an ethnic group and as a commentary on the narrow range of roles for black characters in the show. // Victims of gender-related violence, such as rape, incest, battering, and sexual harassment, have used have used T-shirts as **venues for statements about their experiences** that are exhibited in clotheslines in public plazas.

→key words

→key word

①

→key word
②

→key word

③

모범답안

The T-shirt has been used as a means of social and political expression. T-shirts as a medium to convey messages initially started in the 1940s, with political content, and then commercial logos and designs in the 60s. While previously hats were quick indicators of social status, T-shirts revealed many more facets of a person. People wearing shirts took part of "unpaid advertising," showing their associations with certain products or political or social points. Even T-shirts can be the means to "grassroots resistance," such as when bootleggers fabricated shirts bearing their own African-American versions of the family from the television show *The Simpsons*. Likewise, they can be made in order to make criticisms about gender-related violence or dominant culture.

한글 번역

티셔츠라는 특정 타입의 옷이 다른 형태의 정보와 소통하는 방식으로 활용된 것은 몇몇 얼굴과 정치적 슬로건이 티셔츠 위에 새겨진 1940년대부터이다. 1960년대에는 상업적 로고와 다른 디자인적 요소들이 티셔츠에 나타났다. 1950년대와 1960년대의 기술 발전, 예를 들면 플라스틱 잉크나 플라스틱 트랜스퍼, 스프레이 페인트 같은 것들이 색채화된 디자인의 사용을 이끌었고 티셔츠를 의사소통의 수단으로 사용하는 일의 가능성을 증대시켰다. 미국에서는 연간 대략 10억 장의 티셔츠가 판매된다. 티셔츠는 개인의 사회적 위치를 즉각적으로 나타내 보이는 기능을 수행하고 있는데, 티셔츠 전에는 모자가 이 기능을 담당했다. 사회적 지위만을 나타냈던 19세기의 모자와는 달리, 티셔츠는 이데올로기나 차이 그리고 정치, 인종, 성별, 여가와 같은 신화들에 관련된 문제에 대해 이야기를 한다. 티셔츠에 나타나는 슬로건과 로고의 다양성은 무궁무진하다. 많은 시간 동안 사람들은 옷, 음악, 스포츠, 그리고 오락을 파는 글로벌 회사들을 위한 '무보수 광고'에 끌어들여지는 것에 합의했다. 그 대가로 사람들은 그러한 상품들과 연관이 있다는 사회적 위신을 얻었다. 어떨 때는 사람들은 티셔츠를 그들이 헌신하는 사회적, 정치적 대의명분이나 단체, 기관을 지지하기 위해 사용했다. 때때로, 티셔츠는 서민들의 저항 매개가 되었다. TV쇼 심슨 가족의 캐릭터들이 그려진 짝퉁 티셔츠는 그 쇼가 방영된 방송국이 판매하는 상품에 대응하기 위해 생겨났다. 그 짝퉁 티셔츠는 심슨 가족을 흑인으로 묘사했다. 바트 심슨은 레게머리에 빨간색, 초록색, 금색이 섞인 헤어밴드를 한 라스타 바트, 라스타 민족 바트 말리로, 그리고 넬슨 만델라와 짝을 이루는 흑인 바트로 묘사되었다. 옷을 의견을 내는 것의 수단으로 사용하면서, 티셔츠는 흑인이라는 인종을 지지하고 TV쇼에서 흑인의 입지가 좁은 것에 대한 비판을 시사하기도 했다. 강간, 근친상간, 구타, 성추행과 같은 성별과 관련된 폭력의 피해자들은 티셔츠를 광장의 빨랫줄에 전시하여 그들이 겪은 사건에 대해 진술하는 장소로써 사용했다.

NOTE	
Step 1	**Survey**
Key Words	T-shirt; communicate; functions; expression; grass-roots resistance; The Simpsons; gender-related violence; venues for statements
Signal Words	in the 1960s; Some of the time; Occasionally
Step 2	**Reading**
Purpose	to show how t-shirts have become instruments to convey other types of information
Pattern of Organization	series
Tone	informative; neutral
Main Idea	T-shirts have become a means to convey ideology, associate one with products, and make statements.
Step 3	**Summary**
지문 요약하기 (Paraphrasing)	The T-shirt has been used as a means of commercial, social and political communication. Some people wear T-shirts to take part of "unpaid advertising," showing their associations with certain products. Also, people wear T-shirts to illustrate their support for political or social points. Even T-shirts can be the means to "grassroots resistance," such as when bootleggers fabricated shirts bearing their own African-American versions of the family from the television show The Simpsons. Likewise, they can be made in order to make criticisms about gender-related violence or dominant culture.
Step 4	**Recite**
요약문 말로 설명하기	

03 Read the passage and follow the directions.

MEMO

No artist has reinvented the visible world in a more radical way than Picasso. In his stringent early Cubist paintings, composed with fragmentary geometric planes, the differences between figure and ground are hardly distinguishable, testing the limits of representation. After the First World War, he developed a very different kind of painting, paradoxically both flat and suggestive of intangible depth, hard-edged and often brightly coloured. Recently, T. J. Clark focuses on those paintings of the 1920s and 30s in his book, *Picasso and Truth*. Picasso's works from this period have now become so familiar that their complexity and radical strangeness are often taken for granted, even overlooked. Clark's book sets out to explore just how radical and how strange these paintings are.

Ugliness and monstrosity cannot always be co-opted into another form of beauty; they are sometimes meant to shake the very foundations of the viewer's beliefs and reveal new kinds of truth. Clark sees Picasso as a kind of wizard, who had the uncanny gift of being able to see the world around him in a clearer, more truthful way than his contemporaries. Clark's book attempts to show how Picasso extends and even redefines conventional notions of truth through complex relationships between spaces and objects and subject matter, most especially through a courageous engagement with monstrosity.

Because Picasso's works of these years departed so radically from accepted norms, they were often greeted with hostility or puzzlement. In 1932, the psychologist Carl G. Jung famously compared Picasso's paintings to the pictures made by schizophrenics, and called him an "underworld" personality who followed "the demonic attraction of ugliness and evil." Although Clark does not mention Jung in this context, he casts his own similar position in a positive light, celebrating rather than damning the eerie power of Picasso's paintings. Clark acknowledges that Picasso's art contains pathological elements, but he sees them as reflections of the pathology of an age rather than of an individual. For him, Picasso's art is a judgement on a century that was rife with disaster.

Identify one "disaster" mentioned in the passage that can be inferred to have influenced Picasso's art style. Additionally, explain the aspect of Picasso's work that Jung and Clark agree upon, and how their opinions differ.

_____

_____

_____

_____

_____

03

NOTE ▶

Step 1	Survey
Key Words	
Signal Words	
Step 2	**Reading**
Purpose	
Pattern of Organization	
Tone	
Main Idea	
Step 3	**Summary**
지문 요약하기 (Paraphrasing)	
Step 4	**Recite**
요약문 말로 설명하기	

💡 Answer Key

No artist has reinvented the visible world in a more radical way than **Picasso**. In his stringent early Cubist paintings, composed with fragmentary geometric planes, the differences between figure and ground are hardly distinguishable, testing the limits of representation. After the First World War, he developed a very different kind of painting, paradoxically both flat and suggestive of intangible depth, hard-edged and often brightly coloured. Recently, **T. J. Clark** focuses on those paintings of the 1920s and 30s in his book, *Picasso and Truth*. **Picasso's works** from this period have now become so familiar that their complexity and radical strangeness are often taken for granted, even overlooked. Clark's book sets out to explore just how radical and how strange these paintings are.

→ key words

Ugliness and monstrosity cannot always be co-opted into another form of beauty; they are sometimes meant to shake the very foundations of the viewer's beliefs and reveal new kinds of truth. Clark sees Picasso as a kind of wizard, who had the uncanny gift of being able to see the world around him in a clearer, more truthful way than his contemporaries. Clark's book attempts **to show how Picasso extends and even redefines conventional notions of truth through complex relationships between spaces and objects and subject matter, most especially through a courageous engagement with monstrosity.**

Because Picasso's works of these years departed so radically from accepted norms, they were often greeted with hostility or puzzlement. In 1932, the psychologist Carl G. Jung famously compared Picasso's paintings to the pictures made by schizophrenics, and called him an "underworld" personality who followed "the demonic attraction of ugliness and evil." Although Clark does not mention Jung in this context, he casts his own similar position in a positive light, **celebrating** rather than damning **the eerie power of Picasso's paintings**. Clark acknowledges that Picasso's art contains pathological elements, but he sees them as **reflections of the pathology of an age** rather than of an individual. For him, **Picasso's art is a judgement on a century that was rife with disaster.**

모범답안

One "disaster" to influence Picasso that is referred to in the passage is World War I. Both Jung and Clark agree on the eeriness and pathological quality of Picasso's work, but Jung viewed the work as ugly and akin to schizophrenics' art whilst Clark saw them as reflecting the problem of the era's mindset, not the artist's.

03

어휘

co-opt 선임하다, 끌어들이다

schizophrenic 정신 분열병 환자

hard-edged 냉철한, 철저히 현실에 입각한

stringent 엄중한, 엄격한, 긴박한

한글 번역

피카소보다 더 급진적인 방식으로 가시적인 세상을 보여준 예술가는 없었다. 파편화된 기하학적인 평면들로 구성된 그의 엄격한 초기 입체파 그림들에서는 인물과 배경 사이의 차이점이 거의 구분이 되지 않으며 구상적 재현의 한계를 시험하고 있다. 제1차 세계대전이 끝난 뒤, 그는 역설적으로 평평하면서도 뭐라 꼬집어 말할 수 없는 깊이를 암시하고, 현실을 예리하게 묘사하면서도 종종 밝게 채색된 매우 다른 종류의 그림을 그렸다. 최근에 T. J. 클락은 그의 저서인 *Picasso and Truth*에서 1920년대와 30년대의 피카소 그림들에 초점을 맞추고 있다. 이 시기의 피카소 그림들은 지금은 아주 익숙해져서 그림들의 복잡함과 극단적인 생소함이 종종 당연한 것으로 여겨지고 있고 심지어 간과되기도 한다. 클락의 책은 이 그림들이 얼마나 급진적이고 생소한지를 탐구하고 있다.

추악함과 기괴함이 항상 또 다른 형태의 아름다움이라고 내세워질 수는 없다; 왜냐하면 그러한 것들은 때때로 그림을 보는 사람들의 믿음의 토대를 흔들어 새로운 종류의 진실을 드러내도록 의도되어 있기 때문이다. 클락은 피카소를 동시대인들보다 더 분명하고 더 진실된 방식으로 자신의 주변 세상을 볼 수 있는 초자연적인 재능을 가진 일종의 마법사로 여기고 있다. 클락의 책은 피카소가 어떻게 공간과 물체 그리고 주제 사이의 복잡한 관계를 통해, 특히 기괴함을 대담하게 수용함으로써 틀에 박힌 진실의 개념을 확대하고 심지어 재정의하는지를 보여주고 있다.

이 몇 년간 피카소의 작품들은 보편적인 규범들로부터 아주 급진적으로 이탈되어 있었기 때문에 종종 적대감이나 혼란스러움으로 받아들여졌다. 1932년에 심리학자인 칼 융은 피카소의 그림을 정신분열증 환자가 그린 그림과 비교하여 그를 '추악함과 사악함의 악마적 매력'을 추구하는 '저승에서 온 인간'이라 불렀다. 비록 클락은 이러한 맥락에서 융을 언급하지는 않지만 긍정적인 관점에서 그와 비슷한 자신의 의견을 드러내고 피카소 그림들의 섬뜩한 힘을 혹평하기보다는 오히려 높이 평가하고 있다. 클락은 피카소의 작품에 병적인 요소가 포함되어 있음을 인정하고는 있지만 그는 피카소의 작품들이 한 개인의 병적 상태라기보다는 한 시대의 병적 상태를 반영하고 있다고 보고 있다. 그에게 피카소의 그림은 재난으로 가득했던 한 세기에 대한 판단이다.

NOTE

Step 1	Survey
Key Words	Picasso; T. J. Clark; cubist; representation; monstrosity; conventional; norms
Signal Words	recently; most especially; because; although
Step 2	Reading
Purpose	to summarize author T. J. Clark's view of Picasso's art
Pattern of Organization	unclear
Tone	neutral
Main Idea	Although Picasso's work contains ugly, monstrous elements, T.J. Clark argues it is a radical and truthful reflection of the age and therefore valuable.
Step 3	Summary
지문 요약하기 (Paraphrasing)	Although Picasso's work contains ugly, monstrous elements, T.J. Clark, the author of Picasso and Truth, argues it is a radical and truthful reflection of the age and therefore valuable. Picasso's art was a departure from the norms of art in his time, which some viewed with hostility and puzzlement. However, Clark asserts that Picasso was able to see the world in a more truthful way than his contemporaries and that the pathological elements in Picasso's art reflect the character of an age rather than of the artist himself.
Step 4	Recite
요약문 말로 설명하기	

04 Read the passage and follow the directions.

My first Apple came with video games; I gave them away. Playing games on the computer didn't interest me. If I had free time I'd spend it talking on the telephone to friends. Anthony got hooked. His wife was often annoyed by the hours he spent at his computer and the money he spent upgrading it. My marriage had no such strains—until I discovered email. Then I got hooked. Email draws me the same way the phone does: it's a souped-up conversation. Email deepened my friendship with Anthony. Though his office was next to mine, we rarely had extended conversations, because he is shy. Face to face he mumbled, so I could barely tell he was speaking. But when we both got on _____, I started receiving long, self-revealing messages: we poured our hearts out to each other. A friend discovered that email opened up that kind of communication with her father. He would never talk much on the phone (as her mother would), but have become close since both got on line. Why, I wondered, would some men find it easier to open up on email? It's a combination of the technology (which they enjoy) and the obliqueness of the written word, just as many men will reveal feelings in dribs and drabs while riding in the car or doing something, which they'd never talk about sitting face to face. It's too intense, too bearing-down on them, and once you start you have to keep going. With a computer in between, it's safer.

It was on email, in fact, that I described to Anthony how boys in groups often struggle to get the upper hand whereas girls tend to maintain an appearance of cooperation. And he pointed out that this explained why boys are more likely to be captivated by computers than girls are. Boys are typically motivated by a social structure that says if you don't dominate you will be dominated. Computers, by their nature, balk: you type a perfectly appropriate command and it refuses to do what it should. Many boys and men are incited by their defiance: "I'm going to whip this into line and teach it who's boss! I'll get it to do what I say!" (and if they work hard enough, they always can). Girls and women are more likely to respond, "This thing won't cooperate. Get it away from me!"

3-1. Fill in the blank with the ONE most appropriate word from the passage.

_____

3-2. What does the writer mean by saying "the obliqueness of the written word"? Write down your answer in 15 words or less.

_____

NOTE

Step 1	Survey
Key Words	
Signal Words	
Step 2	**Reading**
Purpose	
Pattern of Organization	
Tone	
Main Idea	
Step 3	**Summary**
지문 요약하기 (Paraphrasing)	
Step 4	**Recite**
요약문 말로 설명하기	

💡 Answer Key

My first Apple came with video games; I gave them away. Playing games on the computer didn't interest me. If I had free time I'd spend it talking on the telephone to friends. Anthony got hooked. His wife was often annoyed by the hours he spent at his computer and the money he spent upgrading it. My marriage had no such strains—until I discovered **email**. Then I got hooked. **Email** draws me the same way the phone does: it's a souped-up conversation. **Email** deepened my friendship with Anthony. Though his office was next to mine, we rarely had extended **conversations**, because he is shy. Face to face he mumbled, so I could barely tell he was speaking. But when we both got on **email**, I started receiving long, self-revealing messages: we poured our hearts out to each other. A friend discovered that email opened up **that kind of communication** with her father. He would never talk much on the phone (as her mother would), but have become close since both **got on line**. Why, I wondered, would some men find it easier to open up on email? It's a combination of the technology (which they enjoy) and the obliqueness of the written word, just as many men will reveal feelings in dribs and drabs while riding in the car or doing something, which they'd never talk about sitting face to face. It's too intense, too bearing-down on them, and once you start you have to keep going. **With a computer in between**, it's safer.

It was on **email**, in fact, that I described to Anthony how **boys** in groups often struggle to get the upper hand whereas **girls** tend to maintain an appearance of cooperation. And he pointed out that this explained why **boys** are more likely to be captivated by computers than **girls** are. **Boys** are typically motivated by **a social structure** that says if you don't dominate you will be dominated. Computers, by their nature, balk: you type a perfectly appropriate command and it refuses to do what it should. Many **boys and men** are incited by their defiance: "I'm going to whip this into line and teach it who's boss! I'll get it to do what I say!" (and if they work hard enough, they always can). **Girls and women** are more likely to respond, "This thing won't cooperate. Get it away from me!"

key words

모범답안

3-1. email

3-2. Email is an indirect form of communication, free of face to face experience.

한글 번역

나의 첫 애플(컴퓨터)은 비디오게임과 함께 왔는데, 난 그것들을 포기해버렸다. 컴퓨터에서 게임을 하는 것은 별 재미가 없었다. 자유시간이 있다면 전화로 친구와 대화하는 데 쓸 것이다. 앤서니는 푹 빠져버렸다. 그의 부인은 컴퓨터에 그가 보내는 시간과 컴퓨터를 업그레이드하는 데 드는 돈 때문에 종종 화를 냈다. 내 결혼생활은 그와 같은 긴장이 없었다. 내가 이메일을 알기 전까지는. 그때 나도 푹 빠져버렸다. 이메일은 전화가 나를 끌어당기듯 나를 똑같이 끌어당겼다: 이메일은 마력을 올린 대화다. 이메일은 나와 앤서니와의 우정을 더욱 깊어지게 했다. 앤서니의 오피스는 내 오피스 옆에 있었지만, 그가 내성적인 관계로 대화를 깊게 나눌 기회가 거의 없었다. 얼굴을 맞대고 얘기할 때 그는 우물우물거렸기에, 그가 말하고 있는지 거의 알아차릴 수 없었다. 하지만 우리 둘이 이메일을 주고받을 때 나는 사적인 감정을 드러낸 긴 메시지들을 받기 시작했다: 우린 우리의 감정을 솔직하게 드러내었다. 한 친구는 그녀의 아버지와 이와 같은 대화를 이메일이 열어주었다는 것을 발견하였다. 그는 전화상으로는 별로 말을 하지 않았지만(그의 어머니도 마찬가지였다), 그들은 온라인을 통해서 가까워지게 되었다. 왜 어떤 남자들은 이메일에서 마음을 터놓기가 더 쉬울까? 그것은 (그들이 좋아하는) 기술과 문자 언어의 완곡한 표현의 결합이 (기 때문이)다. 많은 남성들이 차를 타면서 또는 뭔가를 하면서 찔끔찔끔 자신들의 감정을 드러내듯이, 그들은 이런 것을 얼굴을 맞대고 앉아서는 결코 하지 않는다. 얼굴을 맞대고 앉아서 대화하는 것은 너무 긴장되고, 그들을 너무 압박한다. 그리고 일단 시작하면, 계속 진행해야 한다. 컴퓨터를 사이에 두면(즉, 이메일을 통해 대화하면), 더 안전하다.

사실, 내가 앤서니에게 그룹 내에서 소년들이 종종 상대를 이기기 위해 어떻게 노력하는지를, 그리고 그와는 달리 소녀들은 협력의 모습을 유지하려는 경향이 있음을 묘사한 것도 바로 이 이메일을 통해서였다. 앤서니는 이것이 왜 소년들이 소녀들보다 컴퓨터에 마음이 사로잡히는지를 설명한다고 지적하였다. 소년들은 전형적으로 사회구조에 의해 동기부여가 되는데, 이 사회구조는 '네가 남을 지배하지 못하면, 남들에게 지배당한다.'라고 말한다. 컴퓨터는 그 본성상 멈칫거린다: 당신이 완전히 적절한 명령을 입력했는데, 컴퓨터는 자신이 해야 하는 것을 하기를 거절한다. 많은 소년과 남성들은 이런 컴퓨터의 반항에 분노한다: "이놈을 매질해서 이놈에게 누가 상전인지를 가르치겠어!"(그리고, 그들이 충분히 열심히 일하면, 그들은 항상 할 수 있다). 소녀들과 여성들은 "이것이 협력하려고 하지 않네. 그것 좀 나에게서 치워줘!"라고 할 가능성이 더 많다.

NOTE	
Step 1	**Survey**
Key Words	communication; email; boys; girls
Signal Words	whereas; more likely … than
Step 2	**Reading**
Purpose	to show how email is used differently by men to communicate
Pattern of Organization	comparison&contrast
Tone	subjective; humorous
Main Idea	The nature of email can evoke more open communication among men.
Step 3	**Summary**
지문 요약하기 (Paraphrasing)	The nature of email can evoke more open communication among men. The writer formed a deep bond with his office neighbor, over email rather than in talking due to technological enjoyment and the lessened intensity of writing. Men tend to have a deeper interest in facing the challenges of a computer, while women, who value cooperation, tend to find this unappealing.
Step 4	**Recite**
	요약문 말로 설명하기

05　Read the passage and follow the directions.

MEMO

At precisely 4 P.M., Monday through Friday, Oprah appears on innumerable television sets. First, before the live action starts, a theme song is heard. Oprah sings her own song, in which the main lyrics are, I will rise: Various photographic stills of Oprah are flashed on the screen. Some of these snapshots include Oprah hugging a distraught fan, Oprah laughing with that signature smile, Oprah dancing with her hands clapped together, Oprah bent down on one knee like a preacher holding a young girl's hand. All of these images are there to relax the television viewing audience and to assure them that Oprah is a kind, caring, fun-loving individual who really is real.

　When Oprah first appears, she sets the stage and the mood for what is to come. The show begins after a brief commercial break with an excited-looking Oprah running onto the set to the cheers of a very enthusiastic audience. Oprah gives audience members high fives; on her face is a huge grin as she prances onto the stage. The applause goes on for a moment or two as Oprah bows, and then the cheering dies out. Speaking loudly into her handheld microphone, Oprah greets the audience in a very friendly manner and points out some things about the audience that she finds funny. Often she relates to the audience something that occurred to her backstage. After cheerfully bantering with the audience, Oprah explains what she has in store for them today. Sometimes she has a celebrity guest, other times she has a regular person whose story has inspired her. Her celebrity guests have included stars like Julia Roberts and Will Smith; her regular guests have shared their triumphs and problems. On other shows she picks a topic like how to handle your money and invites financial experts on the show. They may cover such skills as how to save money at the grocery store or how to balance your checkbook.

Describe the main idea of the first paragraph. Second, describe the main idea of the second paragraph.

03

NOTE ►

Step 1	Survey
Key Words	
Signal Words	
Step 2	**Reading**
Purpose	
Pattern of Organization	
Tone	
Main Idea	
Step 3	**Summary**
지문 요약하기 (Paraphrasing)	
Step 4	**Recite**
요약문 말로 설명하기	

☉ Answer Key

At precisely 4 P.M., Monday through Friday, **Oprah** appears on innumerable television sets. First, before the live action starts, [a theme song is heard.] Oprah sings her own song, in which the main lyrics are, "I will rise." [Various photographic stills of Oprah] are flashed on the screen. Some of these snapshots include Oprah ⓐhugging a distraught fan, Oprah ⓑlaughing with that signature smile, Oprah ⓒdancing with her hands clapped together, Oprah bent down on one knee like a preacher ⓓ holding a young girl's hand. All of these images are there to relax the television viewing audience and to assure them that Oprah is a kind, caring, fun-loving individual who really is "real."

When Oprah first appears, she sets the stage and the mood for what is to come. [The show begins after a brief commercial break with an excited-looking Oprah running onto the set] to the ⓐ cheers of a very enthusiastic audience. Oprah gives audience members ⓑ high fives; on her face is a huge grin as she prances onto the stage. The ⓒ applause goes on for a moment or two as Oprah bows, and then the cheering dies out. Speaking loudly into her handheld microphone, Oprah ⓓ greets the audience in a very friendly manner and points out some things about the audience that she finds funny. Often she relates to the audience something that occurred to her backstage. After cheerfully bantering with the audience, [Oprah explains what she has in store for them today.] Sometimes she has ⓐ a celebrity guest, other times she has a "regular" person whose story has inspired her. Her celebrity guests have included stars like Julia Roberts and Will Smith; her "regular" guests have shared their triumphs and problems. On other shows she picks ⓑ a topic like how to handle your money and invites financial experts on the show. They may cover such skills as how to save money at the grocery store or how to balance your checkbook.

▸ key word
- major supporting details: the theme songs
- minor supporting details:
Oprah song
▸*appearance (반복됨)
- major supporting details: the photographic still of Oprah
- minor supporting details:
 ⓐ hugging a fan
 ⓑ laughing
 ⓒ dancing
 ⓓ holding a girl's hand
▸ main idea
- major supporting details: Oprah running onto the set and starts the shows
- minor supporting details:
 ⓐ cheering
 ⓑ high fives
 ⓒ applauding
 ⓓ sharing something funny that occurred backstage
- major supporting details:
 explains the day's program
- minor supporting details:
 ⓐ guests
 ⓑ special topic

모범답안

The main idea of the first paragraph is that all of the images at the beginning of the Oprah show relax and assure the audience that Oprah is a kind, caring, fun-loving individual who really is "real." Second, the main idea of the second one is that when Oprah first appears, she sets the stage and the mood for what is to come.

구문분석

All of these images are there to relax the television viewing audience and to assure them that Oprah is a kind, caring, fun-loving individual who really is "real."
⇨ to relax와 to assure는 병렬구조로 to부정사로 연결되어 있다.

한글 번역

월요일부터 금요일까지 정확히 오후 4시에 오프라는 수많은 티비에 등장한다. 먼저 생방송이 시작되기 전에 주제곡이 흘러나온다. 오프라는 주 가사가 "나는 일어날 거야"라는 자신의 노래를 부른다. 화면에는 수많은 오프라의 스틸 사진이 비친다. 오프라가 (흥분해서) 제정신이 아닌 팬을 끌어안는 장면, 오프라의 그 특유의 미소로 웃는 모습, 오프라가 박수를 치며 춤추는 장면, 오프라가 목사님처럼 한쪽 다리를 구부리고 어린 소녀의 손을 잡고 있는 장면 등이 이들 스냅샷이다. 이 모든 이미지들은 텔레비전을 보는 시청자들을 이완하게 해주고, 오프라가 친절하고, 따뜻하며, 재미있고, 사랑이 많은 '진짜' 인물임을 확신시켜 주기 위함이다.

　오프라가 일단 들어오면, 그녀는 무대와 분위기를 앞으로 진행될 일에 맞춰 놓는다. 쇼는 짧막한 광고 이후에 열광적인 관중들의 환호를 받으며 흥분한 표정의 오프라가 세트로 뛰어 들어오면서 시작된다. 오프라는 관중들과 하이파이브를 하고 무대를 걸어 다니는 동안 얼굴에는 환한 미소를 띠고 있다. 오프라가 인사를 하는 동안 박수는 한동안 계속되고 환호는 가라앉는다. 손에 쥔 마이크에 크게 말을 하면서 오프라는 관중들을 대단히 친근한 매너로 맞이하고 자신이 관중들 사이에서 재미있다고 본 것들을 말한다. 가끔 그녀는 무대 뒤편에서 일어난 일들에 대해 관중들에게 말한다. 관중들과 활기차게 몇 마디를 나눈 후 오프라는 오늘의 주제가 무엇인지를 설명한다. 어떤 때는 유명인사가 손님일 때도 있고, 또 어떤 경우는 그녀에게 인상을 준 '보통 사람'을 데려올 때도 있다. 그녀의 유명인 손님은 줄리아 로버츠나 윌 스미스 같은 스타들은 포함한다. 일반인 손님은 자신들의 성취나 문제점들을 공유한다. 또 어떤 쇼에서는 어떻게 돈을 관리할지와 같은 주제를 선정하고 쇼에 경제 전문가를 초대하기도 한다. 이들 쇼에서는 식품점에서 돈을 아끼는 기술이라든지 어떻게 체크북을 수지타산 맞추는지 등을 알려준다.

NOTE

Step 1	Survey
Key Words	Oprah; appearance; television show
Signal Words	At precisely 4 P.M; First; When; after
Step 2	**Reading**
Purpose	to depict the Oprah Winfrey show
Pattern of Organization	time order; series
Tone	cheerful; informative
Main Idea	Oprah's show presents herself as real and friendly as she gives her thoughts and talks with both celebrity and inspiring guests.
Step 3	**Summary**
지문 요약하기 (Paraphrasing)	Oprah's show opens with images establishing her as real and friendly. After this she gives some thoughts and observations before talking with both celebrity and inspiring guests about various topics.
Step 4	**Recite**
	요약문 말로 설명하기

06   Read the passage and follow the directions.

MEMO

In the Medieval Age, when personal attention was focused more on securing a place in the next world, virtue was what every good Christian aspired to. To lead a virtuous life and to be of good virtue assured eternal salvation. In the Modern Age, virtue began drifting to the margins as society became increasingly production oriented. The bourgeoisie began to substitute character for virtue. By the nineteenth century, character had become one of the most important descriptive words in the English vocabulary. To be of good character was the highest compliment one could extend to a bourgeois man or woman. Character, more than anything else, conjured up the notion of self-control and self-mastery. The term character became associated with citizenship, hard work, industriousness, determination, frugality, integrity, and, above all else, adulthood. It represented both a secularization of the values of the Protestant work ethic and a reaffirmation of the kind of producer values deemed so important to advancing the capitalist agenda and propertied regime. By the early 1920s, however, _____ was beginning to wane in importance and a new concept of self was beginning to emerge, first in the pages of self-improvement manuals and books and later in the popular culture. Commentators of the day urged Americans to develop their personalities. Orison Swett Marden, who just a generation earlier had written on the qualities of good character, published a new book, *The Masterful Personality*, in 1921, in which he urged his readers to learn to exhibit personal charm. Marden reminded his followers that "so much of our success in life depends upon what others think of us." He counseled that manners, proper clothes, good conversation ("to know what to say and how to say it"), energy, life efficiency, and poise all are qualities that everyone can use to "sway great masses." The words used to describe personality were quite different from those used to describe character. Someone is said to have personality if he or she is attractive, creative, fascinating, forceful, magnetic, engaging, vivacious, demonstrative, and warm.

To have personality is to stand out in a crowd, to be noticed, to command attention, to influence others. To "be yourself," to "express your individuality." To "have self-confidence" became the rallying cry of a generation. Those very qualities, in turn, became the psychological raw material for mass marketing techniques and national advertising campaigns designed to turn a nation of savers and producers into a nation of spenders and consumers.

03

Fill in the blank with ONE word from the passage. Also, write a summary following the guidelines below.

⌐ Guidelines ⌐

- Summarize the above passage in ONE paragraph.
- Provide a topic sentence and supporting details from the passage.
- Do NOT copy more than FIVE consecutive words from the passage.

_____

_____

_____

_____

_____

NOTE

Step 1	Survey
Key Words	
Signal Words	
Step 2	**Reading**
Purpose	
Pattern of Organization	
Tone	
Main Idea	
Step 3	**Summary**
지문 요약하기 (Paraphrasing)	
Step 4	**Recite**
요약문 말로 설명하기	

Answer Key

In the Medieval Age, when personal attention was focused more on securing a place in the next world, **virtue** was what every good Christian aspired to. To lead a virtuous life and to be of good virtue assured eternal salvation. In the Modern Age, virtue began drifting to the margins as society became increasingly production oriented. The bourgeoisie began to substitute character for virtue. By the nineteenth century, **character** had become one of the most important descriptive words in the English vocabulary. To be of good character was the highest compliment one could extend to a bourgeois man or woman. **Character**, more than anything else, conjured up the notion of self-control and self-mastery. The term character became associated with citizenship, hard work, industriousness, determination, frugality, integrity, and, above all else, adulthood. It represented both a secularization of the values of the Protestant work ethic and a reaffirmation of the kind of producer values deemed so important to advancing the capitalist agenda and propertied regime. By the early 1920s, however, **character** was beginning to wane in importance and a new concept of self was beginning to emerge, first in the pages of self-improvement manuals and books and later in the popular culture. Commentators of the day urged Americans to develop their **personalities**. Orison Swett Marden, who just a generation earlier had written on the qualities of good **character**, published a new book, *The Masterful Personality*, in 1921, in which he urged his readers to learn to exhibit personal charm. Marden reminded his followers that "so much of our success in life depends upon what others think of us." He counseled that manners, proper clothes, good conversation ("to know what to say and how to say it"), energy, life efficiency, and poise all are qualities that everyone can use to "sway great masses." The words used to describe **personality** were quite different from those used to describe **character**. Someone is said to have personality if he or she is attractive, creative, fascinating, forceful, magnetic, engaging, vivacious, demonstrative, and warm. To have **personality** is to stand out in a crowd, to be noticed, to command attention, to influence others. To "be yourself," to "express your individuality." To "have self-confidence" became the rallying cry of a generation. Those very qualities, in turn, became the psychological raw material for mass marketing techniques and national advertising campaigns designed to turn a nation of savers and producers into a nation of spenders and consumers.

→ key word

→ key word

→ key word

03

모범답안

The value by which people were primarily celebrated and weighed has changed over time. From the Medieval age to the nineteenth century, "virtue" was the primary factor to considering a person's merit. Subsequently, and until the 1920s, "character" became the leading quality. Following this, there was a clear shift towards "personality". Those who stood out and had strengths and unique properties as individuals were given praise(were praised). Second, the word in the blank should be "character".

한글 번역

중세인의 가장 큰 관심사는 내세에서 안전한 자리를 차지하는 것이었다. 그래서 선량한 기독교도라면 누구나 덕을 쌓고 싶어 했다. 덕을 쌓은 사람은 영원한 구원을 받을 수 있다고 그들은 믿었다. 그러나 근대로 들어와 사회가 점점 생산 지향적으로 움직이면서 덕은 변방으로 밀려나기 시작했다. 부르주아는 덕보다는 양식을 강조하기 시작했다. 19세기로 오면 양식이라는 단어는 영어 어휘 중에서 가장 중요한 묘사어의 하나로 굳건히 자리 잡는다. 양식이 있다는 말은 남녀를 불문하고 부르주아가 가장 듣고 싶어하는 말이었다. 양식은 무엇보다도 자기 절제와 자기 통제라는 관념을 연상시켰다. 양식은 시민의식, 근면, 성실, 의지, 검약, 청렴, 그리고 성숙함과 자연스럽게 연결되었다. 그것은 프로테스탄트의 노동 윤리에 담긴 정신을 세속화시키면서 동시에 자본주의와 사유 재산 체제를 앞으로 밀고 나가는 데 중요한 역할을 할 생산자 정신의 가치를 재확인하는 말이었다. 그러나 1920년대부터는 상황이 달라졌다. 양식의 중요성이 점점 약해지고, 새로운 자아의 개념이 처음에는 자아를 향상시키려는 요령을 가르치는 책에서 나타나더니 나중에는 대중문화로까지 침투한다. 당시 이 방면의 전문가들은 매력을 갈고 닦아야 한다고 강조했다. 불과 한 세대 전까지만 하더라도 바람직한 양식의 특성에 대해서 글을 썼던 오리즌 스웨트 마든이 1921년에는 "매력 있는 인간"이라는 책을 써서 독자들에게 개인적 매력을 발산하는 비결을 배우라고 촉구했다. 마든은 그의 추종자들에게 "남들이 우리를 어떻게 생각하느냐에 따라 우리는 성공할 수도 있고 실패할 수도 있다"고 강조했다. 그는 예의범절, 경우에 맞는 옷차림, 원만한 화술(언제 무슨 말을 해야 할지 아는 것), 활력, 절도 있는 생활, 바른 몸가짐만 익히면 누구나 "만인을 자기편으로 만들 수 있다"고 조언했다. 매력 있는 인간을 묘사하는 데 동원되는 단어는 양식 있는 인간을 묘사하는 데 쓰이던 단어와는 판이하게 달랐다. 호감을 주고 창조적이고 흡인력 있고 끄는 힘이 있고 애교 있고 쾌활하고 속을 드러내는 포근한 사람을 두고 우리는 매력 있는 인간이라고 말한다. 그런 사람은 수많은 군중 속에 있어도 단번에 좌중의 시선을 끌어들이는 힘이 있고 남에게 영향을 미칠 수 있는 능력이 있다. "나 자신이 되자", "나의 개성을 표현하자", "자기 확신을 가지자" 같은 구호가 시대를 풍미했다. 이런 구호는 저축과 생산 중심의 사회를 지출과 소비 중심의 사회로 탈바꿈시키기 위해 고안된 마케팅 기법과 국가 차원의 선전을 위한 심리적 재료가 되었다.

Step 1	Survey
Key Words	virtue; character; personalities
Signal Words	In the Medieval Age; By the nineteenth century; By the early 1920s

Step 2	Reading
Purpose	to explain how the value by which people were primarily celebrated and weighed has changed over time.
Pattern of Organization	time order
Tone	neutral
Main Idea	The value by which people were primarily celebrated and weighed has changed over time.

Step 3	Summary
지문 요약하기 (Paraphrasing)	The value by which people were primarily celebrated and weighed has changed over time. From the Medieval age to the nineteenth century, "virtue" was the primary factor to considering a person's merit. Subsequently, and until the 1920s, "character" became the leading quality. Following this, there was a clear shift towards "personality". Those who stood out and had strengths and unique properties as individuals were given praise(were praised).

Step 4	Recite
요약문 말로 설명하기	

07 Read the passage and follow the directions.

Sigmund Freud, the Austrian founder of psychoanalysis, called dreams the "royal road to the unconscious." He therefore paid close attention to their content. Through his study of dreams, Freud identified several specific ways in which they disguise their underlying meaning. According to Freud, dreams make use of condensation. In other words, one dream figure or object might well represent several different real-life people or things. Thus, a person in a dream could look like your instructor yet speak and gesture like your father, which Freud, at least, would say was a condensed figure representing authority. Displacement was another one of Freud's dream disguises. When displacement is at work in a dream, violent or angry actions, unacceptable in real life, are directed toward safe objects. For example, a teenager who goes to sleep furious at parents who are planning to divorce might dream of smashing a set of dishes rather than dreaming about being angry at the parents she loves. In what Freud called "dream work," symbolization is often at play, and he believed that dream imagery should be interpreted in symbolic rather than real terms. A student who dreams of walking into class naked, for example, might well be motivated not by exhibitionist tendencies but by the fear of being weak and vulnerable. Secondary elaboration involves not the dream itself but the memory of it. It was Freud's position that when remembering dreams, we elaborate on them, adding logical connections not originally present in the dream itself.

MEMO

Write a summary following the guidelines below.

Guidelines

- Summarize the above passage in ONE paragraph.
- Provide a topic sentence and supporting details from the passage.
- Do NOT copy more than FIVE consecutive words from the passage.

03

NOTE

Step 1	Survey
Key Words	
Signal Words	
Step 2	**Reading**
Purpose	
Pattern of Organization	
Tone	
Main Idea	
Step 3	**Summary**
지문 요약하기 (Paraphrasing)	
Step 4	**Recite**
요약문 말로 설명하기	

💡 Answer Key

Sigmund Freud, the Austrian founder of psychoanalysis, called **dreams** the "royal road to **the unconscious**." He therefore paid close attention to their content. **Through his study of dreams, Freud identified several specific ways in which they disguise their underlying meaning.** According to Freud, **dreams** make use of **condensation**. In other words, one dream figure or object might well represent several different real-life people or things. Thus, a person in a dream could look like your instructor yet speak and gesture like your father, which Freud, at least, would say was a condensed figure representing authority. // **Displacement** was another one of Freud's dream disguises. When displacement is at work in a dream, violent or angry actions, unacceptable in real life, are directed toward safe objects. For example, a teenager who goes to sleep furious at parents who are planning to divorce might dream of smashing a set of dishes rather than dreaming about being angry at the parents she loves. // In what Freud called "dream work," **symbolization** is often at play, and he believed that dream imagery should be interpreted in symbolic rather than real terms. A student who dreams of walking into class naked, for example, might well be motivated not by exhibitionist tendencies but by the fear of being weak and vulnerable. // **Secondary elaboration** involves not the dream itself but the memory of it. It was Freud's position that when remembering dreams, we elaborate on them, adding logical connections not originally present in the dream itself.

→ key words

① condensation

② displacement

③ symbolization

④ Secondary elaboration

모범답안

Sigmund Freud identified four different ways that dreams disguise their hidden meanings. Through the process of "condensation", one person in a dream may actually represents several different people. Second, "displacement" allows antisocial actions (or emotions) unacceptable in reality to be redirected toward a safe target. Third, "symbolization" means that symbols should be interpreted symbolically, not literally. Finally, "second elaboration" takes place when the dream is over and the dreamer adds logical details to what s/he remembers about the dream.

한글 번역

정신분석학의 오스트리아인 창립자인 지그문트 프로이트는 꿈을 '무의식을 향하는 왕도'라고 불렀다. 따라서 그는 꿈의 내용에 깊은 주의를 기울였다. 자신의 꿈 연구를 통하여, 프로이트는 꿈이 그 기저에 깔린 의미를 숨기는 여러 구체적인 방법을 찾아냈다. 프로이트에 따르면, 꿈은 압축을 사용한다. 다시 말해, 꿈의 어떤 인물이나 대상은 아마 여러 다른 실제 삶의 사람들이나 사물들을 나타낼 수도 있다. 따라서, 꿈속에 있는 어떤 사람은 당신의 교사처럼 보이면서도 당신의 아버지처럼 말하고 몸짓할 수 있는데, 적어도 프로이트는, 이를 권위를 나타내는 응축된 인물이라고 말했을 것이다. 치환은 프로이트의 꿈 위장술의 또 다른 하나이다. 치환이 꿈에서 작동할 때, 실제 생활에서 받아들여질 수 없는 난폭하거나 화난 행동들이 안전한 대상을 향한다. 예를 들어, 이혼을 계획하는 부모에 성이 난 채로 잠자리에 드는 10대는 자신이 사랑하는 부모에 화를 내는 것에 대한 꿈을 꾸기보다는 식기 한 세트를 부수는 것을 꿈꿀지도 모른다. 프로이트가 '꿈 작업'이라고 불렀던 것 중, 상징화가 종종 영향을 미치며, 그는 꿈의 형상이 실제보다는 상징적인 용어로 해석되어야 한다고 믿었다. 예를 들어, 나체로 수업에 걸어 들어가는 꿈을 꾸는 학생은, 아마도 노출증적인 경향보다는 나약해지고 취약해지는 것에 대한 공포에 의해 동기를 받았을지도 모른다. 이차적 정교화는 꿈 자체가 아니라 그 꿈에 대한 기억과 연관되어 있다. 꿈을 기억할 때, 우리는 그 꿈 자체에 원래 존재하지 않았던 논리적인 연관성을 더함으로써, 꿈을 정교화한다는 것이 프로이트의 입장이었다.

NOTE

Step 1	Survey
Key Words	Sigmund Freud; dreams; the unconscious; condensation; Displacement; symbolization; Secondary elaboration
Signal Words	specific ways; another
Step 2	Reading
Purpose	to explain Sigmund Freud's theory about dreams
Pattern of Organization	series
Tone	neutral
Main Idea	Sigmund Freud identified four different ways that dreams disguise their hidden meanings.
Step 3	Summary
지문 요약하기 (Paraphrasing)	Sigmund Freud identified four different ways that dreams disguise their hidden meanings. Through the process of "condensation", one person in a dream may actually represents several different people. Second, "displacement" allows antisocial actions (or emotions) unacceptable in reality to be redirected toward a safe target. Third, "symbolization" means that symbols should be interpreted symbolically, not literally. Finally, "second elaboration" takes place when the dream is over and the dreamer adds logical details to what s/he remembers about the dream.
Step 4	Recite
요약문 말로 설명하기	

03

08   Read the passage and follow the directions.

According to a recent Gallup survey, only 15 percent of Americans think that Homo sapiens evolved through natural selection alone, free of all divine intervention; 32 percent maintain that humans may have evolved from earlier life forms in a process lasting millions of years, but God orchestrated this entire show; 46 percent believe that God created humans in their current form sometime during the last 10,000 years, just as the Bible says. Spending three years in college has absolutely no impact on these views. Though schools evidently do a very poor job teaching evolution, religious zealots still insist that it should not be taught at all. Alternatively, they demand that children must also be taught the theory of intelligent design, according to which all organisms were created by the design of some higher intelligence. "Teach them both theories," say the zealots, "and let the kids decide for themselves."

Why does the theory of evolution provoke such objections, whereas nobody seems to care about the theory of relativity or quantum mechanics? How come politicians don't ask that kids be exposed to alternative theories about matter, energy, space and time? After all, Darwin's ideas seem at first sight far less threatening than the monstrosities of Einstein and Werner Heisenberg. The theory of evolution rests on the principle of the survival of the fittest, which is a clear and simple—not to say humdrum—idea. In contrast, the theory of relativity and quantum mechanics argue that you can twist time and space, that something can appear out of nothing, and that a cat can be both alive and dead at the same time. This makes a mockery of our common sense, yet nobody seeks to protect innocent schoolchildren from these scandalous ideas. The theory of relativity makes nobody angry, because it doesn't contradict any of our cherished beliefs. Most people don't care an iota whether space and time are absolute or relative. If you think it is possible to bend space and time, well, be my guest. Go ahead and bend them. What do I care? In contrast, Darwin has deprived us of our souls. If you really understand the theory of evolution, you understand that there is no soul.

Summarize the passage following the guidelines below.

| Guidelines |

- Summarize the above passage in ONE paragraph.
- Provide a topic sentence and supporting ideas from the passage.
- Be sure to include the main reason the theory of evolution provokes much antagonism in your summary.
- Do NOT copy more than FIVE consecutive words from the passage.

03

_____

_____

_____

_____

_____

NOTE

Step 1	Survey
Key Words	
Signal Words	
Step 2	**Reading**
Purpose	
Pattern of Organization	
Tone	
Main Idea	
Step 3	**Summary**
지문 요약하기 (Paraphrasing)	
Step 4	**Recite**
요약문 말로 설명하기	

💡 **Answer Key**

According to a recent Gallup survey, only 15 percent of Americans think that Homo sapiens evolved through **natural selection** alone, free of all divine intervention; 32 percent maintain that humans may have evolved from earlier life forms in a process lasting millions of years, but God orchestrated this entire show; 46 percent believe that God created humans in their current form sometime during the last 10,000 years, just as the Bible says. Spending three years in college has absolutely no impact on these views. Though schools evidently do a very poor job teaching evolution, **religious zealots** still insist that it should not be taught at all. Alternatively, they demand that children must also be taught the theory of intelligent design, according to which all organisms were created by the design of some higher intelligence. "Teach them both theories," say the zealots, "and let the kids decide for themselves."

➤ key words

Why does the theory of evolution provoke such objections, whereas nobody seems to care about the theory of relativity or quantum mechanics? How come politicians don't ask that kids be exposed to alternative theories about matter, energy, space and time? After all, Darwin's ideas seem at first sight far less threatening than the monstrosities of Einstein and Werner Heisenberg. The theory of evolution rests on the principle of the survival of the fittest, which is a clear and simple—not to say humdrum—idea. In contrast, **the theory of relativity and quantum mechanics** argue that you can twist time and space, that something can appear out of nothing, and that a cat can be both alive and dead at the same time. This makes a mockery of our common sense, yet nobody seeks to protect innocent schoolchildren from these scandalous ideas. **The theory of relativity makes nobody angry, because it doesn't contradict any of our cherished beliefs**. Most people don't care an iota whether space and time are absolute or relative. If you think it is possible to bend space and time, well, be my guest. Go ahead and bend them. What do I care? In contrast, **Darwin has deprived us of our souls**. If you really understand **the theory of evolution**, you understand that there is no soul.

key question

answers
①

②

모범답안

The theory of evolution in the United States elicits strong opposition from people who believe God created the world. Not more than 15 percent of American people believe evolutionary theory while more than 75 percent of Americans reject it. Though other scientific theories, such as quantum theory and the theory of relativity, have much deeper implications about the nature of reality, they face no such challenge. It is because evolutionary theory challenges "cherished beliefs" and proves "that there is no soul".

한글 번역

최근 갤럽조사에 따르면 미국인의 오직 15%만이 호모사피엔스가 신의 개입 없이 자연선택만을 통해 진화했다고 생각한다; 32%는 인간이 초기 생명 형태부터 수백만 년에 걸쳐 진화했을 가능성이 있지만 신이 이 쇼 전체를 지휘했다고 주장한다; 46%의 미국인은 성경에 적힌 그대로 신이 지난 1만 년 동안의 어느 시점에 지금의 형태로 인간을 창조했다고 믿는다. 3년간 대학을 다녀도 이러한 견해는 절대 바뀌지 않는다. 학교가 진화에 대해 제대로 가르치지 못한 것이 분명하지만, 열성적인 신자들은 그것도 모자라 진화를 아예 가르치지 말아야 한다고 주장한다. 혹은 지적설계론도 함께 학생들에게 가르치라고 요구한다. 지적설계론에 따르면 모든 생명체는 어떤 지적 존재(신)의 설계로 창조되었다. 신자들은 "아이들에게 두 이론을 모두 가르치고 아이들 스스로 결정하게 하라"고 주장한다.

그런데 왜 진화론에는 이렇듯 격렬한 반대를 일으키면서도 상대성이론이나 양자역학에는 아무도 신경 쓰지 않을까? 왜 정치인들은 물질, 에너지, 공간, 시간에 대한 대안이론들을 아이들에게 가르치라고 요구하지 않을까? 따지고 보면 다윈의 이론들은 처음에는 아인슈타인과 베르너 하이젠베르크의 기괴한 이론들보다 훨씬 덜 위협적으로 보인다. 진화이론의 토대인 최적자 생존 원리는 단조롭다고 말할 수는 없어도 간단명료한 개념이다. 반면 상대성 이론과 양자역학은 시간과 공간을 구부릴 수 있고 무에서 어떤 것이 출현할 수 있으며 고양이가 살아 있는 동시에 죽은 상태일 수 있다고 주장한다. 이런 주장은 우리의 상식을 조롱하지만, 아무도 이 해괴망측한 이론들에게서 죄 없는 학생들을 보호하려고 하지 않는다. 상대성이론은 아무도 화나게 하지 않는다. 왜냐하면 우리의 소중한 믿음 가운데 어떤 것과도 모순되지 않기 때문이다. 대부분의 사람들은 공간과 시간이 절대적인지 상대적인지 눈곱만큼도 관심이 없다. 만일 당신이 공간과 시간을 구부리는 것이 가능하다고 생각한다면 마음대로 하라는 식이다. 가서 그것을 구부려라. 내가 무슨 상관인가? 반면 다윈은 우리에게서 영혼을 박탈했다. 당신이 진화론을 제대로 이해한다면 그것이 영혼은 없다는 이야기임을 알아차릴 것이다.

Step 1	Survey
Key Words	natural selection; the theory of evolution; religious zealots; the theory of relativity and quantum mechanics
Signal Words	Why; because; in contrast
Step 2	**Reading**
Purpose	to explain why the theory of evolution provokes such objections
Pattern of Organization	cause&effect
Tone	critical
Main Idea	The theory of evolution in the United States elicits strong opposition from people who believe God created the world. It is because evolutionary theory challenges "cherished beliefs" and proves "that there is no soul".
Step 3	**Summary**
지문 요약하기 (Paraphrasing)	The theory of evolution in the United States elicits strong opposition from people who believe God created the world. Not more than 15 percent of American people believe evolutionary theory while more than 75 percent of Americans reject it. Though other scientific theories, such as quantum theory and the theory of relativity, have much deeper implications about the nature of reality, they face no such challenge. It is because evolutionary theory challenges "cherished beliefs" and proves "that there is no soul".
Step 4	**Recite**
	요약문 말로 설명하기

09   Read the passage and follow the directions.

MEMO

One of the most striking tendencies of our time is the expansion of markets and market-oriented reasoning into spheres of life traditionally governed by non-market norms. We consider the moral questions that arise, for example, when countries hire out military service and the interrogation of prisoners to mercenaries or private contractors; or when parents outsource pregnancy and child-bearing to paid laborers in the developing world; or when people buy and sell kidneys on the open market. Other instances abound: Should students in under performing schools be offered cash payments for scoring well on standardized tests? Should teachers be given bonuses for improving the test results of their students? Should states hire for-profit prison companies to house their inmates? Should the United States simplify its immigration policy by adopting the proposal of a University of Chicago economist to sell U.S. citizenship for a $100,000 fee? These questions are not only about utility and consent. They are also about the right ways of valuing key social practices—military service, child-bearing, teaching and learning, criminal punishment, the admission of new citizens, and so on. Since marketizing social practices may corrupt or degrade the norms that define them, we need to ask what non-market norms we want to protect from market intrusion. This is a question that requires public debate about <u>competing conceptions</u> of the right way of valuing goods. Markets are useful instruments for organizing productive activity. But unless we want to let the market rewrite the norms that govern social institutions, we need a public debate about the moral limits of markets.

Summarize the passage following the guidelines below.

⌐ Guidelines ⌐

- Summarize the above passage in ONE paragraph."''
- Provide a topic sentence, supporting ideas from the passage, and a concluding sentence.
- Be sure to identify the "<u>competing conceptions</u>" of the underlined section in your summary.
- Do NOT copy more than FIVE consecutive words from the passage.

03

NOTE

Step 1	Survey
Key Words	
Signal Words	
Step 2	**Reading**
Purpose	
Pattern of Organization	
Tone	
Main Idea	
Step 3	**Summary**
지문 요약하기 (Paraphrasing)	
Step 4	**Recite**
요약문 말로 설명하기	

💡 Answer Key

One of the most striking tendencies of our time is **the expansion of markets and market-oriented reasoning into spheres of life traditionally governed by non-market norms**. We consider the moral questions that arise, for example, when countries hire out military service and the interrogation of prisoners to mercenaries or private contractors; or when parents outsource pregnancy and child-bearing to paid laborers in the developing world; or when people buy and sell kidneys on the open market. Other instances abound: Should students in under performing schools be offered cash payments for scoring well on standardized tests? Should teachers be given bonuses for improving the test results of their students? Should states hire for-profit prison companies to house their inmates? Should the United States simplify its immigration policy by adopting the proposal of a University of Chicago economist to sell U.S. citizenship for a $100,000 fee? // **These questions** are not only about **utility** and **consent**. They are also about the right ways of valuing key social practices—military service, child-bearing, teaching and learning, criminal punishment, the admission of new citizens, and so on. **Since marketizing social practices may corrupt or degrade the norms that define them, we need to ask what non-market norms we want to protect from market intrusion**. This is a question that requires public debate about competing conceptions of the **right way of valuing goods**. Markets are useful instruments for organizing productive activity. But unless we want to let the market rewrite the norms that govern social institutions, we need a **public debate** about **the moral limits of markets**.

→ key words

series

→ key words

key idea

→ key words

모범답안

The marketization of spheres of life traditionally free of this influence is a new and controversial shift. The following social practices and institutes have been influenced by markets in ways that raise ethical questions: military service, the treatment of child-bearing, education, criminal punishment, and immigration. Currently, there are "competing conceptions" that are comprised of those who would see these sectors organized in the morally-questionable terms of markets, and those who would keep them unaffected. Therefore, our society needs to start a serious debate where we apply marketization in the realms of morality and public services.

한글 번역

우리시대에 가장 두드러진 성향 하나는 시장과 시장 친화적 사고가 시장과는 거리가 먼 기준의 지배를 받던 전통적 삶의 영역까지 파고든다는 점이다. 이를테면 국가가 병역이나 죄수 심문을 민간 도급업체나 별도 인력을 고용해 맡길 때, 부모가 개발도상국가 사람들에게 돈을 주고 임신과 출산을 의뢰할 때, 콩팥을 공개시장에서 사고팔 때 어떤 도덕 문제들이 생기는지 앞에서 살펴본 바 있다. 이런 예는 많다. 학업 성취도가 부진한 학교에 다니는 학생들이 표준화된 시험에서 좋은 성적을 낼 경우 상금으로 보상해야 하는가? 학생들의 시험성적이 올라갔다면 교사가 보너스를 받아야 하는가? 국가는 이익을 추구하는 기업에 재소자 수용을 맡겨야 하는가? 미국은 시카고대학 경제학자의 제안을 받아들여 미국 시민권을 10만 달러에 파는 방법으로 외국인 이민 정책을 단순화해야 하는가? 이는 공리와 합의만을 묻는 게 아니다. 그것은 군 복무, 출산, 가르침과 배움, 범죄자 처벌, 새시민을 받아들이는 일 같은 중요한 사회적 행위의 가치를 측정하는 올바른 방법에 관한 물음이기도 하다. 사회적 행위를 시장에 맡기면 그 행위를 규정하는 규범이 타락하거나 질이 떨어질 수 있기에, 시장이 침입하지 못하도록 보호하고 싶은 비시장 규범이 무엇인지 물을 필요가 있다. 이를 위해서는 선의 가치를 측정하는 올바른 방법을 놓고 공개 토론을 벌여야한다. 시장은 생산 활동을 조직하는 데 유용한 도구다. 그러나 사회제도를 지배하는 규범을 시장이 고쳐 쓰기를 원치 않는다면, 시장의 도덕적 한계를 공론에 부칠 필요가 있다.

NOTE

Step 1	Survey
Key Words	the expansion of markets; market-oriented reasoning; spheres of life traditionally governed by non-market norms; utility; consent; public debate; the moral limits of markets
Signal Words	for example; when…; when…; when…; Other instance; Should…;Should…
Step 2	**Reading**
Purpose	to call for a public debate about the moral limits of markets
Pattern of Organization	series
Tone	critical
Main Idea	The marketization of spheres of life traditionally free of this influence is a new and controversial shift.
Step 3	**Summary**
지문 요약하기 (Paraphrasing)	The marketization of spheres of life traditionally free of this influence is a new and controversial shift. The following social practices and institutes have been influenced by markets in ways that raise ethical questions: military service, the treatment of child-bearing, education, criminal punishment, and immigration. Currently, there are "competing conceptions" that are comprised of those who would see these sectors organized in terms of markets, and those who would keep them unaffected. Therefore, our society needs to start a serious debate where we apply marketization in the realms of morality and public services.
Step 4	**Recite**
요약문 말로 설명하기	

10 Read the passage and follow the directions.

MEMO

In 1966, *Time* magazine famously examined whether the United States was on a path to secularization when it published its now-iconic "Is God Dead?" cover. However, the question proved premature.

In fact, Americans pray more often, are more likely to attend weekly religious services and ascribe higher importance to faith in their lives than adults in other wealthy, Western democracies, such as Canada, Australia and most European states. For instance, more than half of American adults (55%) say they pray daily, compared with 25% in Canada, 18% in Australia and 6% in Great Britain. (The average European country stands at 22%.) Actually, when it comes to their prayer habits, Americans are more like people in many poorer, developing nations—including South Africa (52%), Bangladesh (57%) and Bolivia (56%)—than people in richer countries.

As it turns out, the U.S. is the only country out of 102 examined that has higher-than-average levels of both prayer and wealth. In every other country surveyed with a gross domestic product of more than $30,000 per person, fewer than 40% of adults say they pray every day. The U.S. tendency to run counter to international trends on religiosity has long fascinated social scientists. One idea popular among modern sociologists for a number of decades held that America's unregulated and open religious "market"—where different faiths compete freely for new members without government interference—has fostered fertile ground for religious growth. More recently, some sociologists have argued that there is a link between relatively high levels of income inequality in the U.S. and continued high levels of religiosity. These researchers posit that less-well-off people in the U.S. and other countries with high levels of income inequality may be more likely to seek comfort in religious faith because they also are more likely to experience financial and other insecurities.

But even though the U.S. is more religious than other wealthy countries, it hasn't been completely immune from the secularization that has swept across many parts of the Western world. Indeed, previous Pew Research Center studies have shown slight but steady declines in recent years in the overall number of Americans who say they believe in God. This lines up with the finding that American adults under the age of 40 are less likely to pray than their elders, less likely to attend church services and less likely to identify with any religion—all of which may portend future declines in levels of religious commitment.

Write a summary following the guidelines below.

| Guidelines |

- Summarize the above passage in one paragraph.
- Provide a topic sentence, supporting ideas, and a concluding sentence based on the passage.
- Do NOT copy more than FIVE consecutive words from the passage.

_____

_____

_____

_____

_____

NOTE

Step 1	Survey
Key Words	
Signal Words	
Step 2	**Reading**
Purpose	
Pattern of Organization	
Tone	
Main Idea	
Step 3	**Summary**
지문 요약하기 (Paraphrasing)	
Step 4	**Recite**
	요약문 말로 설명하기

Answer Key

In 1966, *Time* magazine famously examined whether the United States was on a path to **secularization** when it published its now-iconic "Is God Dead?" cover. However, the question proved premature. → key word

In fact, Americans pray more often, are more likely to attend weekly **religious services** and ascribe higher importance to faith in their lives than adults in other wealthy, Western democracies, such as Canada, Australia and most European states. For instance, more than half of American adults (55%) say they pray daily, compared with 25% in Canada, 18% in Australia and 6% in Great Britain. (The average European country stands at 22%.) Actually, when it comes to their prayer habits, Americans are more like people in many poorer, developing nations— including South Africa (52%), Bangladesh (57%) and Bolivia (56%)— than people in richer countries.

As it turns out, the U.S. is the only country out of 102 examined that has higher-than-average levels of both prayer and wealth. In every other country surveyed with a gross domestic product of more than $30,000 per person, fewer than 40% of adults say **they pray every day**. The U.S. tendency to run counter to international trends on **religiosity** has long fascinated social scientists. One idea popular among modern sociologists for a number of decades held that America's **unregulated and open religious "market"**—where different faiths compete freely for new → key word members without government interference—has fostered fertile ground for **religious growth**. More recently, some sociologists have argued that there is a link between relatively high levels of **income inequality** in the U.S. and continued high levels of **religiosity**. These researchers posit that less-well-off people in the U.S. and other countries with high levels of **income inequality** may be more likely to seek comfort in religious faith → key word because they also are more likely to experience financial and other insecurities.

But even though the U.S. is **more religious** than other wealthy countries, it hasn't been completely immune from the **secularization** that has swept across many parts of the Western world. Indeed, previous Pew Research Center studies have shown slight but steady declines in recent years in the overall number of Americans who say they believe in God. This lines up with the finding that American adults under the age of 40 are less likely to **pray** than their elders, less likely to **attend church services** and less likely to **identify with any religion**—all of which may portend future declines in levels of **religious commitment**.

The U.S. remains a robustly religious country and the most devout of all the rich Western democracies. Americans' prayer habits exceed other wealthy democracies and are more like people of poorer, developing nations. The unique combination of high prayer and wealth levels has been attributed to the U.S.'s open religious situation encouraging growth, and, on the other hand, to the nation's income inequality creating a need for people to use faith for comfort. However, secularization is slightly growing in the U.S. as more young people show less likelihood to believe in God or practice prayer.

한글 번역

지난 1966년, "타임"은 이제는 매우 유명한 "신은 죽었는가?"라는 표지를 펴내며 미국이 세속화로 향하는 길에 있는가에 대해 공공연하게 질문을 던졌다. 그러나, 그 질문은 너무 이른 것이었던 것으로 나타났다.

실제로, 미국인은 캐나다, 호주, 그리고 다른 대부분 유럽 국가와 같은 부유한 서구 민주주의의 성인들보다 더 자주 기도하고, 매주 교회를 비롯한 종교 시설에 가는 사람도 많았으며, 자신의 삶에서 신앙이 중요하다고 생각하는 사람도 더 많다. 예를 들어 미국인 성인의 과반수(55%)가 매일 기도한다고 답했으며, 이는 캐나다 25%, 호주 18%, 영국 6%와 비교된다. (유럽 국가들의 평균은 22%이다.) 사실, 그들의 기도 습관에 대해 말하자면, 미국들은 선진국에 있는 사람들보다는 남아프리카공화국(52%), 방글라데시(57%), 볼리비아(56%)와 같은 경제적으로 더 궁핍한 개발도상국의 사람들과 더 비슷하다.

드러난 바와 같이, 미국은 조사 대상 102개국 가운데 기도하는 사람의 비율과 부유한 정도 둘 다 평균을 웃도는 유일한 나라이다. 1인당 국내총생산이 3만 달러를 넘는 나머지 모든 나라는 매일 기도한다고 응답하는 국민의 비율이 40%가 되지 않는다. 종교적 독실함에 대한 국제적인 추세에 역행하는 미국의 경향은 여러 사회과학자의 마음을 오랫동안 사로잡아왔다. 현대 사회학자들 사이에서 지난 수십 년간 널리 받아들여진 한 가설은 미국의 규제 없고 개방된 종교 '시장', 즉 서로 다른 신앙이 정부의 개입 없이 자유롭게 새 신도를 위해 경쟁하는 장이 종교의 성장을 위한 비옥한 토지를 조성해왔다는 것이다. 최근에는 일부 사회학자들이 미국 내에서 상대적으로 높은 수준의 수입 불평등과 계속해서 높은 수준으로 유지되는 신앙적 독실함 간에 연관성이 있음을 주장해왔다. 이 연구자들은 미국이나 소득 불평등이 심한 다른 나라에 사는 저소득층 사람들이 재정적인 불안함과 그 외 다른 종류의 불안함을 겪을 가능성이 더 높기 때문에 종교적 신앙 안에서 위안을 구하려고 할 가능성도 더 높다고 주장한다.

하지만 비록 미국이 다른 선진국보다는 더 종교적이기는 해도, 서구 국가 대부분을 휩쓴 세속화의 물결로부터 완전히 영향을 받지 않았던 것은 아니다. 실제로, 퓨 리서치 센터가 앞서 진행한 조사 결과들은 신을 믿는다고 말하는 미국인의 전반적인 숫자가 미세하지만, 꾸준히 감소함을 보여주었다. 이는 40세 미만 성인 미국인들은 더 나이 든 미국인들보다 기도도 덜 하고, 교회 등 종교 행사에도 덜 나갔으며, 자신을 어떤 종교와도 동일시하는 경향이 더 적다는 연구 결과와 일맥상통한다. 이 모두는 종교적 헌신의 수위가 미래에 감소할 것이라는 전조가 될 수 있다.

NOTE

Step 1	Survey
Key Words	secularization; religiosity; pray; unregulated and open religious market; income inequality
Signal Words	For instance; One idea; because
Step 2	**Reading**
Purpose	to explain why the U.S. remains a robustly religious country
Pattern of Organization	series; cause&effect
Tone	objective
Main Idea	The U.S. remains a robustly religious country and the most devout of all the rich Western democracies.
Step 3	**Summary**
지문 요약하기 (Paraphrasing)	The U.S. remains a robustly religious country and the most devout of all the rich Western democracies. Americans' prayer habits exceed other wealthy democracies and are more like people of poorer, developing nations. The unique combination of high prayer and wealth levels has been attributed to the U.S.'s open religious situation encouraging growth, and, on the other hand, to the nation's income inequality creating a need for people to use faith for comfort. However, secularization is slightly growing in the U.S. as more young people show less likelihood to believe in God or practice prayer.
Step 4	**Recite**
	요약문 말로 설명하기

03

11 Read the passage and follow the directions.

As Theodor Adorno stressed, the essential characteristic of the culture industry is repetition. Adorno illustrates this by contrasting 'popular' and 'serious' music. As early as his 1936 essay 'On Jazz,' Adorno had argued that an essential characteristic of popular music was its standardization. 'On Popular Music', written in 1941, repeats this point. "The whole structure of popular music is standardized, even where the attempt is made to circumvent standardization. Standardization extends from the most general features to the most specific ones." Standardization implies the interchangeability, the substitutability of parts. By contrast, serious music is a 'concrete totality' for Adorno, whereby every detail derives its musical sense from the concrete totality of the piece. This is a dialectical relationship, whereby the totality is constituted of the organic interrelation of the particulars. In the case of serious music, interchangeability is not possible; if a detail is omitted, all is lost.

Other illustrations could be given, such as the soap operas with their substitutable episodes, horror films with their formulas, etc. This repetition is due to the reflection in the sphere of cultural production of the standardized and repetitive processes of monopoly capitalist industry. Under late capitalism, what happens at work in the factory or in the office can only be escaped by approximating it in one's leisure time. This sets the terms for cultural products: "no independent thinking must be expected from the audiences" instead, "the product prescribes every reaction." The standardization of the cultural product leads to the standardization of the audience. "Man as a member of a species has been made a reality by the culture industry. Now any person signifies only those attributes by which he can replace everybody else; he is interchangeable." Standardization, says Adorno, "divests the listener of his spontaneity and promotes conditioned reflexes." To this point, the argument suggests that both popular culture and its audience suffer a radical loss of significance under late capitalism.

MEMO

What is the main idea of the passage? Write down your answer in about 15 words. Also, describe what "concrete totality" is in approximately 10 words.

_____

_____

_____

NOTE

Step 1	Survey
Key Words	
Signal Words	
Step 2	Reading
Purpose	
Pattern of Organization	
Tone	
Main Idea	
Step 3	Summary
지문 요약하기 (Paraphrasing)	
Step 4	Recite
요약문 말로 설명하기	

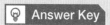

Answer Key

As **Theodor Adorno** stressed, the essential characteristic **of the culture industry** is **repetition**. Adorno illustrates this by contrasting 'popular' and 'serious' music. As early as his 1936 essay *On Jazz*, Adorno had argued that an essential characteristic of popular music was its **standardization**. *On Popular Music*, written in 1941, repeats this point. "The whole structure of popular music is **standardized**, even where the attempt is made to circumvent **standardization**. **Standardization** extends from the most general features to the most specific ones." **Standardization** implies the **interchangeability**, the substitutability of parts. By contrast, serious music is a 'concrete totality' for Adorno, whereby every detail derives its musical sense from the concrete totality of the piece. This is a dialectical relationship, whereby the totality is constituted of the organic interrelation of the particulars. In the case of serious music, **interchangeability** is not possible; if a detail is omitted, all is lost.

> → key words

Other illustrations could be given, such as the soap operas with their substitutable episodes, horror films with their formulas, etc. **This repetition is due to the reflection in the sphere of cultural production of the standardized and repetitive processes of monopoly capitalist industry. Under late capitalism, what happens at work in the factory or in the office can only be escaped by approximating it in one's leisure time.** This sets the terms for cultural products: "no independent thinking must be expected from the audiences" instead, "the product prescribes every reaction." **The standardization of the cultural product leads to the standardization of the audience**. "Man as a member of a species has been made a reality by the culture industry. Now any person signifies only those attributes by which he can replace everybody else; he is interchangeable." **Standardization**, says Adorno, "divests the listener of his spontaneity and promotes conditioned reflexes." To this point, the argument suggests that both **popular culture** and **its audience** suffer **a radical loss of significance under late capitalism**.

> key point

> key idea

> key idea

모범답안

The main idea is that the standardization of the culture industry leads to that of popular music and its audience. Second, the concrete totality is the whole(or totality) which consists of the organic interrelation of the parts.

한글 번역

테오도르 아도르노가 강조했듯이, 문화산업의 본질적 특성은 반복이다. 아도르노는 '대중'음악과 '순수'음악을 대조함으로써 이것을 설명한다. 일찍이 1936년도에 쓴 논문 "재즈에 대하여"에서, 아도르노는 대중음악의 본질적 특성은 그것의 표준화라고 주장했다. 1941년에 쓴 "대중음악에 대하여"가 이 주장을 반복하고 있다. "대중음악의 전체 구조는 표준화되어 있는데 심지어 표준화를 회피하려는 시도가 이루어지는 곳에서조차 그렇다. 표준화는 가장 일반적인 작품에서부터 가장 구체적인 작품에까지 퍼져 있다." 표준화는 호환성(교체할 수 있는), 즉 부분적인 것들의 대체 가능성을 의미한다. 이와는 대조적으로, 아도르노에게 있어서 순수음악은 '구체적 전체'인데, 여기선 모든 세부적인 것들은 그 작품의 구체적 전체로부터 음악적 의미를 얻게 된다. 이것은 변증법적 관계로, 그에 따라 전체는 세부사항들의 유기적 상호관계로 구성된다. 순수음악의 경우, 호환성은 불가능하다. 왜냐면 하나의 세부사항이 빠지면, 모든 것이 상실되기 때문이다.
　(이와 유사한) 다른 예들이 주어질 수 있는데, 대체 가능한 에피소드를 가진 연속극, 일정한 형식을 가진 공포영화 등과 같은 것들이다. 이러한 반복은 독점 자본주의 산업의 표준화되고 반복적인 과정들이 문화 생산의 영역에 반영되기 때문이다. 후기 자본주의에서, 공장이나 사무실에서 근무 중에 일어나는 일은 여가 시간에 그것을 전유함으로써 벗어나질 수 있을 뿐이다. 이것이 문화 상품들의 조건을 정한다: 즉 "어떠한 독립적 사고도 청중에게서 기대되지 말아야 하고" 그 대신에 "상품이 모든 반응을 규정한다." 문화 상품의 표준화는 청중의 표준화를 낳는다. "하나의 종의 일원으로서의 인간은 문화 산업에 의해 실재가 된다. 이제 어떤 사람도 그가 다른 모든 사람을 대신할 수 있는 그러한 부속물일 뿐임을 의미한다. 즉 그는 (다른 사람과) 교환 가능한 것이다. 아도르노는 "표준화는 청취자에게서 자발성을 박탈하고 조건 반사적 반응을 촉진한다"고 말한다. 이러한 점에서, 그 주장은 대중문화와 그 청중이 모두 후기 자본주의하에서 급격한 의미의 상실을 겪는다는 것을 암시한다.

NOTE

Step 1	Survey
Key Words	Thedodre Adormol, the culture industry; repetition; standardization; late capitalism; popular culture; radical loss of meaning
Signal Words	due to; leads to
Step 2	Reading
Purpose	to explain how capitalism's standardization of work leads to various effects
Pattern of Organization	cause&effect
Tone	critical
Main Idea	Standardization of the cultural product after capitalism's standardization of work, leading to a standardization of the audience and thus total direction of audience's reactions and a loss of their significance.
Step 3	Summary
지문 요약하기 (Paraphrasing)	Standardization means that parts of the music can be adapted, substituted and changed, a contrast to the totality of 'serious music' which lacks interchangeability. Standardization of cultural production models itself after capitalism's standardization of work, leading to a standardization of the audience and thus total direction of audience's reactions and a loss of their significance.
Step 4	Recite
	요약문 말로 설명하기

12 Read the passage and follow the directions.

Many scientists believe that the aging process is caused by the gradual buildup of a huge number of individually tiny faults—some damage to a DNA strand here, a deranged protein molecule there, and so on. This degenerative buildup means that the length of our lives is regulated by the balance between how fast new damage strikes our cells and how efficiently this damage is corrected. The body's mechanisms to maintain and repair our cells are wonderfully effective—which is why we live as long as we do—but these mechanisms are not perfect. Some of the damage passes unrepaired and accumulates as the days, months and years pass by. We age because our bodies keep making mistakes.

We might well ask why our bodies do not repair themselves better. Actually we probably could fix damage better than we do already. In theory at least, we might even do it well enough to live forever. The reason we do not is because it would have cost more energy than it was worth when our aging process evolved long ago, when our hunter-gatherer ancestors faced a constant struggle against hunger. Under the pressure of natural selection to make the best use of scarce energy supplies, our species gave higher priority to growing and reproducing than to living forever. Our genes treated the body as a short-term vehicle, to be maintained well enough to grow and reproduce, but not worth a greater investment in durability when the chance of dying an accidental death was so great. In other words, genes are immortal, but the body—what the Greeks called soma—is disposable.

Since the late 1970s, the evidence to support this <u>disposable soma theory</u> has grown significantly. In my laboratory some years ago we showed that longer-lived animals have better maintenance and repair systems than short-lived animals do. If you can avoid the hazards of the environment for a bit longer by flying away from danger or being cleverer or bigger, then the body is correspondingly a bit less disposable, and it pays to spend more energy on repair.

The writer proposes a "disposable soma theory" to provide an answer to why human bodies do not repair themselves better. What is the "disposable soma theory"? Do not copy more than SIX consecutive words from the passage.

NOTE

Step 1	Survey
Key Words	
Signal Words	
Step 2	Reading
Purpose	
Pattern of Organization	
Tone	
Main Idea	
Step 3	Summary
지문 요약하기 (Paraphrasing)	
Step 4	Recite
요약문 말로 설명하기	

💡 **Answer Key**

Many scientists believe that **the aging process** is caused by the gradual buildup of a huge number of individually tiny faults—some damage to a DNA strand here, a deranged protein molecule there, and so on. This degenerative buildup means that the length of our lives is regulated by the balance between how fast new damage strikes our cells and how efficiently this damage is corrected. The body's mechanisms to maintain and repair our cells are wonderfully effective—which is why we live as long as we do—but these mechanisms are not perfect. Some of the damage passes unrepaired and accumulates as the days, months and years pass by. We age because our bodies keep making mistakes.

> key word

We might well ask why our bodies do not repair themselves better. Actually we probably could **fix damage** better than we do already. In theory at least, we might even do it well enough to live forever. The reason we do not is because **it would have cost more energy than it was worth when our aging process evolved long ago, when our hunter-gatherer ancestors faced a constant struggle against hunger**. Under the pressure of natural selection to make the best use of **scarce energy supplies**, our species gave higher priority **to growing and reproducing** than to **living forever. Our genes** treated the body as a short-term vehicle, to be maintained well enough to grow and reproduce, but not worth a greater investment in **durability** when the chance of dying an accidental death was so great. In other words, **genes are immortal**, but **the body**—what the Greeks called **soma**—is **disposable**.

> key question
> key words

Since the late 1970s, the evidence to support **this disposable soma theory** has grown significantly. In my laboratory some years ago we showed that longer-lived animals have better maintenance and repair systems than short-lived animals do. If you can avoid the hazards of the environment for a bit longer by flying away from danger or being cleverer or bigger, then the body is correspondingly a bit less **disposable**, and it pays to spend more **energy** on **repair**.

> key words

모범답안

It is a theory that explains why human beings' bodies do not repair themselves better than now. According to the theory, human beings only have a limited amount of energy that has to be divided between reproductive activities and the repair of the non-reproductive aspects of the body(soma). In that situation, human beings tend to give high priority to reproductive activities at the expense of maintaining of the non-reproductive activities.

한글 번역

많은 과학자들은 노화 과정은 개별적으로 작은 결함들(DNA사의 어느 정도의 손상과 저기의 비정상적인 단백질 분자 등)의 엄청난 수의 점차적인 축적에 의해 야기된다고 믿는다. 이 퇴행성 축적이 의미하는 것은 우리의 수명이 얼마나 빠르게 새로운 손상이 세포에 타격을 주고 얼마나 효과적으로 이 손상이 복구되는지 사이의 균형에 의해 조정된다는 것이다. 우리 신체의 세포를 유지하고 복구하는 매커니즘은 놀라울 정도로 효과적이다. 그것이 왜 우리가 지금처럼 오래 사는지에 대한 이유이다. 그러나 이러한 매커니즘은 완벽하진 않다. 몇몇의 손상은 복구되지 않은 채로 매일, 매달, 매년이 지나면서 축적된다. 우리의 신체가 이런 실수를 거듭하기 때문에 나이가 드는 것이다.

우리는 왜 우리 신체가 더 잘 스스로를 복구하지 못하는지에 대해 질문할 지도 모른다. 사실상 우린 지금보다 더 손상을 잘 복구할 수 있을지도 모른다. 적어도 이론적으로는, 우린 영원히 살 수 있을 만큼 복구를 잘 할 수 있을지도 모른다. 그렇지 못한 이유는 수렵, 채집을 하던 우리 조상들이 굶주림에 맞서 지속적인 고통을 마주하였을 때, 우리의 노화 과정이 오래전 진화할 당시에 그것의 가치보다 더 많은 에너지를 소비하였기 때문이다. 부족한 에너지 공급원들의 사용을 극대화하기 위한 자연 선택의 원리 때문에, 우리 종족은 평생 사는 것보다 성장하고 번식하는 것에 더 우선순위를 부여하였다. 우리 유전자들은 성장하고 번식하기 충분하게 유지되기 위하여 신체를 단기적 기관으로 간주하였으나, 사고사의 확률이 높았던 당시 내구성을 위한 큰 투자는 가치가 없었다. 다시 말해서, 유전자들은 죽지 않지만, 그리스인들이 소마라고 부르는 신체는 소멸할 수 있는 것이다.

1970년도 후기 이래로, 이러한 소멸할 수 있는 소마 이론을 지지하는 증거들은 점점 막대해졌다. 내 실험실에서 몇 년 전 우리는 오래 사는 동물들은 짧게 사는 동물들보다 유지 능력과 치유 시스템이 더 뛰어났다는 것을 증명했다. 만약 환경의 위험을 위험 요소로부터 멀리 날아가거나 더 영리하거나 더 큰 신체를 이용해 피할 수 있다면, 신체는 덜 소멸 가능하게 될 것이며, 치유에 더 투자하게 될 것이다.

NOTE

Step 1	Survey
Key Words	the aging process; repair; to live forever; reproducing; soma; disposable; energy
Signal Words	why; the reason; in other words
Step 2	Reading
Purpose	to explain why our bodies do not repair themselves better
Pattern of Organization	cause&effect
Tone	neutral
Main Idea	The disposable soma theory proposes that bodies are treated as disposable by genes and given the ability to repair based on their reproduction rather than on living forever.
Step 3	Summary
지문 요약하기 (Paraphrasing)	The disposable soma theory proposes that bodies are treated as disposable by genes and given the ability to repair based on their reproduction rather than on living forever. Aging is understood by scientists to be the accumulation of damage that our bodies aren't able to repair over time. The reason for this is that it would cost more energy to perfectly repair than natural selection could allow, so instead the species made growing and reproducing higher priorities.
Step 4	Recite
요약문 말로 설명하기	

13 Read the passage and follow the directions.

Popular among laymen but not fully confirmed by empirical research, greater fool theory portrays bubbles as driven by the behavior of a perennially optimistic market participants (the fools) who buy overvalued assets in anticipation of selling it to other speculators (the greater fools) at a much higher price. According to this explanation, the bubbles continue as long as the fools can find greater fools to pay up for the overvalued asset. The bubbles will end only when the greater fool becomes the greatest fool who pays the top price for the overvalued asset and can no longer find another buyer to pay for it at a higher price. Some argue that the cause of bubbles is excessive monetary liquidity in the financial system, inducing lax or inappropriate lending standards by the banks, which then causes asset markets to be vulnerable to volatile hyperinflation caused by short-term, leveraged speculation. According to the explanation, excessive monetary liquidity (easy credit, large disposable incomes) potentially occurs while fractional reserve banks are implementing expansionary monetary policy (i.e. lowering of interest rates and flushing the financial system with money supply). When interest rates are going down, investors tend to avoid putting their capital into savings accounts. Instead, investors tend to leverage their capital by borrowing from banks and invest the leveraged capital in financial assets such as equities and real estate. Simply put, economic bubbles often occur when too much money is chasing too few assets, causing both good assets and bad assets to appreciate excessively beyond their fundamentals to an unsustainable level. Once the bubble bursts the central bank will be forced to reverse its monetary accommodation policy and soak up the liquidity in the financial system or risk a collapse of its currency. The removal of monetary accommodation policy is commonly known as a contractionary monetary policy. When the central bank raises interest rates, investors tend to become risk averse and thus avoid leveraged capital because the cost of _____ may become too expensive.

MEMO

Complete the last sentence by filling in the blank with the ONE most appropriate word from the passage.

Step 1	Survey
Key Words	
Signal Words	
Step 2	**Reading**
Purpose	
Pattern of Organization	
Tone	
Main Idea	
Step 3	**Summary**
지문 요약하기 (Paraphrasing)	
Step 4	**Recite**
요약문 말로 설명하기	

Answer Key

Popular among laymen but not fully confirmed by empirical research, **greater fool theory** portrays **bubbles** as driven by the behavior of a perennially optimistic market participants (the fools) who buy overvalued assets in anticipation of selling it to other speculators (the greater fools) at a much higher price. According to this explanation, the **bubbles** continue as long as the fools can find greater fools to pay up for the overvalued asset. The bubbles will end only when the greater fool becomes the greatest fool who pays the top price for the overvalued asset and can no longer find another buyer to pay for it at a higher price. Some argue that **the cause of bubbles** is **excessive monetary liquidity** in the financial system, inducing lax or inappropriate lending standards by the banks, which then causes asset markets to be vulnerable to volatile hyperinflation caused by short-term, leveraged speculation. According to the explanation, **excessive monetary liquidity** (easy credit, large disposable incomes) potentially occurs while fractional reserve banks are implementing expansionary monetary policy (i.e. lowering of interest rates and flushing the financial system with money supply). When interest rates are going down, investors tend to avoid putting their capital into savings accounts. Instead, investors tend to leverage their capital by borrowing from banks and invest the leveraged capital in financial assets such as equities and real estate. Simply put, **economic bubbles** often occur when too much money is chasing too few assets, causing both good assets and bad assets to appreciate excessively beyond their fundamentals to an unsustainable level. Once the bubble bursts the central bank will be forced to reverse its monetary accommodation policy and soak up the liquidity in the financial system or risk a collapse of its currency. The removal of monetary accommodation policy is commonly known as a contractionary monetary policy. When the central bank raises interest rates, investors tend to become risk averse and thus avoid leveraged capital because the cost of borrowing may become too expensive.

> key word 1
> one explanation of the bubbles by the theory definition (the great fool theory)

> key word 2

> another explanation of the bubbles definition(excessive monetary liquidity)

> key word 3

> summary of the explanation 2

borrowing

구문분석

이 글을 두 문단으로 나눈다면, "Some argue~"에서 시작된다. 이 글의 제목은 'What is the cause of bubbles?'이고, 이 질문에 대한 답이 글 전체의 내용이 된다. 거품의 원인에 대한 첫 번째 설명은 "greater fool theory"이며; 두 번째는 "금융시스템에서의 과잉 유동성(excessive monetary liquidity in the financial system)"이다. 따라서 나머지 내용들은 이 두 이론의 구체적 내용을 설명하는 supporting details에 해당한다.

어휘

be driven by ~에 의해 추동되다(움직이다)	burst 터지다
disposable 처분 가능한, 가처분	equities 주식
flush 홍수가 나게 하다, 범람시키다	in anticipation of ~을 기대하며
induce ~을 장려하다, 유발하다	leverage (자금을) 조달하다
liquidity 유동성	perennially 영원히, 항상, 지속적으로
reverse 뒤바꾸다	risk averse 위험 회피
speculation 투기	

한글 번역

보통 사람들 사이에서 인기가 있지만, 실증적 연구에 의해서는 아직 확증되지 않은, '더 큰 바보 이론'은 거품이 시장을 항상 낙관적으로 바라보는 시장 참여자(바보)의 행위에 의해 추동되는 것으로 설명한다. 이들은 과잉 평가된 자산을 그것보다 더 높은 가격에 다른 투기자(더 큰 바보)에게 팔려는 기대를 가지고 산다. 이 이론에 따르면, 거품은 과잉 평가된 자산을 산 바보들이 그 과잉 평가된 자산을 사줄 수 있는 더 큰 바보들을 발견할 수 있을 때까지 지속된다. 버블은 오직 '더 큰 바보'가 '가장 큰 바보'가 될 때 꺼지게 된다. 이때 '가장 큰 바보'는 과잉 평가된 자산을 가장 높은 가격에 지불하여 더 이상 그 높게 올라간 가격으로 사줄 사람을 찾을 수 없게 된다. 어떤 사람들은 버블의 원인을 느슨하거나 부적절한 은행의 대출 관행을 포함한, 금융시스템에서의 과잉 유동성에서 찾고 있다. 그런데 이것은 자산시장이 단기로 차입된 투기자본에 의해 야기되는 폭발적인 하이퍼인플레이션에 취약해지도록 만든다. 이 설명에 따르면, 각 준비은행의 지점들에서 통화 팽창 정책(예를 들어, 이자율을 낮춘다든가, 돈을 공급하여 금융시스템이 굴러가도록 하는 것 등)을 시행하고 있을 때, 금융시스템에서의 과잉 유동성(손쉬운 신용, 풍부한 가처분소득 등)은 잠재적으로 발생한다. 이자율이 낮아지면, 투자자들은 자신들의 자본을 저축통장에 넣는 것을 피하는 경향이 있다. 오히려, 투자자들은 은행으로부터 자본을 빌려 그 차입된 자본을 주식이나, 부동산 등 금융자산에 투자한다. 간단히 말하면, 경제 거품은 너무나 많은 돈이 너무나 적은 자산을 추구할 때 종종 발생하는데, 이것에 의해서 건전한 자산이든 불량자산이든 모두 자신들의 기초 체력을 넘어서 지속 불가능한 수준까지 과하게 평가받게 된다. 일단 거품이 터지면, 중앙은행은 통화 대부 정책을 되돌려, 금융시스템에서 유동성을 회수할 수밖에 없는데 그렇지 않으면, 통화 붕괴라는 위험을 감수해야만 하기 때문이다. 통화 대부 정책을 되돌리는 것은 보통 통화 수축 정책이라 불린다. 중앙은행이 이자율을 올리면, 투자자는 위험을 회피하는 경향이 있으며, 따라서 (은행으로부터) 돈을 빌리는 비용이 너무나 높기 때문에 자본을 차입하는 것을 피하게 된다.

NOTE

Step 1	Survey
Key Words	greater fool theory; (economic) bubbles; excessive monetary liquidity
Signal Words	According to this explanation; Some; causes; According to this explanation; Simply put
Step 2	**Reading**
Purpose	to give the two explanations of the cause of the bubbles
Pattern of Organization	definition; cause&effect; series
Tone	neutral (objective)
Main Idea	There are a few of explanations of the causes of economic bubbles.
Step 3	**Summary**
지문 요약하기 (Paraphrasing)	There are several explanations of the causes of economic bubbles. According to the great fool theory bubbles are fed by optimism towards assets which become heavily over-valued to a breaking point, at which point they burst and the value descends rapidly, causing the market to once again adjust to the reversal. Second, according to the second explanation, excessive monetary liquidity cause bubbles in the financial system.
Step 4	**Recite**
	요약문 말로 설명하기

14 Read the passage and follow the directions.

The Civil War preserved the unity of the American nation while ousting from power a planter class that had controlled the national government since its inception. It made the Republican Party the dominant political force for the next six decades. It created a new banking and tariff system that set the stage for the rapid expansion of industrial capitalism. It destroyed the largest slave system the modern world has known and established equality before the law, regardless of race, as an essential element of American citizenship. All these results produced winners and losers. Among the winners were African-Americans, Union veterans, the Republican party, industrialists and Wall Street bankers. The _____ⓐ_____ included anyone who had tied his or her fortunes to the struggle for southern independence, believers in white supremacy and many farmers and laborers whose protests against the new fiscal-industrial system help to shape the volatile politics of the Gilded Age. From the vantage point of 1900, after the experiment in interracial democracy during postwar Reconstruction failed, it seemed that the white South, in some ways, had won the war. Racism pervaded the nation, and sharecropping, disenfranchisement, lynching and other elements of the Jim Crow system severely proscribed blacks' freedom. But despite the disappointments that followed, it is important to remember that the Union's triumph foreclosed an even more oppressive outcome. Had the Confederacy emerged victorious, not only would _____ⓑ_____ there have lasted into the 20th century, but an independent South would have moved to create a slave empire encompassing much of the Caribbean and Central America. Union victory helped to propel Cuba and Brazil, the last great slave systems, down the road to abolition. Southern victory would have reinvigorated slavery throughout the hemisphere.

Fill in each blank with the ONE most appropriate word from the passage.

NOTE

Step 1	Survey
Key Words	
Signal Words	
Step 2	**Reading**
Purpose	
Pattern of Organization	
Tone	
Main Idea	
Step 3	**Summary**
지문 요약하기 (Paraphrasing)	
Step 4	**Recite**
요약문 말로 설명하기	

03

💡 Answer Key

The Civil War ① <u>preserved</u> the unity of the American nation while ousting from power **a planter class** that had controlled the national government since its inception. It ② <u>made</u> the Republican Party the dominant political force for the next six decades. It ④ <u>created</u> a new banking and tariff system that set the stage for the rapid expansion of industrial capitalism. It ⑤ <u>destroyed</u> the largest slave system the modern world has known and established equality before the law, regardless of race, as an essential element of American citizenship. // All these **results** produced **winners and losers**. Among **the winners** were African-Americans, Union veterans, the Republican party, industrialists and Wall Street bankers. **The losers** included anyone who had tied his or her fortunes to the struggle for southern independence, believers in white supremacy and many farmers and laborers whose protests against the new fiscal-industrial system help to shape the volatile politics of the Gilded Age. // From the vantage point of 1900, after the experiment in interracial democracy during postwar Reconstruction failed, it seemed that the white South, in some ways, had won the war. Racism pervaded the nation, and sharecropping, disenfranchisement, lynching and other elements of the Jim Crow system severely proscribed blacks' freedom. But despite the disappointments that followed, **it is important to remember that the Union's triumph foreclosed an even more oppressive outcome**. Had the Confederacy emerged victorious, not only would **slavery** there have lasted into the 20th century, but an independent South would have moved to create a slave empire encompassing much of the Caribbean and Central America. Union victory helped to propel Cuba and Brazil, the last great slave systems, down the road to abolition. Southern victory would have reinvigorated slavery throughout the hemisphere.

key words

results:
- ①
- ②
- ③
- ④
- ⑤

main idea

evidence

모범답안
ⓐ losers   ⓑ slavery

어휘

abolition 폐지	**down the road** 장래에	**foreclose** ~을 막다; (가능성)을 배제하다
hemisphere 반구	**oppressive** 억압적인	**oust** 몰아내다
pervade 만연하다	**proscribe** 금지하다	**reinvigorate** 활기를 불어넣다
vantage point (무엇을 지켜보기에) 좋은 위치; (특히 과거를 생각해 보는) 시점[상황]		

한글 번역

남북전쟁은 그것의 시초부터 중앙 정부를 통제했던 농장주 계급을 권력에서 몰아내는 동안에도 미국의 통일을 지켰다. 그것은 그 후 60년간 공화당을 주도적인 정치 세력으로 만들었다. 그것은 산업 자본주의의 급격한 팽창을 준비시킬 수 있었던 새로운 금융과 관세 제도를 만들어냈다. 그것은 현대 세계가 알고 있는 가장 큰 노예 제도를 부숴버렸고, 미국 시민권의 중요한 요소로서 인종에 상관없이 법 앞에 평등을 확립시켰다. 이러한 모든 것의 결과들은 승자와 패자를 양산시켰다. 승자들은 미국 흑인, 참전 용사, 공화당, 기업가와 월 스트리트 자본가들이었다. 패자는 남부 독립을 위한 투쟁을 위해 그들의 미래를 건 사람들, 백인 우월주의를 믿는 사람들, 그리고 새롭게 등장하던 금융 산업제도에 대항해 싸웠던 많은 농부와 노동자들이었다. 그런데 이 농부와 노동자들의 투쟁이 도금시대(미국 남북전쟁 후의 대호황 시대)의 불안한 정치를 형성하는 데 일조하였다. 1900년이라는 역사적으로 유리한 시점에서 보면, 전후의 재건운동(1865–1877년 있었던 남북전쟁 후 미국을 새롭게 건설하는 것) 동안에 서로 다른 인종 간의 민주주의 실험이 실패했기 때문에, 어떤 면에서 보면 남부 백인들이 전쟁에서 이겼다고 보일 수도 있다. 인종차별주의가 미국 전반에 만연했고 소작, 시민권 박탈, 억압과 짐 크로우 법(재건시대부터 1965년까지 남부에서 흑인을 비롯한 유색인종을 차별하던 법)의 여러 다른 요소들이 흑인의 자유를 엄격히 금했다. 하지만 그 이후에 이뤄진 실망스러운 결과에도 불구하고, 우리가 중요하게 기억해야 할 것이 있다. 즉, 미합중국(북군)의 승리는 훨씬 더 억압적인 결과가 일어나지 못하게 했다는 사실 말이다. 만일 남부 연합(남군)이 승리했었더라면, 노예제도가 20세기까지 이어졌을 뿐만 아니라 독립적인 남부가 캐리비안과 중앙아메리카를 둘러싼 노예 제국을 건설하기 위해 움직였을 것이다. 미합중국의 승리는 쿠바와 브라질이라는 마지막으로 남은 최대 규모의 노예제를 장차 폐지하도록 몰고 갔다. 남부 연합이 승리했다면 반구 전역(중남미)의 노예제에 활기를 불어넣었을 것이다.

NOTE

Step 1	Survey
Key Words	Civil War; equality; postwar; slavery
Signal Words	
Step 2	**Reading**
Purpose	to clarify the changes following the Civil War and how they benefited the disenfranchised
Pattern of Organization	cause&effect; series
Tone	critical; optimistic
Main Idea	The Union's victory in The Civil War has several crucial contributions to the history of USA. Though there were limitations, the Union's victory excluded a much more oppressive result.
Step 3	**Summary**
지문 요약하기 (Paraphrasing)	The Union's victory in The Civil War has several crucial contributions to the history of USA. The Union's victory expelled southern rullers, created a new financial system, and above all destroyed slavery. Though there were limitations such as severe racism in the southern states of United States, the Union's victory excluded a much more oppressive result. Also, it helped other slave nations to abolish slavery.
Step 4	**Recite**
요약문 말로 설명하기	

15 Read the passage and follow the directions.

In a culture in which organ transplants, life-extension machinery, microsurgery, and artificial organs have entered everyday medicine, we seem to be on the verge of the realization of the seventeenth century European view of the body as a machine. But if we seem to have realized that conception, it can also be argued that we have in a sense turned it inside out. In the seventeenth century, machine imagery reinforced the notion of the human body as a totally determined mechanism whose basic functionings the human being is helpless to alter. The then-dominant metaphors for this body—clocks, watches, collections of springs—imagined a system that is set, wound up, whether by nature or God the watchmaker, ticking away in a predictable, orderly manner, regulated by laws over which the human being has no control. Understanding the system, we can help it perform efficiently and intervene when it malfunctions, but we cannot radically alter the configuration of things. Western science and technology have now arrived, paradoxically but predictably (for it was a submerged, illicit element in the mechanistic conception all along), at a new, post-modern conception of human freedom from bodily determination. Gradually and surely, a technology that was first aimed at the replacement of malfunctioning parts has generated an industry and a value system fueled by fantasies of rearranging, transforming, and correcting, an ideology of limitless improvement and change, defying the historicity, the mortality, and indeed the very materiality of the body. In place of that materiality, we now have what I call "cultural plastic." In place of God the watchmaker, we now have ourselves, the master sculptors of that plastic.

MEMO

Complete the main idea of the passage by using the words from the passage.

The notion of the human body as a _____ⓐ_____ in the 17th century has now changed to the conception of _____ⓑ_____.

NOTE

Step 1	Survey
Key Words	
Signal Words	
Step 2	**Reading**
Purpose	
Pattern of Organization	
Tone	
Main Idea	
Step 3	**Summary**
지문 요약하기 (Paraphrasing)	
Step 4	**Recite**
요약문 말로 설명하기	

03

🅹 Answer Key

In a culture in which organ transplants, life-extension machinery, microsurgery, and artificial organs have entered everyday medicine, we seem to be on the verge of the realization of the seventeenth century **European view of the body as a machine**. But if we seem to have realized that conception, it can also be argued that we have in a sense turned it inside out. In the seventeenth century, **machine imagery reinforced the notion of the human body as a totally determined mechanism** whose basic functionings the human being is helpless to **alter**. The then-dominant metaphors for this body—clocks, watches, collections of springs—imagined a system that is set, wound up, whether by nature or God the watchmaker, ticking away in **a predictable, orderly manner, regulated by laws over which the human being has no control**. Understanding the system, we can help it perform efficiently and intervene when it malfunctions, but we cannot radically **alter** the configuration of things. // Western science and technology have now arrived, paradoxically but predictably (for it was a submerged, illicit element in the mechanistic conception all along), at a new, post-modern conception of **human freedom from bodily determination**. Gradually and surely, a technology that was first aimed at the replacement of malfunctioning parts has generated an industry and a value system fueled by fantasies of rearranging, transforming, and correcting, an ideology of limitless improvement and change, defying the historicity, the mortality, and indeed the very materiality of the body. In place of that materiality, we now have what I call **"cultural plastic."** In place of God the watchmaker, we now have ourselves, **the master sculptors of that plastic**.

➤ key word 1

17C
: the notion of the human body as a totally determined mechanism

▶ change

now
: post-modern conception of human freedom from bodily determination

➤ key word 2

➤ creator

모범답안

ⓐ totally determined mechanism(또는 machine)
ⓑ human freedom from bodily determination

구문분석

1. we seem to be on the verge of the realization of the seventeenth century European view of the body as a machine.
   ⇨ **be on the verge of** : ~하기 직전에 있는
   ⇨ **European view of the body as a machine** : 인간의 몸을 기계로 바라보았던 유럽의 관점

2. The then-dominant metaphors for this body—clocks, watches, collections of springs—imagined a system (that is set, wound up, whether by nature or God the watchmaker, ticking away in a predictable, orderly manner, regulated by laws over which the human being has no control).
   ⇨ **주어** : The then-dominant metaphors for this body, **동사** : imagined, **목적어** : a system (that is ~ no control)

3. Gradually and surely, / a technology (that was first aimed at the replacement of malfunctioning parts) has generated an industry and a value system (fueled by fantasies of rearranging, transforming, and correcting), / an ideology of limitless improvement and change, defying the historicity, the mortality, and indeed the very materiality of the body).

⇨ **주어**: a technology, **동사**: has generated, **목적어**: an industry and a value system, **목적어와 동 격관계**: an ideology of limitless improvement and change

어휘

be on the verge of ~하기 직전에 있는
helpless 무기력한
in place of ~의 대신에
malfunction 오작동하다
submerged 감춰진
tick away 째깍째깍 흘러가다

configuration 구성, 배열
illicit 불법적인, 부정한
intervene 사이에 끼어들다, 중재하다
mortality 죽을 운명
then-dominant 당시의 지배적인

한글 번역

장기 이식, 생명 연장 기계, 현미경 외과수술, 그리고 인공 장기가 일상의 의학에 들어와 있는 문화 속에서, 17세기 유럽인들이 인간을 바라보았던, 즉 인간의 몸을 기계로 바라보았던 관점이 바야흐로 현실화되는 것처럼 보인다. 하지만 우리가 그 개념을 현실화하는 것처럼 보인다면, 또한 어떤 의미에선 그 개념을 뒤집는 것일 수도 있다는 주장을 할 수도 있다. 17세기에 기계란 이미지는 인간의 몸이 인간 스스로 자신들의 기본적 기능들을 바꿀 수 없는 완전히 미리 결정되어 있는 기계라고 하는 개념을 강화하였다. 이런 인간의 몸에 대한 그 당시의 지배적인 은유-벽걸이 시계, 손목시계, 스프링들의 집합들-는 어떤 한 체계를 상상했는데, 거기선 자연이든 또는 신과 같은 시계 제작자이든 간에, 그것들에 의해 정해져 태엽이 감겨지는데, 예측 가능한 질서 있는 방식으로, 똑딱똑딱 나아가며 인간이 통제할 수 없는 법칙에 따라 통제된다. 이 체계를 이해하면, 우리는 그 체계가 효과적으로 작동하도록 도울 수 있고 잘 작동하지 않으면 개입할 수는 있지만, 그렇다고 해서 사물이나 일들의 배열을 근본적으로 변화시킬 수는 없다. 서구의 과학과 기술은, 역설적으로 그러나 예측 가능하게(이것의 이유는 이 새로운 개념은 기계론적 개념에서는 겉으로 드러날 수 없는 불법적인 것이었기 때문이다), 이제 육체적 결정으로부터의 인간의 자유라는 새로운 포스트 모던적 개념에 도달했는데, 점진적으로 그리고 확실히, 처음엔 잘 작동하지 않는 부분을 대체하는 것을 목적으로 삼았던 기술은 이제 재배치, 변형, 수정이라는 환상—이것은 무한 진보와 변화라는 이데올로기인데, 육체의 역사성이나 죽음, 그리고 바로 육체의 물질성 자체를 부정하는 것이다—에 의해 더욱 부채질되고 있는 하나의 산업과 하나의 가치체계를 생성하고 있다. 그 물질성 대신에 우리는 이제 내가 "문화적 성형물"이라 부르는 것을 가지게 된다. 우리는 신과 같은 시계 제작자 대신에, 이제 그 성형물을 능수능란하게 조각하는 우리 자신을 가지게 된다.

NOTE

Step 1	Survey
Key Words	European view of the body as a machine; the notion of the human body; a totally determined mechanism
Signal Words	In the 17th century; now; alter; gradually
Step 2	**Reading**
Purpose	to explain the changing conceptions adddressing the human body
Pattern of Organization	comparison&contrast
Tone	neutral
Main Idea	The concept of the human body has changed over time from an inalterable machine in the 17th century into a transformable or "plastic" form.
Step 3	**Summary**
지문 요약하기 (Paraphrasing)	The concept of the human body has changed over time from an inalterable machine in the 17th century into a transformable or "plastic" form now. The first European view of the body as a machine meant it was seen as a predictable machine. Now though, technology not only replaces parts of the body but also can transform it and made humans the sculptors of the system.
Step 4	**Recite**
요약문 말로 설명하기	

16   Read the passage and follow the directions.

In history war has served sport and sport has served war. The sports field and battlefield are linked as locations for the demonstration of legitimate patriotic aggression. The one location sustains the other, and both sustain the image of the powerful nation. Furthermore, the sports field throughout history has prepared the young for the battlefield. Throughout history sport and militarism have been inseparable. Heroes of sports field and battlefield have much in common. They are both viewed as symbols of national prowess, quality and virtue. The warrior and the athlete are crucial to the perceived success of the nation, imagined community. Sport reinforces antagonisms bred on battlefields, keeps alive memories of "battles long ago," defeats deep in the past and victories recorded in history books, and as such exacerbates antipathy, fuels hostility and extends dislike. Sport can be sublimated warfare kept alive repeatedly year after year, in "conflicts without casualties" in national stadiums keeping vivid past conflicts with casualties, and perhaps contributing to future conflicts with casualties. What is clear is the extent to which nations have used, and use, sport as a form of cultural conditioning to project images of desirable masculinity which lead directly to desirable images of martial masculinity. _____ⓐ_____ has a special power. The memory of war is one of the most significant ways of shaping national identity: images of sacrifice, heroism, mourning and loss provide symbols of unity in suffering, in sadness, in valediction. Sharply focused memories of sporting moments—played or watched—are among the most frequently recalled and infrequently forgotten. Sporting memories often offer the security of belonging. In the modern world, therefore, war and sport have been potent forces in the creation of an imagined community.

MEMO

Fill in the blank ⓐ with the ONE most appropriate word from the passage. Do not consider the capitalization. Then, describe the main idea of the passage by filling in the blank ⓑ with ONE word from the passage.

> Throughout history sport and war have been inseparable and have served as powerful factors in the construction of a(n) _____ ⓑ _____.

03

Step 1	Survey
Key Words	
Signal Words	
Step 2	**Reading**
Purpose	
Pattern of Organization	
Tone	
Main Idea	
Step 3	**Summary**
지문 요약하기 (Paraphrasing)	
Step 4	**Recite**
요약문 말로 설명하기	

Answer Key

In history **war** has served **sport** and **sport** has served **war**. The sports field and battlefield are linked as locations for the demonstration of legitimate patriotic aggression. The one location sustains the other, and both sustain the image of the powerful nation. Furthermore, the sports field throughout history has prepared the young for the battlefield. **Throughout history sport and militarism have been inseparable.** Heroes of sports field and battlefield have much in common. They are both viewed as symbols of national prowess, quality and virtue. The warrior and the athlete are crucial to the perceived success of **the nation, imagined community**. **Sport** reinforces antagonisms bred on battlefields, keeps alive memories of "battles long ago," defeats deep in the past and victories recorded in history books, and as such exacerbates antipathy, fuels hostility and extends dislike. **Sport** can be sublimated warfare kept alive repeatedly year after year, in "conflicts without casualties" in national stadiums keeping vivid past conflicts with casualties, and perhaps contributing to future conflicts with casualties. What is clear is the extent to which nations have used, and use, sport as a form of cultural conditioning to project images of desirable **masculinity** which lead directly to desirable images of **martial masculinity**. Memory has a special power. **The memory of war** is one of the most significant ways of shaping **national identity**: images of sacrifice, heroism, mourning and loss provide symbols of unity in suffering, in sadness, in valediction. Sharply focused **memories** of sporting moments—played or watched—are among the most frequently recalled and infrequently forgotten. **Sporting memories** often offer the security of belonging. In the modern world, therefore, **war and sport have been potent forces in the creation of an imagined community**.

➤ key words
➤ signal words

main idea

nation = imagined community

➤ key words

main idea

모범답안

ⓐ Memory   ⓑ nation

03

한글 번역

역사적으로 전쟁은 스포츠에 기여했고 스포츠는 전쟁에 기여하였다. 스포츠 경기장과 전쟁터는 합법적인 애국주의적 공격성을 느러내는 장소로서 연관이 되어 있다. 한 장소는 다른 장소를 지속하게 하고, 두 곳 모두 강한 국가의 이미지를 지속시킨다. 게다가, 전 역사에 걸쳐 경기장은 젊은이들을 전쟁에 대비시켰다. 전 역사에 걸쳐 스포츠와 군국주의는 분리할 수 없었다. 스포츠와 전쟁터에서의 영웅들은 큰 공통점이 있었다. 그들 모두 국가의 기량, 우수함, 그리고 미덕의 상징들로 여겨졌다. 전사들과 운동선수들은 상상의 공동체, 그 나라의 성공 인식도에 결정적이다. 스포츠는 전쟁터에서 야기된 적대감을 강화하고, 역사책에 기록된 '옛날 옛적 전쟁들'의 극심한 패배와 승리들에 대한 생생한 기억을 간직하고, 그런 식으로 반감을 악화시키고 적대심에 불을 붙이며 혐오감을 확장시켰다. 스포츠는 과거의 사상자를 낳은 전투들을 생생하게 기억하며 아마도 미래의 사상자를 낳게 되는 전투들에 기여하며, 국립 경기장에서 사상자 없이 싸우는 매년 반복적으로 불이 꺼지지 않는 승화된 의미의 전투로 볼 수 있다. 분명한 것은 국가가 어느 정도까지 스포츠를 바람직한 전쟁터 남성성 이미지로 직접적으로 이어지는 바람직한 남성성 이미지를 투영하는 문화적 길들이 기로 사용해왔고, 사용하는지이다. 기억은 특별한 힘을 가지고 있다. 전쟁에 대한 기억은 민족 정체성을 형성하는 가장 중요한 방법들 중 하나이다: 희생, 영웅주의, 애도와 인명 손실에 대한 이미지들은 고통, 슬픔, 고별 속에서 단결의 상징들을 제공한다. 경기를 하고 그것을 관람했던 스포츠 순간들의 첨예하게 집중된 기억들은 가장 빈번하게 회상되고 드물게 망각된다. 스포츠 순간들은 가끔 소속의 안전을 제공한다. 현대 사회에서는, 그러므로, 전쟁과 스포츠는 상상의 공동체를 창조하는 데에 강력한 위력이 되어 왔다.

NOTE

Step 1	Survey
Key Words	war; sport; nation; imagined community; memory; national identity
Signal Words	linked; both; inseparable; Furthermore; have much in common; both
Step 2	Reading
Purpose	to explain how sport and war have served in the construction of a nation
Pattern of Organization	comparison
Tone	persuasive
Main Idea	Throughout history sport and war have been inseparable and have served as powerful factors in the construction of a nation, that is, an imagined community.
Step 3	Summary
지문 요약하기 (Paraphrasing)	Throughout history sport and war have been inseparable and have served as powerful factors in the construction of an imagined community. The two contribute to the one another, with sport reinforcing itself through memory, while also shaping masculinity to serve the nation's continued wars and creating an imagined community within the nation.
Step 4	Recite
요약문 말로 설명하기	

17 Read the passage and follow the directions.

MEMO

A man awakens with chest pain and writes it off as indigestion. His wife urges him to go to the emergency room, where he is diagnosed as having a heart attack. A woman awakens with chest pain and thinks she might be having a heart attack. She goes immediately to the emergency room, where all tests of her heart function are normal. Doctors throw up their hands and send her on her way.

Possible explanations for these differences are complex, ranging from the physiological to the cultural. It's not clear whether women actually feel pain more intensely, as some—but not all—laboratory experiments have found, or whether they simply tend to describe their pain more expansively. Women do have thinner skin and a higher density of nerve fibers than men. And estrogen, the so-called female hormone, influences women's pain response in many ways. Fluctuations in hormone levels might contribute to variations in the severity of women's pain symptoms across the menstrual cycle, during pregnancy and immediately after delivery, and during and after menopause. Menstrual cramps and childbirth themselves might help explain differences in how women and men perceive pain. When women feel pain, their brains don't respond the same as men's do. Because women are brought up to be more nurturing than men, they're more likely to regard pain as a call to action. In other words, women tend to think, "OK, it hurts. Now, let's go do something about it." Men, on the other hand, are taught from boyhood that crying and other expressions of distress are for sissies. Partly because women tend to seek medical help more often than men, their pain complaints are often less likely to be taken seriously. Some doctors might discount a woman's pain because they think it's all in her head. Even if doctors do acknowledge the validity of a woman's pain, they may think she has a higher pain tolerance because she's built to give birth. Either way, they say the outcome is the same: less aggressive treatment of women's pain.

menopause: the permanent cessation of ovarian function occurring some time before the end of the natural lifespan

Summarize the above passage. What primary differences are described regarding the genders' behavior, physiology and the reactions they receive. Make sure to address all major supporting details in the passage. Use specific citation, but no more than SIX consecutive words. [Approximately 100-150 words]

NOTE

Step 1	Survey
Key Words	
Signal Words	
Step 2	**Reading**
Purpose	
Pattern of Organization	
Tone	
Main Idea	
Step 3	**Summary**
지문 요약하기 (Paraphrasing)	
Step 4	**Recite**
요약문 말로 설명하기	

💡 **Answer Key**

A man awakens with chest **pain** and writes it off as indigestion. His wife urges him to go to the emergency room, where he is diagnosed as having a heart attack. **A woman** awakens with chest **pain** and thinks she might be having a heart attack. She goes immediately to the emergency room, where all tests of her heart function are normal. Doctors throw up their hands and send her on her way.

Possible explanations for these differences are complex, ranging from **the physiological** to **the cultural**. It's not clear whether women actually feel pain more intensely, as some—but not all—laboratory experiments have found, or whether they simply tend to describe their pain more expansively. **Women** do have thinner skin and a higher density of nerve fibers than men. And estrogen, the so-called female hormone, influences **women's pain** response in many ways. Fluctuations in hormone levels might contribute to variations in the severity of women's pain symptoms across the menstrual cycle, during pregnancy and immediately after delivery, and during and after menopause. Menstrual cramps and childbirth themselves might help explain differences in how **women and men perceive pain**. When **women** feel **pain**, their brains don't respond the same as men's do. Because **women** are brought up to be more nurturing than **men**, they're more likely to regard pain as a call to action. In other words, **women** tend to think, "OK, it hurts. Now, let's go do something about it." **Men**, on the other hand, are taught from boyhood that crying and other expressions of distress are for sissies. Partly because women tend to seek medical help more often than men, their pain complaints are often less likely to be taken seriously. Some doctors might discount a **woman's pain** because they think it's all in her head. Even if doctors do acknowledge the validity of a woman's pain, they may think she has a higher pain tolerance because she's built to give birth. Either way, they say the outcome is the same: less aggressive treatment of **women's pain**.

key word
① behavioral

② physiological

signal words

③ cultural

모범답안

In the realm of pain, men and women differ in their behavioral responses, the way their bodies sense and the way their pain is perceived by others. First, concerning behavior, a man would be less likely to respond to pain with urgency, while a woman might misread a slight pain as being something more serious. Additionally, research has proven women have more thorough ways to describe pains, as well as hormonal and nervous systems that may in fact explain the differences in how women perceive pain. Finally, in terms of how they are perceived by others, men are expected to be strong and showing pain defines them as "sissies," while women see pain as a "call to action," and even can be ignored by some doctors for being so sensitive.

한글 번역

한 남자가 흉부 통증이 있는 채로 잠에서 깨어나고 그 통증을 소화불량 정도로 치부한다. 그의 아내는 그에게 응급실에 가라고 강력히 권고했고, 거기서 그는 심근경색이 있다고 진단받는다. 한 여성이 흉부 통증이 있는 채로 잠에서 깨어나고 자신이 심근경색이 있을 지도 모른다고 생각한다. 그녀는 곧장 응급실로 가며, 거기서 그녀의 심장 기능에 대한 모든 검사는 정상으로 나온다. 의사들은 손을 들고 그녀를 보낸다.

이러한 여러 차이점에 대해 가능한 설명들은 복합적인데, 생리적인 설명에서부터 문화적인 설명까지 이른다. 일부—그러나 전부는 아닌—실험실 실험이 발견해왔듯, 여성이 실제로 고통을 더 강렬하게 느끼는지, 혹은 여성들이 그저 자신의 고통을 더 크게 묘사하는 것인지는 분명하지 않다. 여성은 남성에 비해 더 얇은 피부와 더 높은 신경 섬유 밀도를 가지고 있다. 그리고 소위 여성 호르몬이라 불리는 에스트로겐은 여성이 고통에 반응하는 것에 많은 방식으로 영향을 미친다. 호르몬 레벨의 변동은 월경 주기, 임신 기간 동안과 출산 직후, 그리고 폐경기 동안과 이후에 걸쳐서 여성의 통증의 강도 변화에 일조할 수도 있다. 월경통과 출산 그 자체가 여성과 남성이 고통을 어떻게 받아들이는지의 차이들을 설명하는 것을 도울 수도 있다. 여성이 고통을 느낄 때, 그들의 뇌는 남성의 뇌가 하는 것처럼 반응하지 않는다. 여성이 남성보다 더 보살핌을 받도록 키워지기 때문에, 여성들은 고통을 조치가 필요한 신호로 간주할 가능성이 더 높다. 다시 말해, 여성은 "아, 아프네. 이제, 이 고통에 뭘 좀 해보러 가야겠네."라고 생각하는 경향이 있다. 반면에, 남성은 소년기부터 울음이나 그 외에 고통에 대한 다른 표현들은 계집애들이나 하는 것이라고 배운다. 부분적으로는 여성이 남성보다 더 자주 의학적 도움을 구하는 경향이 있기 때문에, 여성들의 고통 불평은 종종 진지하게 받아들여질 가능성이 더 적다. 일부 의사는 여성의 고통이 모두 그녀의 상상에서 나온 것이라고 생각하기 때문에 그 고통을 무시할 지도 모른다. 비록 의사들이 어떤 여성의 고통이 유효함을 깨닫는다 할 지라도, 그들은 그 여성이 아이를 낳도록 만들어졌기 때문에 더 높은 고통 저항력을 가진다고 생각할 수도 있다. 어느 쪽이든, 그 의사들은 결과는 같다고 말한다: 결과는 여성의 고통에 덜 적극적인 치료이다.

NOTE

Step 1	Survey
Key Words	a man; a woman; pain
Signal Words	these differences; differences; on the other hand
Step 2	**Reading**
Purpose	to show how men and women are different concerning pain
Pattern of Organization	contrast
Tone	subjective
Main Idea	In the realm of pain, men and women differ in their behavioral responses, the way their bodies sense and the way their pain is perceived by others.
Step 3	**Summary**
지문 요약하기 (Paraphrasing)	In the realm of pain, men and women differ in their behavioral responses, the way their bodies sense and the way their pain is perceived by others. First, concerning behavior, a man would be less likely to respond to pain with urgency, while a woman might misread a slight pain as being something more serious. Additionally, women have more thorough ways to describe pains, as well as hormonal and nervous systems that may in fact explain the differences in how women perceive pain. Finally, in terms of how they are perceived by others, men are expected to be strong and showing pain defines them as "sissies," while women see pain as a "call to action," and even can be ignored by some doctors for being so sensitive.
Step 4	**Recite**
요약문 말로 설명하기	

18 Read the passage and follow the directions.

By 1880 several hundred medicine shows were traveling in the United States, giving performances varying from simple magic acts to elaborate "med-presentations." Among the largest of such operations from 1880 to 1910 was the Kickapoo Indian Medicine Company, "The King of Road Shows." Founded by two veteran troupers, John E. "Doc" Healy and Charles H. "Texas Charlie" Bigelow, the Kickapoo Company maintained a large headquarters building, "The Principal Wigwam," in New Haven, Connecticut, and from there sent out shows, as many as twenty-five at a time, to cities and villages throughout the country. Doc Healy hired performers, both Indian and white—dancers, singers, jugglers, fire-eaters, acrobats, comedians, fiddlers—and Texas Charlie managed the medicine business and trained the "doctors" and "professors" who gave "medical lectures." All troupe members were distinctively garbed. The Indians—including Mohawks, Iroquois, Crees, Sioux, and Blackfeet—billed as "all pure-blooded Kickapoos, the most noted of all Indian medical people," were adorned with colored beads and feathers and loaded down with primitive weapons; they trailed great strings of unidentified hairy objects. Some lecturers wore western-style leather clothes and boots with silver-capped toes. Others wore fancy silk shirts, frock coats, and high silk hats. One of the most colorful Kickapoo figures was smooth-talking Ned T. Oliver— "Nevada Ned, the King of Gold"— who wore an enormous sombrero from the brim of which dangled 100 gold coins, and a fancy suit loaded with buttons made of gold pieces. The Kickapoo shows were presented under canvas at "Kickapoo Camps" during the summer and in opera houses and town halls in winter. On many nights the show was free to all, on others each adult was charged 10¢. The money poured in from medicine sales. The wonder-working Kickapoo concoctions were "compounded according to secret ancient Kickapoo Indian tribal formulas" from "bloodroot, feverwort, spirit gum, wild pokeberries,

MEMO

sassafras, slippery elm, wintergreen, white oak bark, yellow birch bark, dock root, sarsaparilla, and other natural products." The medicines were made in the Connecticut factory in vats so huge the "mixers" had to perch on ladders and wield long paddles. The leader of the Kickapoo line was Sagwa, which sold at 50¢ and $1 per bottle—"Sagwa, the wonderful remedy for catarrh, pulmonary consumption, and all ills that afflict the human body. It is made from roots, barks, gums, leaves, oils, and berries gathered by little Kickapoo children from God's great laboratory, the fertile fields and vast forests. Sagwa, Nature's own great secret cure, now available to all mankind!" Long after the Kickapoo Company was dissolved, a woman who had worked in the medicine factory recalled that one of the ingredients of Kickapoo Cough Syrup was Jamaica rum. Could this "cure" have been the inspiration for the "Kickapoo Joy Juice" Al Capp featured in his popular comic strip?

Fill in each blank with THREE words or TWO words from the passage.

The writer of the passage uses concrete examples to give the reader a clear picture of the _____ⓐ_____. Also, the great number and the variety of minor examples give the reader a good idea of the crazy-quilt nature of _____ⓑ_____ in general.

NOTE

Step 1	Survey
Key Words	
Signal Words	
Step 2	**Reading**
Purpose	
Pattern of Organization	
Tone	
Main Idea	
Step 3	**Summary**
지문 요약하기 (Paraphrasing)	
Step 4	**Recite**
요약문 말로 설명하기	

Answer Key

By 1880 several hundred medicine shows were traveling in the United States, giving performances varying from simple magic acts to elaborate "med-presentations." Among the largest of such operations from 1880 to 1910 was **the Kickapoo Indian Medicine Company**, "The King of Road Shows." Founded by two veteran troupers, John E. "Doc" Healy and Charles H. "Texas Charlie" Bigelow, the Kickapoo Company maintained a large headquarters building, "The Principal Wigwam," in New Haven, Connecticut, and from there sent out shows, as many as twenty-five at a time, to cities and villages throughout the country. // Doc Healy hired performers, both Indian and white—dancers, singers, jugglers, fire-eaters, acrobats, comedians, fiddlers—and Texas Charlie managed the medicine business and trained the "doctors" and "professors" who gave "medical lectures." // All troupe members were distinctively garbed. The Indians—including Mohawks, Iroquois, Crees, Sioux, and Blackfeet—billed as "all pure-blooded Kickapoos, the most noted of all Indian medical people," were adorned with colored beads and feathers and loaded down with primitive weapons; they trailed great strings of unidentified hairy objects. Some lecturers wore western-style leather clothes and boots with silver-capped toes. Others wore fancy silk shirts, frock coats, and high silk hats. One of the most colorful Kickapoo figures was smooth-talking Ned T. Oliver—"Nevada Ned, the King of Gold"—who wore an enormous sombrero from the brim of which dangled 100 gold coins, and a fancy suit loaded with buttons made of gold pieces. // The Kickapoo shows were presented under canvas at "Kickapoo Camps" during the summer and in opera houses and town halls in winter. On many nights the show was free to all, on others each adult was charged 10¢. The money poured in from medicine sales. // The wonder-working Kickapoo concoctions were "compounded according to secret ancient Kickapoo Indian tribal formulas" from "bloodroot, feverwort, spirit gum, wild pokeberries, sassafras, slippery elm, wintergreen, white oak bark, yellow birch bark, dock root, sarsaparilla, and other natural products." The medicines were made in the Connecticut factory in vats so huge the "mixers" had to perch on ladders and wield long paddles. The leader of the Kickapoo line was Sagwa, which sold at 50¢ and $1 per bottle— "Sagwa, the wonderful remedy for catarrh, pulmonary consumption, and all ills that afflict the human body. It is made from roots, barks, gums, leaves, oils, and berries gathered by little Kickapoo children from God's great laboratory, the fertile fields and vast forests. Sagwa, Nature's own great secret cure, now available to all mankind!" // Long after the Kickapoo

thesis statement

major extended example from here to end of essay

key words

minor examples of performers who were hired

minor examples of distinctively garbed troupe members

Company was dissolved, a woman who had worked in the medicine factory recalled that one of the ingredients of Kickapoo Cough Syrup was Jamaica rum. Could this "cure" have been the inspiration for the "Kickapoo Joy Juice" Al Capp featured in his popular comic strip?

모범답안

ⓐ Kickapoo medicine show　　ⓑ medicine shows

한글 번역

1880년대까지, 단순한 마술 공연부터 정교화한 의약 프리젠테이션까지 포함한 다양한 공연을 보여주며, 수백 개의 의약품선전판매 쇼가 미국 전역을 순회하였다. 1880년부터 1910년까지 가장 유명한 것 중 하나는 '순회 공연의 왕'이라 불린 킥카푸 인디언 약품회사였다. 두 명의 숙련된 연예인인 존 E. 닥 힐리와 찰스 H. 텍사스 찰리 비글로에 의해 설립된 킥카푸 회사는 코네티컷주의 뉴헤이븐에 "The Principal Wigwam"이라는 큰 본사 건물을 유지할 수 있었다. 그곳에서 한 번에 스물다섯 개나 되는 쇼를 전국의 각 도시와 마을에 내보냈다. 닥 힐리는 인디언과 백인을 포함한 무용가, 가수, 저글링하는 사람, 불로 묘기를 부리는 사람, 곡예사, 코미디언, 바이올린 연주자 등을 연기자로 고용하였고, 텍사스 찰리는 의약업을 경영하였고, '의약 강의'를 해줄 '의사'와 '교수'를 훈련하였다. 극단의 모든 구성원은 눈에 띄는 의상을 입었다. 모호크족, 이로쿼이족, 크리족, 수족과 블랙풋족을 포함하는 "순수혈통의 킥카푸족인 가장 저명한 인디언 의학 관련 사람들"이라고 광고한 인디언들은 색깔 있는 구슬과 깃털로 장식되었고, 원시의 무기를 장전하였다. 그들은 털이 난 정체불명의 것들의 줄기를 끌고 다녔다. 몇몇의 강연자들은 서부식의 가죽 옷과 은으로 발 앞부분이 장식된 부츠를 착용하였고, 다른 이들은 화려한 실크 셔츠, 긴 코트, 높은 실크 모자를 착용하였다. 가장 다채로운 킥카푸 인물 중 하나는 말을 잘하는 "Nevada Ned, 금의 왕"인 네드 T. 올리버였다. 그는 굉장한 100개의 금 동전이 가장자리에 달린 솜브레로(멕시칸들이 쓰는 것 같은 챙 넓은 모자)를 썼고, 금 조각들의 단추가 달린 화려한 양복을 입었다. 킥카푸 쇼는 여름 동안은 "Kickapoo Camps"의 천막 아래에서, 겨울에는 오페라하우스나 마을회관에서 공연을 했다. 그 쇼는 모두에게 무료로 제공되는 밤이 많았지만, 다른 어떤 날에는 성인 한 명당 10센트의 요금이 부과되기도 했다. 돈은 약 판매로부터 많이 얻어졌다. 킥카푸의 혼합물들은 '혈근초, 피버워트, 고무풀, 야생 미국자리공 열매, 사사프라스, 느릅나무, 노루발풀, 떡갈나무 껍질, 자작나무 껍질, 소리쟁이 뿌리, 청미래덩굴 뿌리'와 그리고 다른 '천연 재료로부터 나온 비밀스러운 고대의 킥카푸 인디언 부족들이 만들던 방식으로 제조되었다.' 약은 코네티컷 공장에 있는 거대한 통에서 만들어졌다. 이 통은 너무 커서 약을 섞는 사람들이 사다리 위에서 앉아서 긴 노로 휘저어야만 했다. 킥카푸 라인에서 가장 잘 팔린 것은 한 병에 50센트나 1달러로 팔리는, 카타르(점막 염증), 폐결핵, 인간 몸에 해를 끼치는 모든 병에 대한 훌륭한 치료법인 Sagwa였다. 그것은 신의 훌륭한 실험인 비옥한 들판과 광활한 숲으로부터 작은 킥카푸 아이들에 의해 모아진 뿌리, 껍질, 나무 진, 잎, 기름, 열매로 만들어졌다. 자연 고유의 훌륭한 비밀 치료제인 Sagwa를 이제 모든 인류가 사용할 수 있게 되었다! 킥카푸 회사가 사라진 뒤 오랜 이후에 약품 공장에서 일했던 한 여자는 킥카푸 기침 시럽의 하나의 원료가 자메이카 럼주라는 것을 기억해냈다. 이 '치료제'가 (미국 만화작가인) Al Capp이 그의 인기 있는 만화에서 그린 "Kickapoo Joy Juice"의 영감이 될 수 있었을까?

NOTE

Step 1	Survey
Key Words	medicine; concoction; performance; show
Signal Words	by 1880; varying from ⋯ to; from there; some ⋯ others

Step 2	Reading
Purpose	to describe the medicine shows of the late 19th and early 20th centuries and the concoctions they sold
Pattern of Organization	series (examples)
Tone	informative; light
Main Idea	The Kickapoo Indian Medicine Company, which traveled all over America in the late 19th and early 20th centuries, presented entertainment and medicine shows using Native American actors and props in order to promote sales of the medical concoctions.

Step 3	Summary
지문 요약하기 (Paraphrasing)	The Kickapoo Indian Medicine Company, which traveled all over America in the late 19th and early 20th centuries, presented entertainment and medicine shows using Native American actors and props in order to promote sales of the medical concoctions. The performers of such shows were white posing as doctors and professors and Indians who pretended to be of the "Kickapoo" tribe. The troupe members' clothing was distinctive and peculiar. Some performances were free and some charged adults a dime to get in, but the shows made most of their money by selling "medicinal" concoctions such as "Sagwa" that were supposed to be able to cure all ills

Step 4	Recite
요약문 말로 설명하기	

19   Read the passage and follow the directions.

MEMO

To find out whether a person means us well there is one almost infallible criterion : how he passes on unkind or hostile remarks about us. Usually such reports are superfluous, nothing but pretexts to help ill-will on its way without taking responsibility. Just as all feel an inclination to say something disparaging about everyone occasionally, so at the same time each is sensitive to the views of others, and secretly wishes to be loved even where he does not himself love: no less indiscriminate and general than the alienation between people is the longing to breach it. In this climate the passer-on flourishes, never short of damaging material and ever secure in the knowledge that those who wish to be liked by everyone are always avidly on the lookout for evidence of the contrary. One ought to transmit denigratory remarks only when they relate directly and transparently to shared decisions, to the assessment of people on whom one has to rely, for example in working with them. It is relatively harmless if the teller simply wants to set the two parties against each other while showing off his own qualities. The more disinterested the report, the murkier the interest, the warped desire, to cause pain. More frequently he comes forward as the appointed mouthpiece of public opinion, and by his very dispassionate objectivity lets the victim feel the whole power of anonymity to which he must bow. The lie is manifest in the unnecessary concern for the honor of the injured party ignorant of his injury, for everything being above board, for inner cleanliness. By dint of moral zeal, the well-meaning become destroyers.

Describe the main idea of the passage in 10 words or so.

NOTE

03

Step 1	Survey
Key Words	
Signal Words	
Step 2	**Reading**
Purpose	
Pattern of Organization	
Tone	
Main Idea	
Step 3	**Summary**
지문 요약하기 (Paraphrasing)	
Step 4	**Recite**
요약문 말로 설명하기	

💡 Answer Key

To find out whether a person means us well there is one almost infallible criterion : **how he passes on unkind or hostile remarks about us**. Usually such reports are superfluous, nothing but pretexts to help ill will on its way without taking responsibility. Just as all feel an inclination to say something disparaging about everyone occasionally, so at the same time each is sensitive to the views of others, and secretly wishes to be loved even where he does not himself love: no less indiscriminate and general than the alienation between people is the longing to breach it. In this climate **the passer-on** flourishes, never short of damaging material and ever secure in the knowledge that those who wish to be liked by everyone are always avidly on the lookout for evidence of the contrary. One ought to transmit denigratory remarks only when they relate directly and transparently to shared decisions, to the assessment of people on whom one has to rely, for example in working with them. It is relatively harmless if the teller simply wants to set the two parties against each other while showing off his own qualities. The more disinterested the report, the murkier the interest, the warped desire, to cause pain. More frequently he comes forward as the appointed mouthpiece of public opinion, and by his very dispassionate objectivity lets the victim feel the whole power of anonymity to which he must bow. The lie is manifest in the unnecessary concern for the honor of the injured party ignorant of his injury, for everything being above board, for inner cleanliness. **By dint of moral zeal, the well-meaning become destroyers.**

➤ key word

main idea

모범답안

The way people deal with hostile gossip reveals something about their character.

한글 번역

어떤 사람이 우리에게 좋은 의도를 갖고 있는지 확인할 수 있는 틀림없는 기준이 있다: 그것은 그 사람이 우리에 대한 불친절하거나 적대적인 언급을 어떻게 전달하는가 하는 것이다. 보통 그런 보고는 불필요하고, 책임지는 일 없이도 악감정이 분출되도록 돕는 핑계에 불과하다. 모두가 때로는 다른 모든 이에게 험담하는 말을 하고 싶어 하는 것처럼 동시에 각자는 다른 이들의 견해에 민감하고 심지어 그 자신조차 사랑할 수 없는 부분까지 사랑받기를 속으로는 바란다: 사람들 사이의 소외만큼이나 그 소외감을 깨고자 하는 바람도 무차별적이고 일반적이다. 상처 주는 소재가 결코 부족하지 않고, 모두에게 사랑받고자 하는 자들이 항상 그 반대의 증거를 찾아다니는 것이 확실한 분위기에서는, 말을 전해주는 사람들이 많아진다. 우리는 예를 들면 함께 일하며 우리가 의지해야 할 사람에 대해 평가하는 경우처럼, 합의하에 결정을 내리는 일과 직접적이고 명백하게 부합하는 경우에만 악의적인 언급을 해야 한다. 화자가 단순히 그 자신의 자질을 뽐내면서 두 당사자를 대립시키려고 한다면 그것은 상대적으로 무해하다. 뒷담화가 더 객관적이면 객관적일수록, 고통을 야기시키는 왜곡된 욕망인 이해관계가 더욱 불분명하게 드러난다. 그 사람이 더 자주 여론의 지정된 대변자로서 앞으로 나서고 그와 바로 그 냉정한 객관성이 그 희생자로 하여금 굴복해야 하는 익명의 거대한 힘을 느끼게 한다. 자신의 상처를 모르는 상처 입은 당사자의 명예에 대한 불필요한 관심, 공명정대한 상태의 모든 일에 대한 불필요한 관심, 내면적 깨끗함에 대한 불필요한 관심 등에서 거짓은 명백히 드러난다. 도덕적 열정에 의해서, 선의는 파괴자가 된다.

NOTE

Step 1	Survey
Key Words	hostile remarks; passing on; wish to be liked
Signal Words	Usually such reports; In this climate; More frequently
Step 2	Reading
Purpose	to show the deeper significance of trading in negative gossip
Pattern of Organization	series
Tone	critical
Main Idea	The manner in which one relays malicious remarks, which are sometimes useful, is often damaging and counter-productive and reveals more about the messenger than the target.
Step 3	Summary
지문 요약하기 (Paraphrasing)	The manner in which one relays malicious remarks is often damaging and counter-productive and reveals more about the messenger than the target. Only hostile remarks that are relevant to assessment on those one has to rely on are directly useful. Often the gossip is presented in a mock-objective manner, which is just as damaging, despite seeming well-meaning.
Step 4	Recite
	요약문 말로 설명하기

20 Read the passage and follow the directions.

Two of the main principles of the existentialist human condition are: that man exists and then creates himself, and what man chooses for himself he chooses for everyone else as well. Man is created on this earth and is nothing but a body, blood and guts. What he chooses to do and to be is what makes him a man. If a man comes into this world and chooses to steal, cheat, kill and lie, then that is what that man has made himself to be. While society may see him as an "evil" person, that is what is right for him. Now, on the other hand, if a person _____ⓐ_____ to be generous, kind, honest and loving, society may see him as a "good" person while it is still right for him. According to the existentialists, a person is placed on this earth with no predisposed "good" or "evil" values; one man is not created with any more good or evil than the next. By the decisions we make in life we create ourselves. The second view is a view I really believe in. Everything we do in life _____ⓑ_____ someone else, whether we know it or not. Every time we drive our car. Every time we eat something, spend money, go for a jog someone else is affected. For an example, a man goes to the store and buys a stereo, and the clerk is affected because they have to check you out, so you have taken some of their time. The store is affected because they are minus one radio from their store. The manufacturer now has to make one more to replace the one that was bought from the store. The manufacturing employees are affected because they put the radio together, and so on. On the other hand, a man who chooses to steal that same stereo will affect even more people. If he gets caught, the store, the manufacturer, the police, the courts, the jails and all the people who are involved with those organizations will be affected.

Fill in each blank with ONE word from the passage. If necessary, you may change the form(s) of the word(s).

NOTE

Step 1	Survey
Key Words	
Signal Words	
Step 2	Reading
Purpose	
Pattern of Organization	
Tone	
Main Idea	
Step 3	Summary
지문 요약하기 (Paraphrasing)	
Step 4	Recite
요약문 말로 설명하기	

03

💡 Answer Key

Two of the main principles of the **existentialist human condition** are: that man exists and then creates himself, and what man chooses for himself he chooses for everyone else as well. // **Man** is created on this earth and is nothing but a body, blood and guts. What he **chooses** to do and to be is what makes him a man. If a man comes into this world and **chooses** to steal, cheat, kill and lie, then that is what that man has made himself to be. While society may see him as an "evil" person, that is what is right for him. Now, on the other hand, if **a person chooses** to be generous, kind, honest and loving, society may see him as a "good" person while it is still right for him. According to the **existentialists**, a person is placed on this earth with no predisposed "good" or "evil" values; one man is not created with any more good or evil than the next. By the decisions we make in life we create ourselves. // The second **view** is a **view** I really believe in. **Everything we do in life affects someone else, whether we know it or not**. Every time we drive our car. Every time we eat something, spend money, go for a jog someone else is affected. For an example, a man goes to the store and buys a stereo, and the clerk is **affected** because they have to check you out, so you have taken some of their time. The store is **affected** because they are minus one radio from their store. The manufacturer now has to make one more to replace the one that was bought from the store. The manufacturing employees are **affected** because they put the radio together, and so on. On the other hand, a man who chooses to steal that same stereo will **affect** even more people. If he gets caught, the store, the manufacturer, the police, the courts, the jails and all the people who are involved with those organizations will be **affected**.

main idea
(two principles of existentialists)

principle 1
→ key word 1
→ key word 2

example:
suggesting two sides

principle 2

examples
①
②

③

④

모범답안
ⓐ chooses   ⓑ affects

구문분석

1. <u>what man chooses for himself</u> <u>he</u> <u>chooses</u> for everyone else as well.
   ⇨ what man chooses for himself : 목적어, he : 주어, chooses : 동사

2. one man is **not** created with **any more** good or evil/ **than** the next.
   ⇨ A is **not** B **any more** than C is D 구문 (A는 B가 아니다; C가 D가 아닌 것과 마찬가지로)
      = A is **no more** B than C is D
   ⇨ the next 다음에 man (is created with good or evil)이 생략되어 있다.
   cf) A whale is not a fish any more than a horse (is a fish).
   = A whale is no more a fish than a horse (is a fish). 고래가 물고기가 아닌 것은 말이 물고기가 아닌 것과 마찬가지다.

어휘

existentialist 실증주의자

predisposed 미리 정해진

gut 내장

put together 짜 맞추다, 구성하다, 종합하다

nothing but 단지 ~일 뿐 (only)

한글 번역

실존주의 인간 조건의 주된 원칙 중 두 가지는, 인간은 존재하고 나서 자신을 창조하며, 자신을 위해 선택한 것을 또한 다른 모든 사람들을 위해 선택한다는 것이다. 인간은 이 지구에서 창조되었고 그저 신체, 혈액, 내장일 뿐이다. 그가 하려고 선택하는 일이 바로 그를 인간으로 만든다. 인간이 이 세상에 와서 절도, 사기, 살인, 그리고 거짓을 선택한다면 그것은 그가 그런 사람이 되도록 할 것이다. 사회는 그를 악인으로서 보지만, 그것은 그의 권리이다. 반면에 이제 어떤 이가 관대하고 친절하고 정직하고 사랑하는 것을 선택한다면 그것은 여전히 그의 권리이며, 사회는 그를 선인으로 본다. 실존주의자들에 따르면 인간은 미리 결정된 선악의 가치 없이 이 지구상에 존재한다. 인간은 선하게 혹은 악하게 창조되지 않는다; 다른 인간이 선하게 혹은 악하게 창조되지 않는 것과 마찬가지로. 우리는 삶에서 우리가 하는 결정에 의해 만들어진다. 두 번째 견해는 내가 정말 신봉하는 견해이다. 살면서 우리가 행하는 모든 것들은 우리가 알든 모르든 다른 누군가에게 영향을 준다. 우리가 운전을 하거나 뭔가를 먹거나 돈을 쓰거나 조깅을 하러 갈 때마다 다른 누군가에게 영향을 끼친다. 예를 들어 한 사람이 가게에 가서 라디오를 산다면 그들은 당신에게 물건을 판매해야 하므로 당신이 그들의 시간을 뺏기 때문에 점원은 영향을 받는다. 그 가게는 그들의 가게에서 라디오가 하나 빠졌기 때문에 영향을 받는다. 제조자는 이제 가게에서 팔린 라디오를 대신하기 위해 하나를 더 만들어야 한다. 공장 노동자들은 라디오를 조립해야 하기 때문에 영향을 받는다. 반면에 그 똑같은 라디오를 훔치기로 결정한 사람은 훨씬 더 많은 사람에게 영향을 줄 것이다. 그가 그 가게에서 잡히면 제조자, 경찰, 법원, 교도소 그리고 그런 조직화에 관련된 모든 사람들에게 영향을 끼칠 것이다.

NOTE

Step 1	Survey
Key Words	existentialist human condition; chooses; creates; affects
Signal Words	Two; The second view
Step 2	**Reading**
Purpose	to explain two main principles of existentialist human condition
Pattern of Organization	definition; series
Tone	neutral
Main Idea	Two main principles of existentialist human condition is following: what a man chooses to do and to be is what makes him a man, everything we do in life affects someone else.
Step 3	**Summary**
지문 요약하기 (Paraphrasing)	Two main principles of existentialist human condition is following: what a man chooses to do and to be is what makes him a man, everything we do in life affects someone else.
Step 4	**Recite**
요약문 말로 설명하기	

21 Read the passage and follow the directions.

More than forty years since the beginning of affirmative action programs and the social change that led to them, Jews, women, African Americans, Latinos, and Asian Americans sit on the boards of the country's largest corporations; presidential cabinets have become increasingly diverse; and the highest ranks of the military are no longer filled solely by white men. The rules, however remain the same as in 1956 when C. Wright Mills' *The Power Elite* described the exclusively white, male, and Christian makeup of the leading members of America's political, military, and business institutions. The broad social movements of the 1960s and '70s sought to diversify this elite—and, in the process, shift its values to reflect greater social equity—but failed to change <u>the three most important factors</u> in attaining membership. Indeed, the diversity "forced" upon the power elite has given it buffers, ambassadors, and tokens, through the women and minorities who share its prevailing values. For the most part, it takes at least three generations to rise from the bottom to the top. Fully one-third of women in the elite are from the upper class. Most of the Cuban Americans and Chinese Americans come from ruling-class families displaced by political upheaval. The Jews and Japanese Americans are the products of two-and three- generational climbs up the social ladder. And the first African Americans to serve in cabinets and on the boards of large corporations tended to come from the small black middle class that predated the civil rights movement. Also, the women and minorities who make it into the corporate elite are typically better educated than the white males who are already a part of it, but time and again they emerge from the same institutions Harvard, Yale, Princeton, and MIT on the East Coast; the University of Chicago in the Midwest; Stanford and the University of California at Berkeley on the West Coast. Finally, African Americans and Latinos who do make it into the power elite are lighter-skinned than other prominent members of their racial group. As Colin Powell told Henry Louis Gates Jr. in the *New Yorker*, explaining his popularity among whites: "Thing is, I ain't that black."

03

Summarize the above passage in a well-formed paragraph. Your summary must contain the main idea and identify the underlined "the three most important factors" clearly. You must not include any of your own idea. Do NOT copy more than SIX consecutive words from the passage.

_____

_____

_____

_____

_____

NOTE

Step 1	Survey
Key Words	
Signal Words	
Step 2	Reading
Purpose	
Pattern of Organization	
Tone	
Main Idea	
Step 3	Summary
지문 요약하기 (Paraphrasing)	
Step 4	Recite
	요약문 말로 설명하기

🔘 **Answer Key**

More than forty years since the beginning of affirmative action programs and the social change that led to them, Jews, women, African Americans, Latinos, and Asian Americans sit on the boards of the country's largest corporations; presidential cabinets have become increasingly diverse; and the highest ranks of the military are no longer filled solely by white men. The rules, however remain the same as in 1956 when C. Wright Mills' *The Power Elite* described the exclusively white, male, and Christian makeup of the leading members of America's political, military, and business institutions. The broad social movements of the 1960s and '70s sought to diversify **this elite**—and, in the process, shift its values to reflect greater social equity—but failed to change the **three most important factors** in attaining membership. Indeed, the diversity "forced" upon the power elite has given it buffers, ambassadors, and tokens, through the women and minorities who share its prevailing values. For the most part, it takes at least three generations to rise from the bottom to the top. Fully one-third of **women** in **the elite** are from **the upper class**. Most of the Cuban Americans and Chinese Americans come from ruling-class families displaced by political upheaval. The Jews and Japanese Americans are the products of two-and three-generational climbs up the social ladder. And the first African Americans to serve in cabinets and on the boards of large corporations tended to come from the small **black middle class** that predated the civil rights movement. // Also, the women and minorities who make it into the corporate elite are typically **better educated** than the white males who are already a part of it, but time and again they emerge from the same institutions Harvard, Yale, Princeton, and MIT on the East Coast; the University of Chicago in the Midwest; Stanford and the University of California at Berkeley on the West Coast. // Finally, African Americans and Latinos who do make it into **the power elite** are **lighter-skinned** than other prominent members of their racial group. As Colin Powell told Henry Louis Gates Jr. in the *New Yorker*, explaining his popularity among whites: "Thing is, I ain't that black."

① class

② education

③ skin color

모범답안

Despite major changes in society to better minorities' place in the workforce and to diversify "the elite" due to social movements and the affirmative action policies, there are still lingering problems. Some of the most important factors have not changed in the slightest, specifically, such issues as class, education, and skin-color. It still takes several generations to enter the highest rung of society. So the high-standing among minorities are those which, exceptionally, have had wealthy and successful parents. With regard to education, minorities who achieve high positions often greatly outmatch their White counterparts in the elite, while emerging from the very same schools. Finally, the Africans and Latino-Americans who do manage to enter into the upper crust of society are "lighter-skinned," or more like Whites in their appearance.

한글 번역

소수자들에게 혜택을 주는 정책과 사회 변동의 시작 이래 40년 이상 유대인들, 여성들, 아프리카계 미국인들, 라틴계 사람들, 동양계 미국인들은 그 나라의 가장 큰 기업의 이사회에 앉았다. 대통령의 내각은 점점 다양해졌고, 군대의 가장 높은 계급은 더 이상 오로지 백인들로만 채워지지 않았다. 하지만 원칙은 C. 라이트 밀스의 "The Power Elite"가 미국의 정치, 군대, 사업 기관의 주도적인 멤버들의 구성은 독점적으로 백인, 남성, 그리고 기독교인이라고 묘사하던 1956년과 같이 남아 있다. 폭넓은 사회적인 움직임인 1960~70년대 이러한 엘리트를 다양화하기 위한 추구는, 더 큰 사회적인 공평함을 반영하기 위한 가치를 바꾸었지만 회원 자격을 얻는 데 3가지 가장 중요한 요인들을 변화시키는 데는 실패했다. 정말로 힘 있는 엘리트에게 강제된 다양성은 힘 있는 엘리트의 우세한 가치들을 공유하는 여성들과 소수집단들을 통해서 완충제, 대사, 토큰들을 주었다. 보통, 바닥에서 꼭대기까지 올라가는 데는 3세대가 걸린다. 엘리트 집단 여성 중 무려 1/3은 상류층 출신이다. 대부분의 쿠바계 미국인과 중국계 미국인은 정치적 변동에 의해 대체된 지배계급으로부터 왔다. 유대인과 일본계 미국인은 사회계층에 오른 2~3세대의 결과물이다. 그리고 내각과 큰 기업의 위원회에 종사하는 첫 번째 아프리카계 미국인들은 시민권 운동보다 앞선 흑인들의 중간 계층으로부터 오는 경향이 있다. 또한 기업의 엘리트가 된 여성들과 소수집단들은 전형적으로 이미 엘리트 집단에 속한 백인 남성보다 더 잘 교육받았다. 하지만 되풀이해서 그들은 동부의 하버드, 예일, 프린스턴, MIT 또는 중부의 시카고 대학, 서부의 스탠퍼드, UC 버클리 같은 기관에서 나왔다. 마지막으로, 힘 있는 엘리트가 된 아프리카계 미국인과 라티노들은 그들의 인종집단에서 저명한 다른 인물들보다 밝은 피부색을 갖고 있다. 뉴요커 잡지에서 콜린 파월은 헨리 루이스 게이츠 주니어에게 백인들 사이에서의 자신의 인기를 다음과 같이 설명했다. "실은 내가 그렇게까지 흑인은 아니어서였지."

Step 1	Survey
Key Words	the power elite; women from the upper class; more educated; lighter-skinned
Signal Words	Also; Finally
Step 2	**Reading**
Purpose	to point out lingering problems despite major changes in society to better minorities' place in the workforce and to diversify "the elite" due to social movements and the affirmative action policies
Pattern of Organization	series
Tone	critical
Main Idea	Despite major changes in society to better minorities' place in the workforce and to diversify "the elite" due to social movements and the affirmative action policies, there are still lingering problems.
Step 3	**Summary**
지문 요약하기 (Paraphrasing)	Despite major changes in society to better minorities' place in the workforce and to diversify "the elite" due to social movements and the affirmative action policies, there are still lingering problems. Some of the most important factors have not changed in the slightest, specifically, such issues as class, education, and skin-color. It still takes several generations to enter the highest rung of society. So the high-standing among minorities are those which, exceptionally, have had wealthy and successful parents. With regard to education, minorities who achieve high positions often greatly outmatch their White counterparts in the elite, while emerging from the very same schools. Finally, the Africans and Latino-Americans who do manage to enter into the upper crust of society are "lighter-skinned," or more like Whites in their appearance.
Step 4	**Recite**
요약문 말로 설명하기	

유희태 일반영어 ①
2S2R 기본

초판 1쇄	2009년 12월 1일	
2쇄	2010년 1월 5일	
3쇄	2010년 5월 10일	
2판 1쇄	2010년 12월 15일	
2쇄	2011년 1월 30일	
3쇄	2012년 2월 23일	
4쇄	2012년 12월 30일	
5쇄	2013년 7월 25일	
3판 1쇄	2014년 11월 30일	
2쇄	2015년 1월 25일	
4판 1쇄	2016년 4월 29일	
5판 1쇄	2017년 1월 3일	
2쇄	2017년 12월 20일	
6판 1쇄	2019년 1월 3일	
2쇄	2019년 3월 20일	
7판 1쇄	2022년 1월 10일	
2쇄	2022년 4월 15일	
3쇄	2023년 8월 25일	
4쇄	2025년 1월 20일	

저자와의
협의하에
인지생략

저자 유희태 **발행인** 박 용 **발행처** (주)박문각출판
표지디자인 박문각 디자인팀
등록 2015. 4. 29. 제2015-000104호
주소 06654 서울시 서초구 효령로 283 서경 B/D
팩스 (02)584-2927
전화 교재 문의 (02)6466-7202 동영상 문의 (02)6466-7201

정 가 28,000원
ISBN 979-11-6704-344-3